X/1999

VOL. 16
NOCTURNE
Shōjo Edition

STORY & ART BY CLAMP

ENGLISH ADAPTATION BY FRED BURKE

Translation/Lillian Olsen
Touch-Up Art & Lettering/Stephen Dutro
Cover and Graphic Design/Yuki Ameda
Editor/P. Duffield

Supervising Editor/Megan Bates
Managing Editor/Annette Roman
Director of Production/Noboru Watanabe
Editorial Director/Alvin Lu
Sr. Director of Licensing & Acquisitions/Rika Inouye
Vice President of Marketing/Liza Coppola
Vice President of Sales/Joe Morici
Executive Vice President/Hyoe Narita
Publisher/Seiji Horibuchi

X/1999 Volume 16 © 2001 CLAMP. Originally published in 2001 by KADOKAWA SHOTEN PUBLISHING CO., LTD., Tokyo.
English translation rights arranged with KADOKAWA SHOTEN PUBLISHING CO., LTD., Tokyo.

Printed in Canada.

Published by VIZ, LLC
P.O. Box 77010
San Francisco, CA 94107

10 9 8 7 6 5 4 3 2 1
First printing, October 2004

www.viz.com

www.animerica-mag.com

X/1999™

Vol. 16
NOCTURNE

Shōjo Edition

Story and Art by
CLAMP

X/1999

THE STORY THUS FAR

The End of the World has been prophesied… and time is running out. Kamui Shiro is a young man who was born with a special power—the power to decide the fate of the Earth itself.

Kamui had grown up in Tokyo, but had fled with his mother after the suspicious death of a family friend. Six years later, his mother too, dies under suspicious circumstances, engulfed in flames. Her last words to him are that he should return to Tokyo…that his destiny awaits.

Kamui obeys his mother's words, but almost immediately upon his arrival, he's challenged to a psychic duel—a first warning that others know of his power, and of his return.

Kamui is also reunited with his childhood friends, Fuma and Kotori Monou. Although Kamui attempts to push his friends away, hoping to protect them, they too are soon drawn into the web of destiny that surrounds him.

Meanwhile, the two sides to the great conflict to come are being drawn. On one side is the dreamseer Hinoto, a blind princess who lives beneath Japan's seat of government, the Diet Building. On the other side is Kanoe, Hinoto's dark sister with similar powers, but a different vision of Earth's ultimate future. Around these two women gather the Dragons of Heaven and the Dragons of Earth, the forces that will fight to decide the fate of the planet. The only variable in the equation is Kamui, whose fate it will be to choose which side he will join.

And Kamui finally does make a choice. He chooses to defend the Earth as it stands now. But by making this choice, he pays a terrible price. For fate has chosen his oldest friend to be his "twin star"—the other "Kamui" who will fight against him. And in this first battle, the gentle Kotori is the first casualty.

Now Kamui must face the consequences of his decision…and try to come to terms with not only his ultimate fate, but that of the Earth…

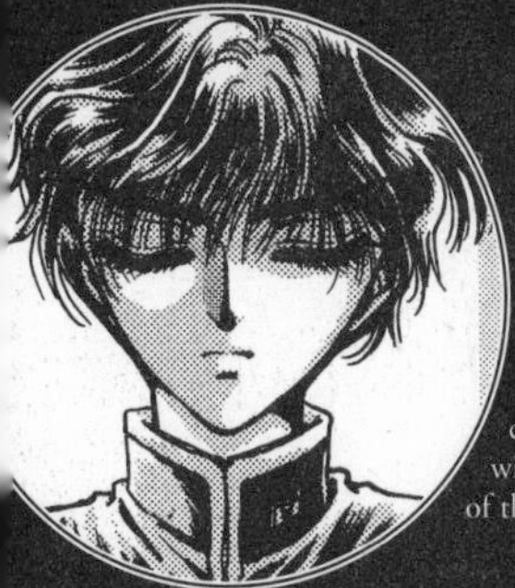

Kamui Shiro
A young man with psychic powers whose choice of destiny will decide the fate of the world.

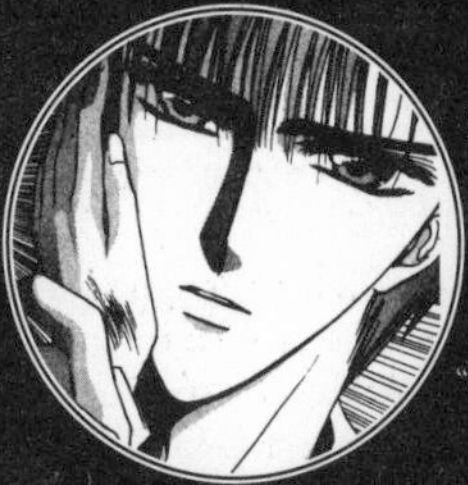

Fuma Monou
Kamui's childhood friend. When Kamui made his choice, Fuma was chosen by fate to become his "Twin Star"—the other "Kamui."

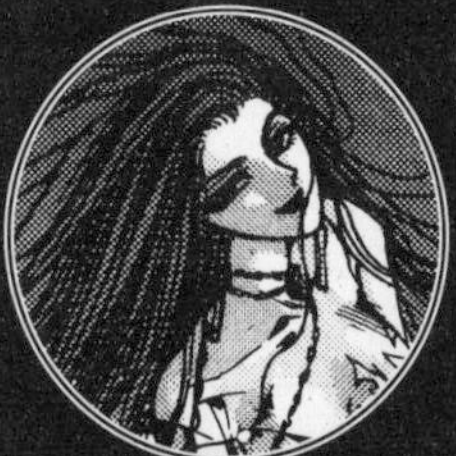

Kanoe
Hinoto's sister shares her ability to see the future… but Kanoe has predicted a different final result.

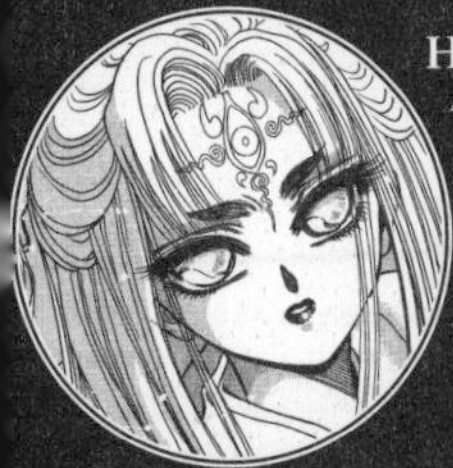

Hinoto
A powerful prophetess who communicates with the power of her mind alone. She lives in a secret shrine located beneath Tokyo's Diet Building.

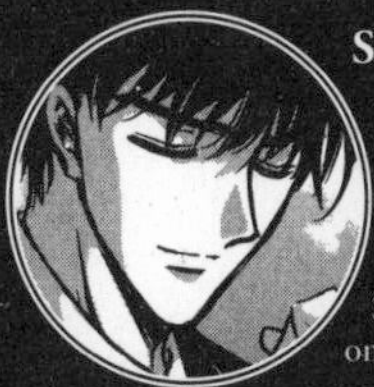

Seishiro Sakurazuka
Also called *Sakurazukamori*, the mysterious Seishiro shares a deep rivalry with Subaru. It was during past experiences connected to Subaru that he lost vision in one eye.

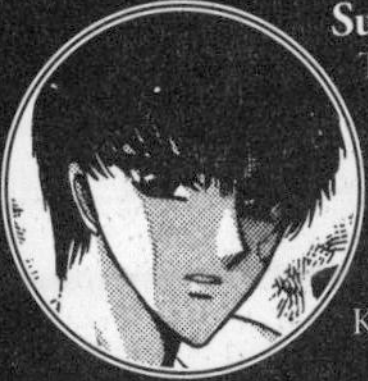

Subaru Sumeragi
The 13th family head of a long line of spiritualists, he is a powerful medium and exorcist. He lost vision in one eye after his encounter with Kamui, Dragon of Earth.

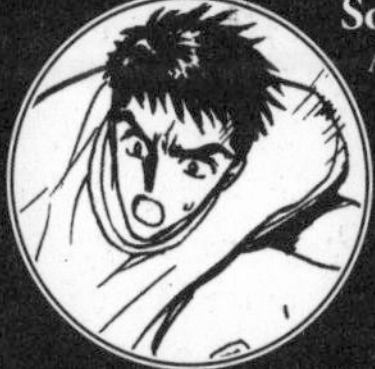

Sorata Arisugawa
A brash, but good-natured priest of the Mt. Koya shrine.

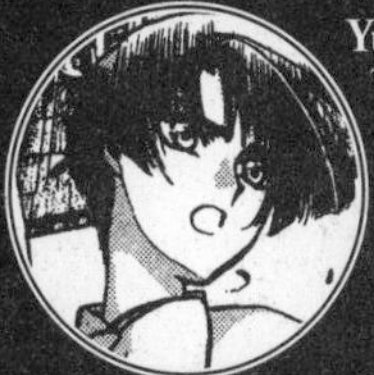

Yuziriha Nekoi
The youngest of the Dragons, she is always accompanied by a spirit dog named Inuki.

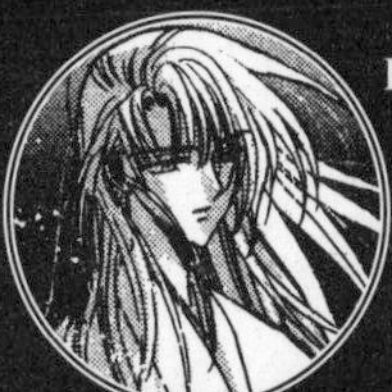

Kakyo Kuzuki
A dreamseer like Hinoto, Kakyo is a hospital-bound invalid kept alive by machines.

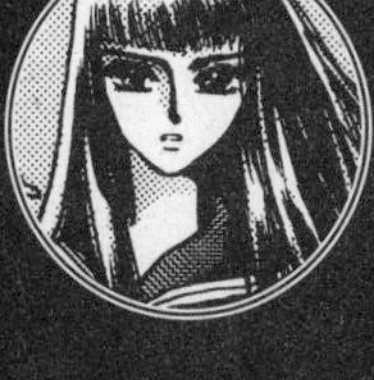

Arashi Kishu
Priestess of the Ise Shrine, Arashi can materialize a sword from the palm of her hand.

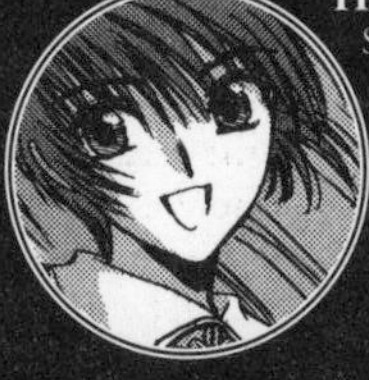

Hokuto Sumeragi
Subaru's beloved twin sister, she and Kakyo met in his dreams.

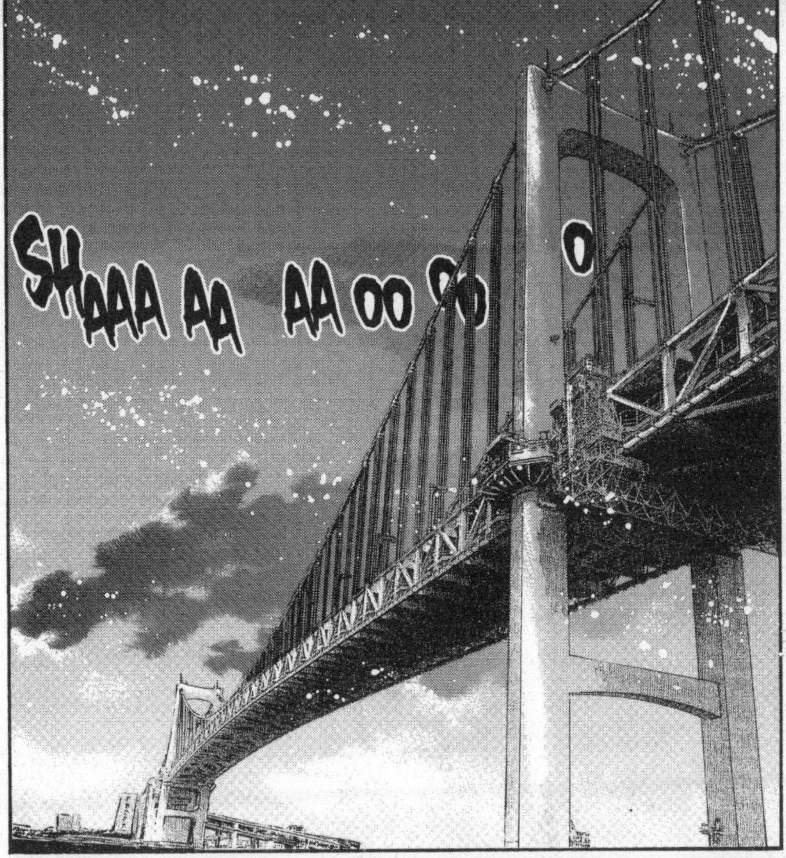
SHAAA AA AA OO OO O

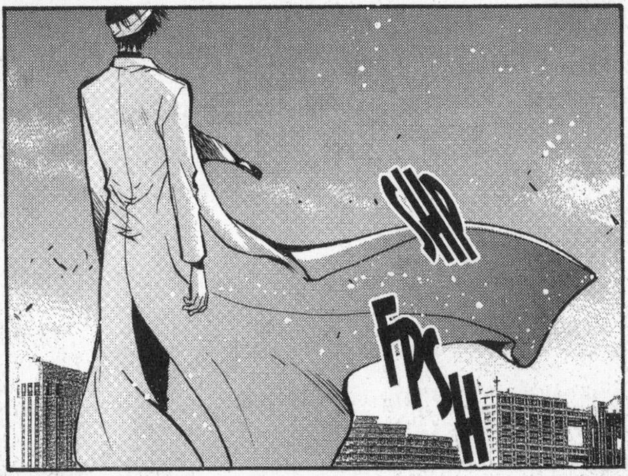
SHAP
FPSH

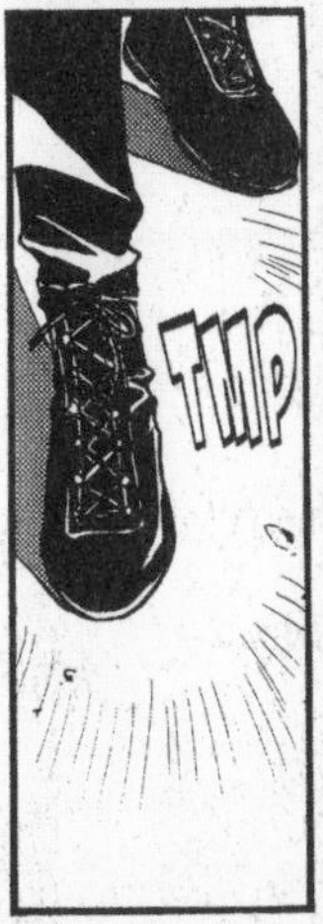
TMP

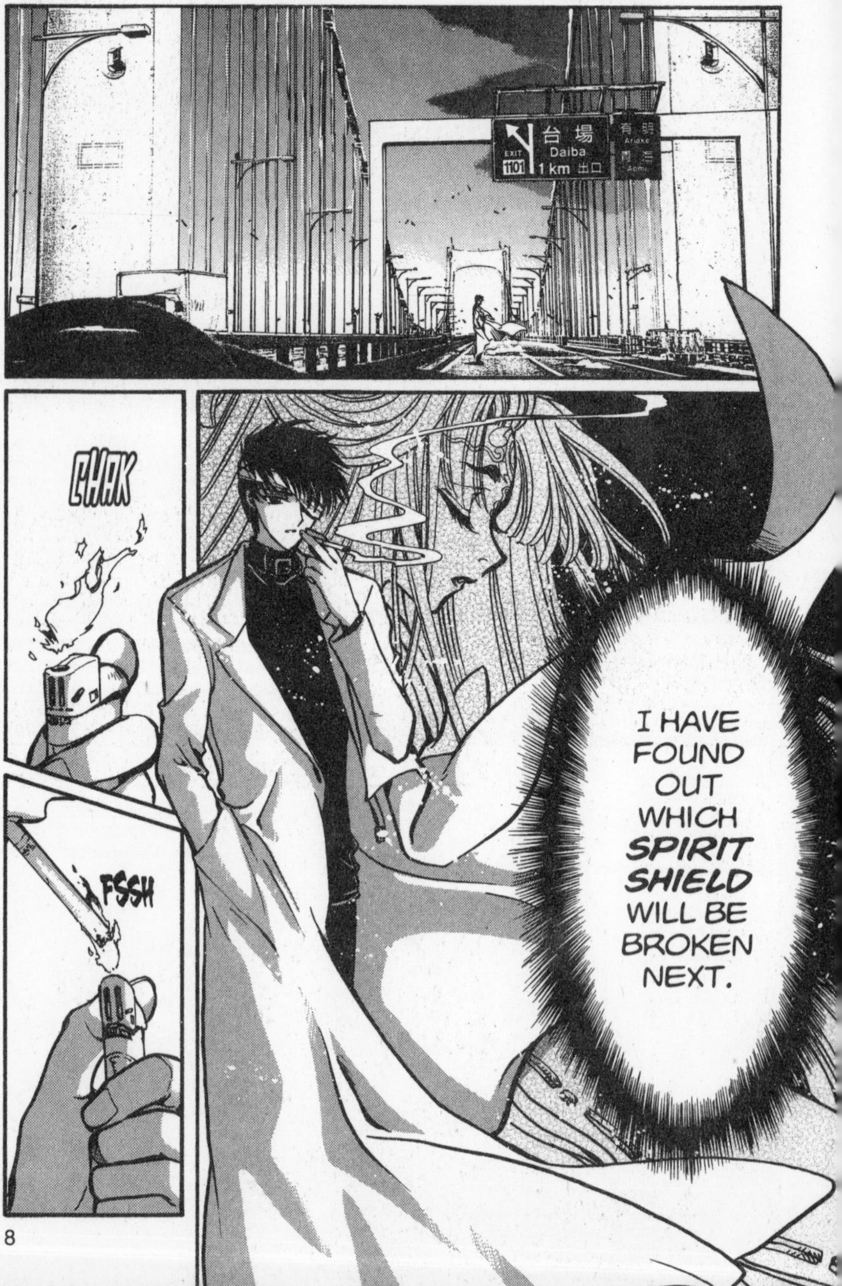
台場
EXIT
1101
Daiba
1 km 出口
有明
Ariake
青海
Aomi
I HAVE FOUND OUT WHICH **SPIRIT SHIELD** WILL BE BROKEN NEXT.
CHAK
FSSH

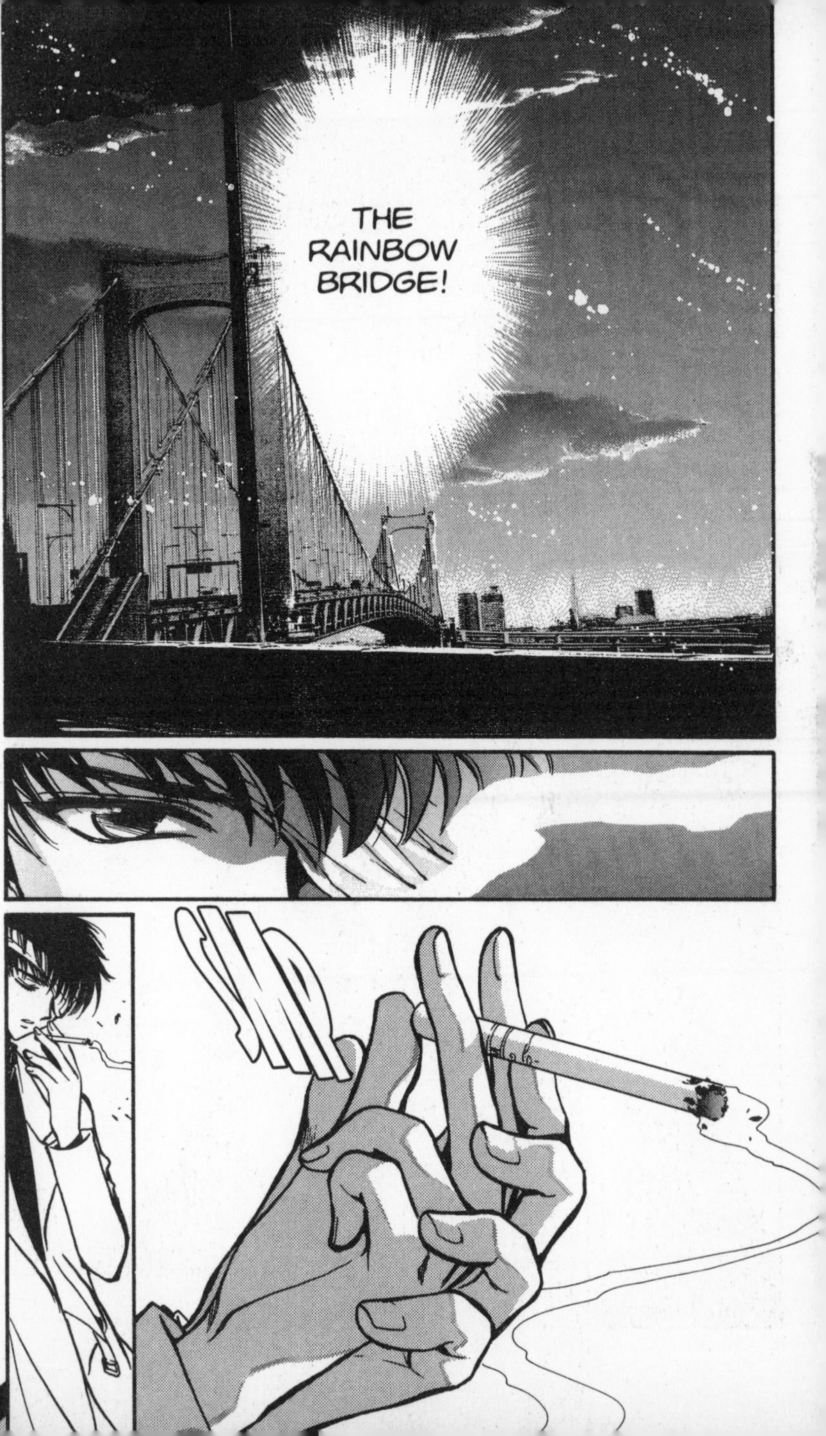
THE RAINBOW BRIDGE!

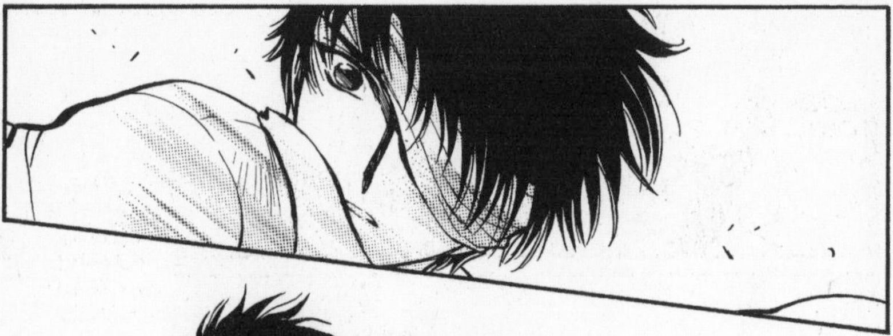
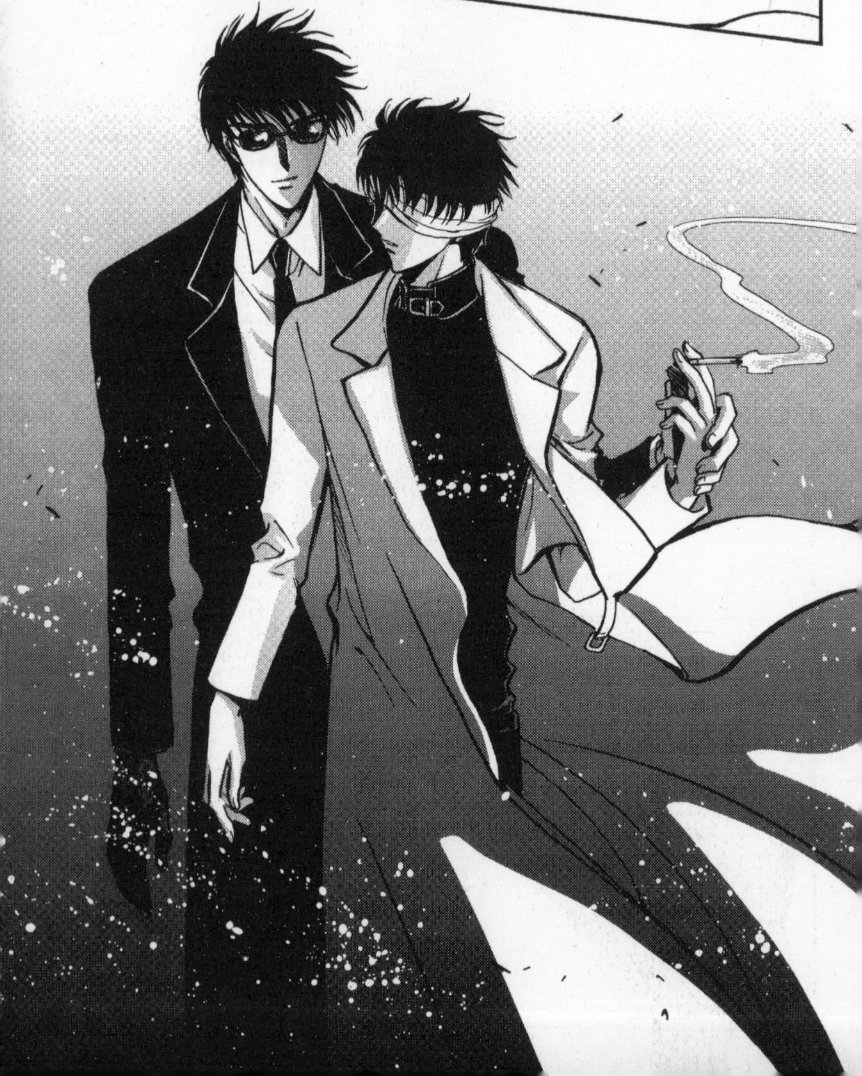

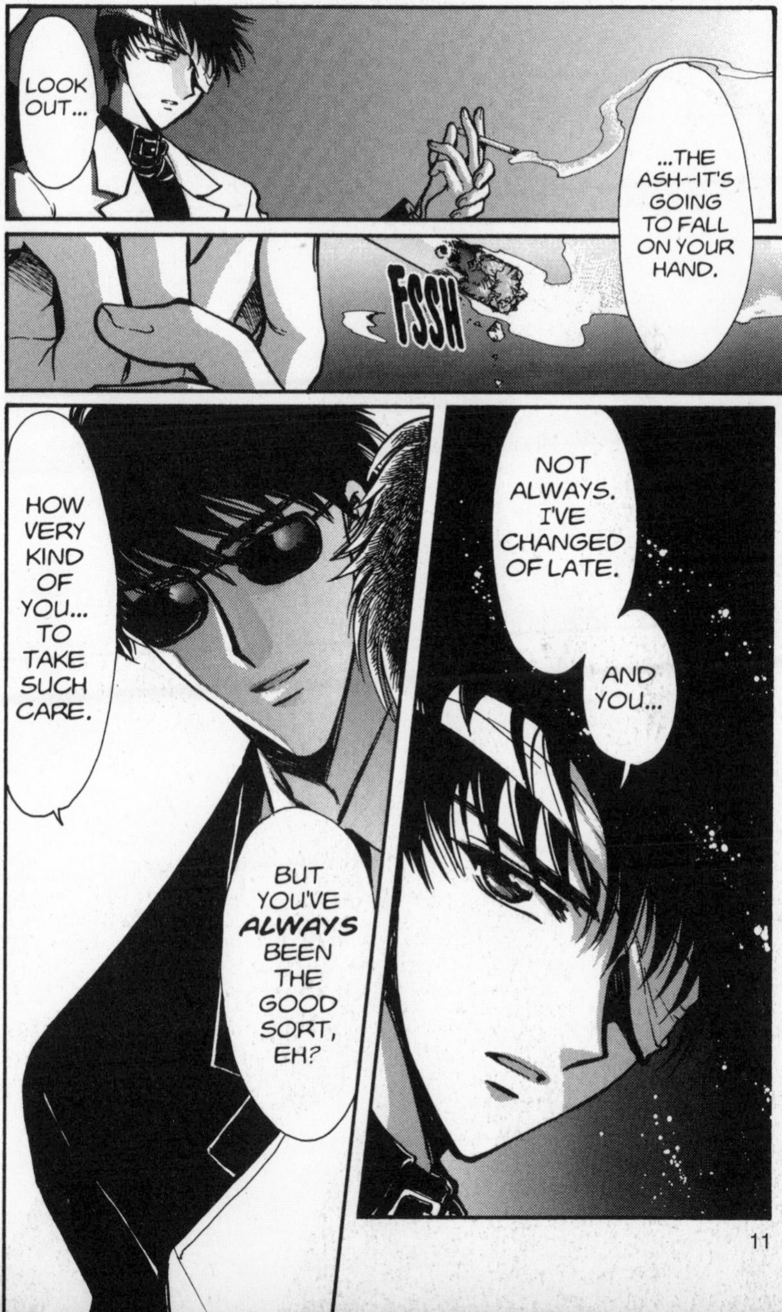

LOOK OUT...
...THE ASH--IT'S GOING TO FALL ON YOUR HAND.
FSSH
HOW VERY KIND OF YOU... TO TAKE SUCH CARE.
NOT ALWAYS. I'VE CHANGED OF LATE.
AND YOU...
BUT YOU'VE ALWAYS BEEN THE GOOD SORT, EH?

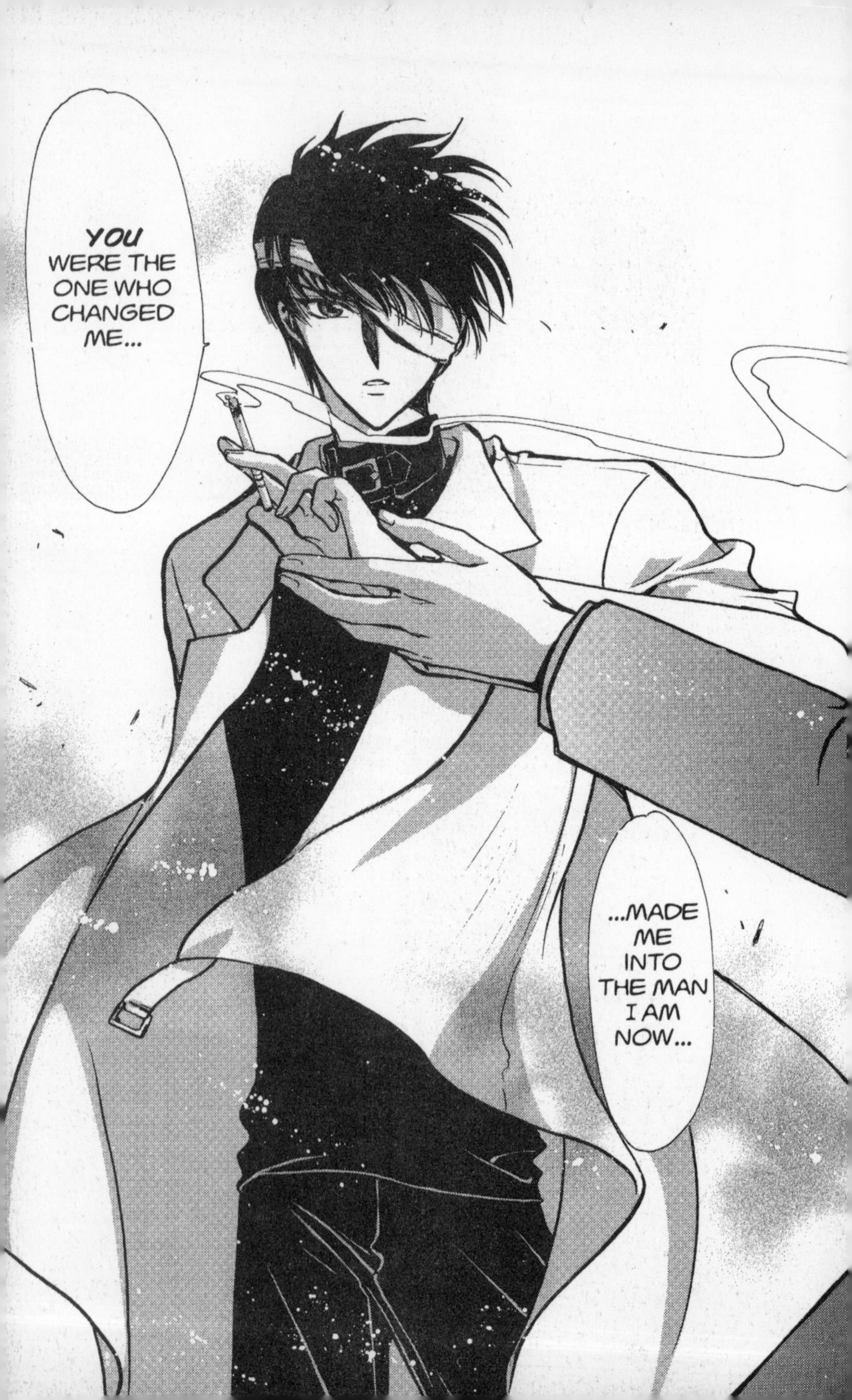
YOU WERE THE ONE WHO CHANGED ME...
...MADE ME INTO THE MAN I AM NOW...

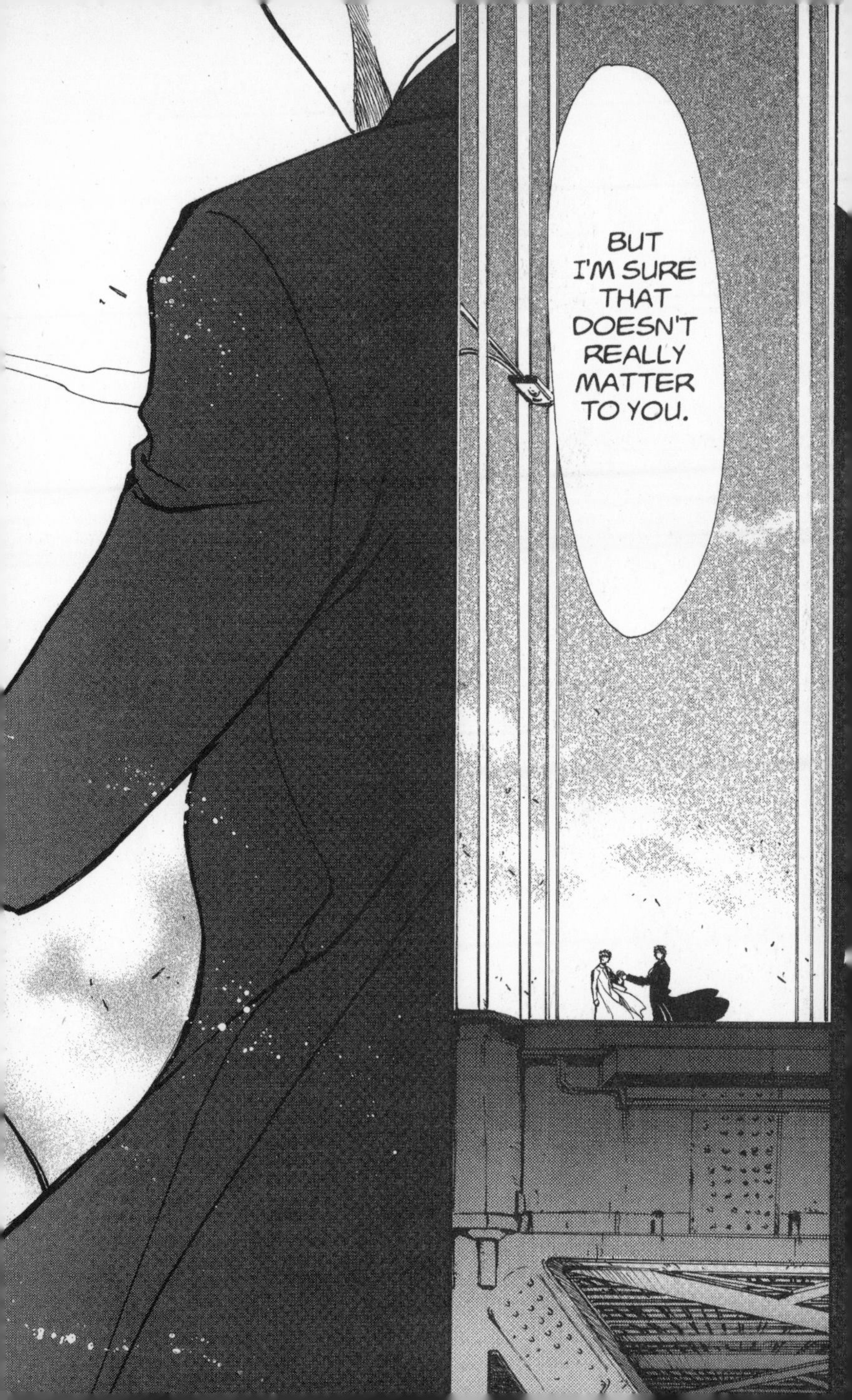
BUT I'M SURE THAT DOESN'T REALLY MATTER TO YOU.

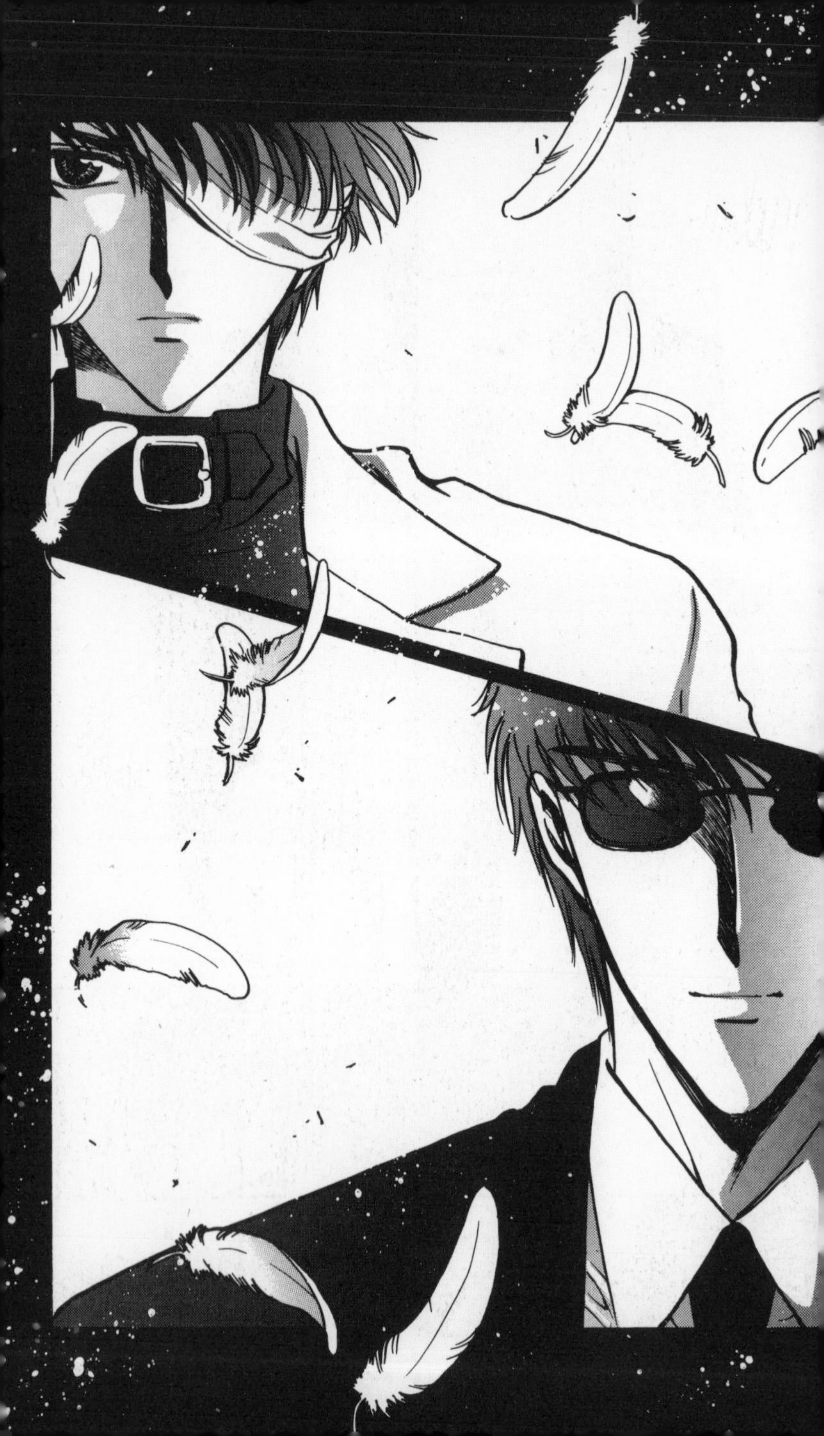

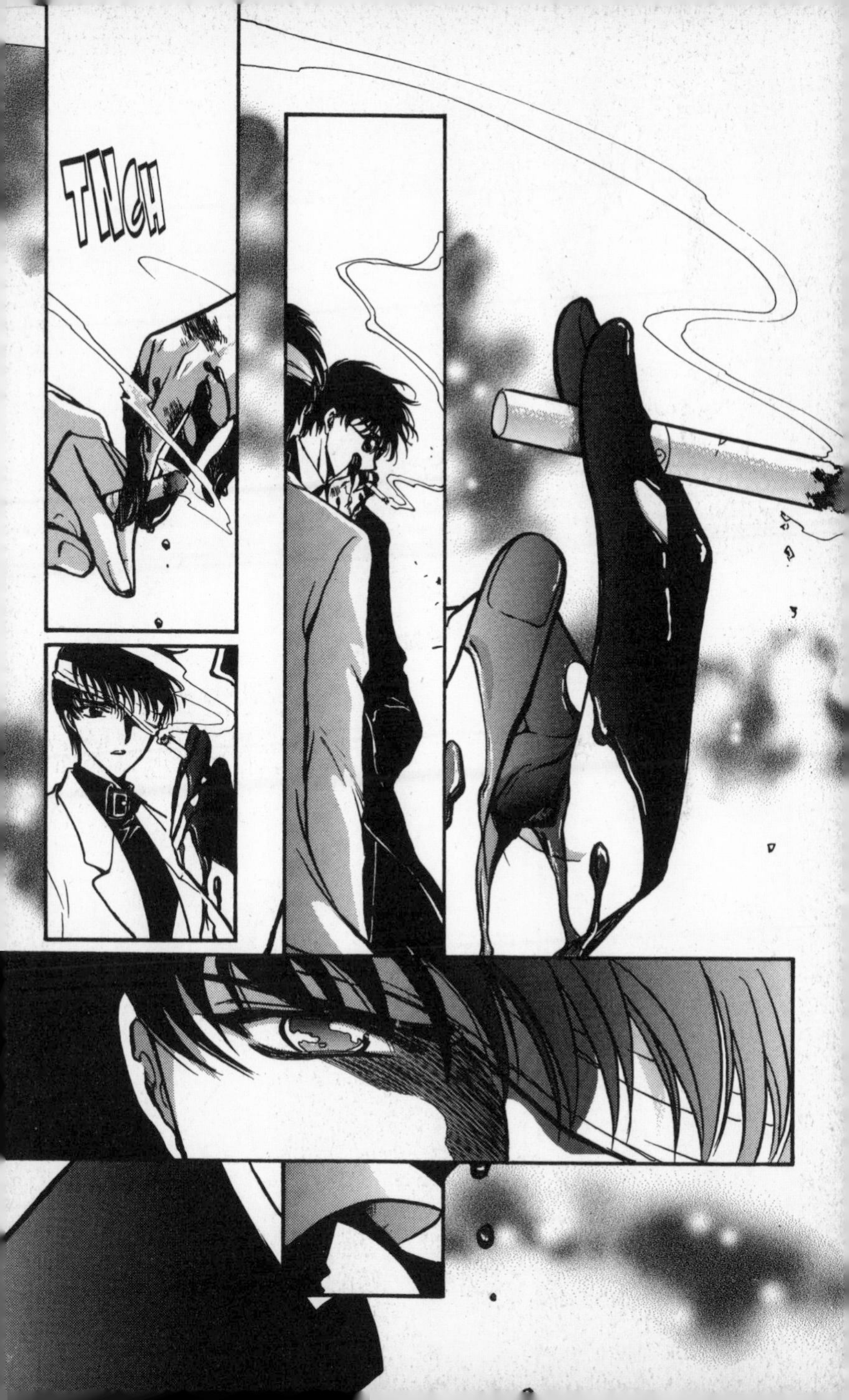
TNCH

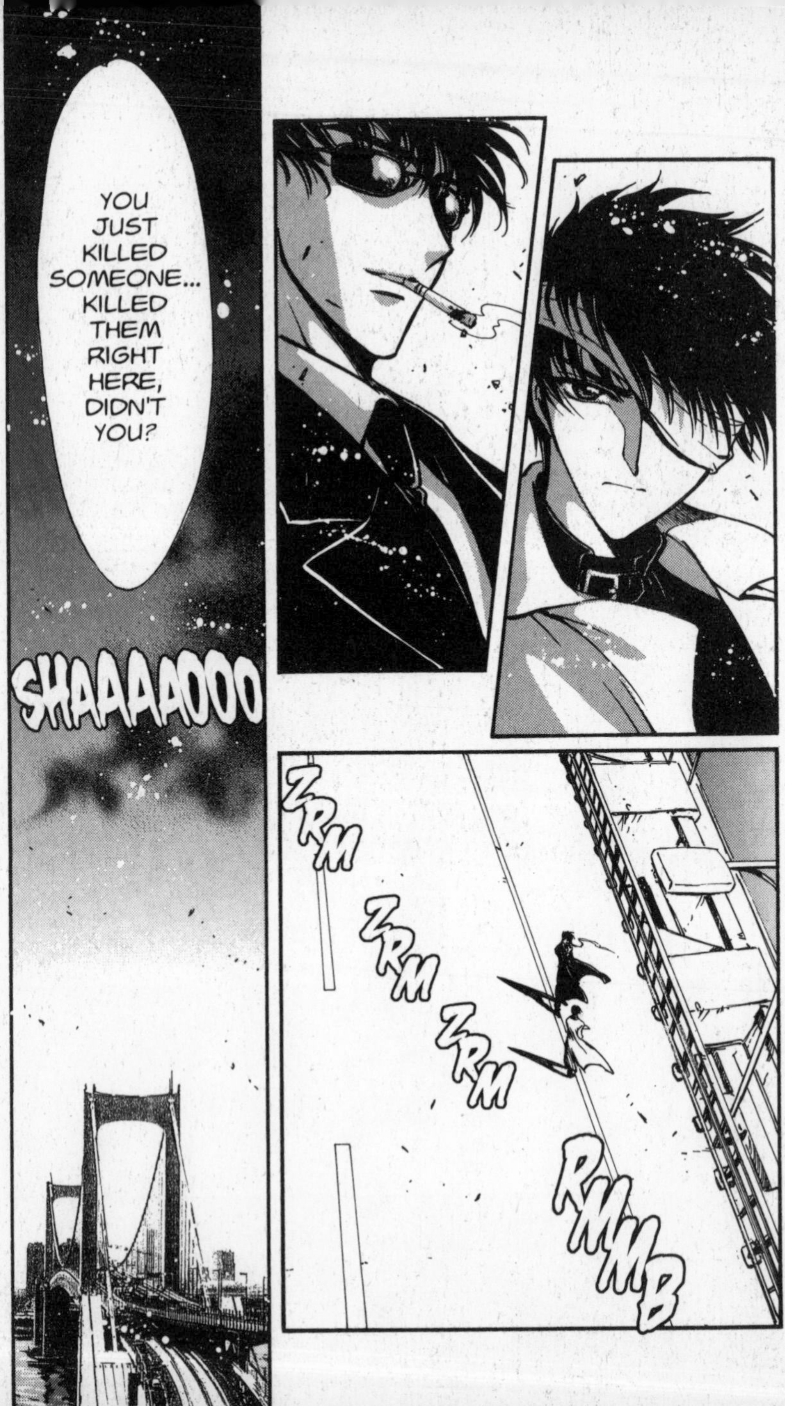
ZRM
ZRM
ZRM
RMMB
YOU JUST KILLED SOMEONE... KILLED THEM RIGHT HERE, DIDN'T YOU?
SHAAAAOOO

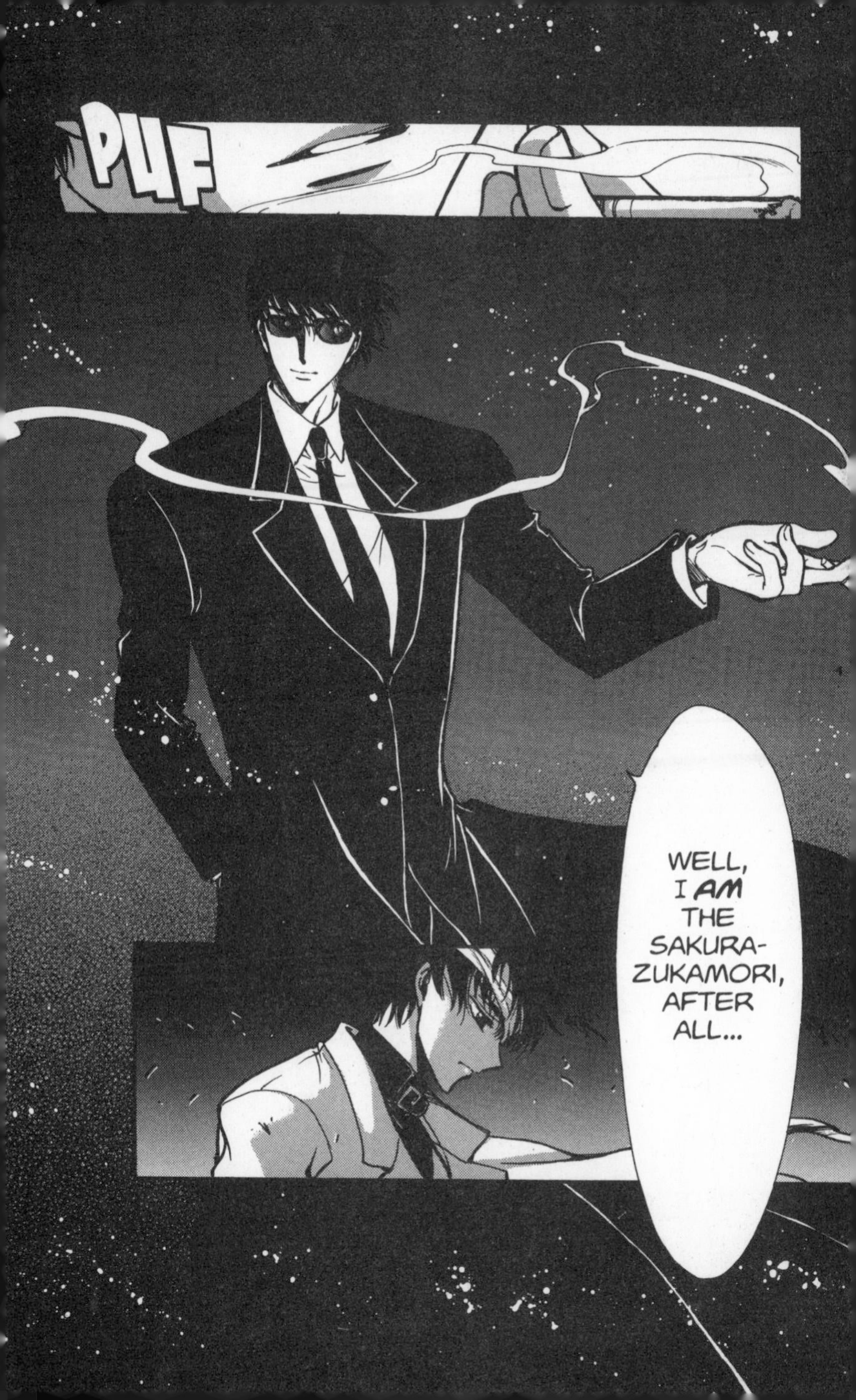
PUF
WELL, I AM THE SAKURA-ZUKAMORI, AFTER ALL...

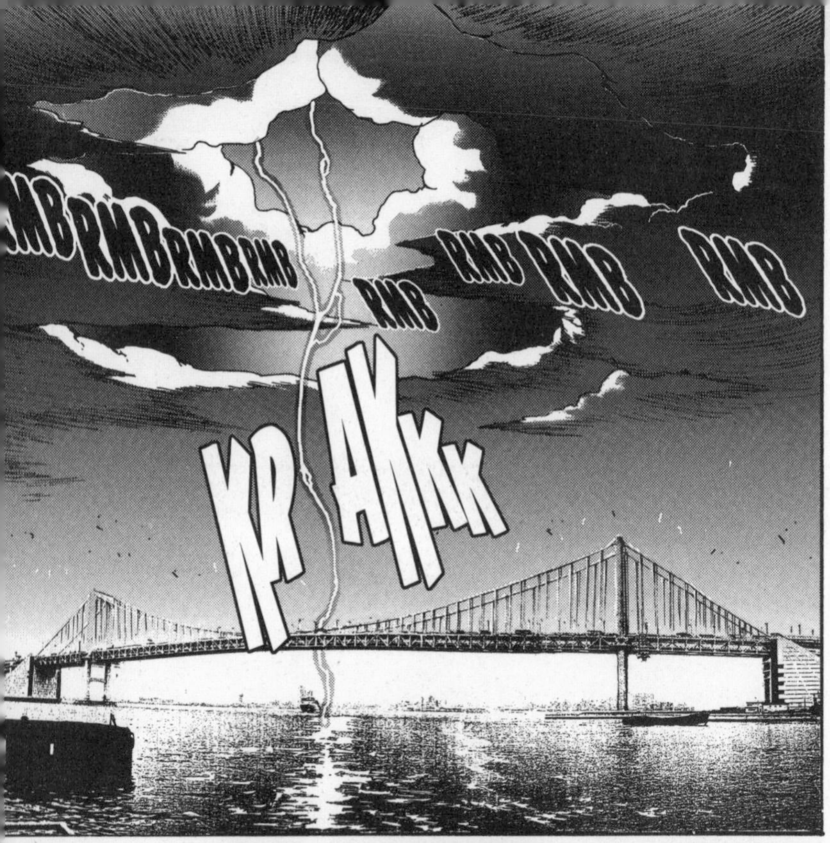
RMBRMBRMBRMB
RMB
RMB RMB
RMB
KRAKKK
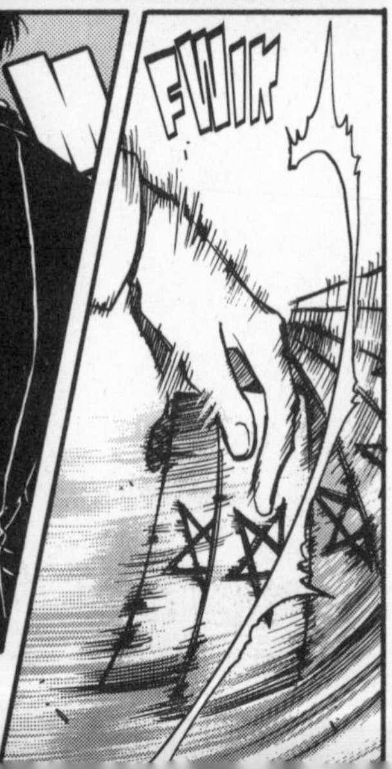
FWIK
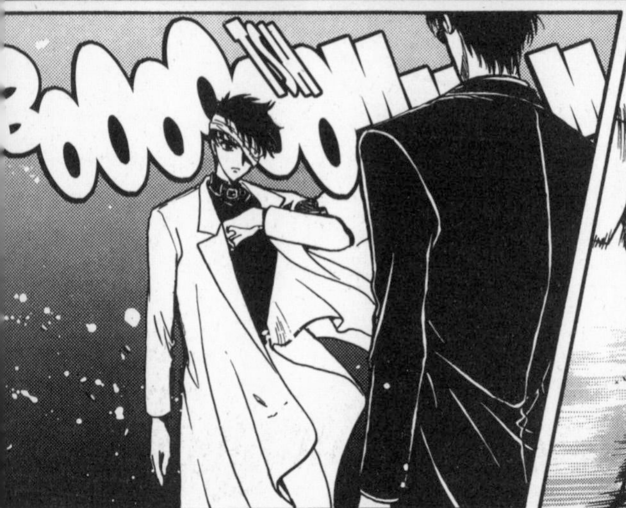
BOOOOOM--M
TSH

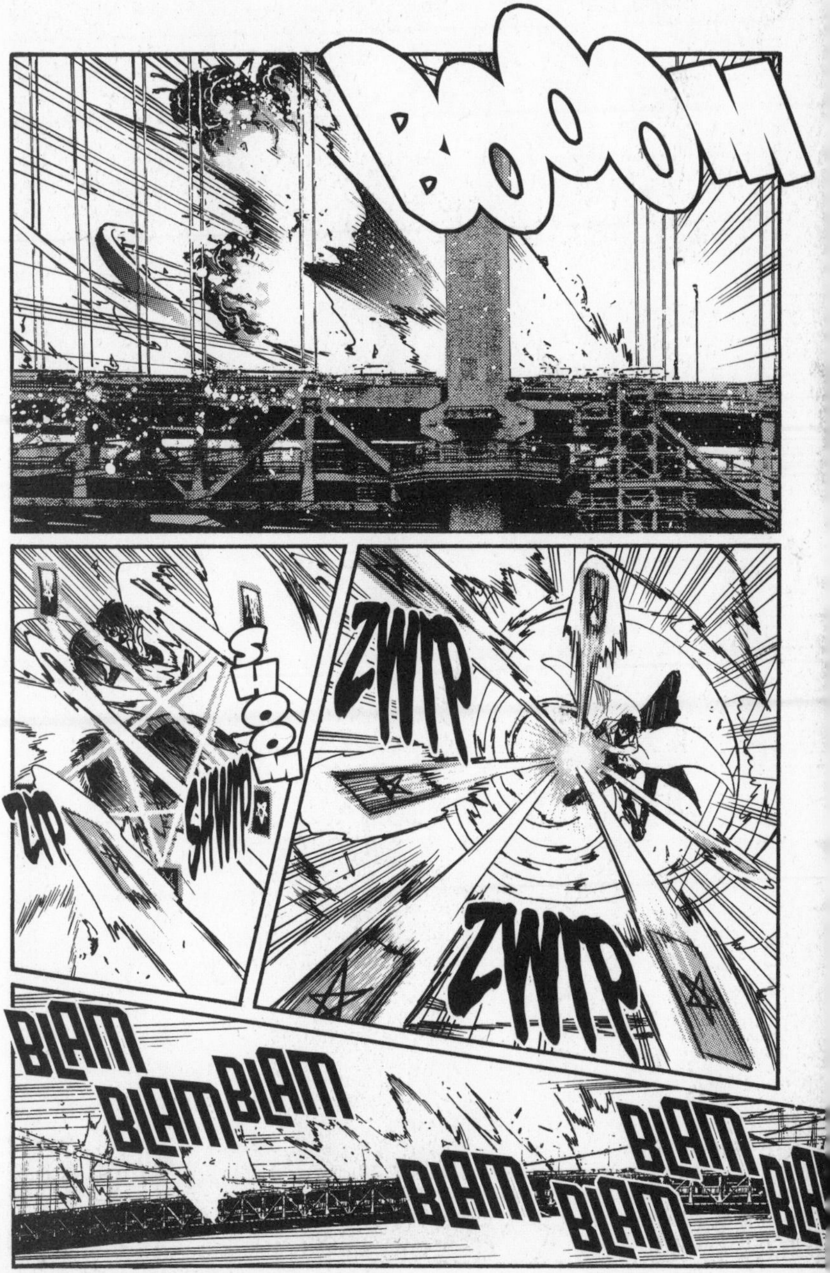
BOOOOM
ZWIP
ZWIP
SHOOOM
SHWIP
ZIP
BLAM
BLAM
BLAM
BLAM
BLAM
BLAM

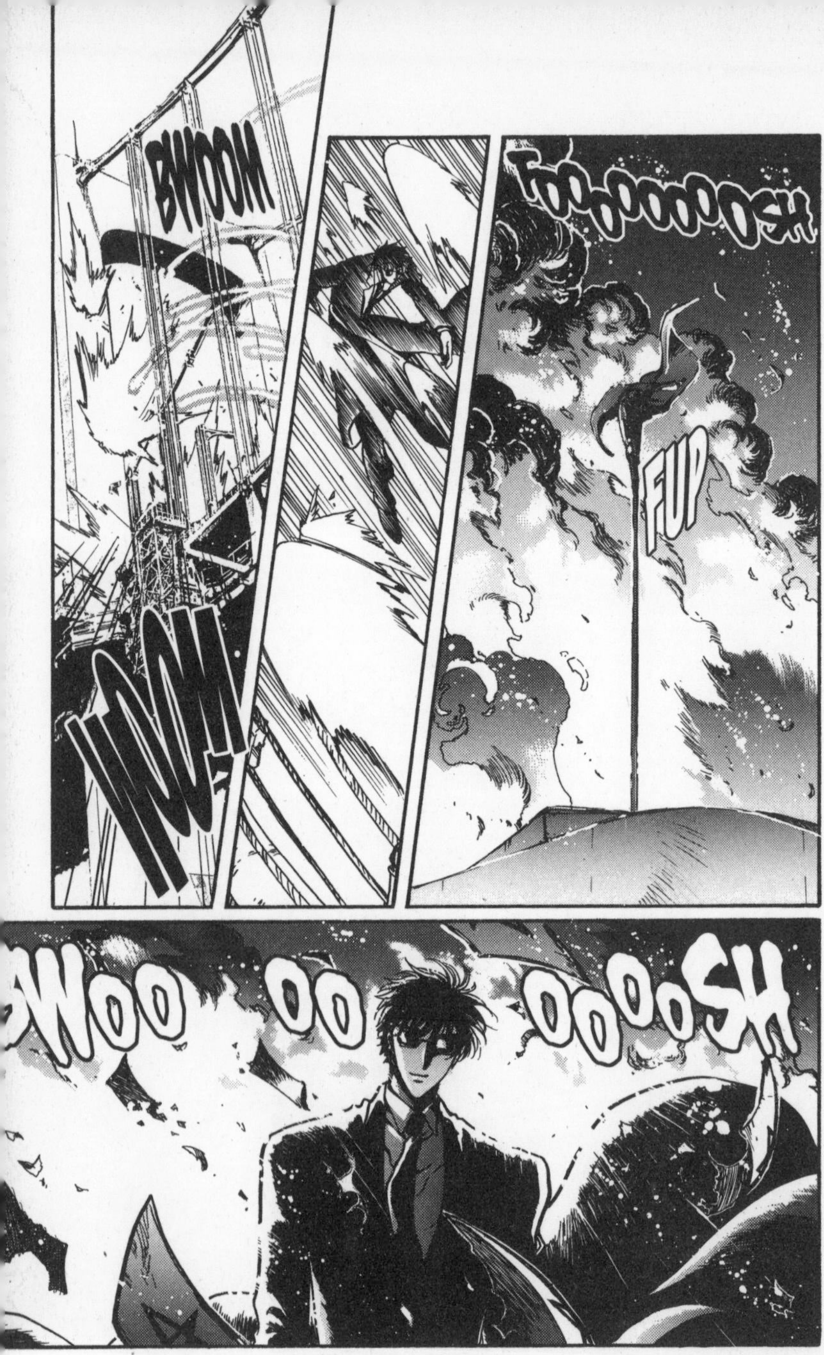
FOOOOOOOOSH
FUP
BWOOM
WOO OO OOOOSH

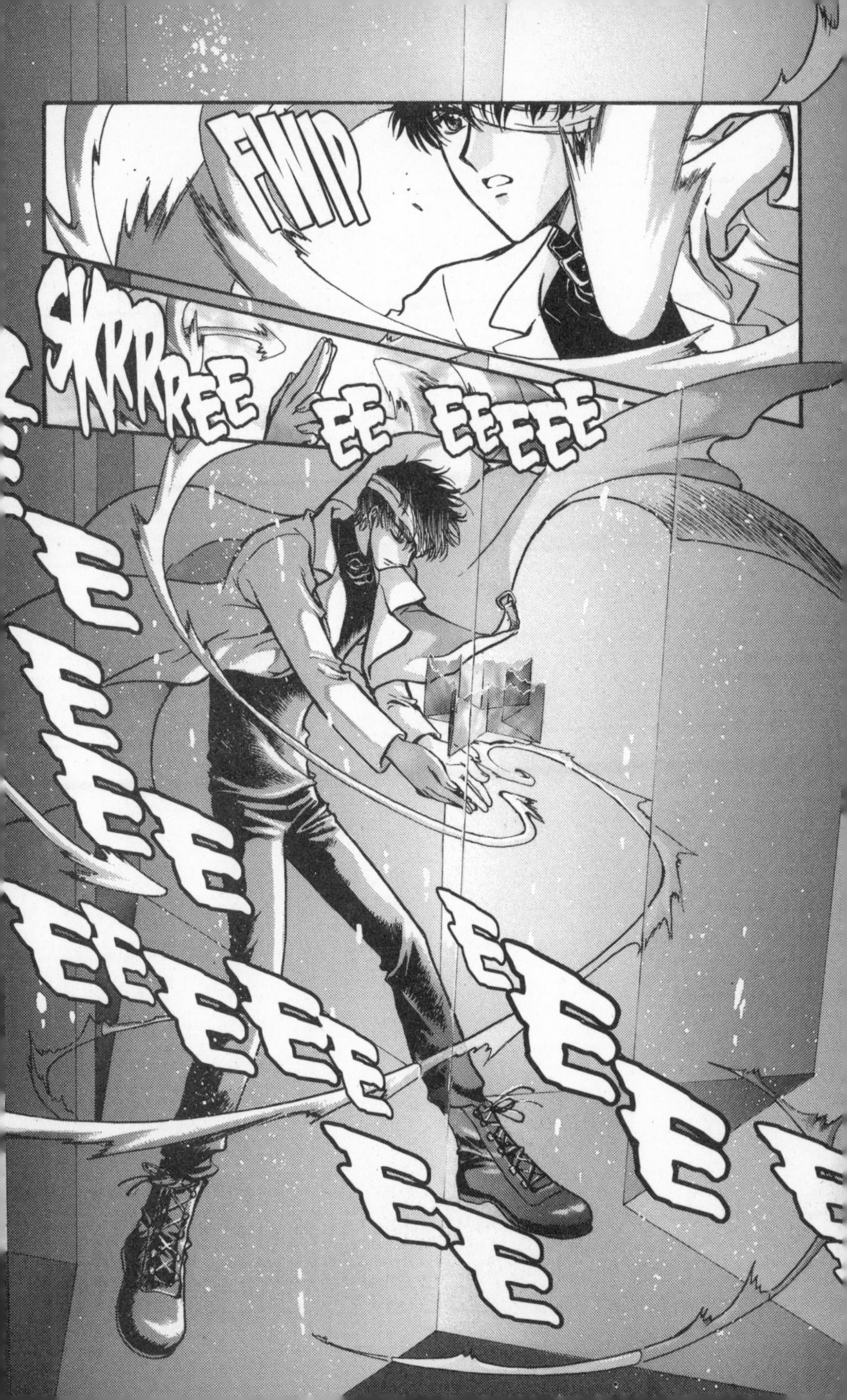
FWIP
SKRRREE
EE
EEEEE

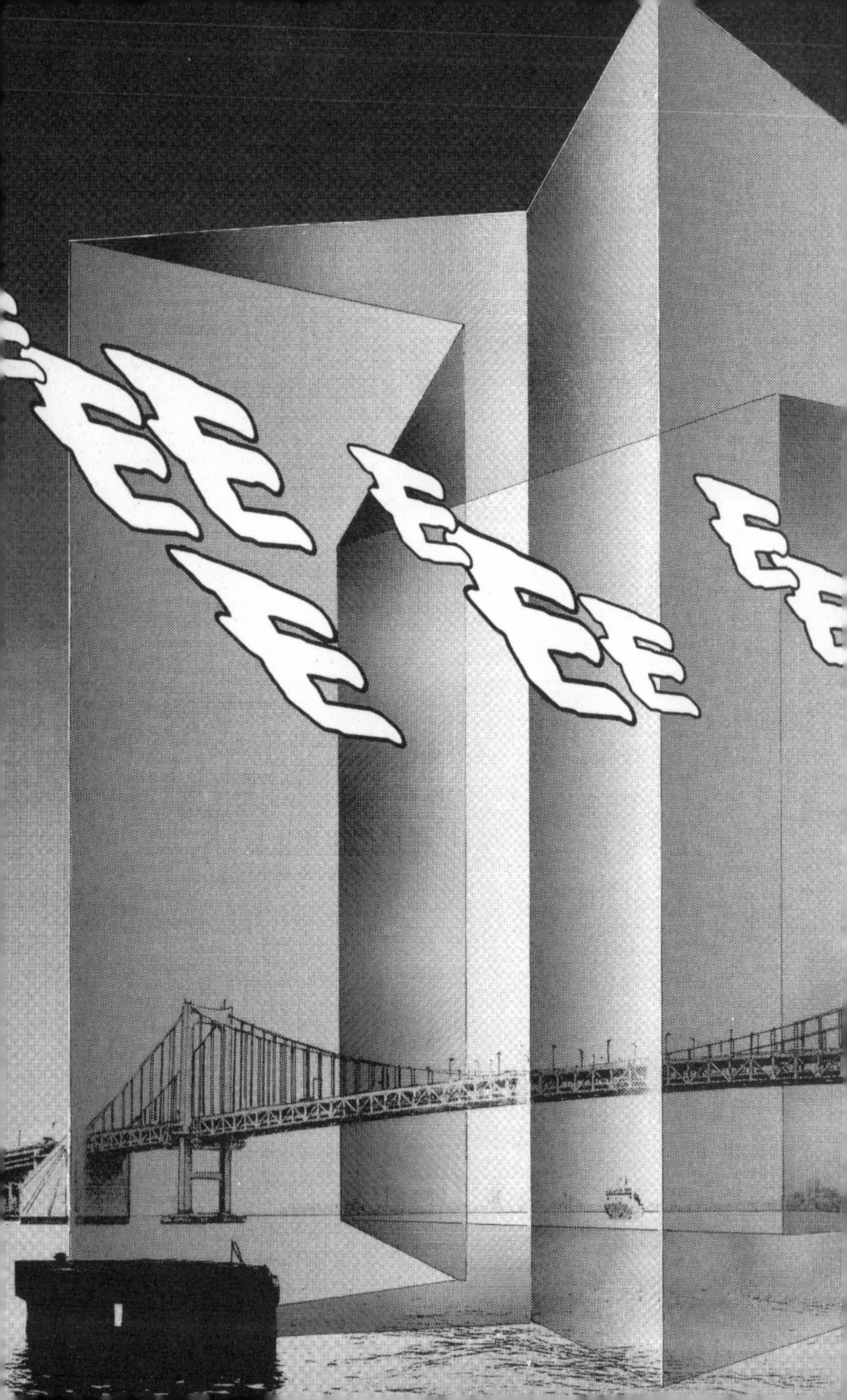

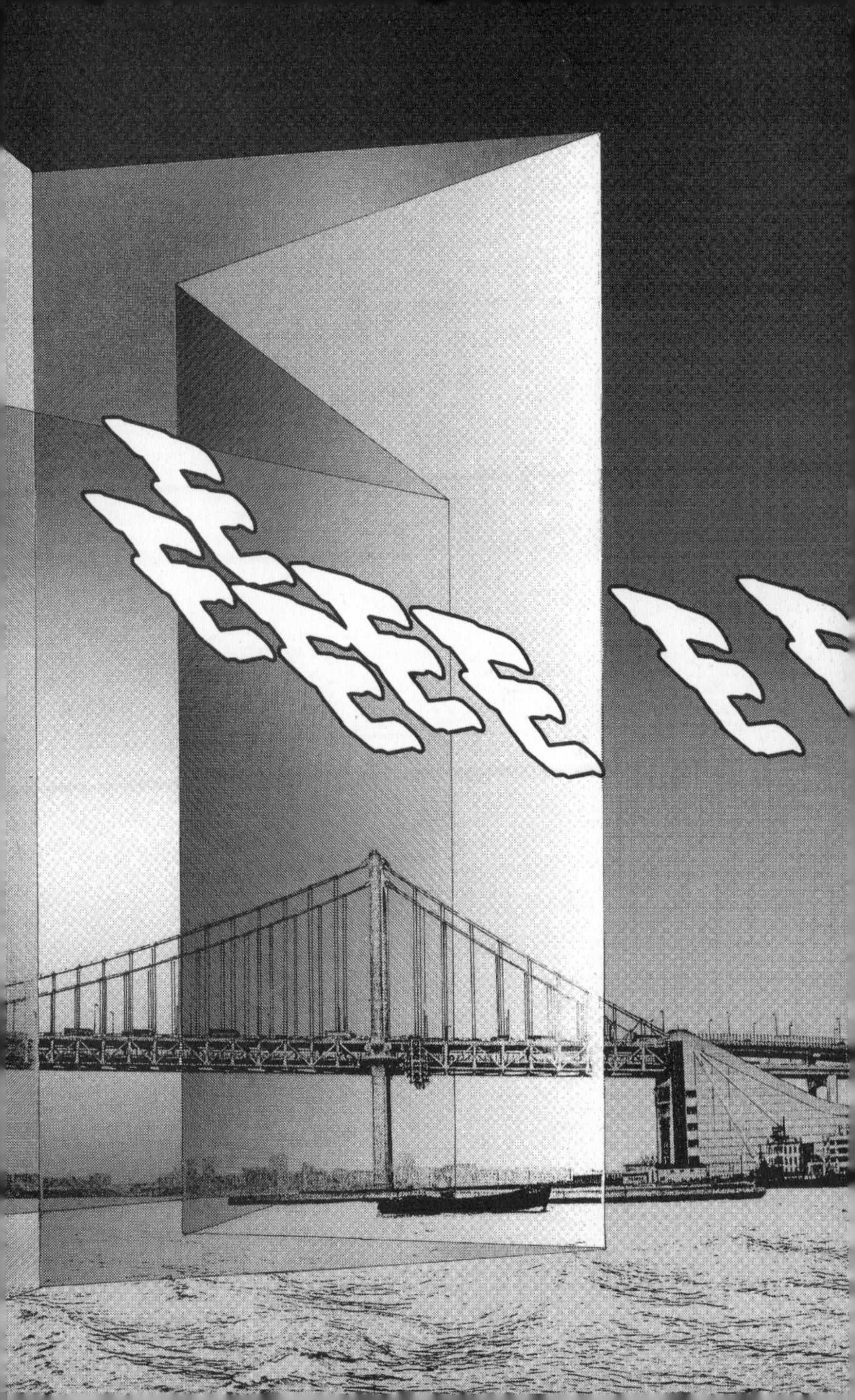

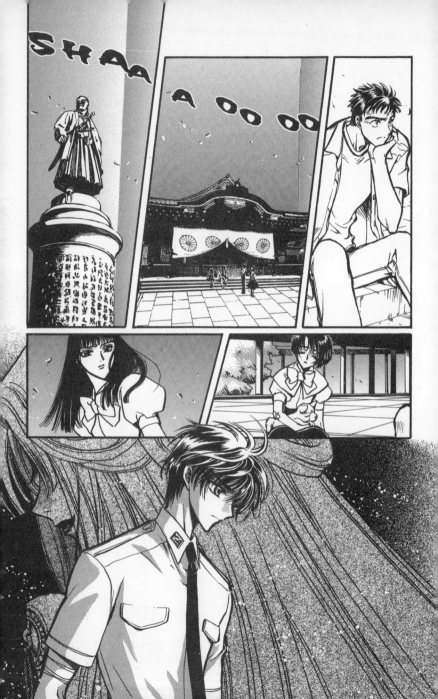

SHAAA OO OO

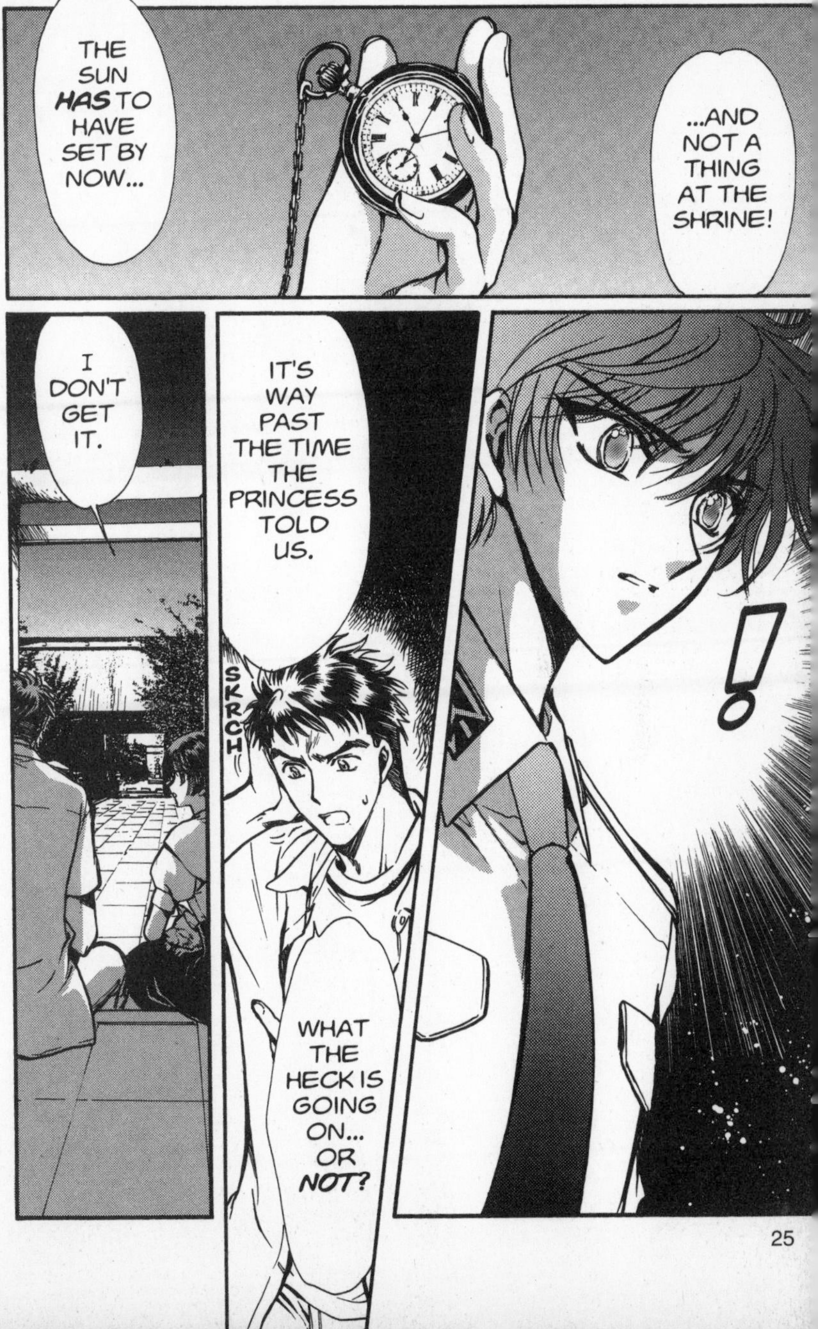
THE SUN HAS TO HAVE SET BY NOW...
...AND NOT A THING AT THE SHRINE!
I DON'T GET IT.
IT'S WAY PAST THE TIME THE PRINCESS TOLD US.
SKRCH
WHAT THE HECK IS GOING ON... OR NOT?
!

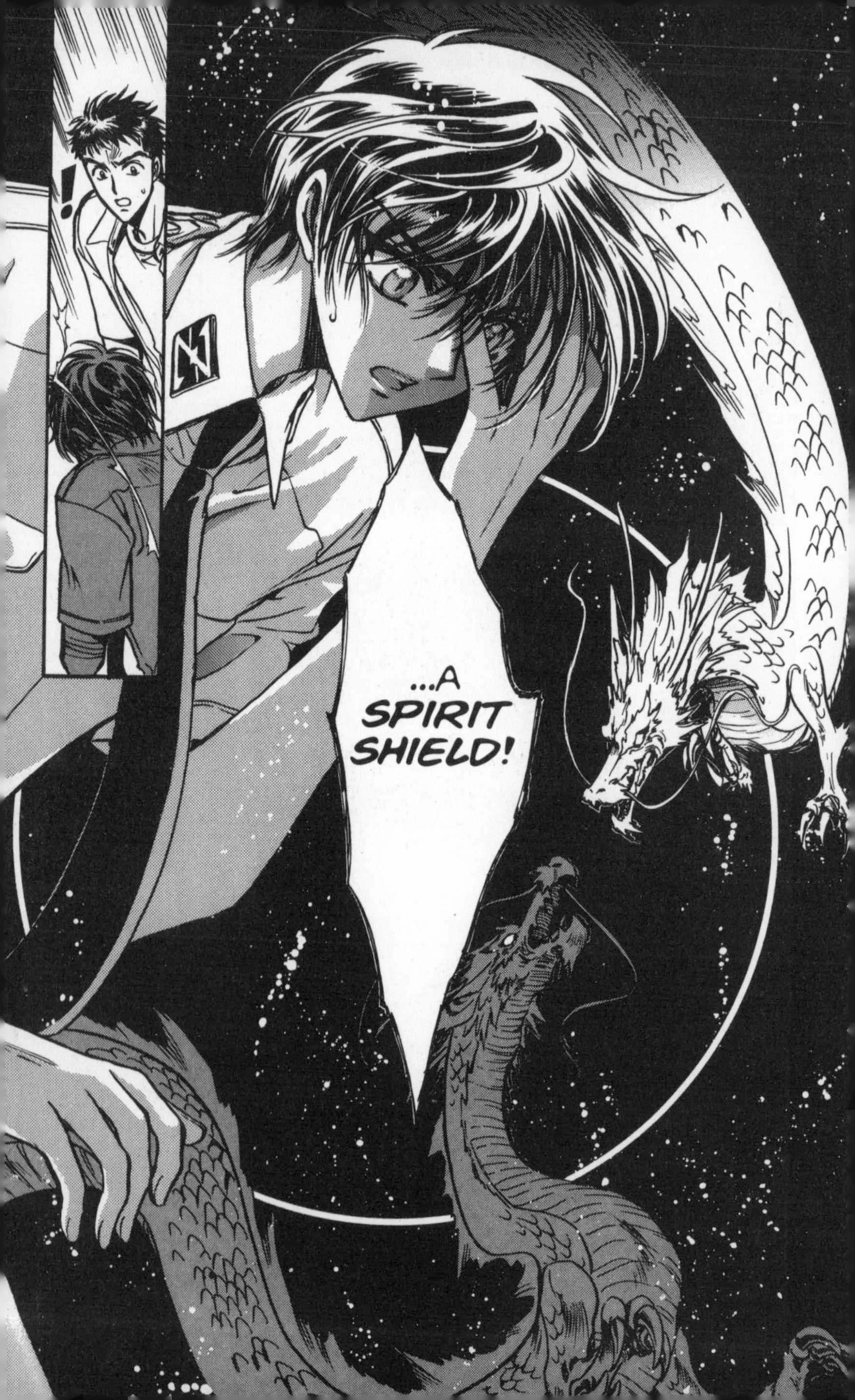
!
...A SPIRIT SHIELD!

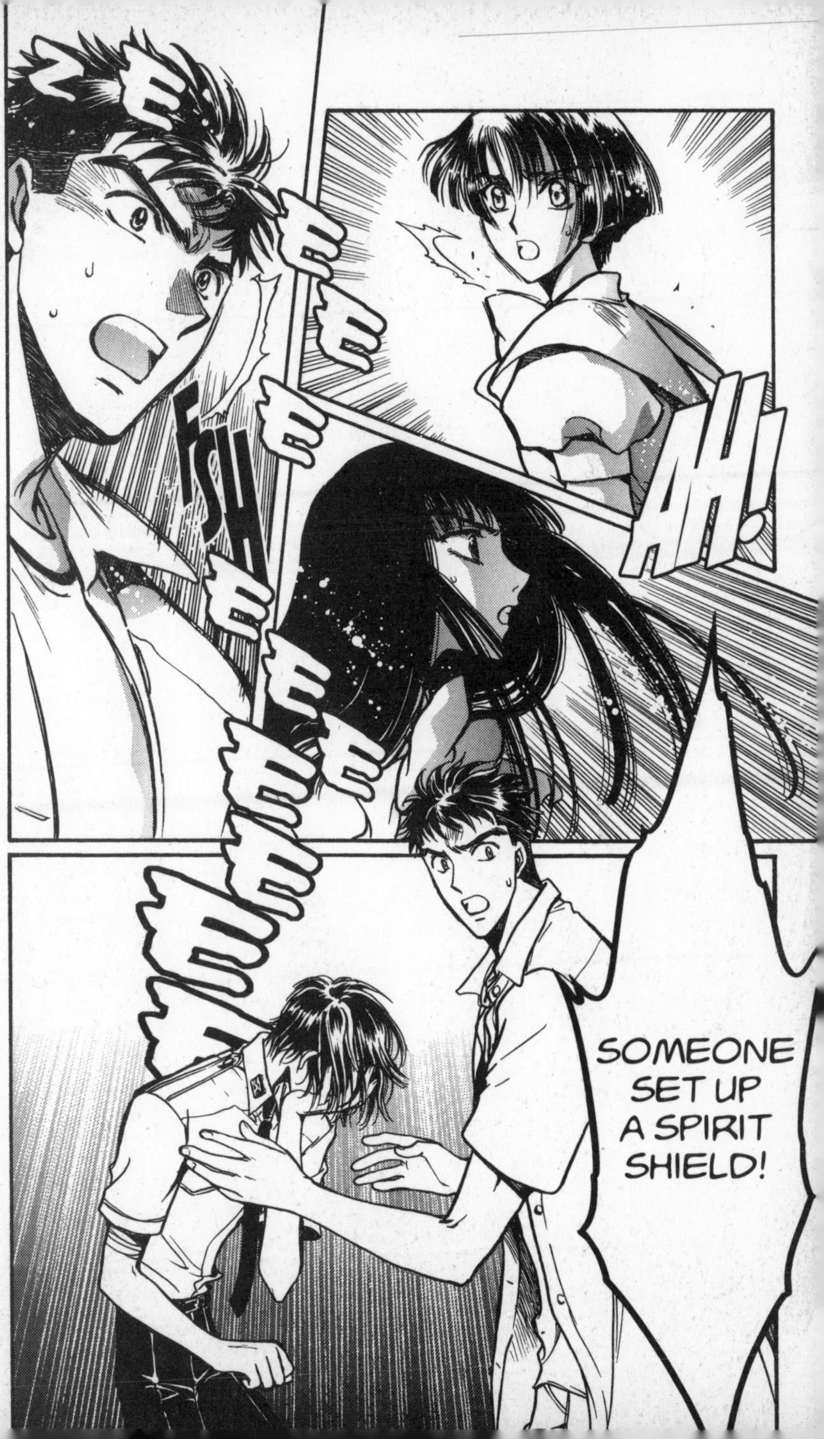
AH!
FSH
SOMEONE SET UP A SPIRIT SHIELD!

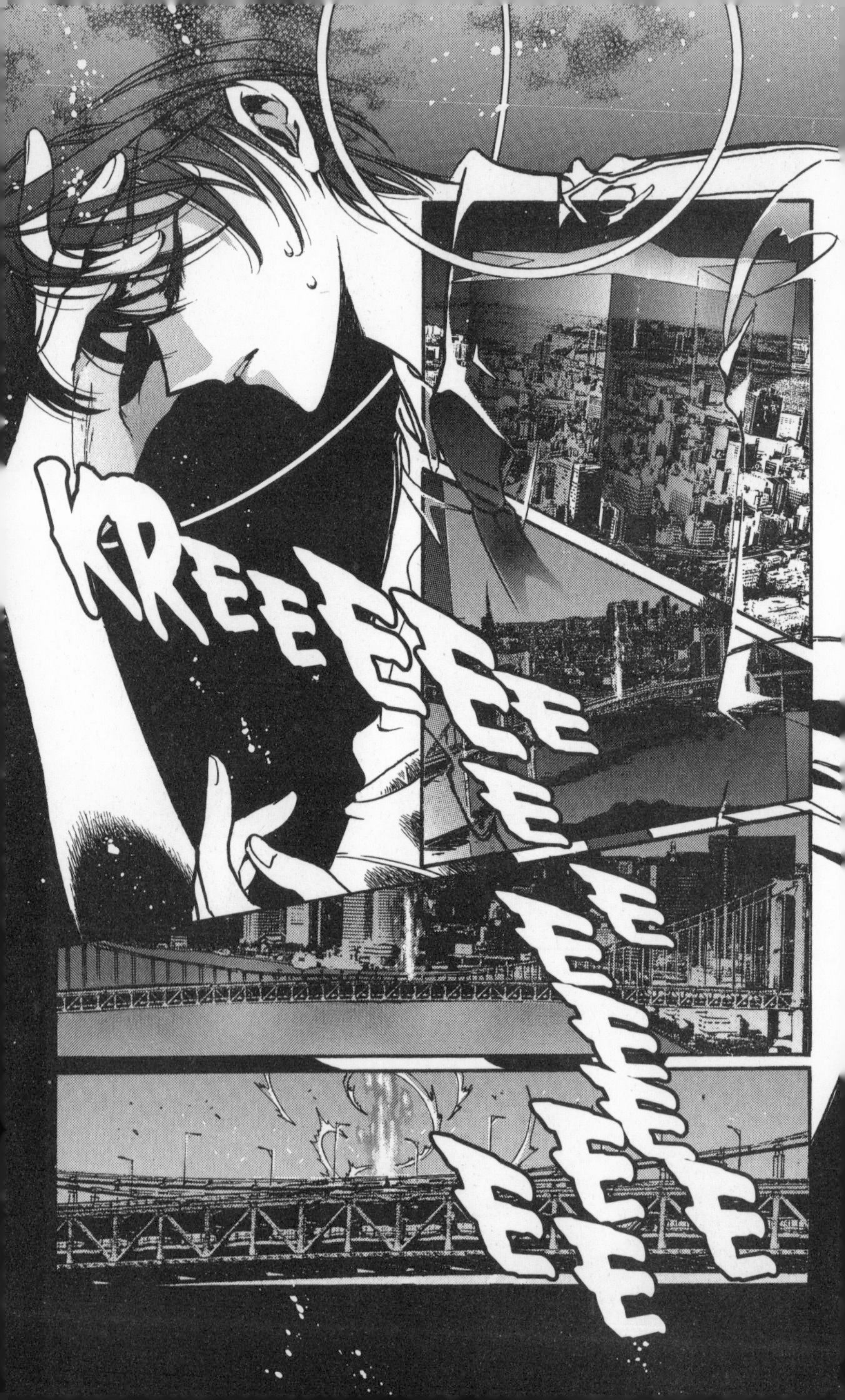
KREEEEEEEEEEEEEE

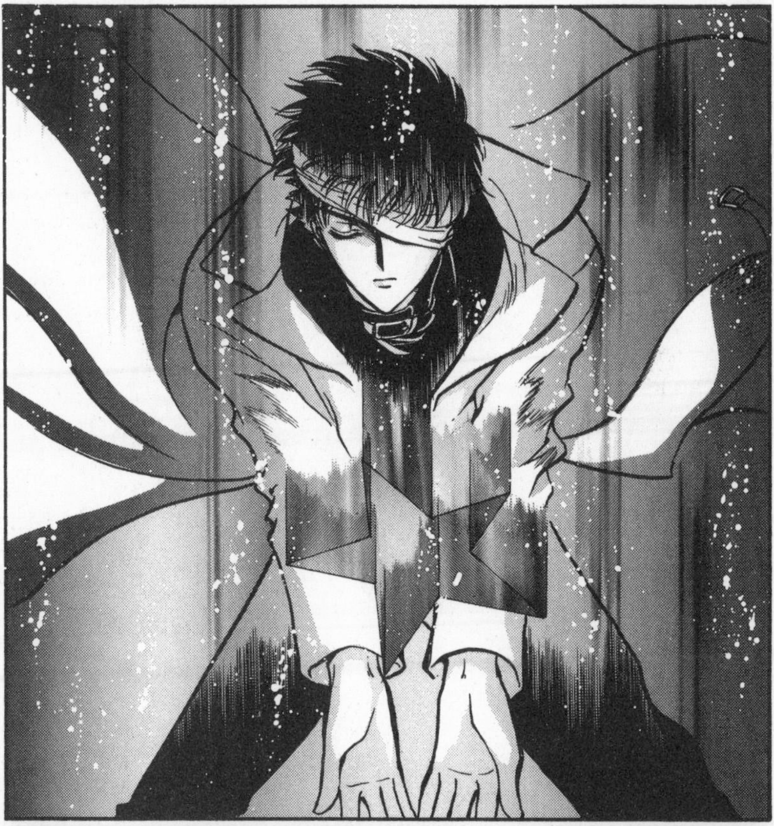
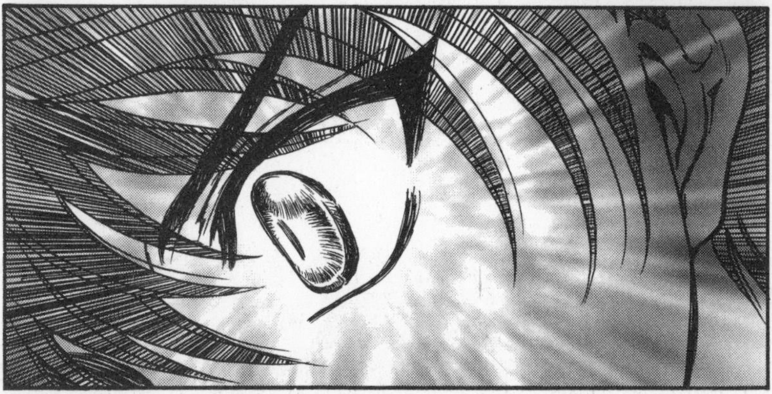

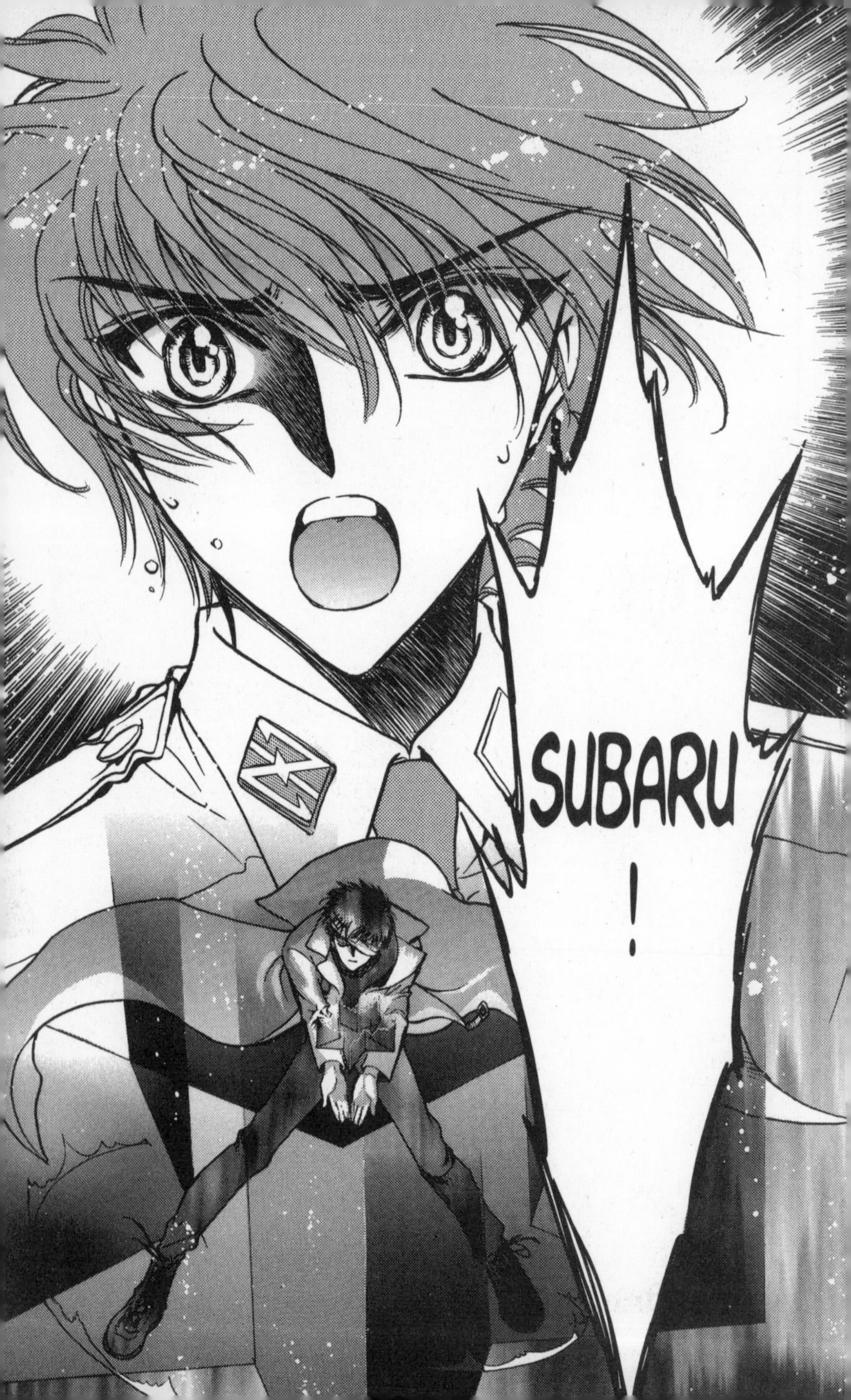
SUBARU!

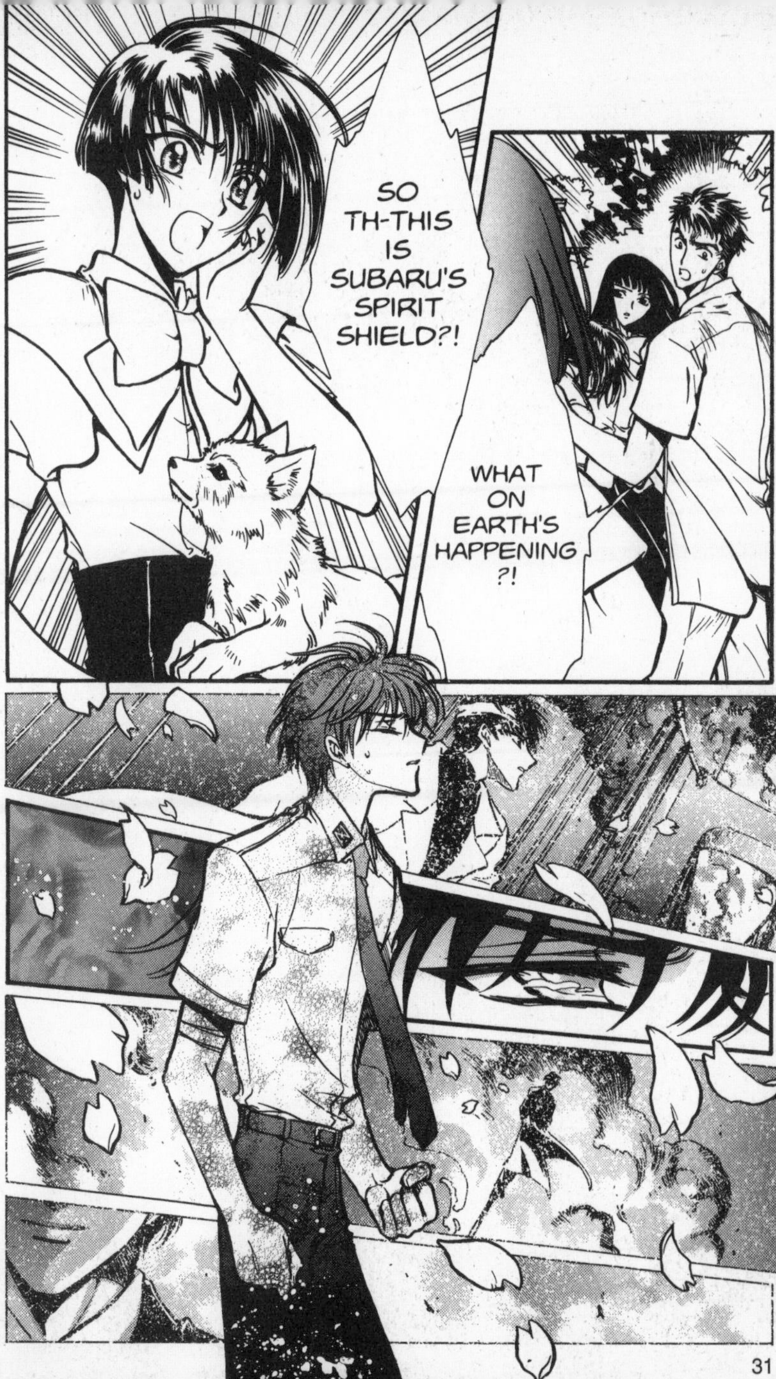
SO TH-THIS IS SUBARU'S SPIRIT SHIELD?!
WHAT ON EARTH'S HAPPENING ?!

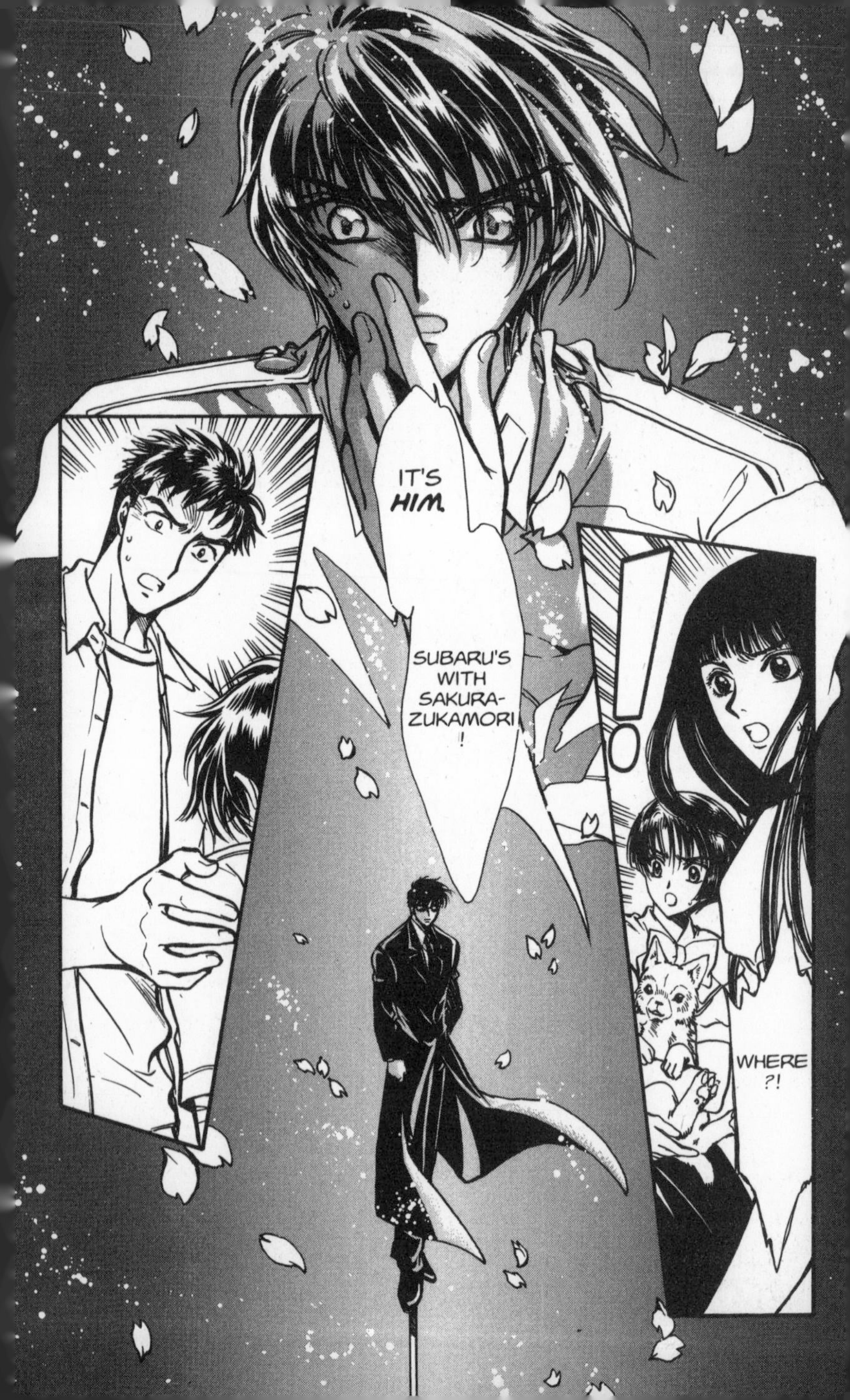
IT'S HIM.
SUBARU'S WITH SAKURA-ZUKAMORI!
!
WHERE?!

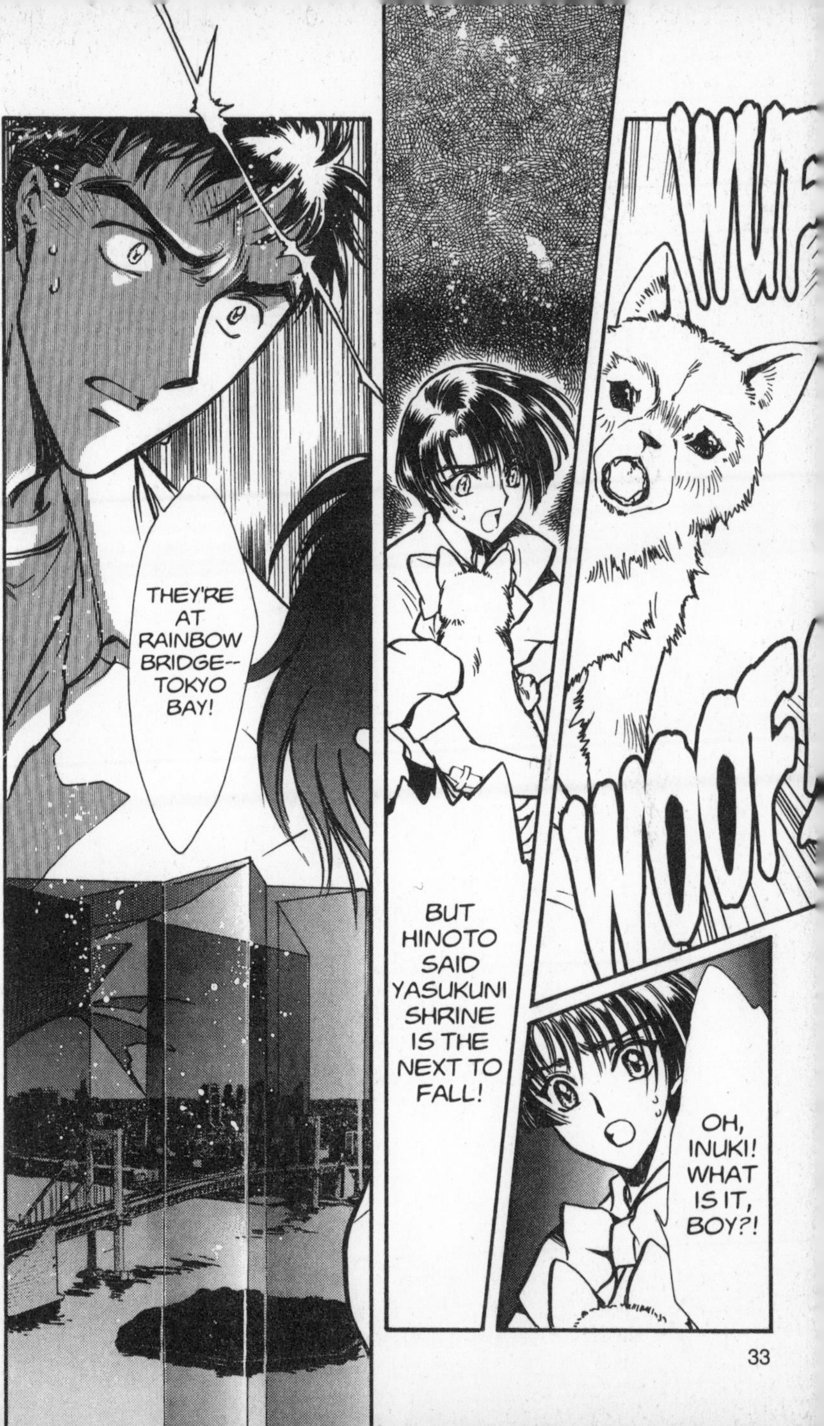
THEY'RE AT RAINBOW BRIDGE-- TOKYO BAY!
BUT HINOTO SAID YASUKUNI SHRINE IS THE NEXT TO FALL!
WUF
WOOF!
OH, INUKI! WHAT IS IT, BOY?!

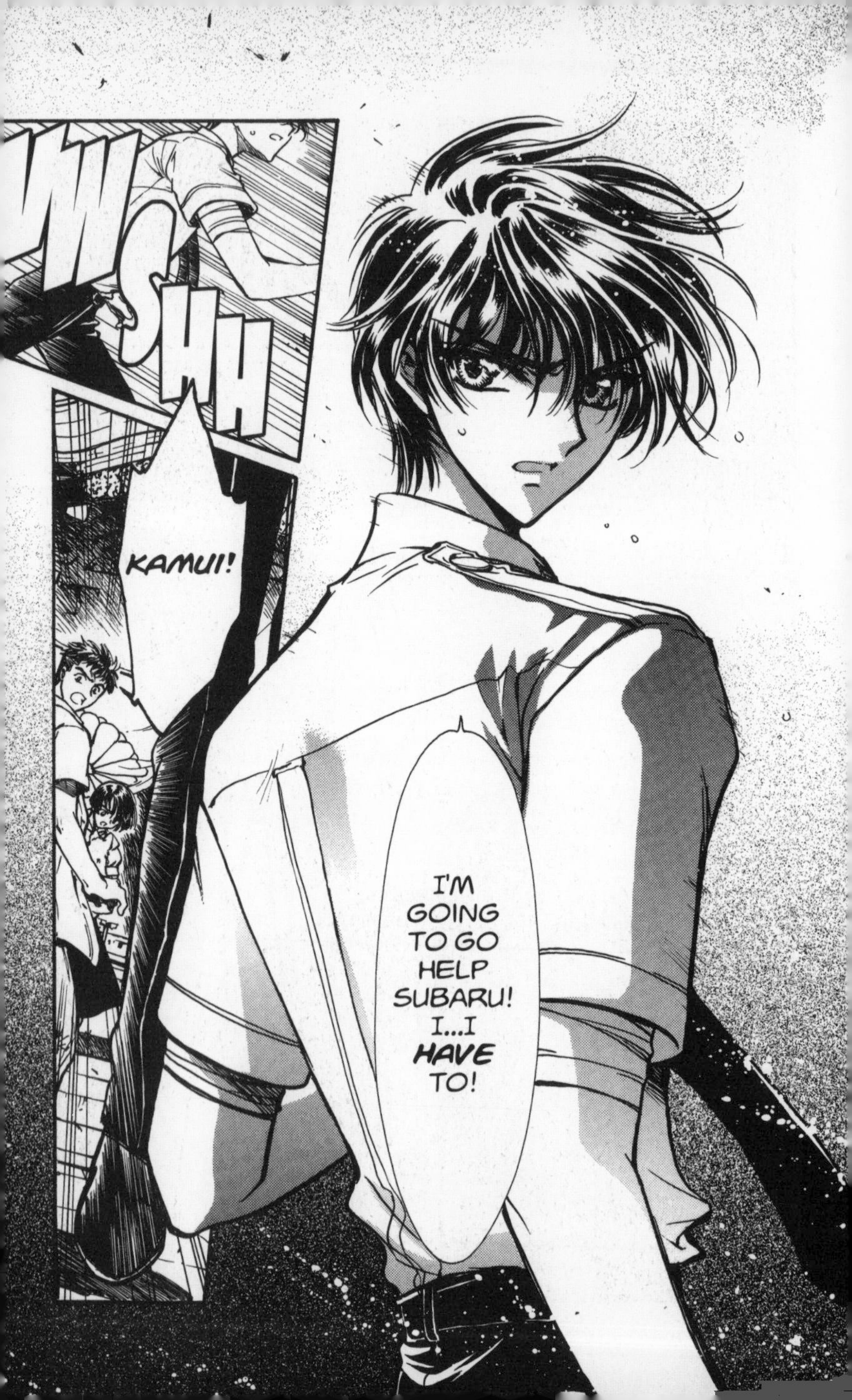
KAMUI!
I'M GOING TO GO HELP SUBARU! I...I *HAVE* TO!

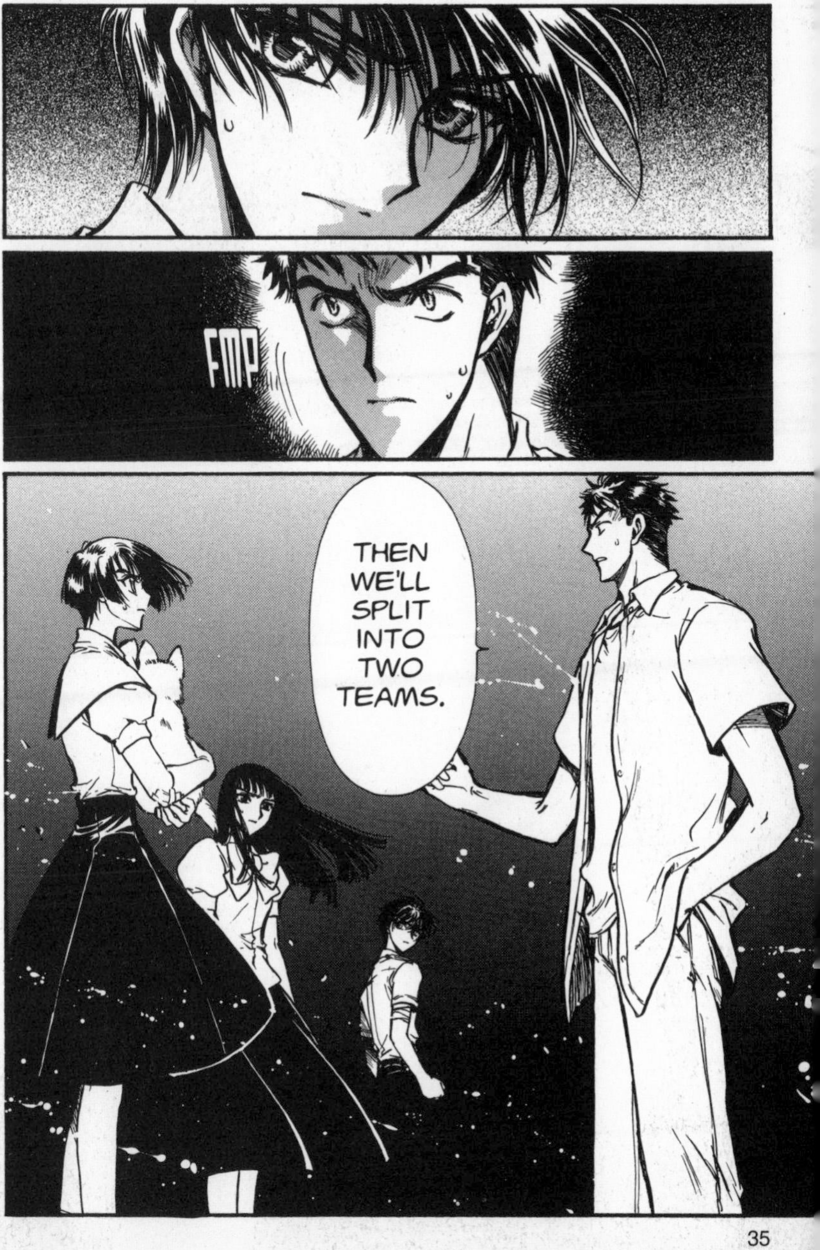
FMP
THEN WE'LL SPLIT INTO TWO TEAMS.

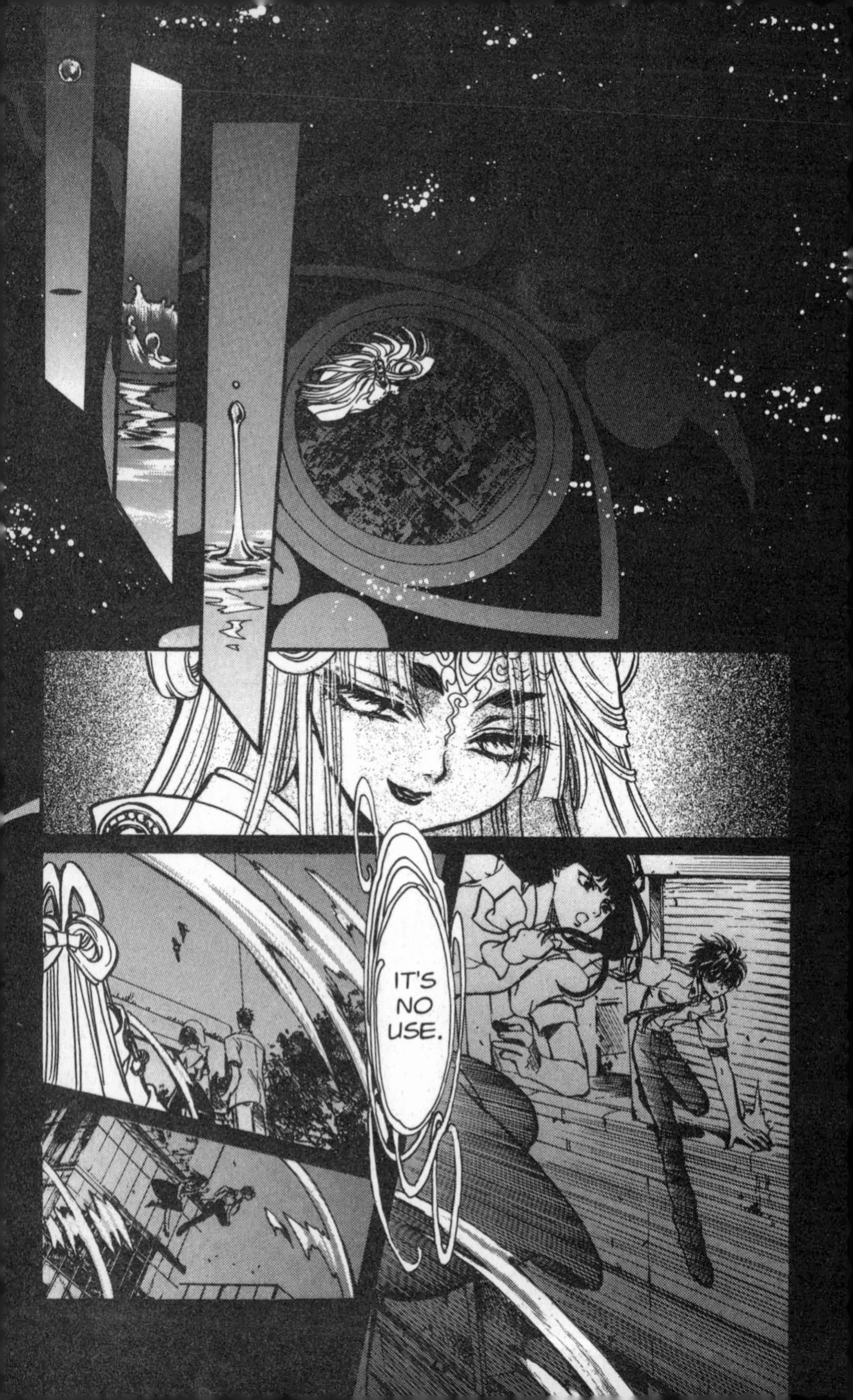
IT'S NO USE.

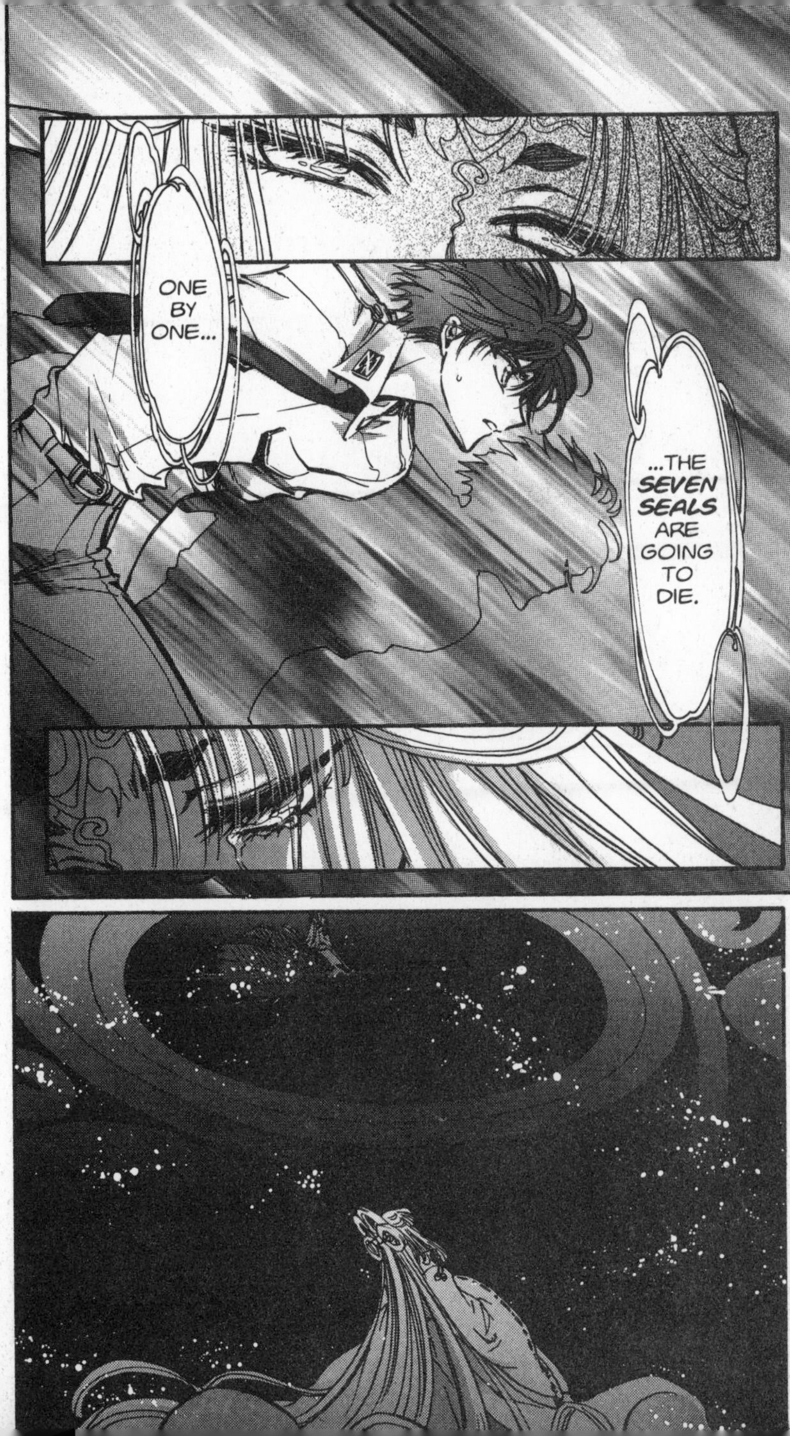
ONE BY ONE...
...THE SEVEN SEALS ARE GOING TO DIE.

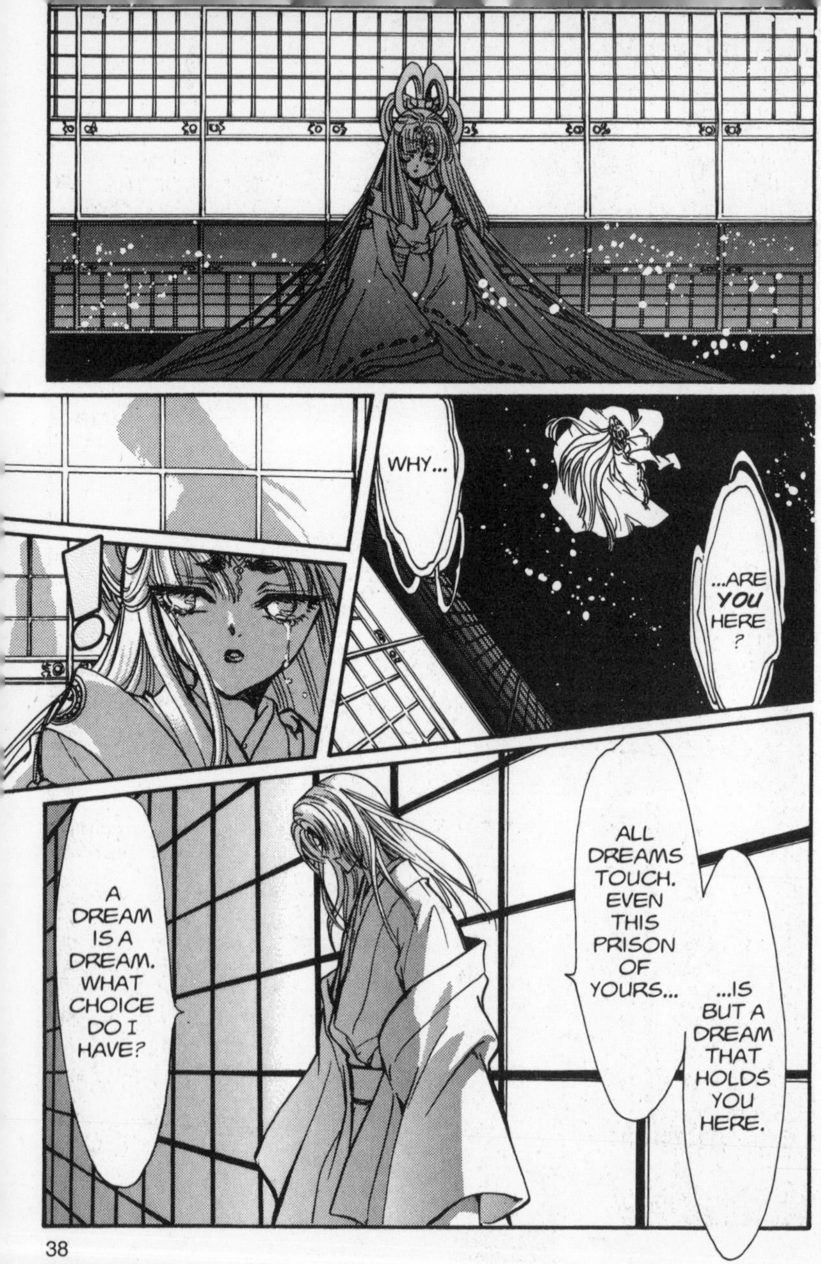
WHY...
...ARE YOU HERE?
ALL DREAMS TOUCH. EVEN THIS PRISON OF YOURS...
...IS BUT A DREAM THAT HOLDS YOU HERE.
A DREAM IS A DREAM. WHAT CHOICE DO I HAVE?

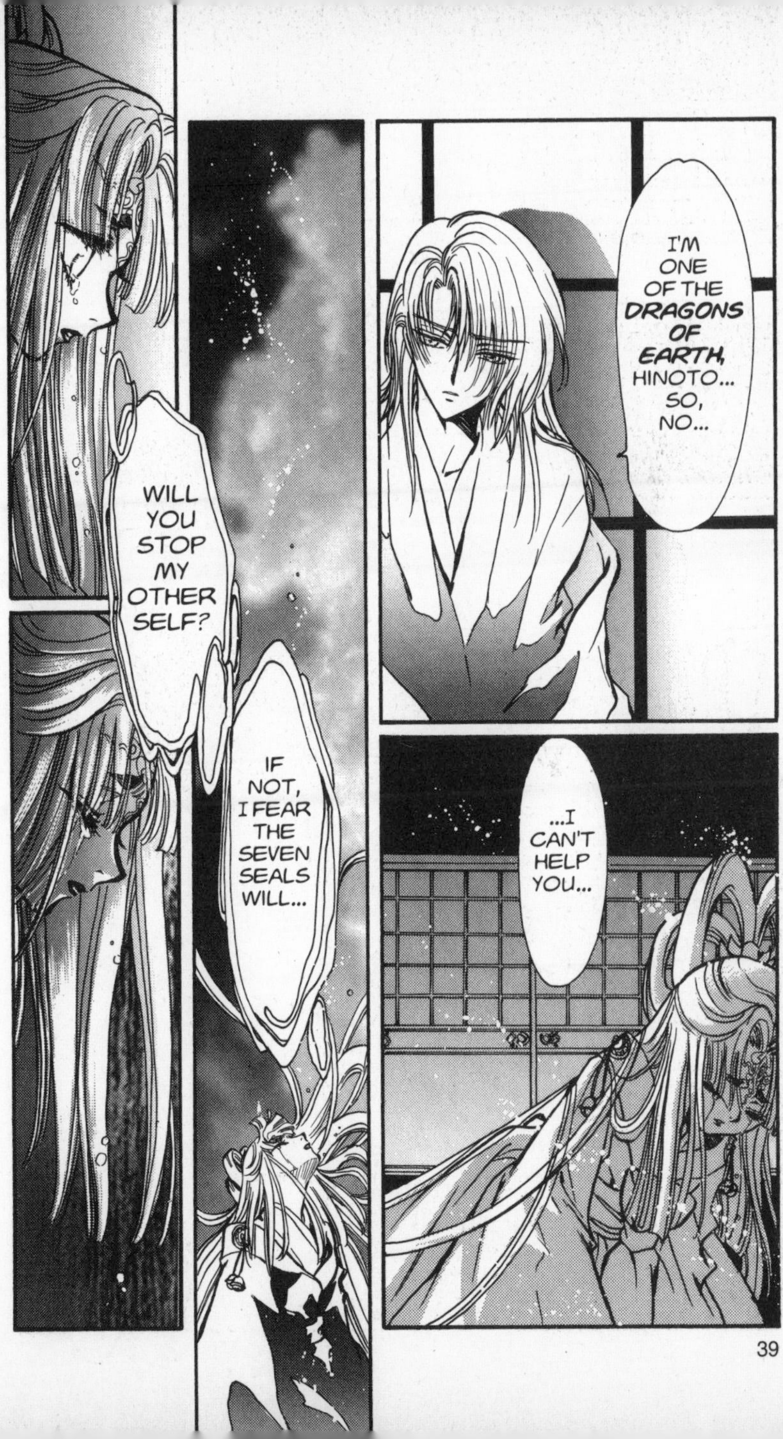
WILL YOU STOP MY OTHER SELF?
IF NOT, I FEAR THE SEVEN SEALS WILL...
I'M ONE OF THE *DRAGONS OF EARTH,* HINOTO... SO, NO...
...I CAN'T HELP YOU...

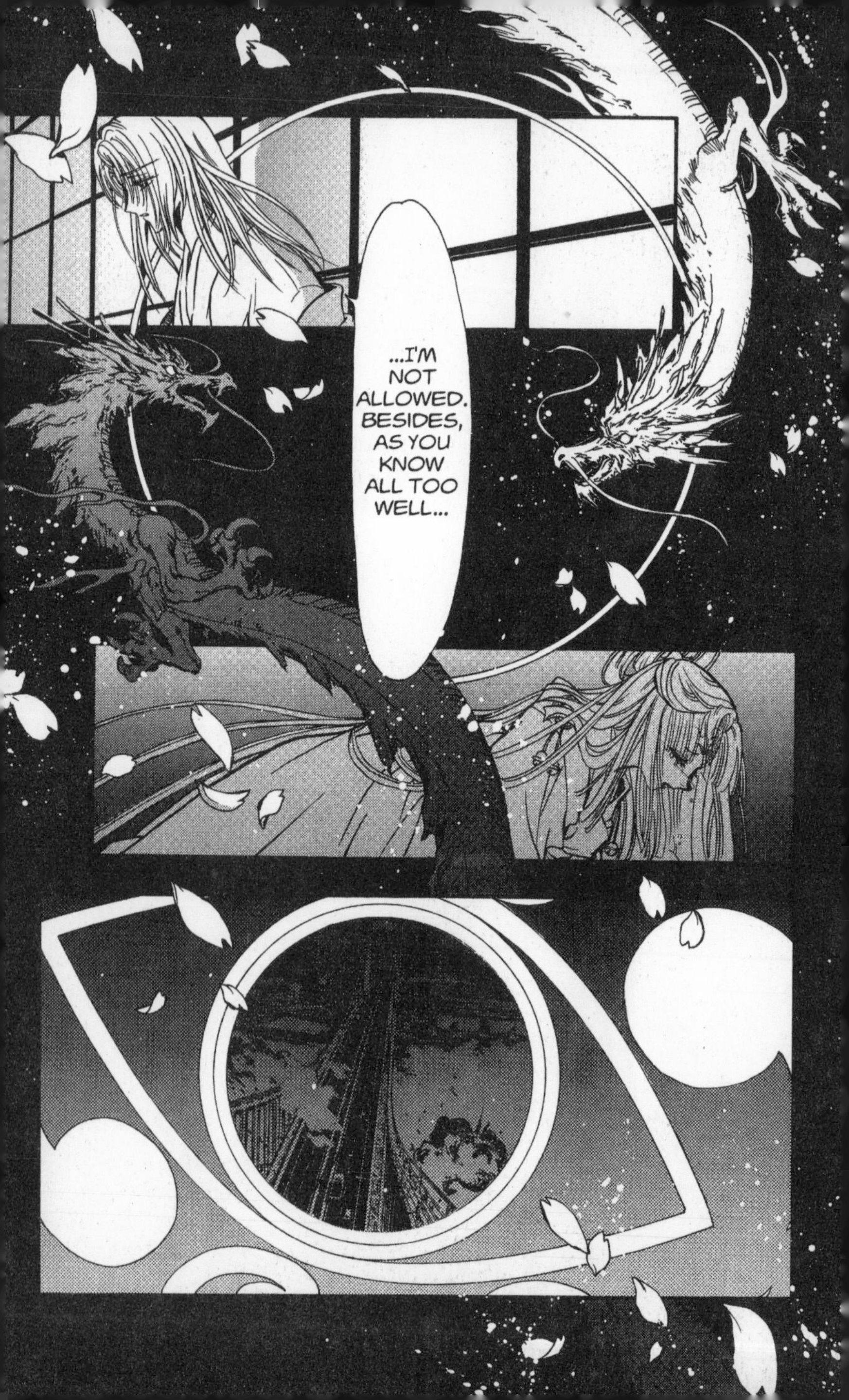
...I'M NOT ALLOWED. BESIDES, AS YOU KNOW ALL TOO WELL...

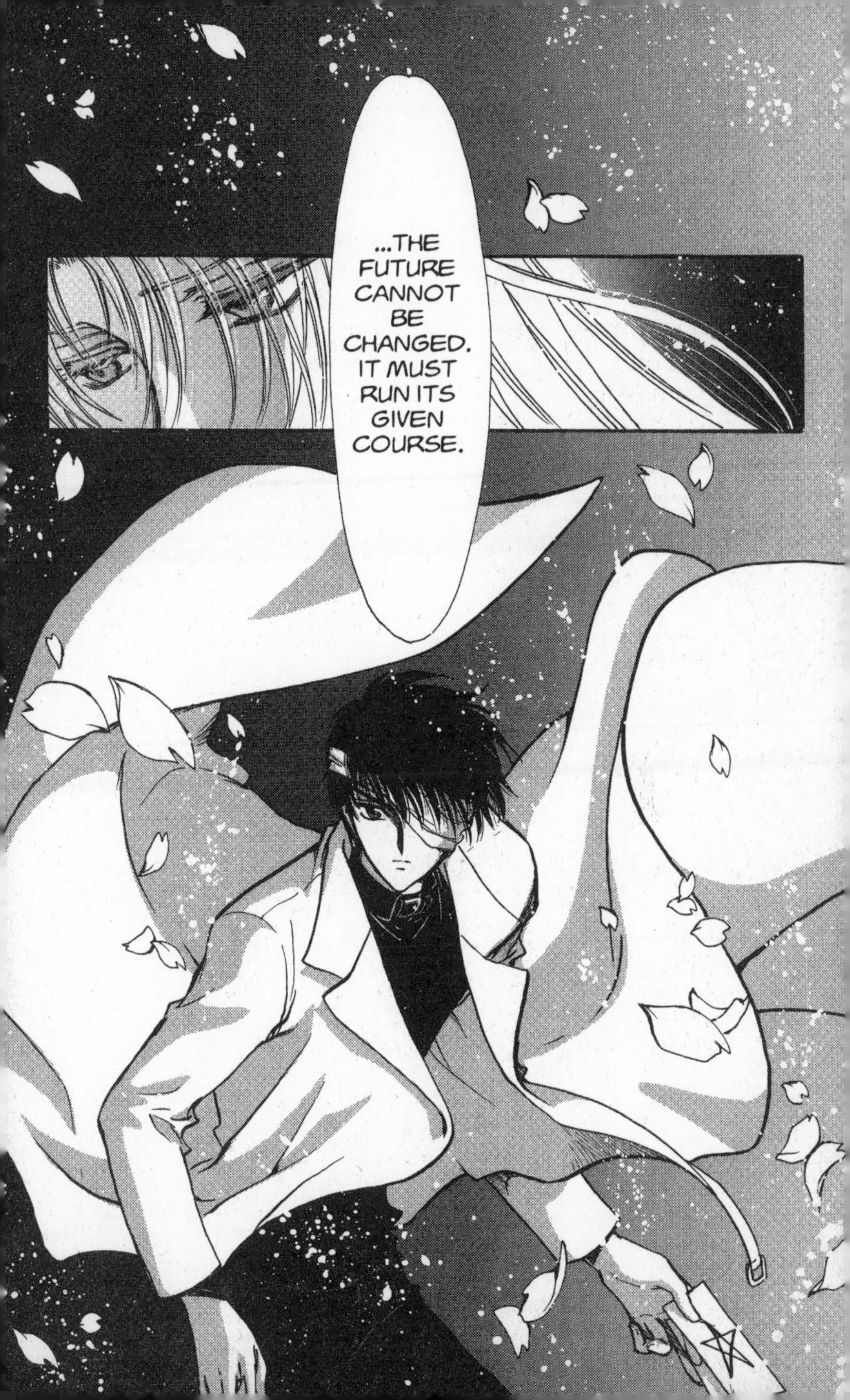
...THE FUTURE CANNOT BE CHANGED. IT MUST RUN ITS GIVEN COURSE.

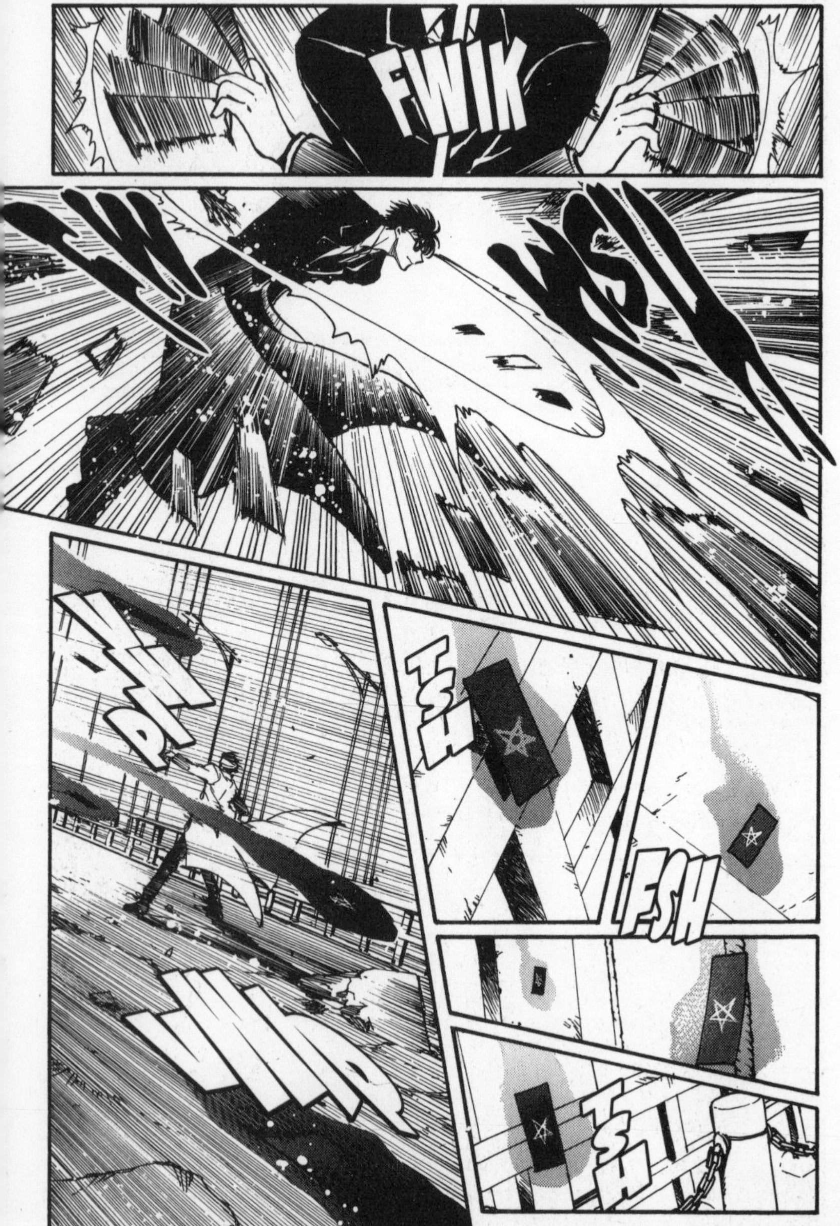
FWIK
TSH
FSH
TSH
WHIP
WHIP

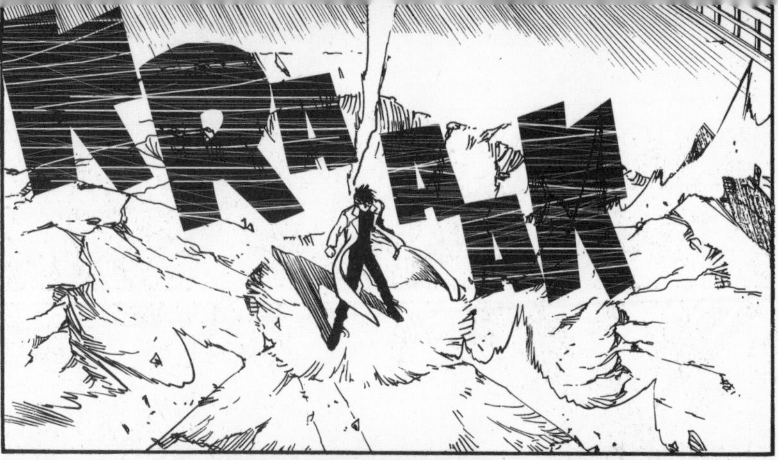
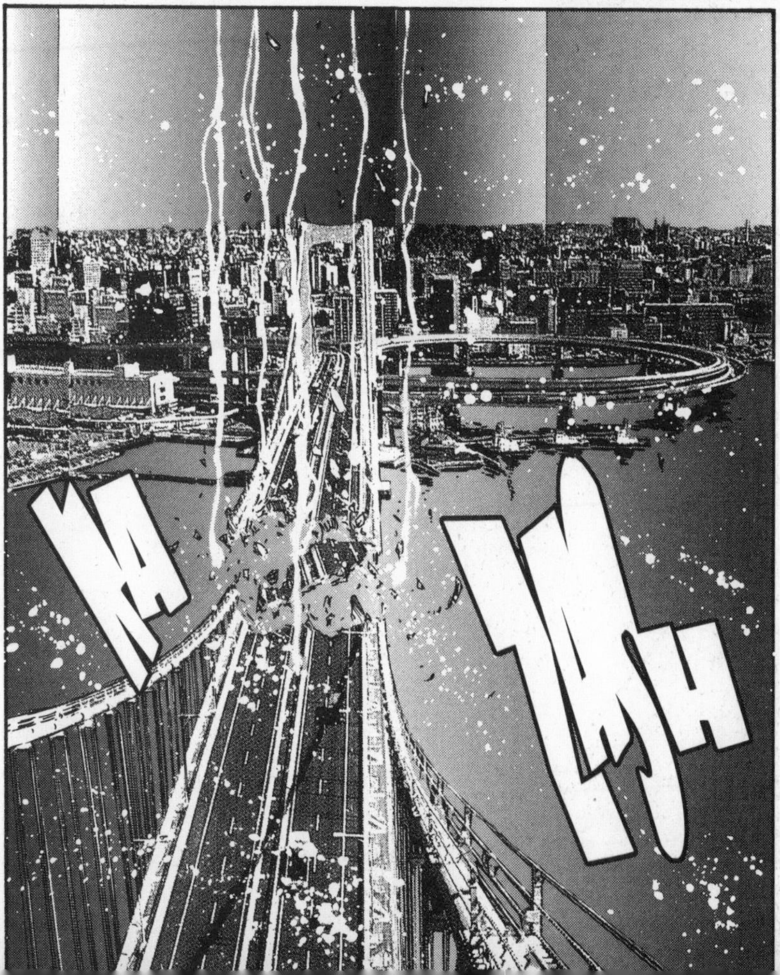

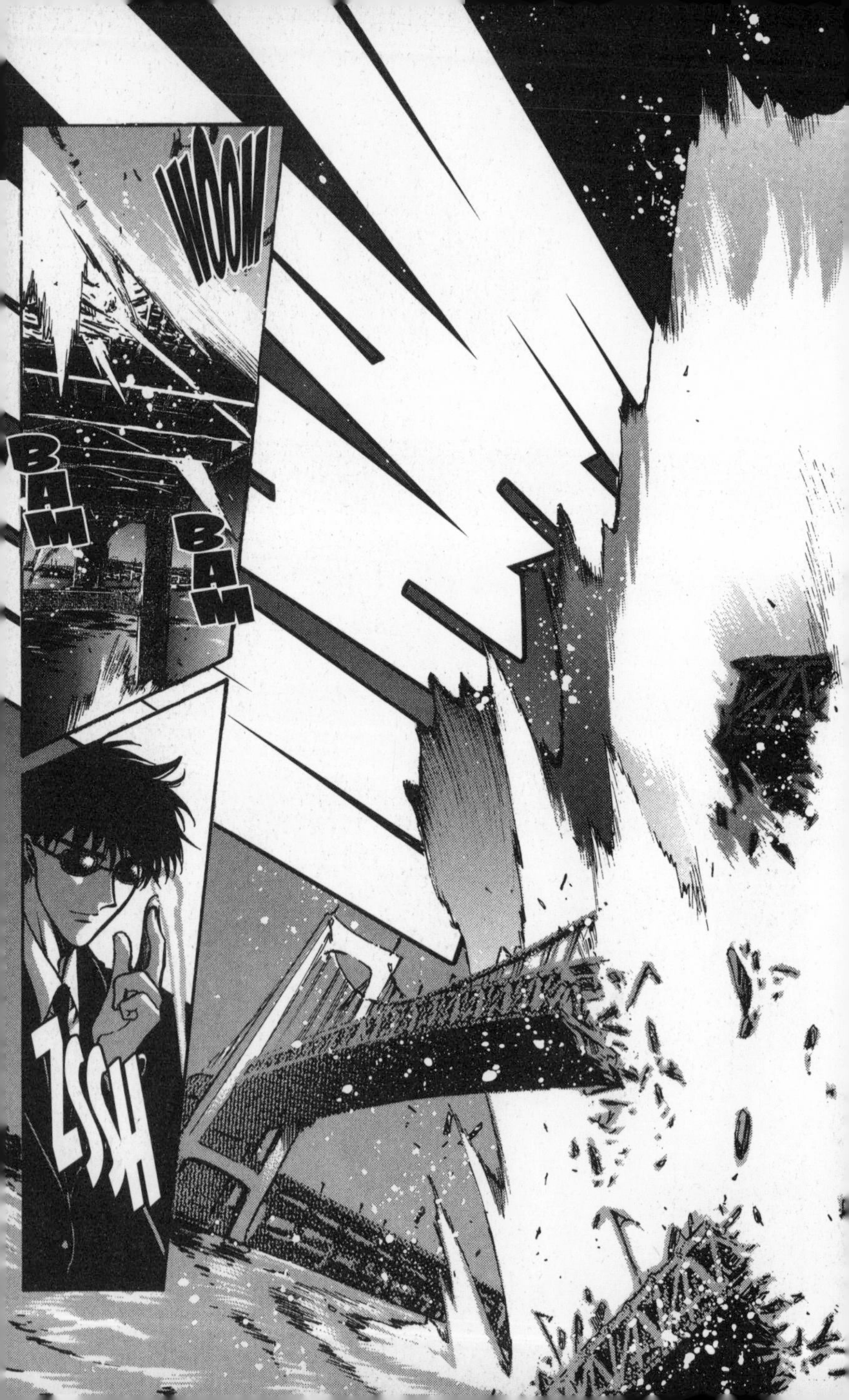
WOOM
BAM
BAM
ZSSH

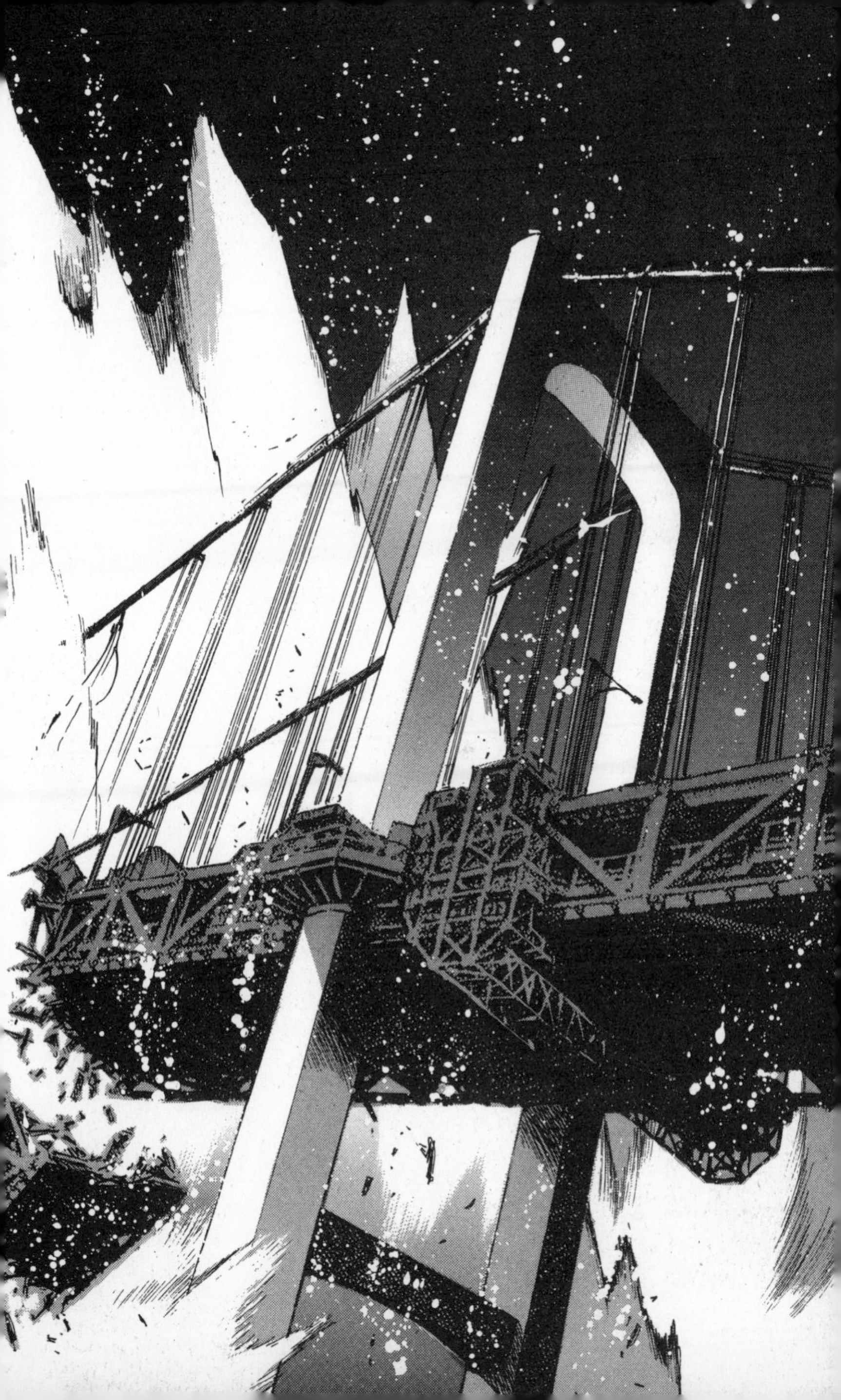

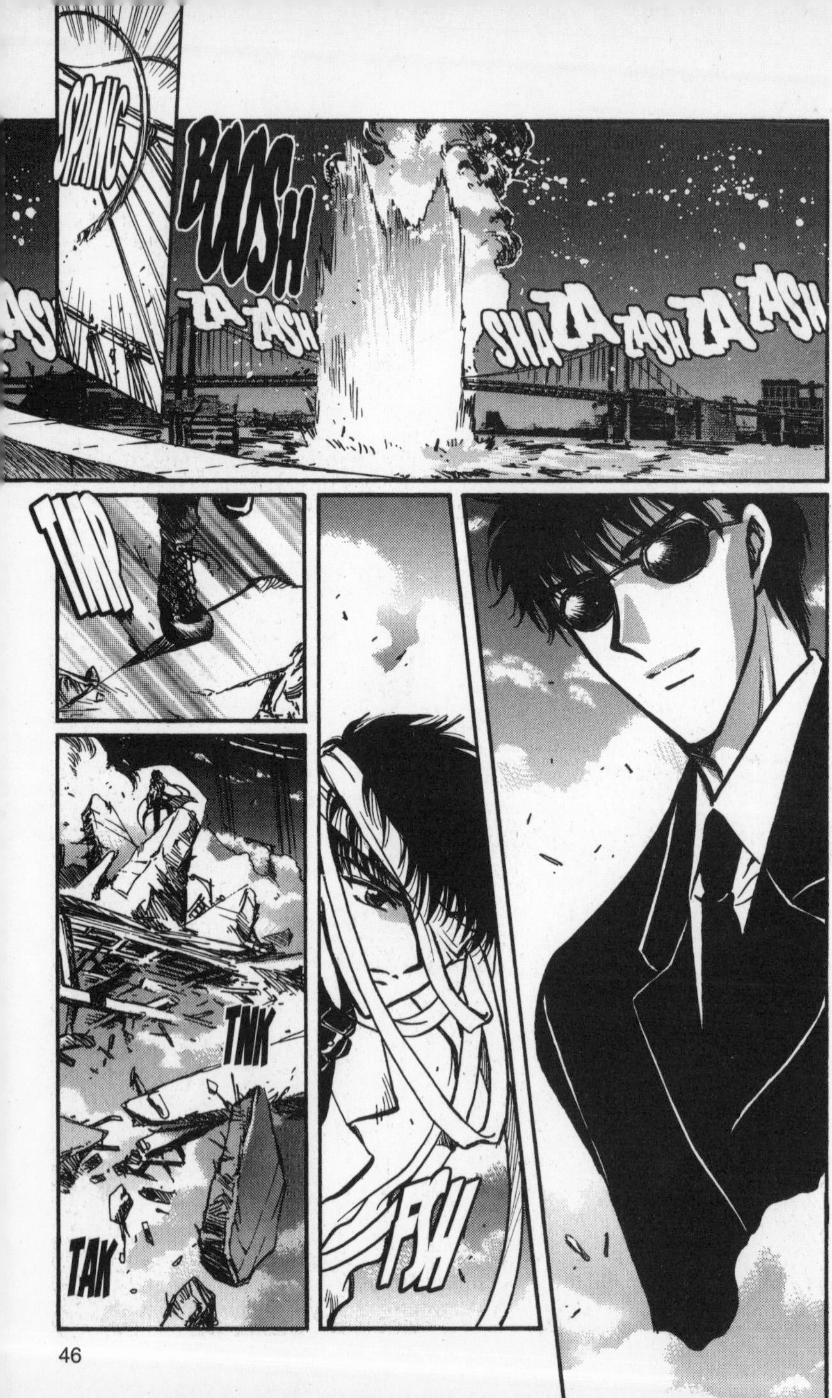
SHA TA TASH TA TASH
BOOSH
TA TASH
SPANG
FSH
TWR
TNK
TAK

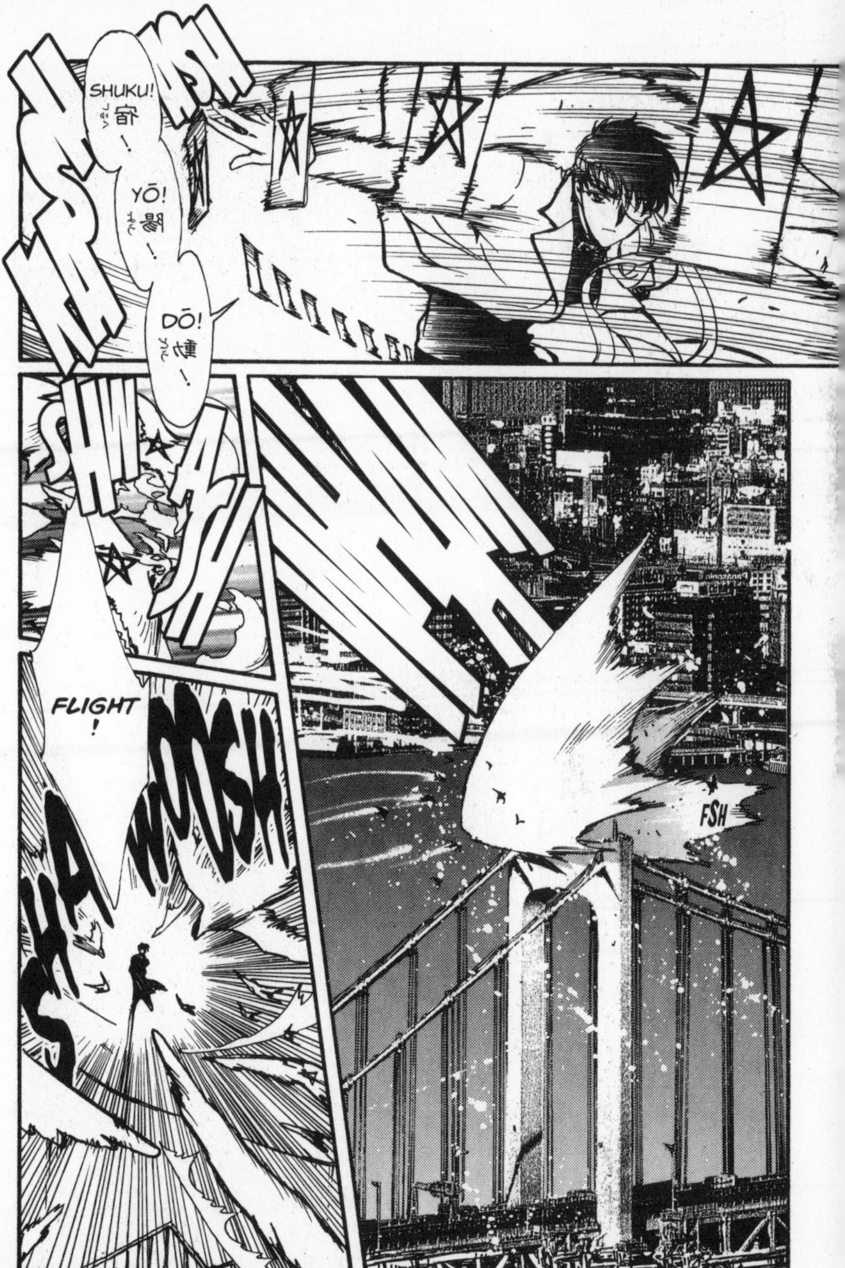
SHUKU! 宿!
YŌ! 陽!
DŌ! 動!
FLIGHT !
FSH

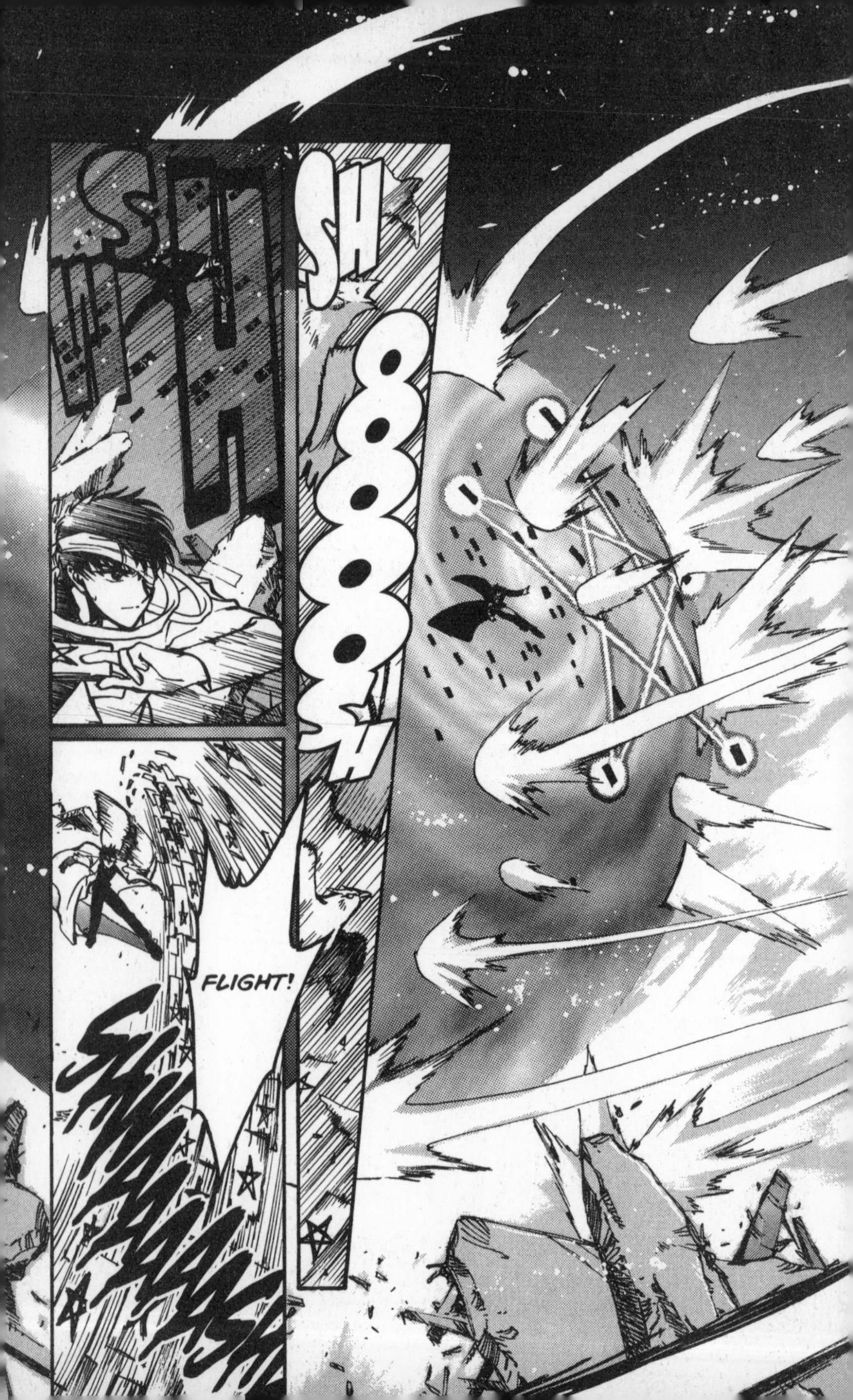
FLIGHT!

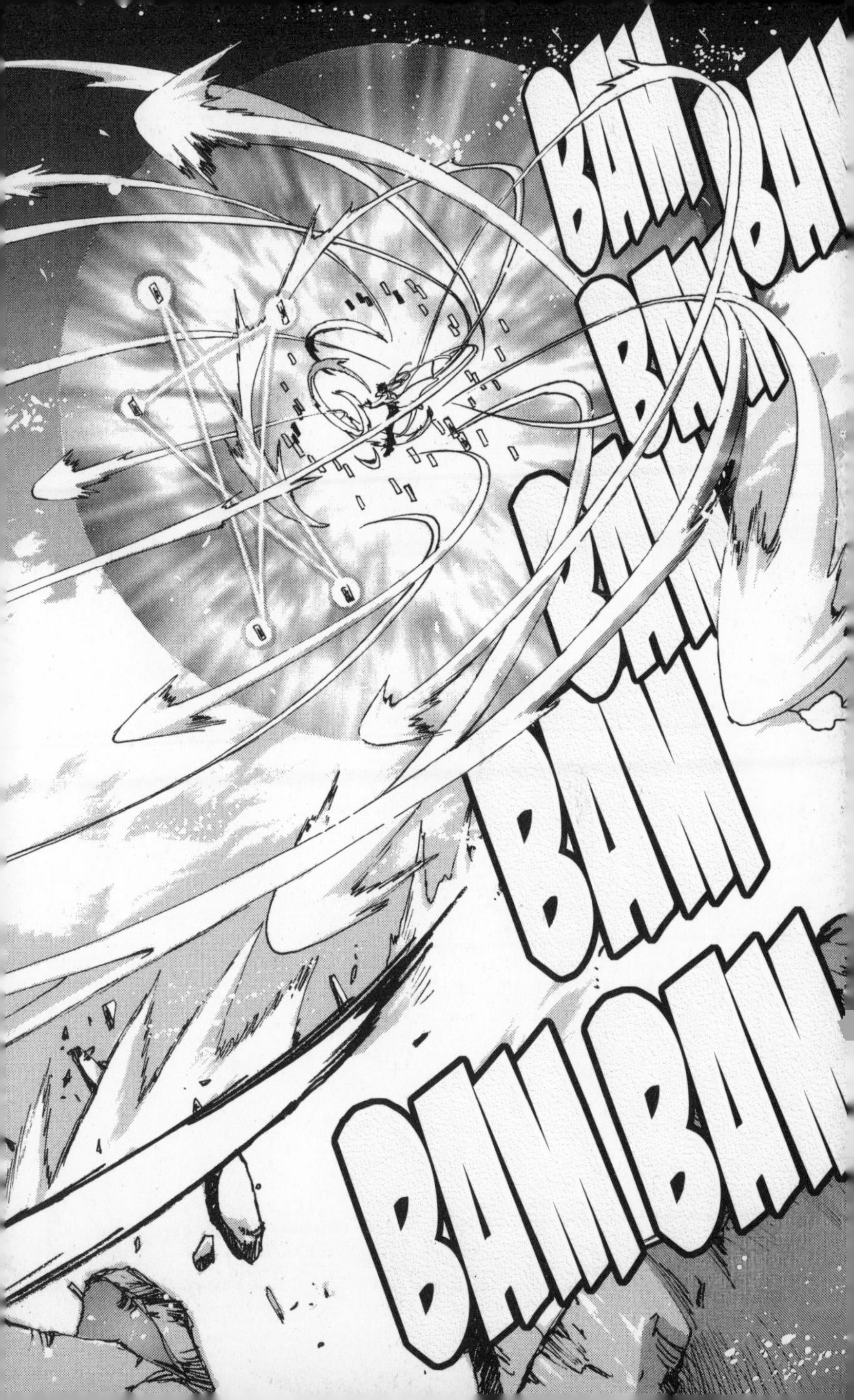
BAM
BAM
BAM
BAM
BAM
BAMBAM

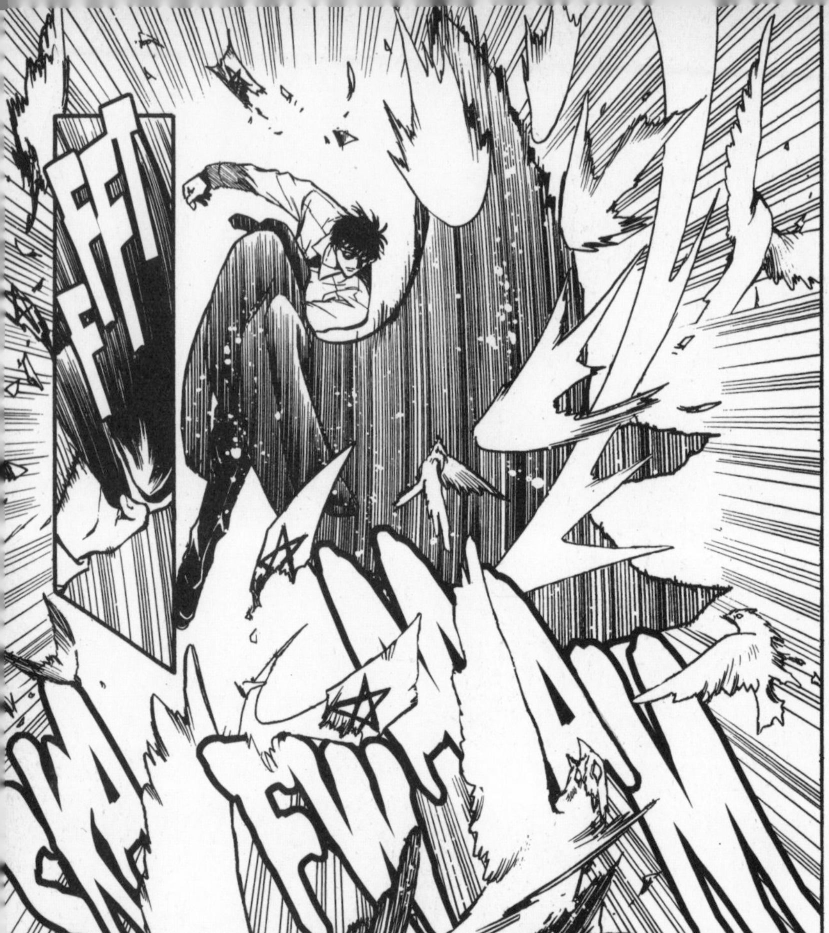
FFT
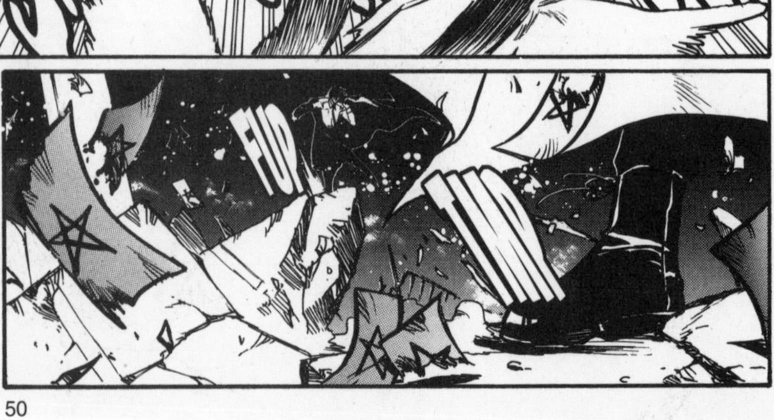

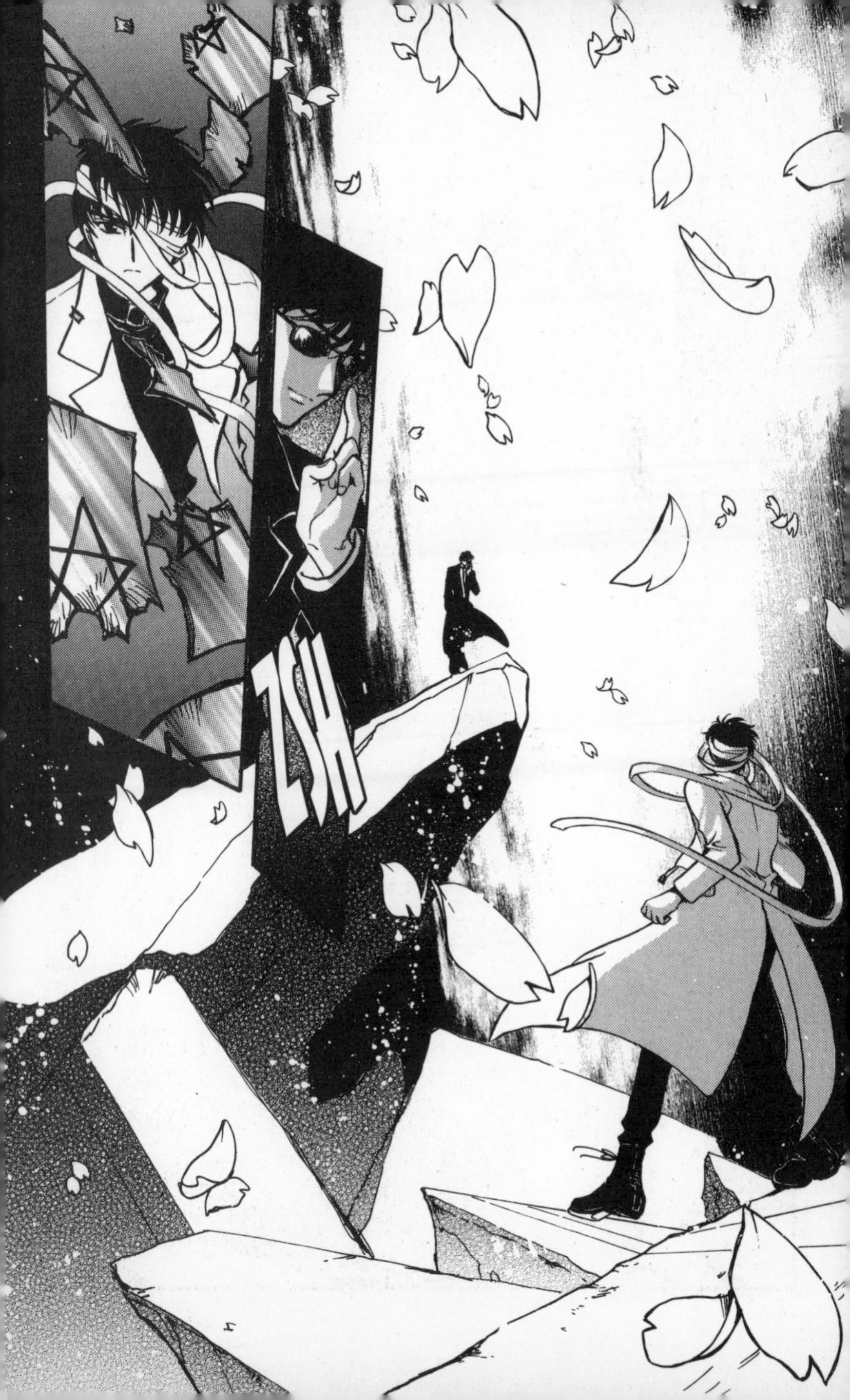
ZSH

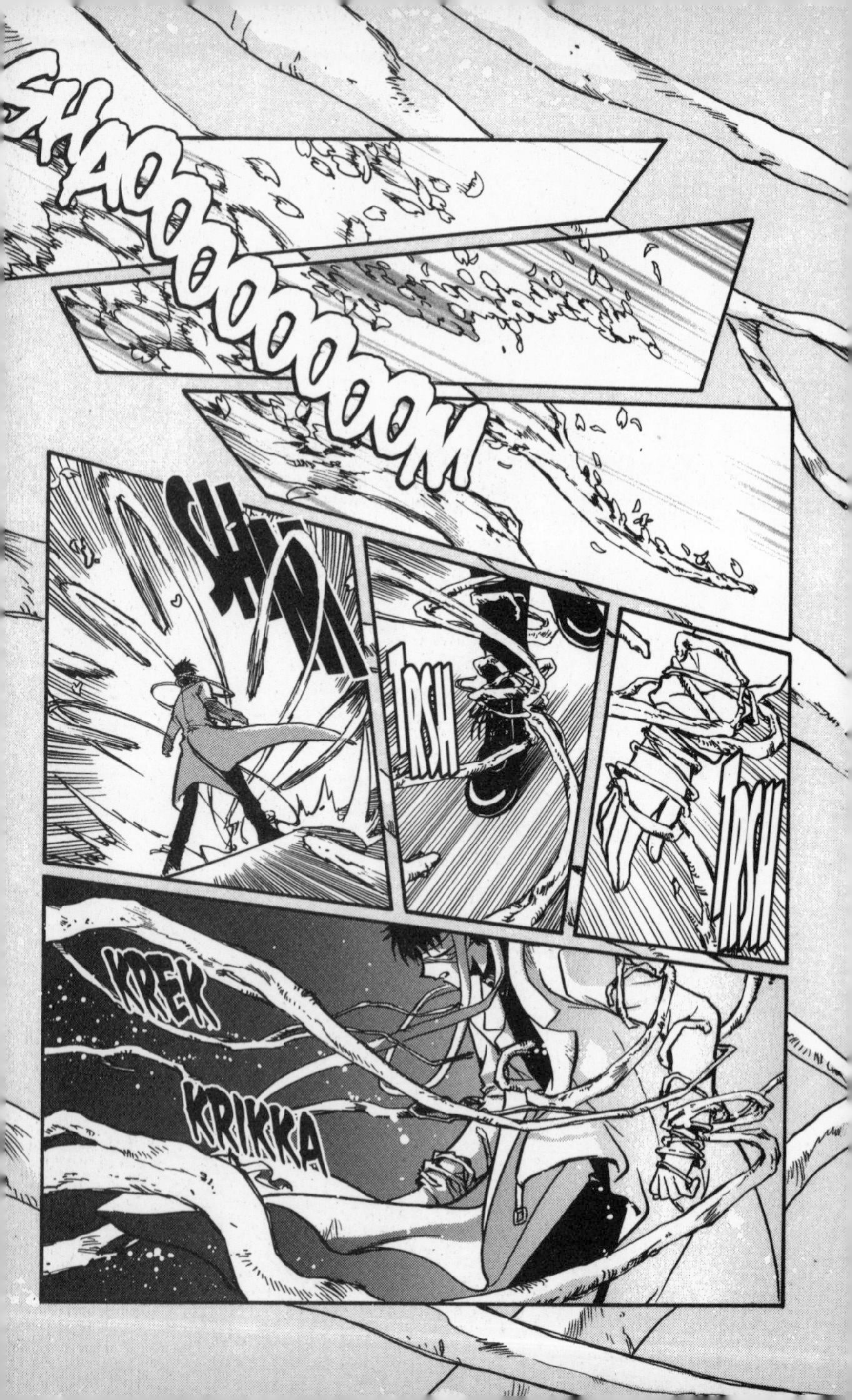
SHAOOOOOOOOM
TRSH
TRSH
KREK
KRIKKA

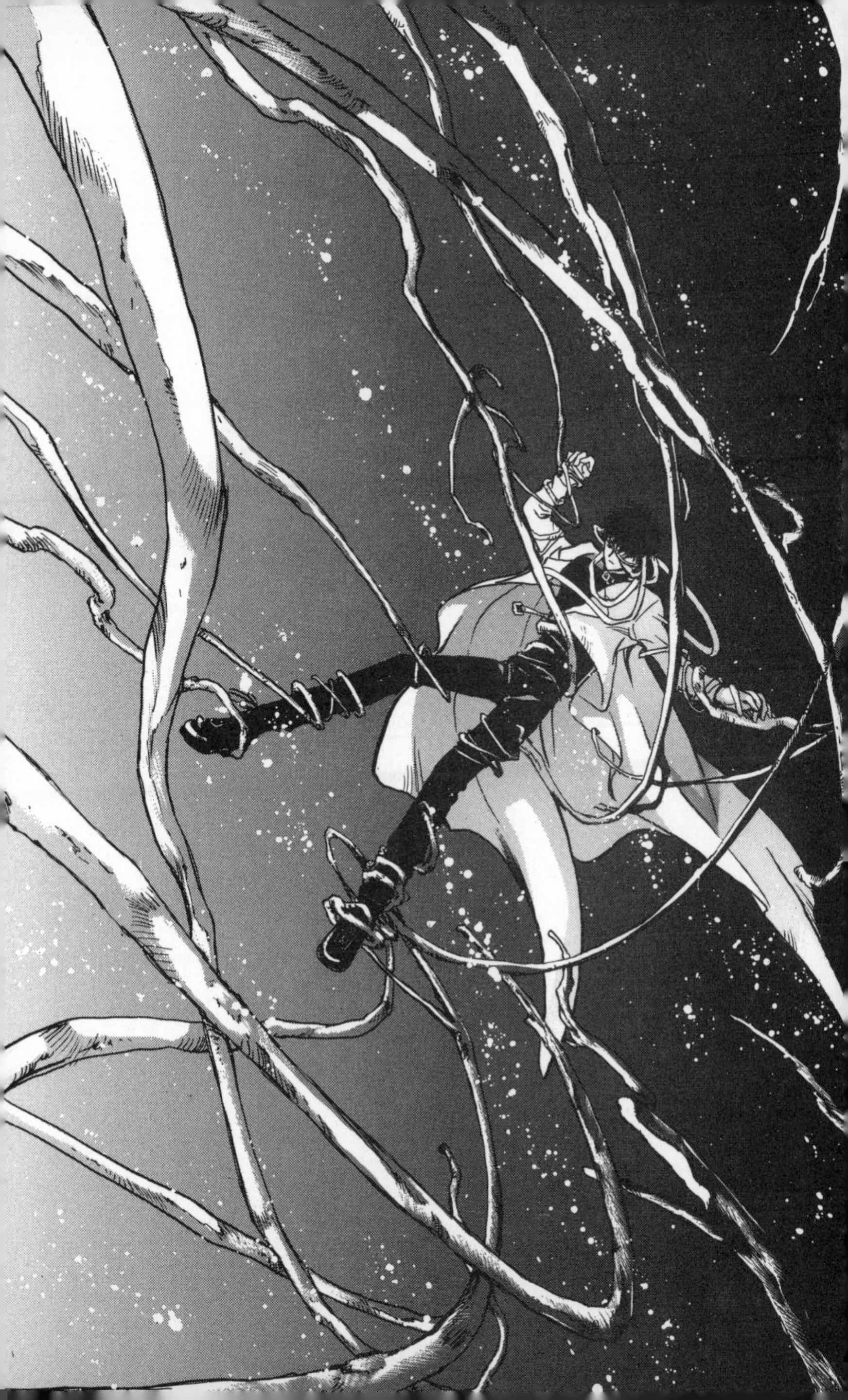

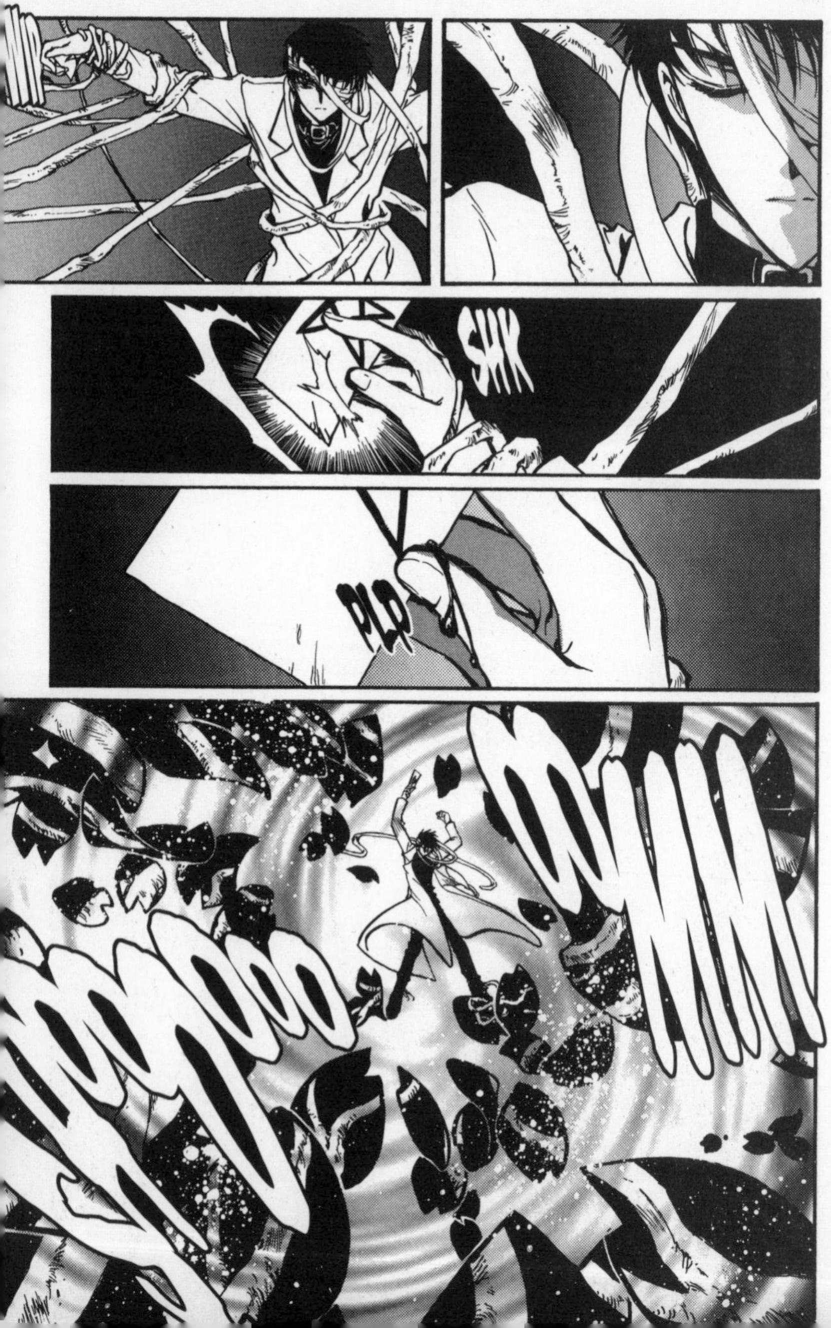
SHK
PLP

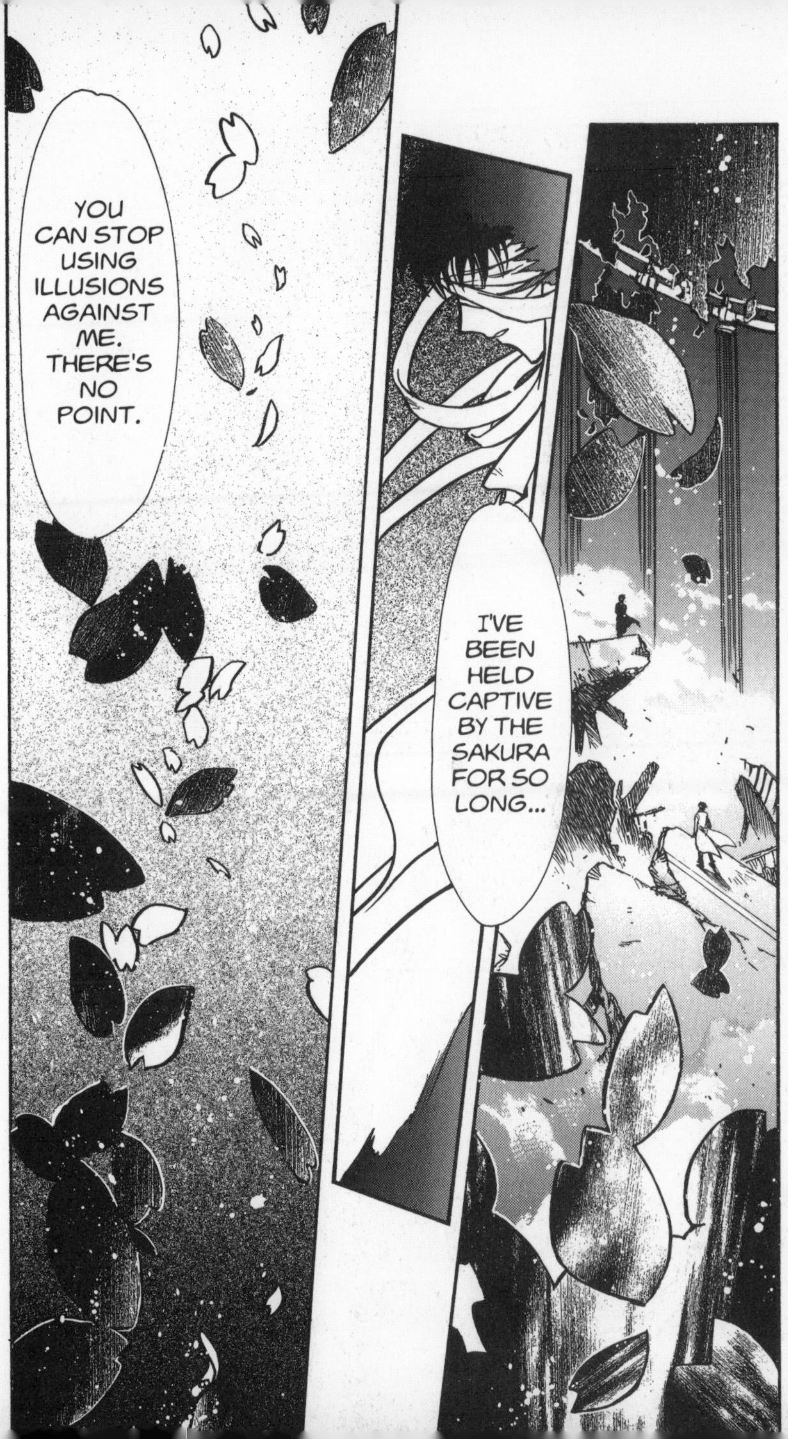
I'VE BEEN HELD CAPTIVE BY THE SAKURA FOR SO LONG...
YOU CAN STOP USING ILLUSIONS AGAINST ME. THERE'S NO POINT.

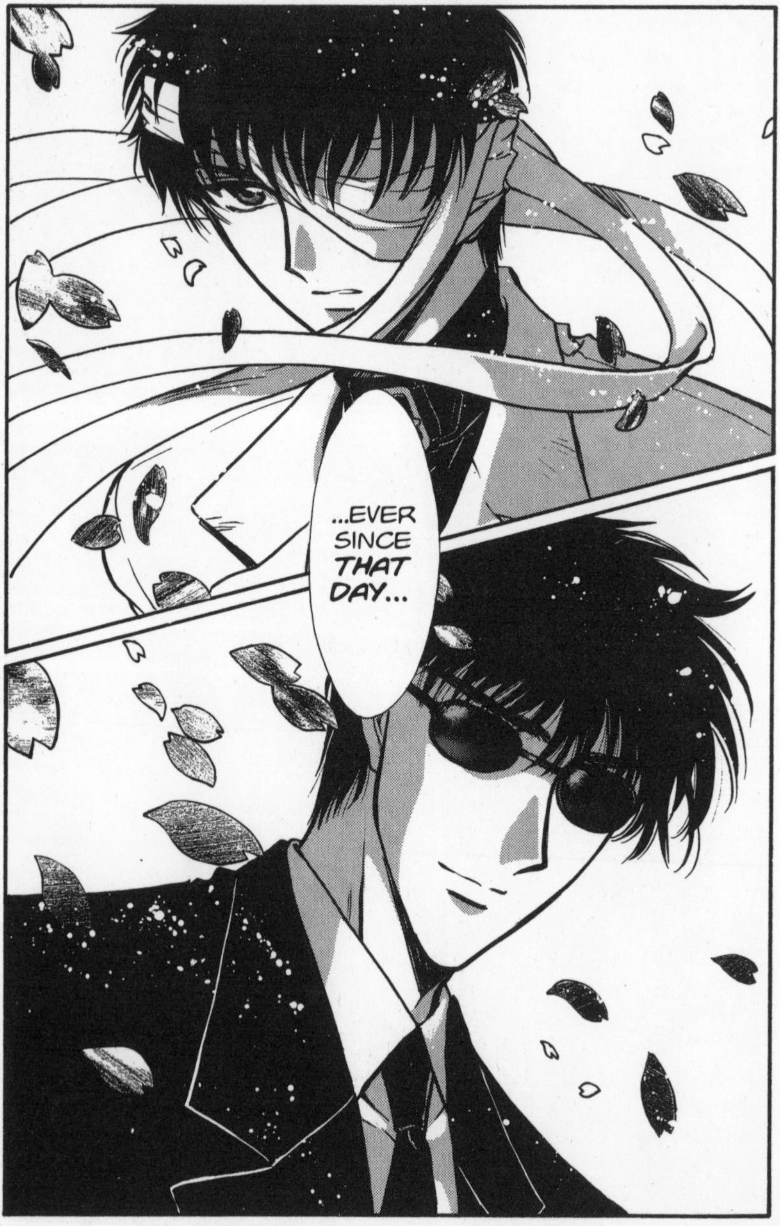
...EVER SINCE *THAT DAY*...

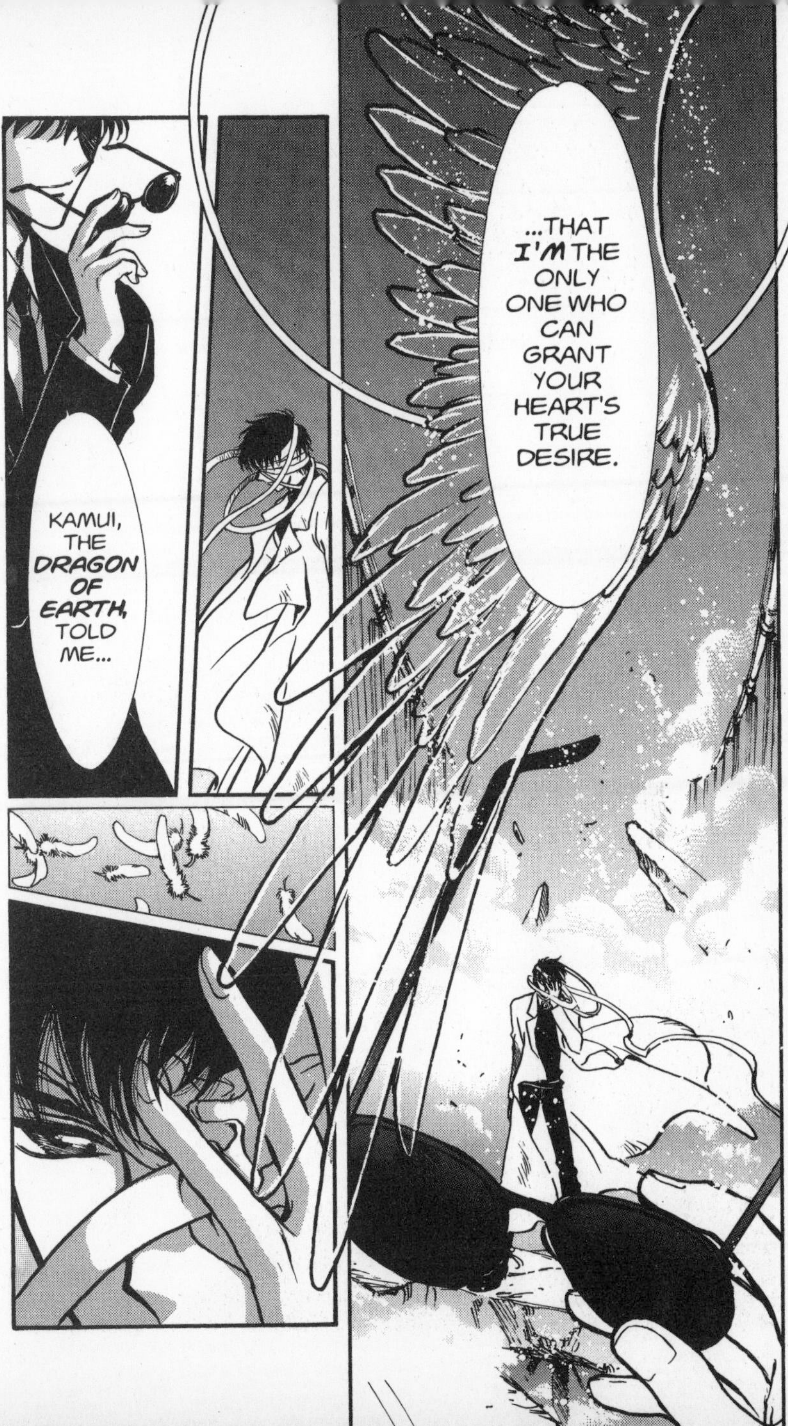
KAMUI, THE DRAGON OF EARTH, TOLD ME...
...THAT I'M THE ONLY ONE WHO CAN GRANT YOUR HEART'S TRUE DESIRE.

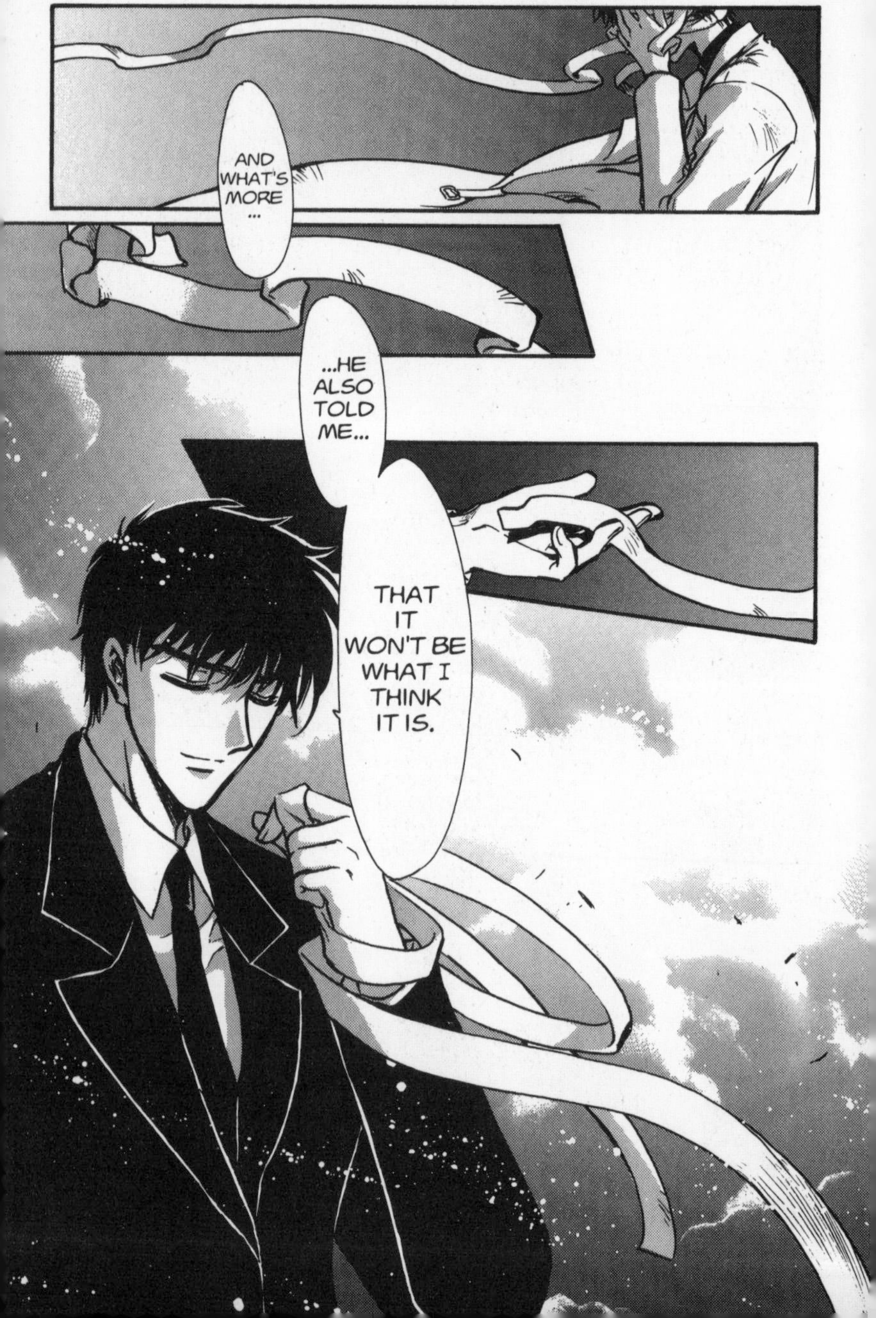
AND WHAT'S MORE ...
...HE ALSO TOLD ME...
THAT IT WON'T BE WHAT I THINK IT IS.

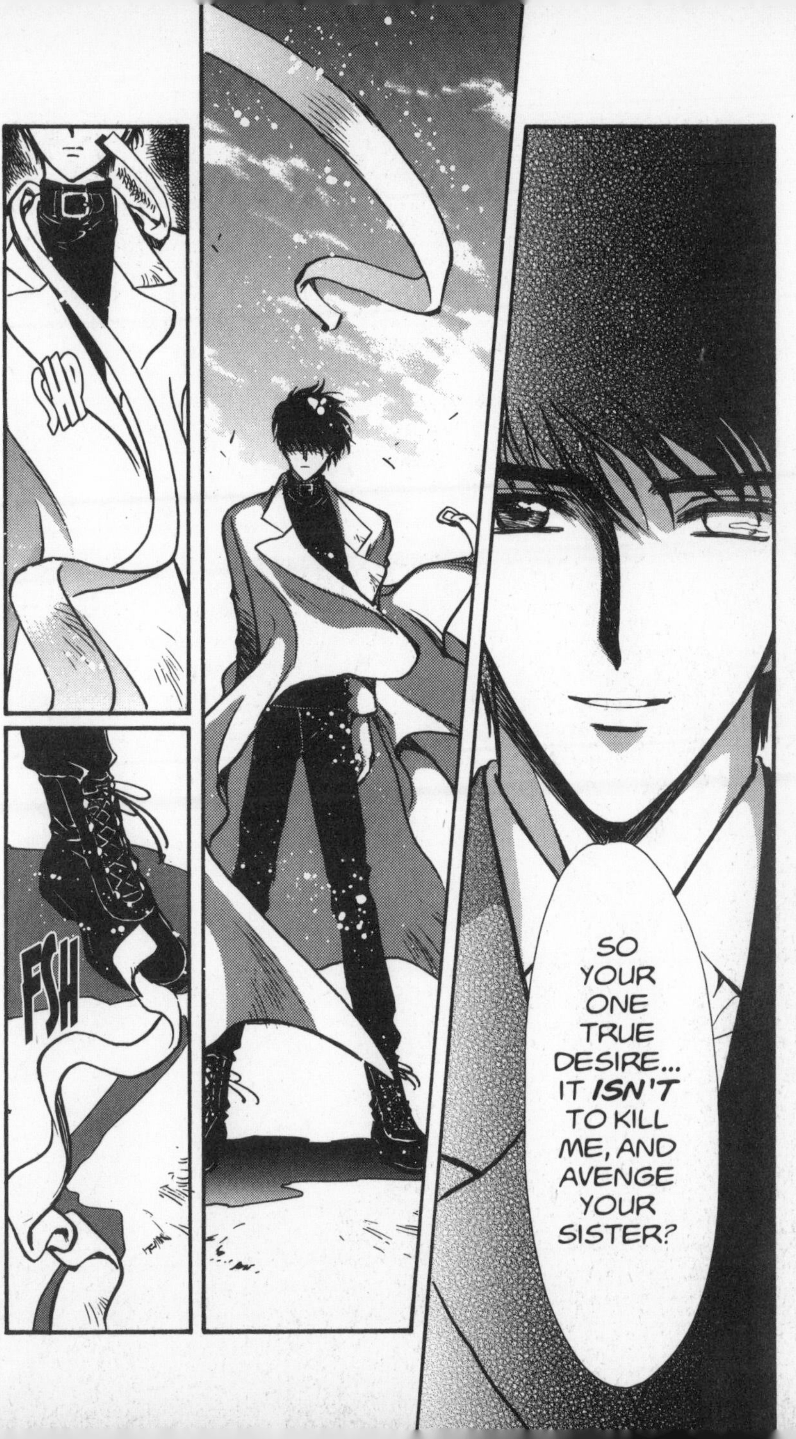
SO YOUR ONE TRUE DESIRE... IT ***ISN'T*** TO KILL ME, AND AVENGE YOUR SISTER?
SHP
FSH

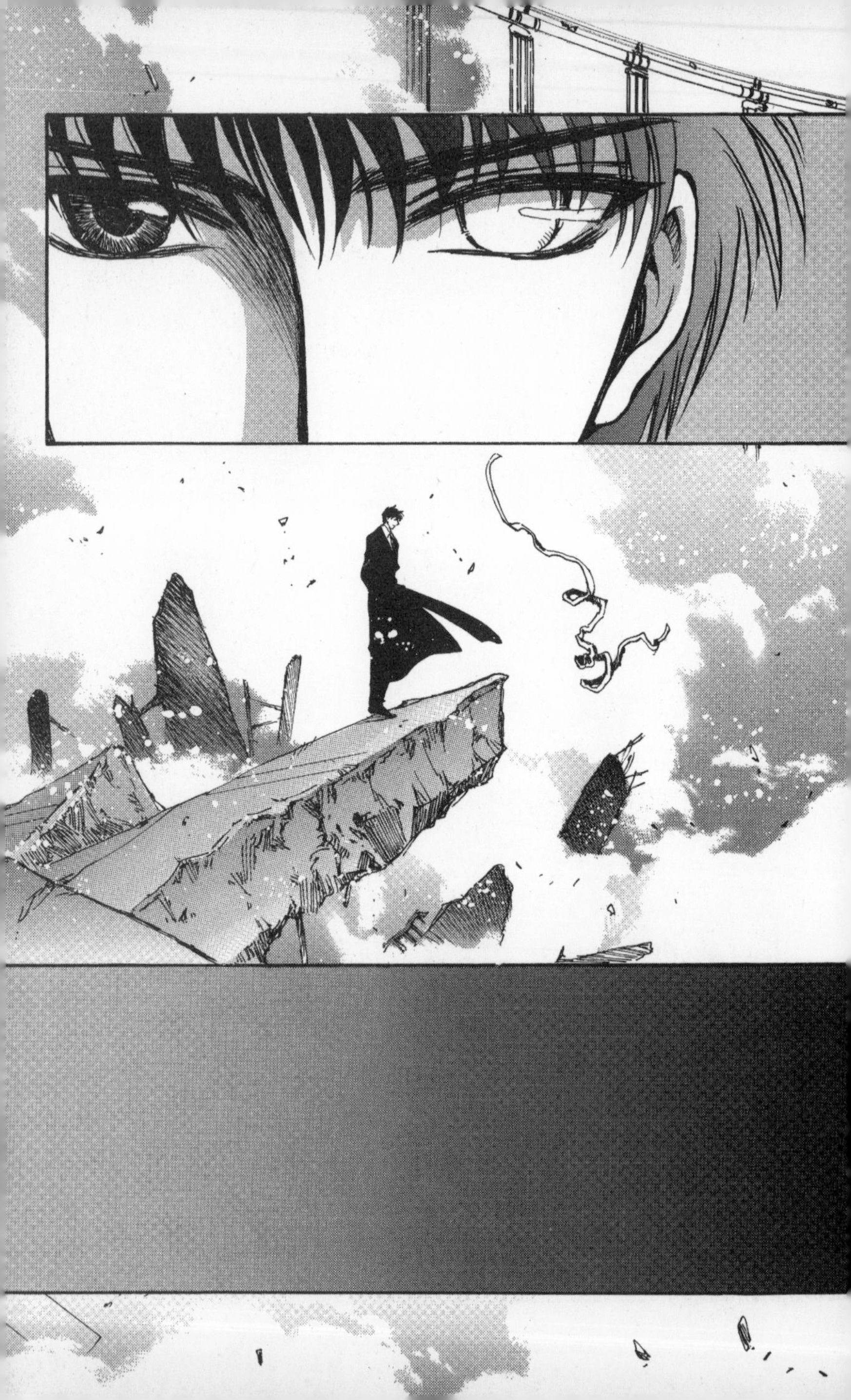

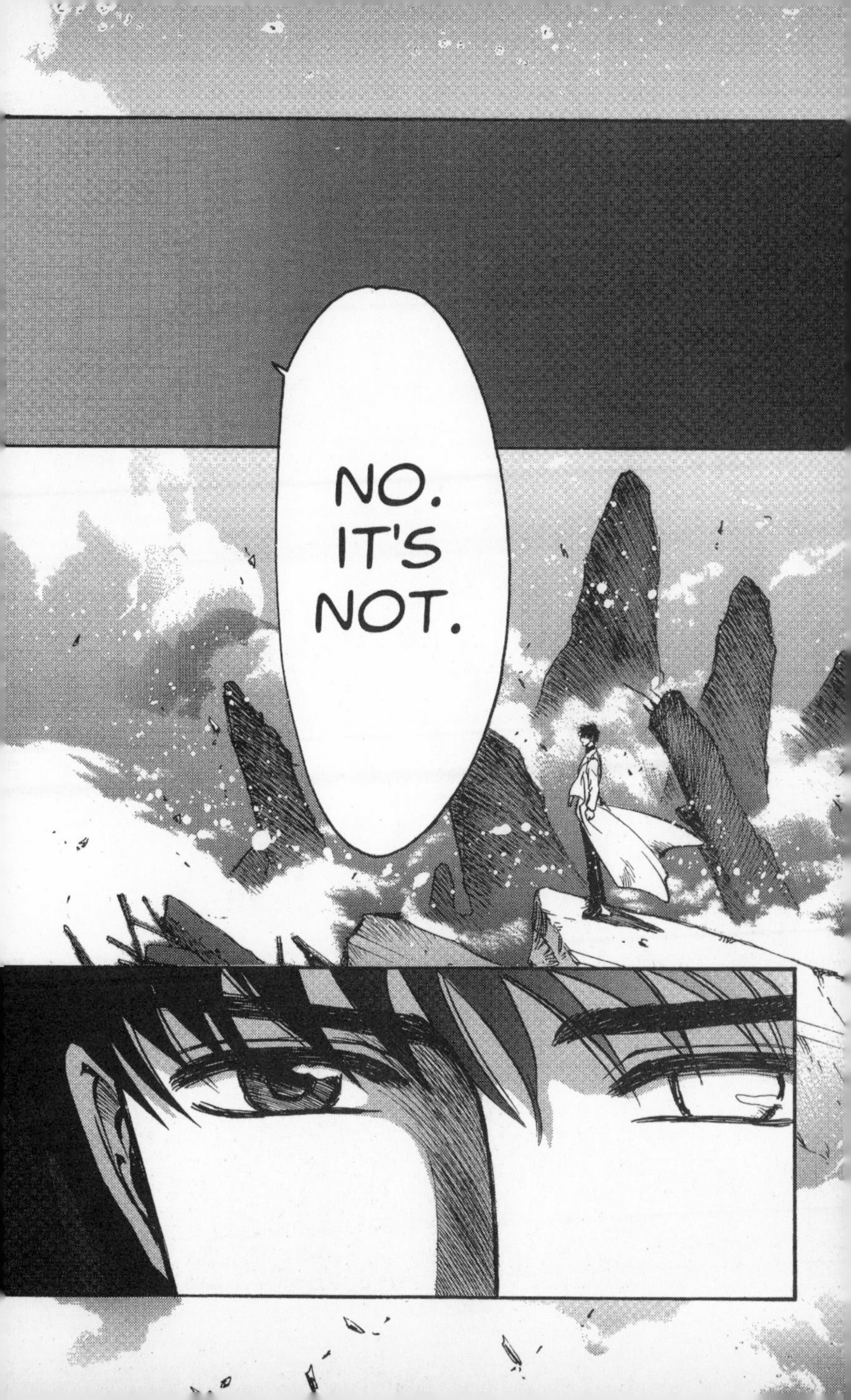
NO. IT'S NOT.

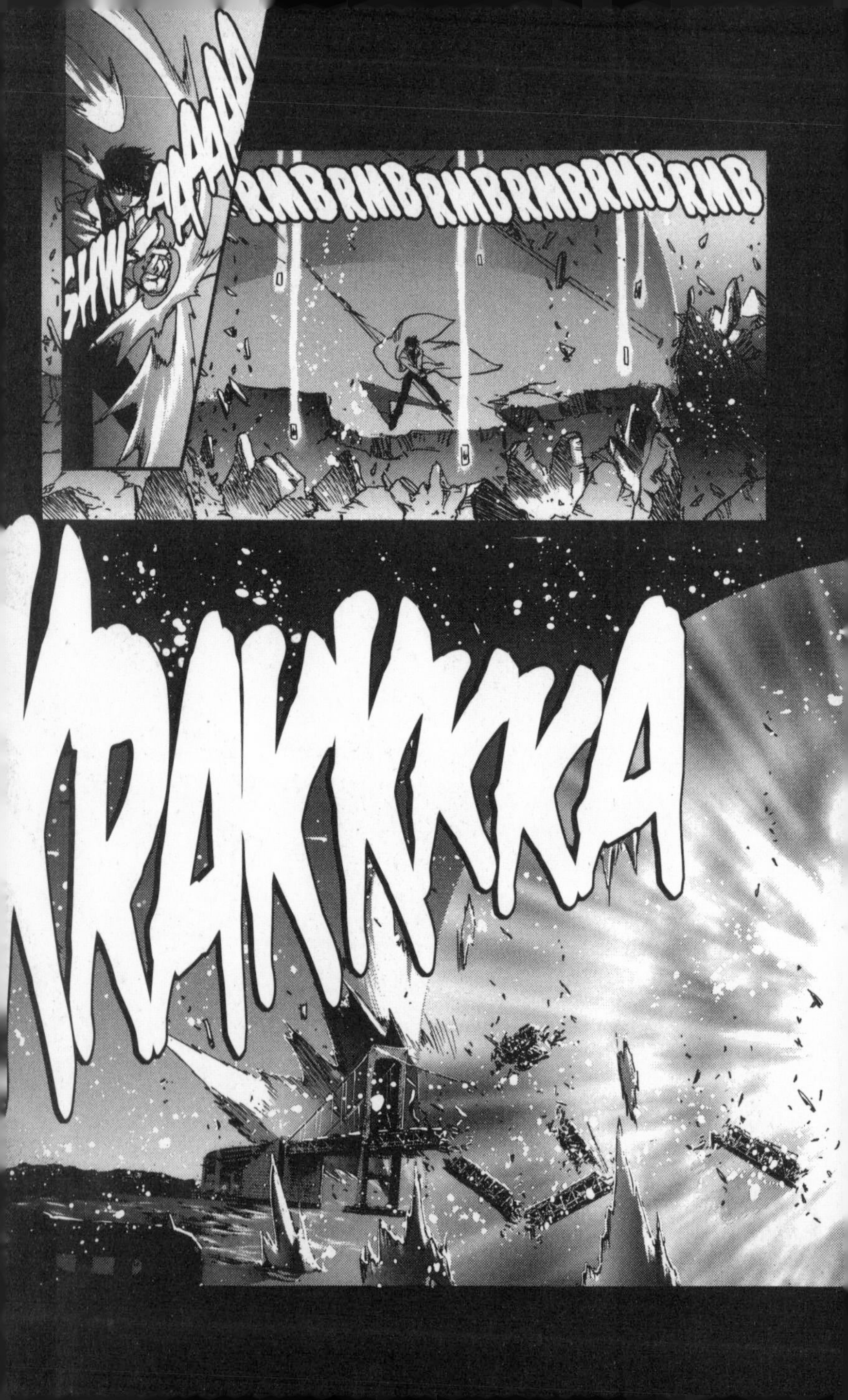
RMBRMBRMBRMBRMBRMB
SHWAAAAAA
KRAKKKKA

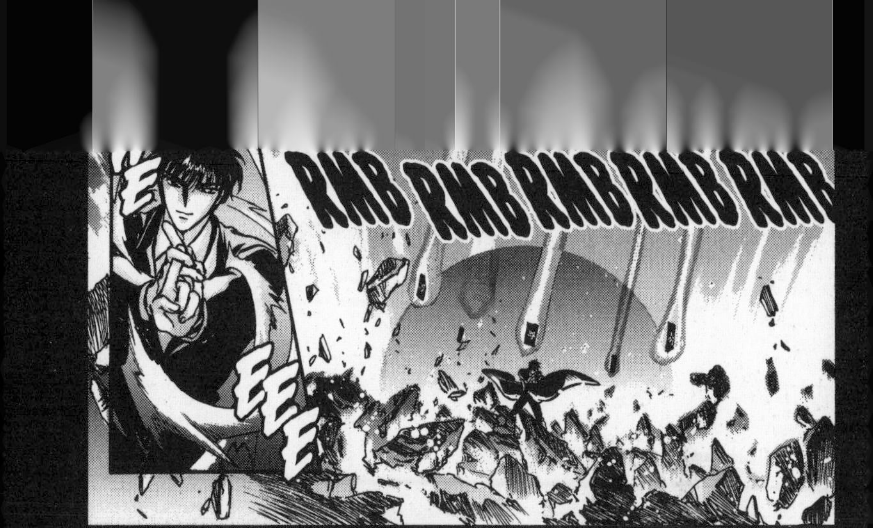
RMB RMB RMB RMB RMB
E
EEE

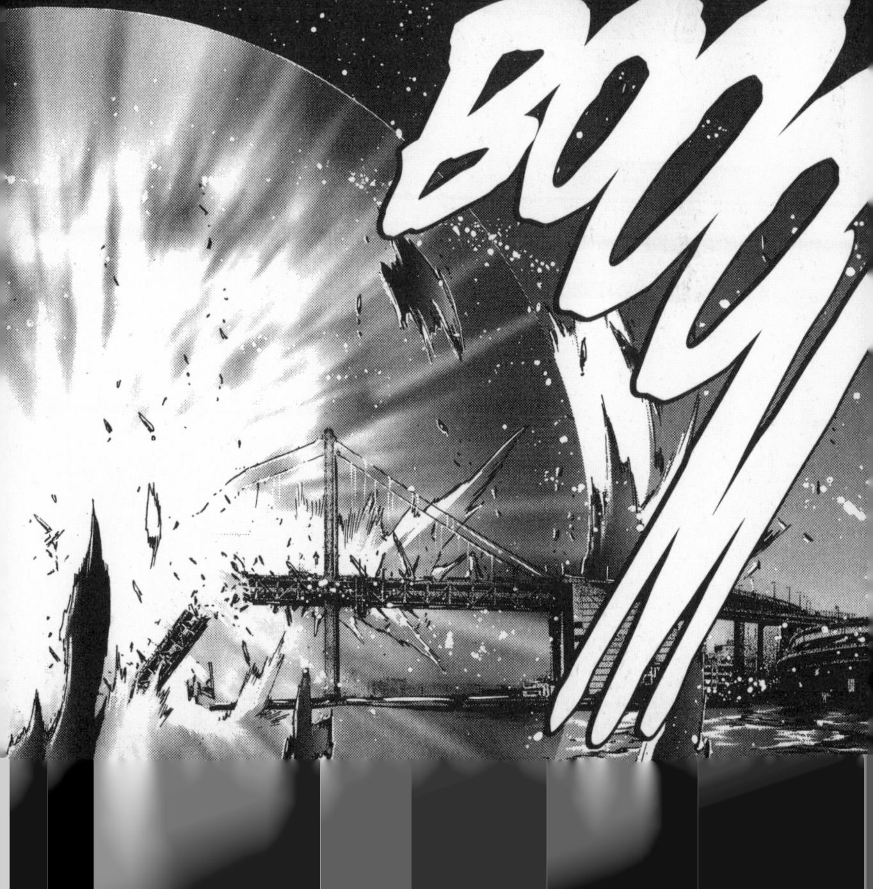
BOOM

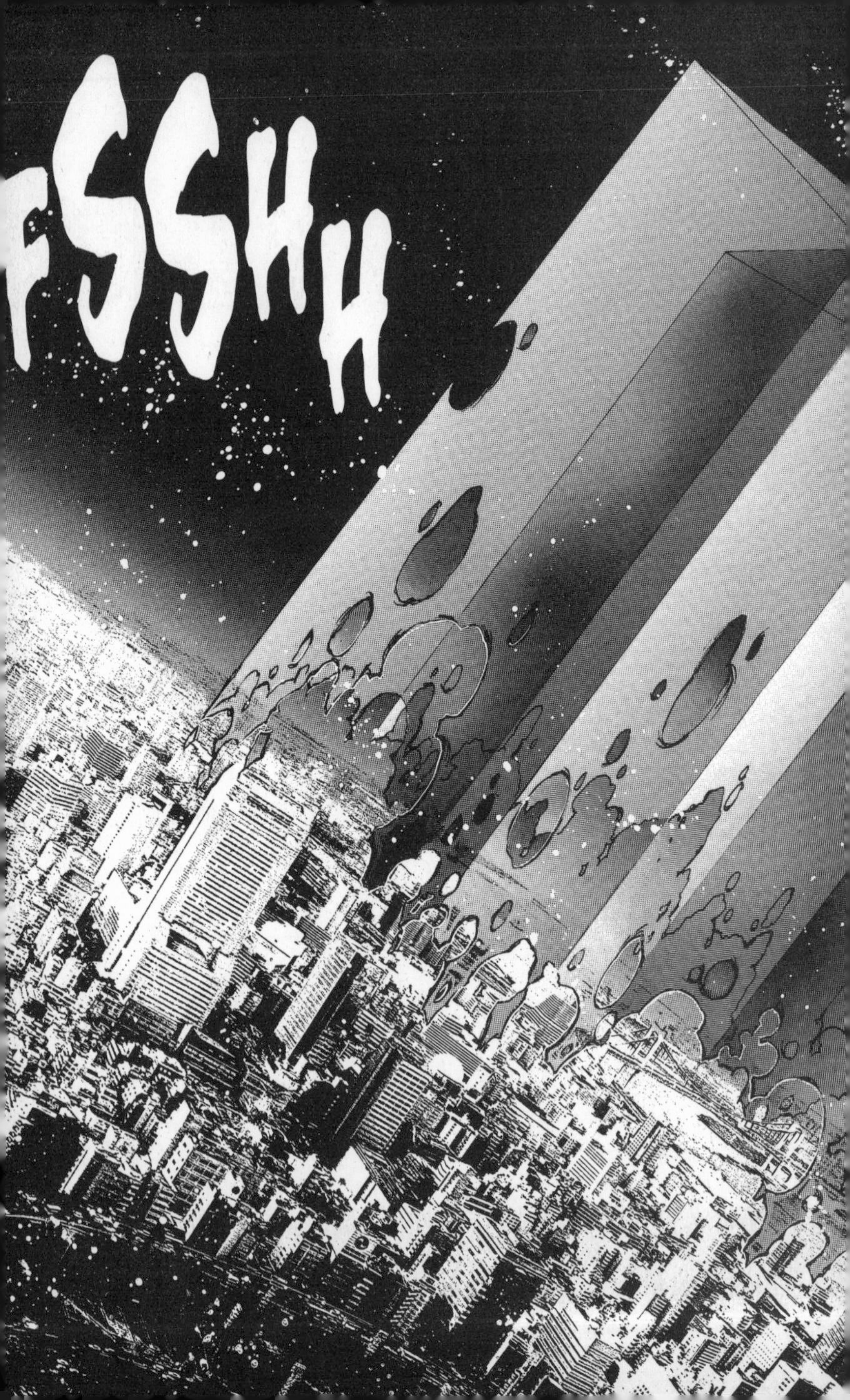
FSSHH

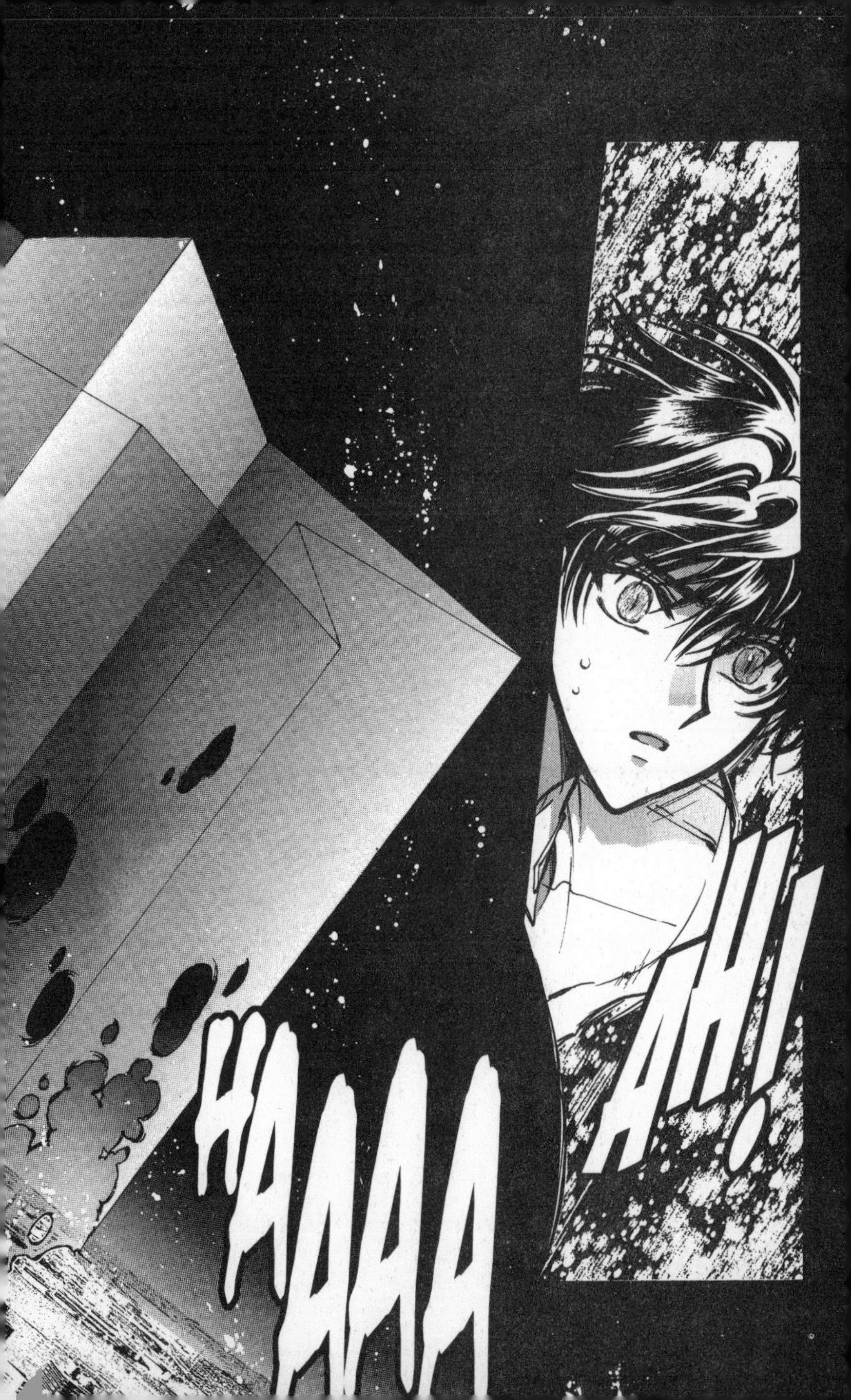
HAAAAAH!

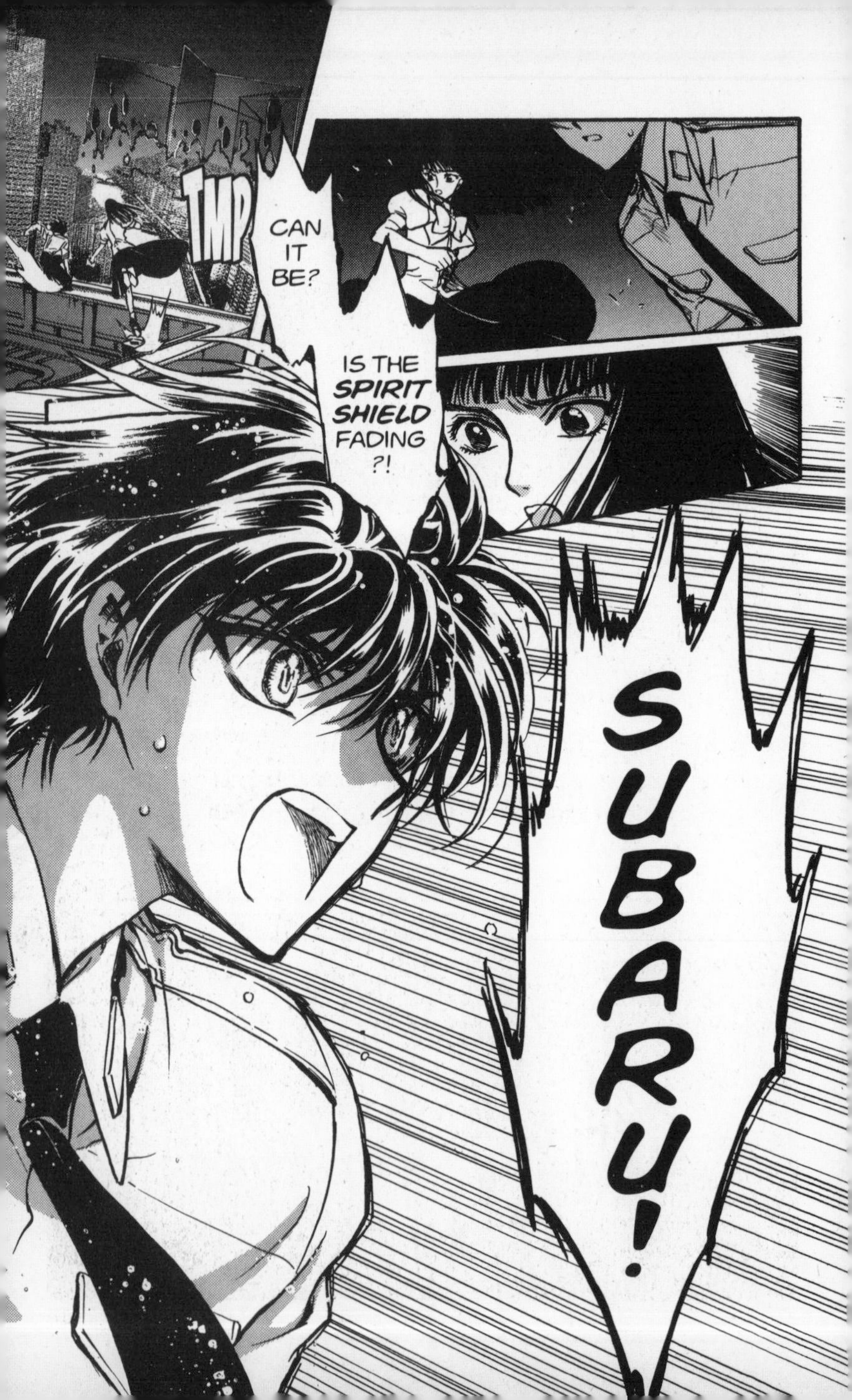
TMP
CAN IT BE?
IS THE **SPIRIT SHIELD** FADING ?!
SUBARU!

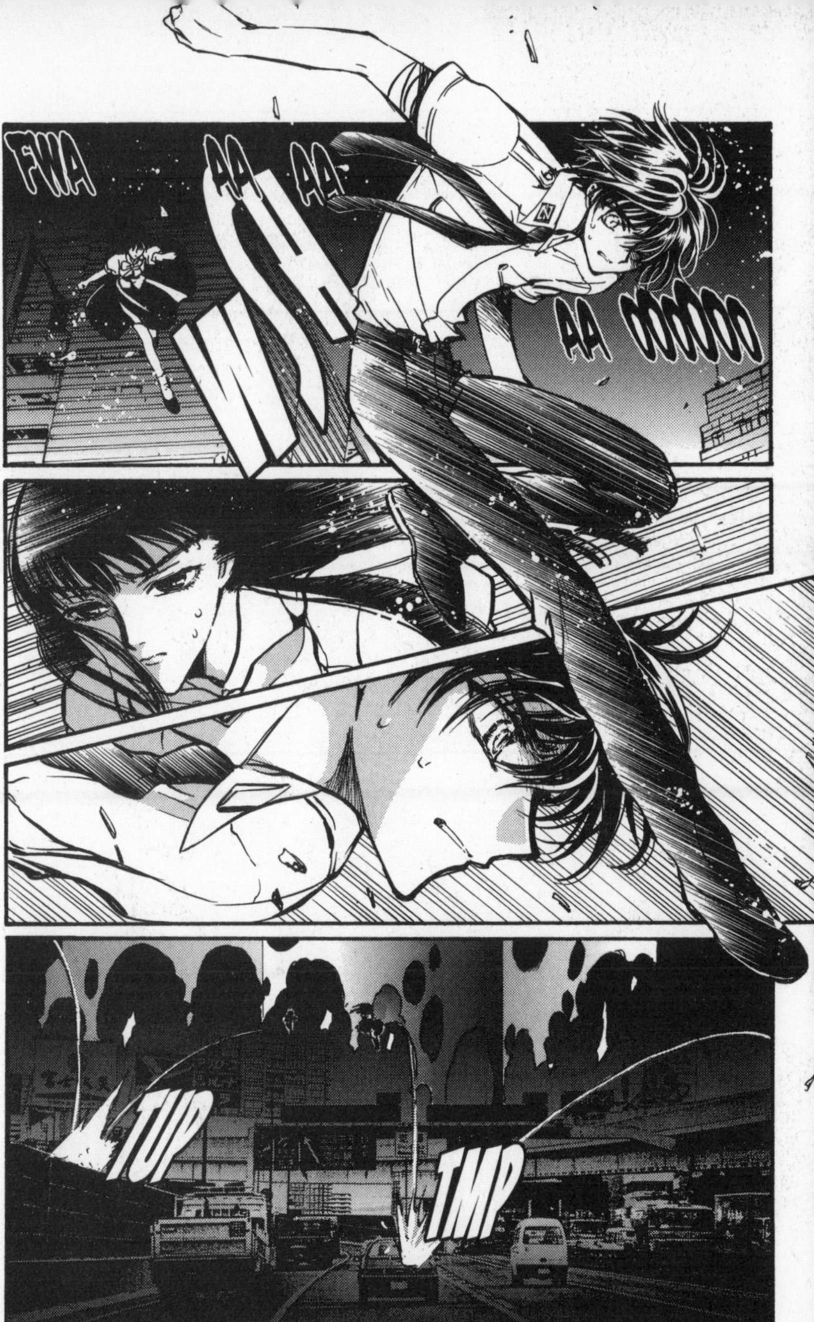
FWA AA AA
AA OOOOOO
TMP
TUP

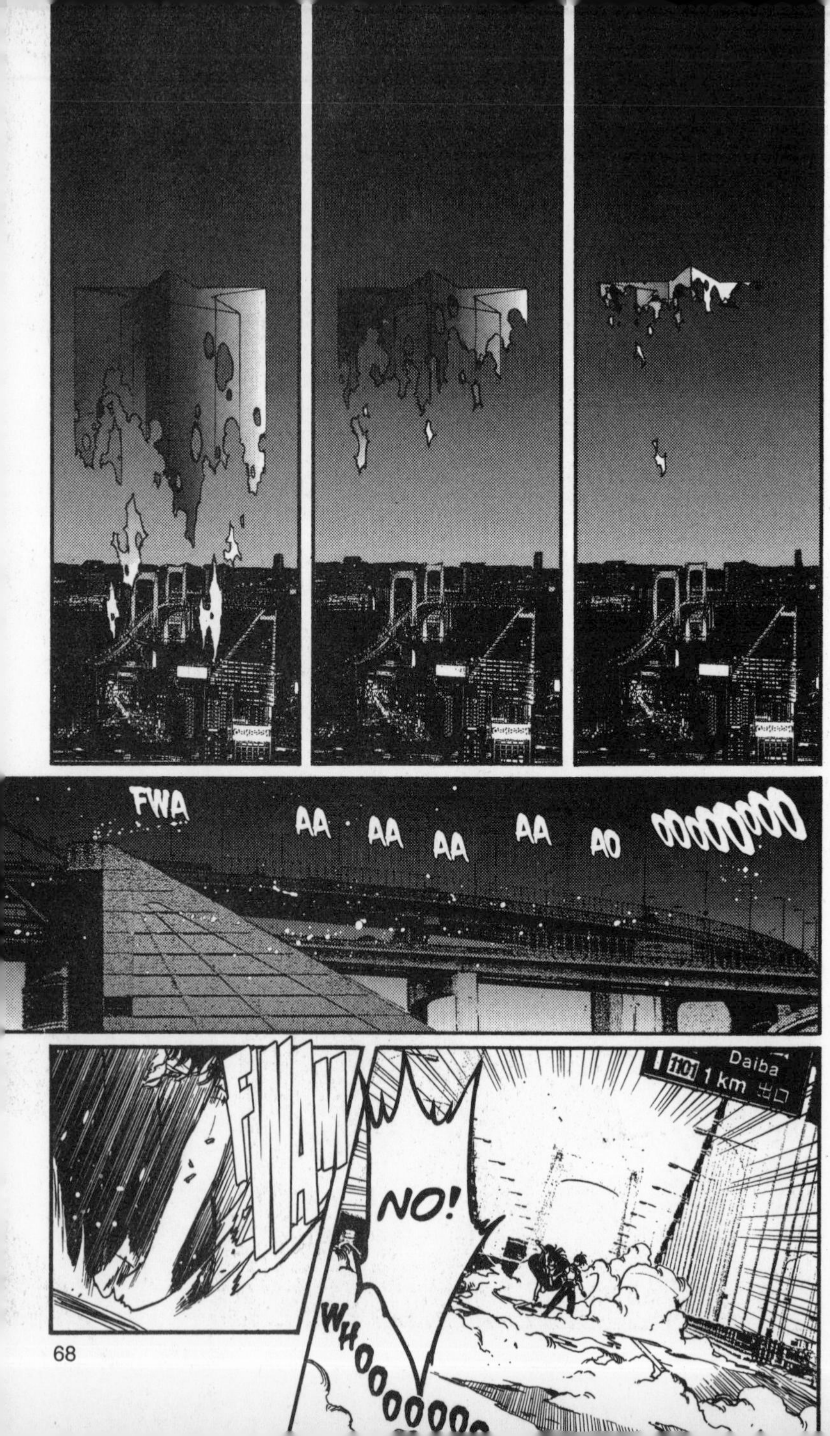
FWA AA AA AA AA AO OOOOOOOO
1101 1 km Daiba 出口
NO!
FWAM
WHOOOOOOO

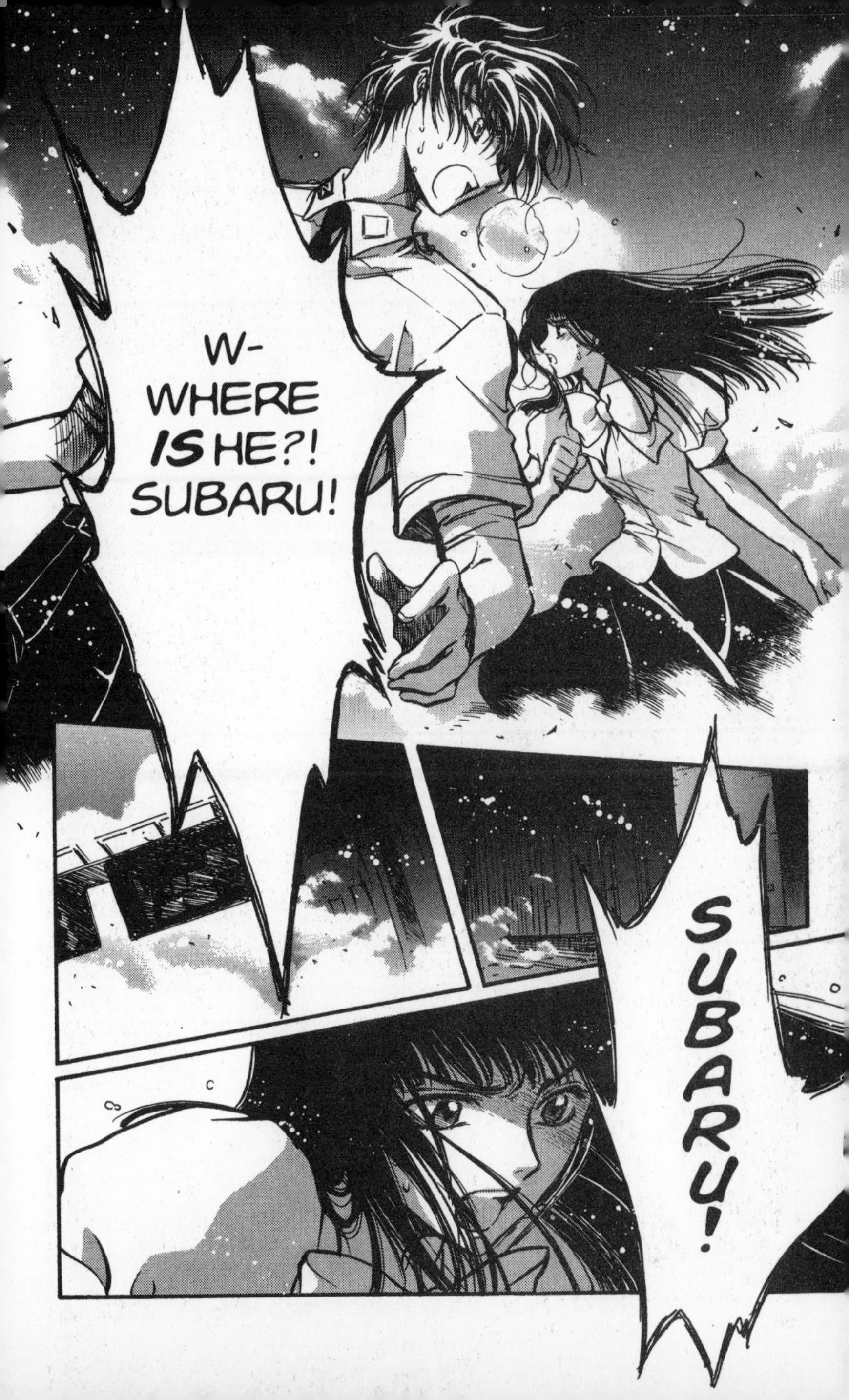
W-
WHERE
IS HE?!
SUBARU!
SUBARU!

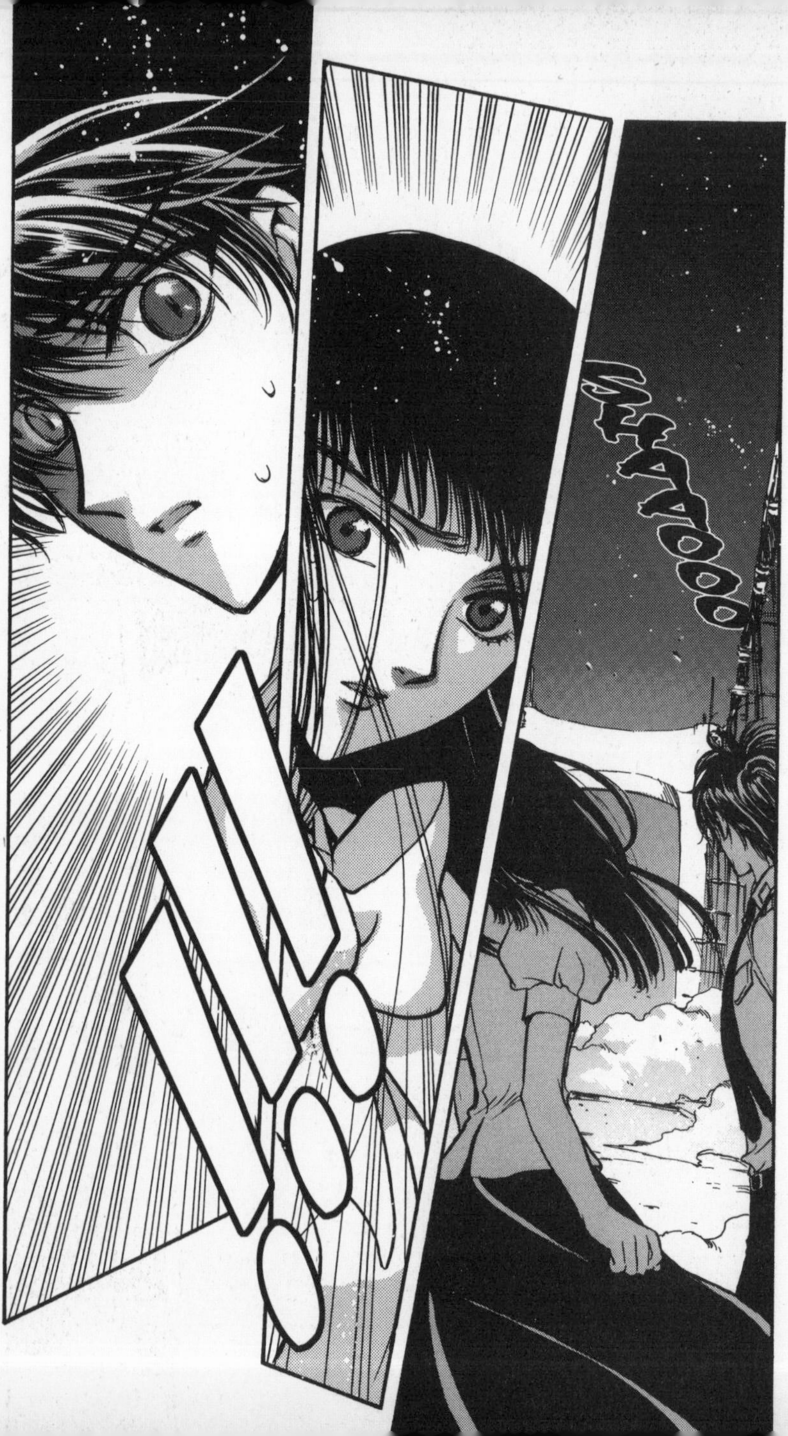
SHAAOOO

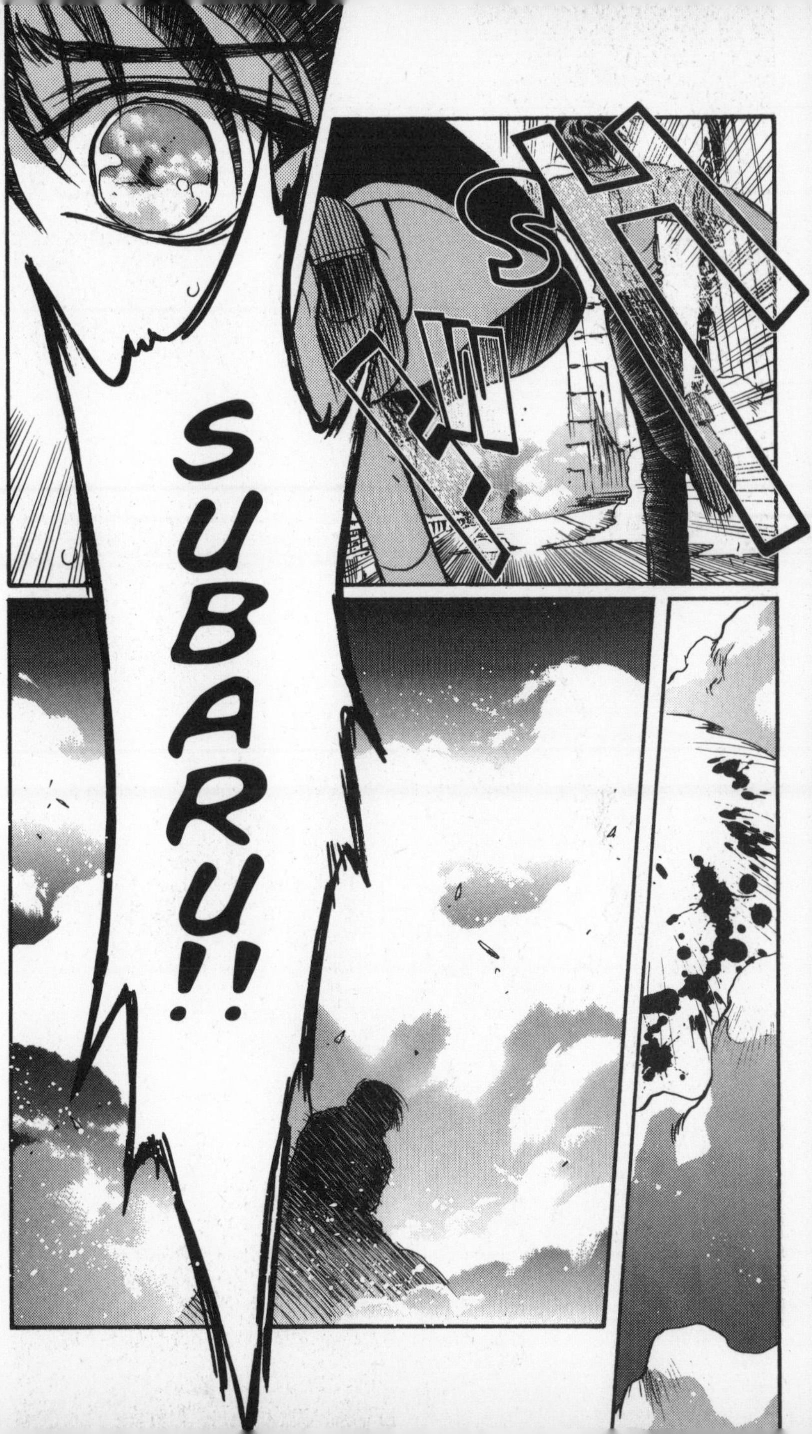
SUBARU!!

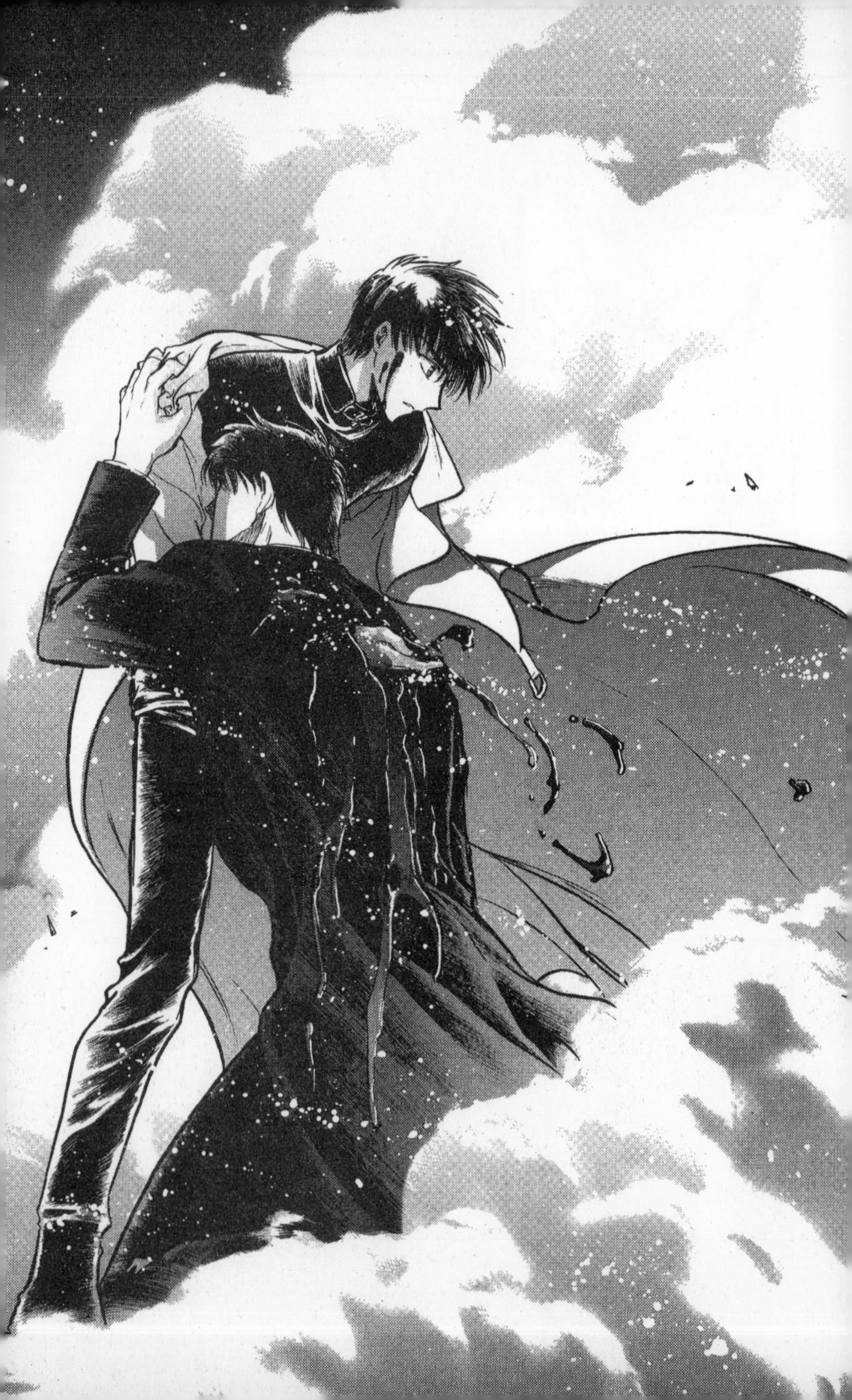

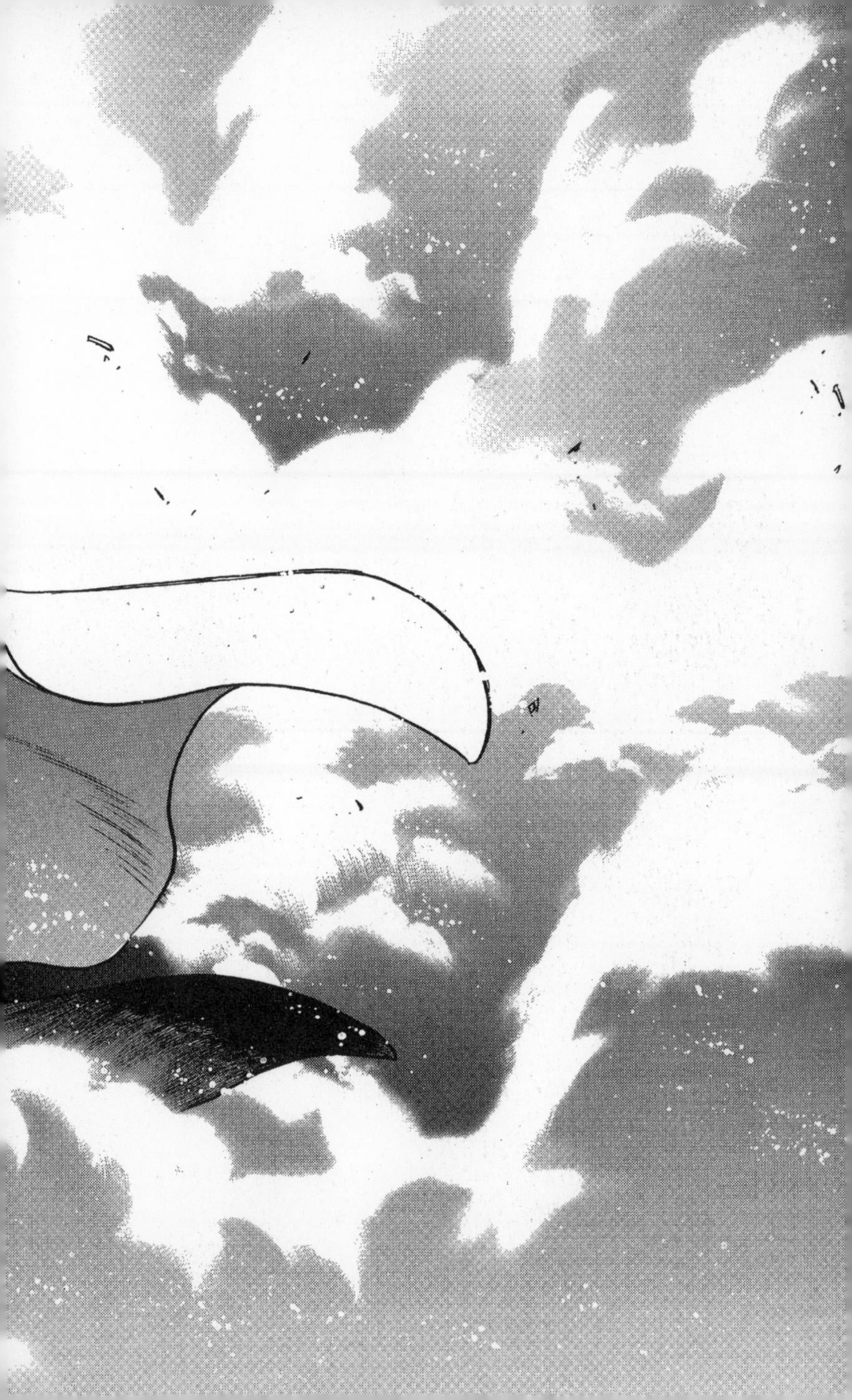

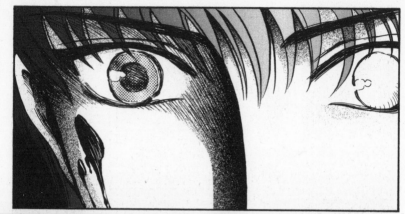

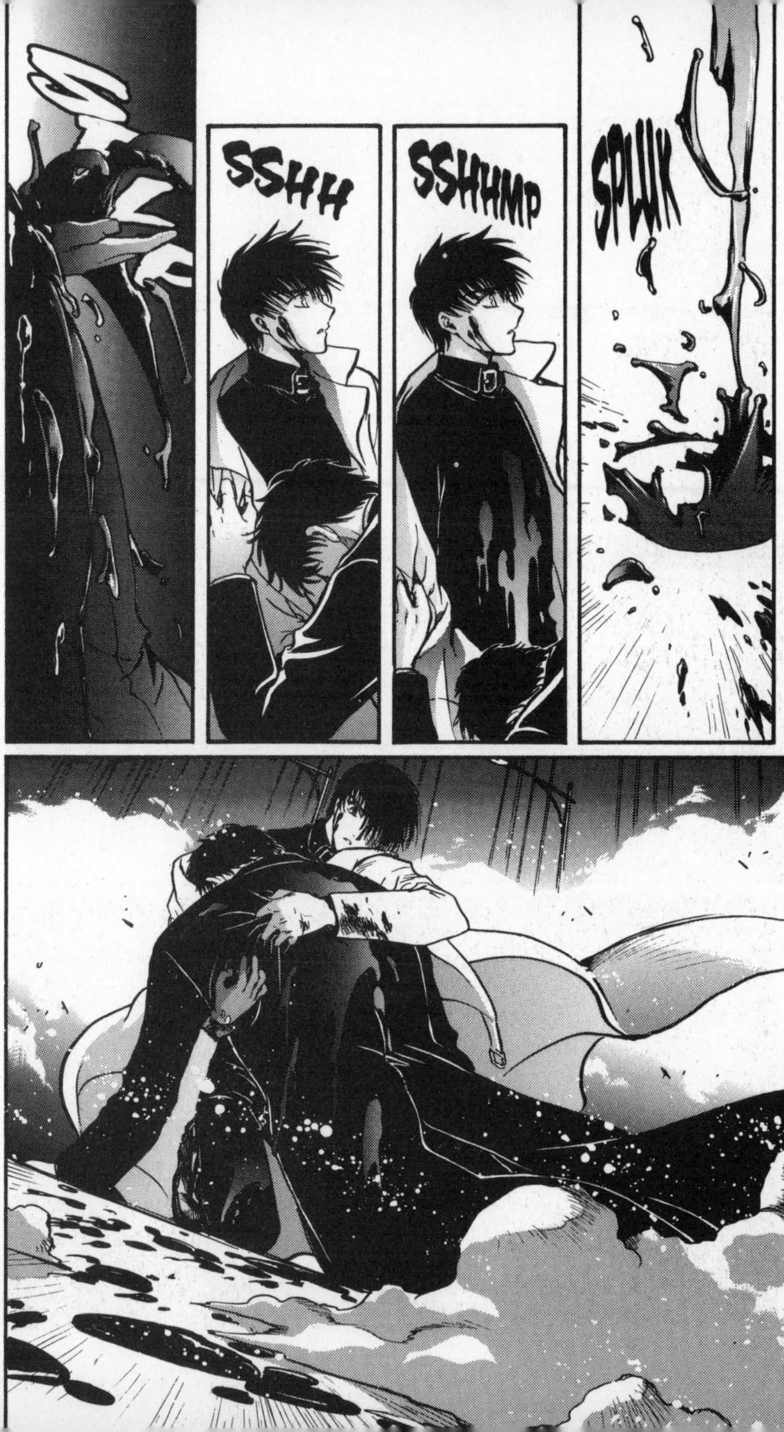
SPLUK
SSHHUMP
SSHH

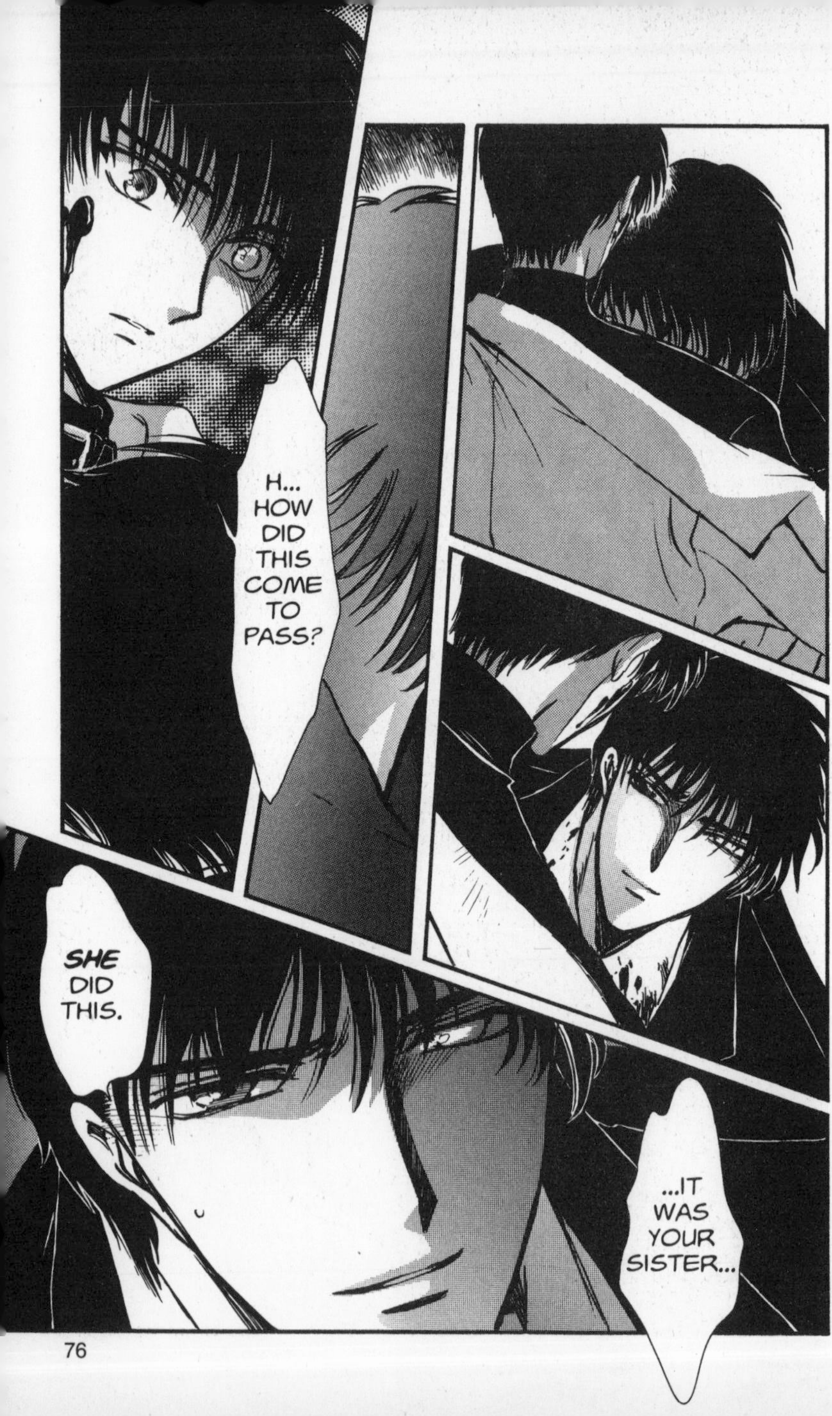
H... HOW DID THIS COME TO PASS?
...IT WAS YOUR SISTER...
SHE DID THIS.

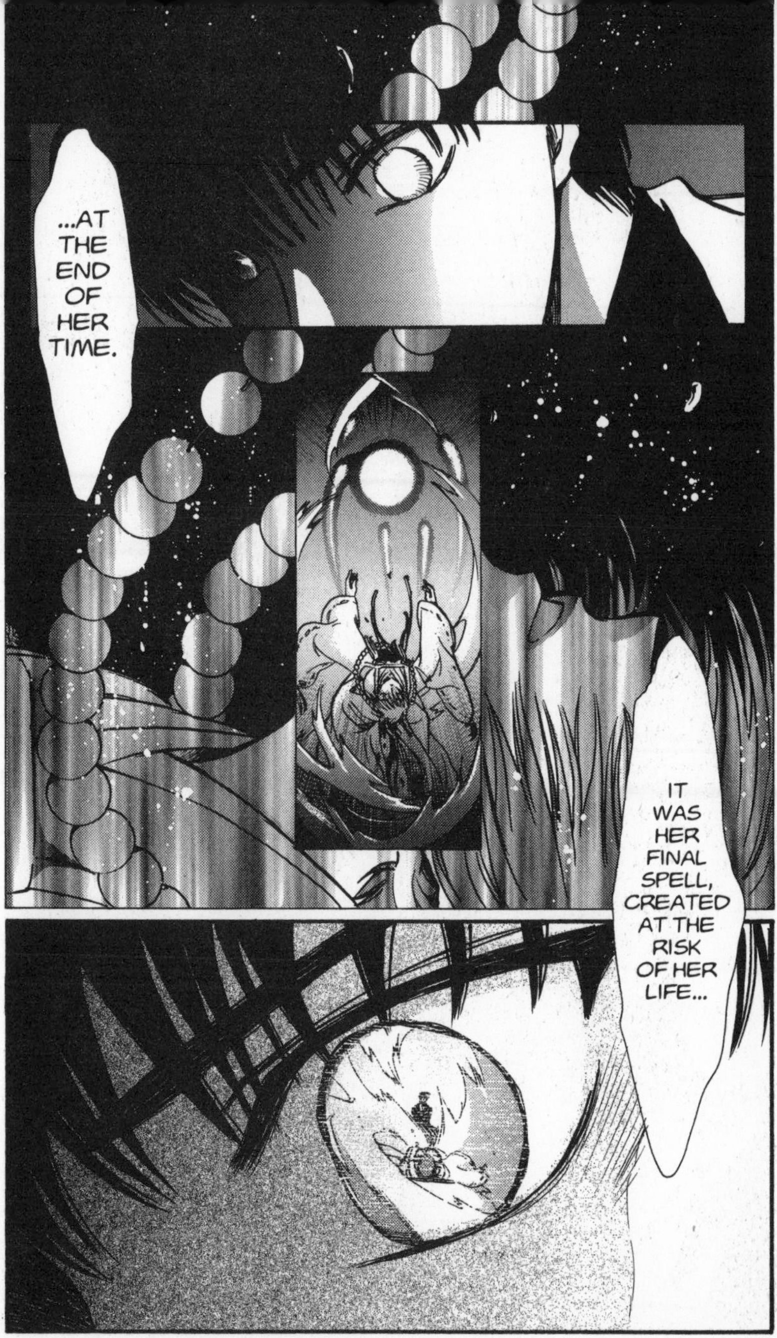
...AT THE END OF HER TIME.
IT WAS HER FINAL SPELL, CREATED AT THE RISK OF HER LIFE...

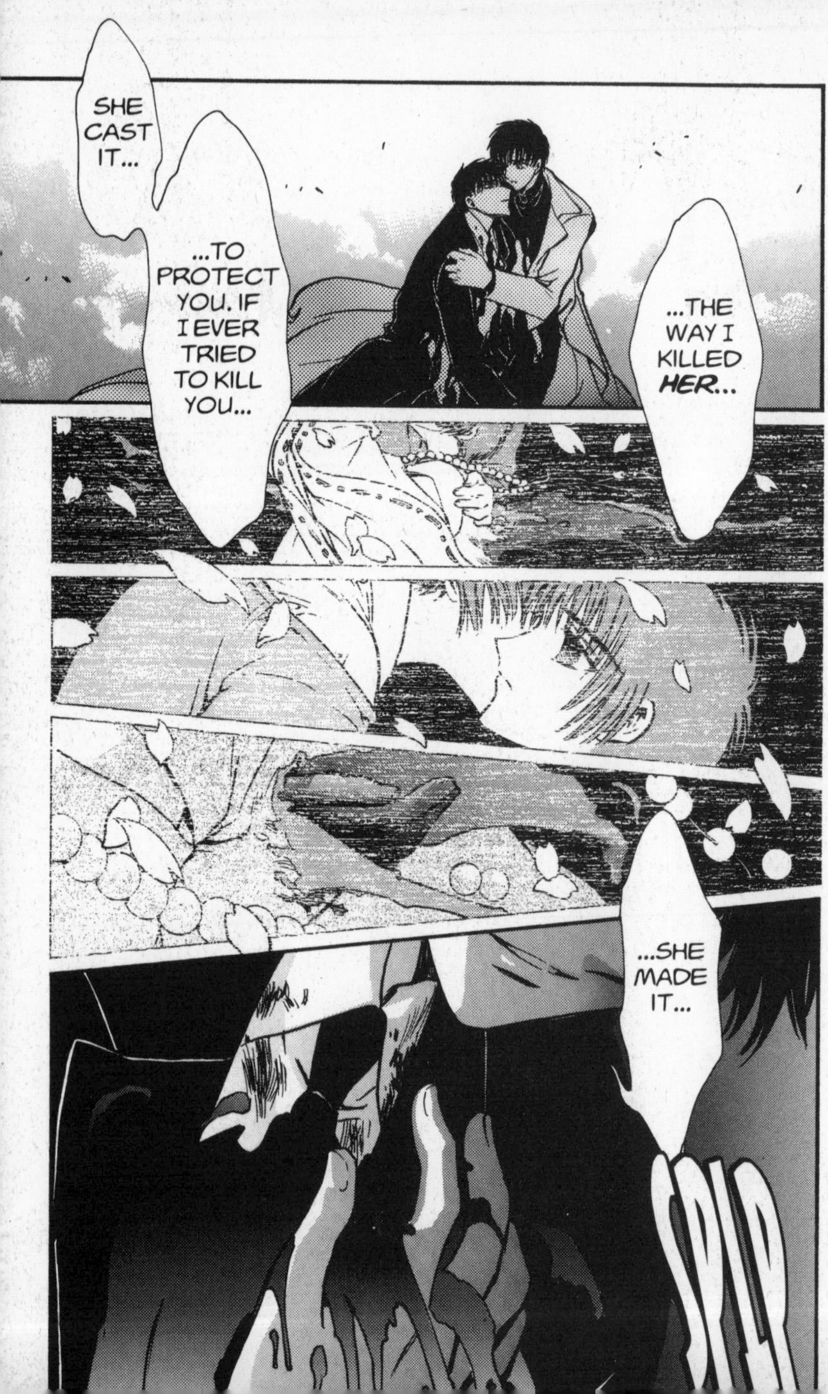
SHE CAST IT...
...TO PROTECT YOU. IF I EVER TRIED TO KILL YOU...
...THE WAY I KILLED HER...
...SHE MADE IT...

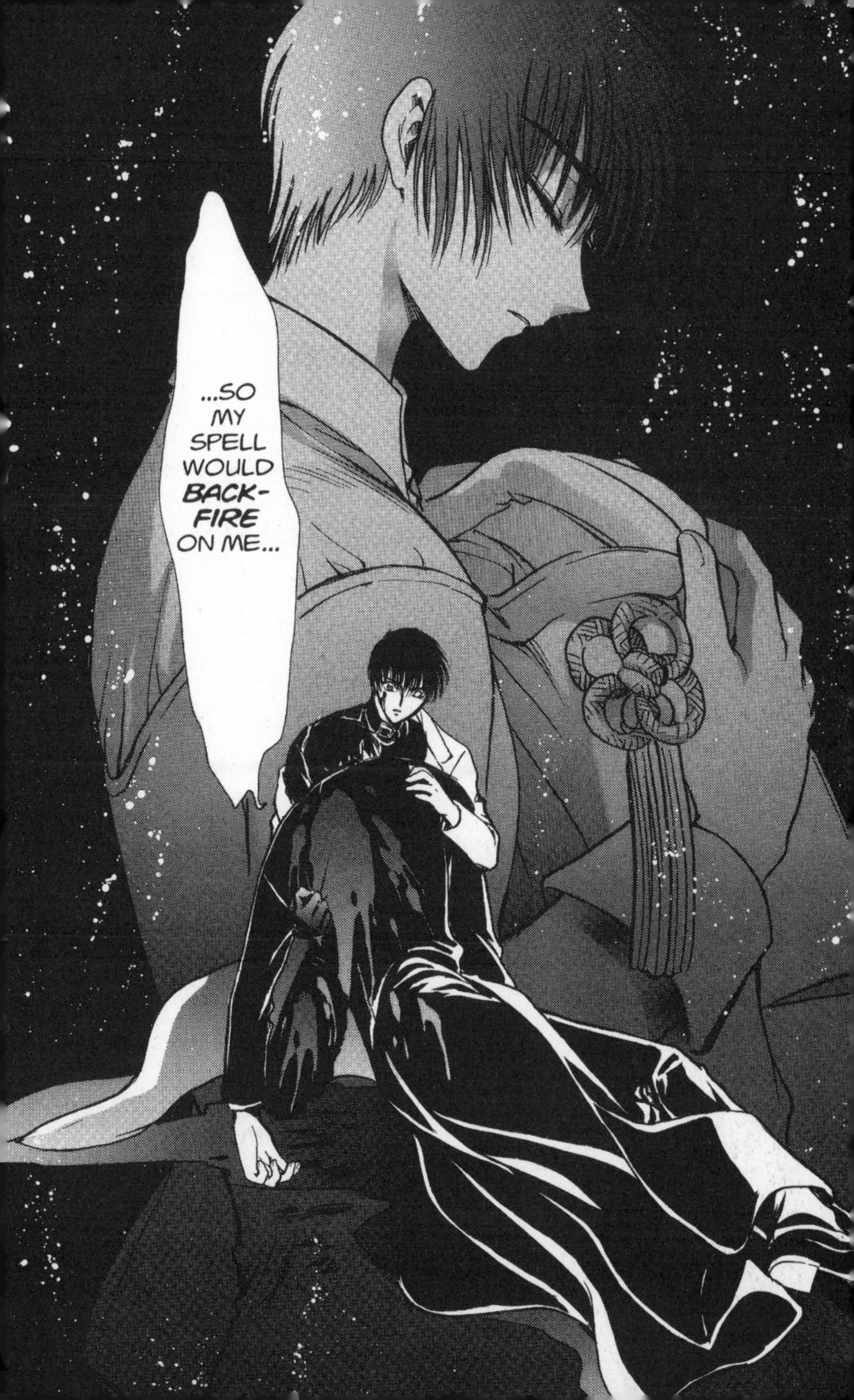
...SO MY SPELL WOULD **BACK-FIRE** ON ME...

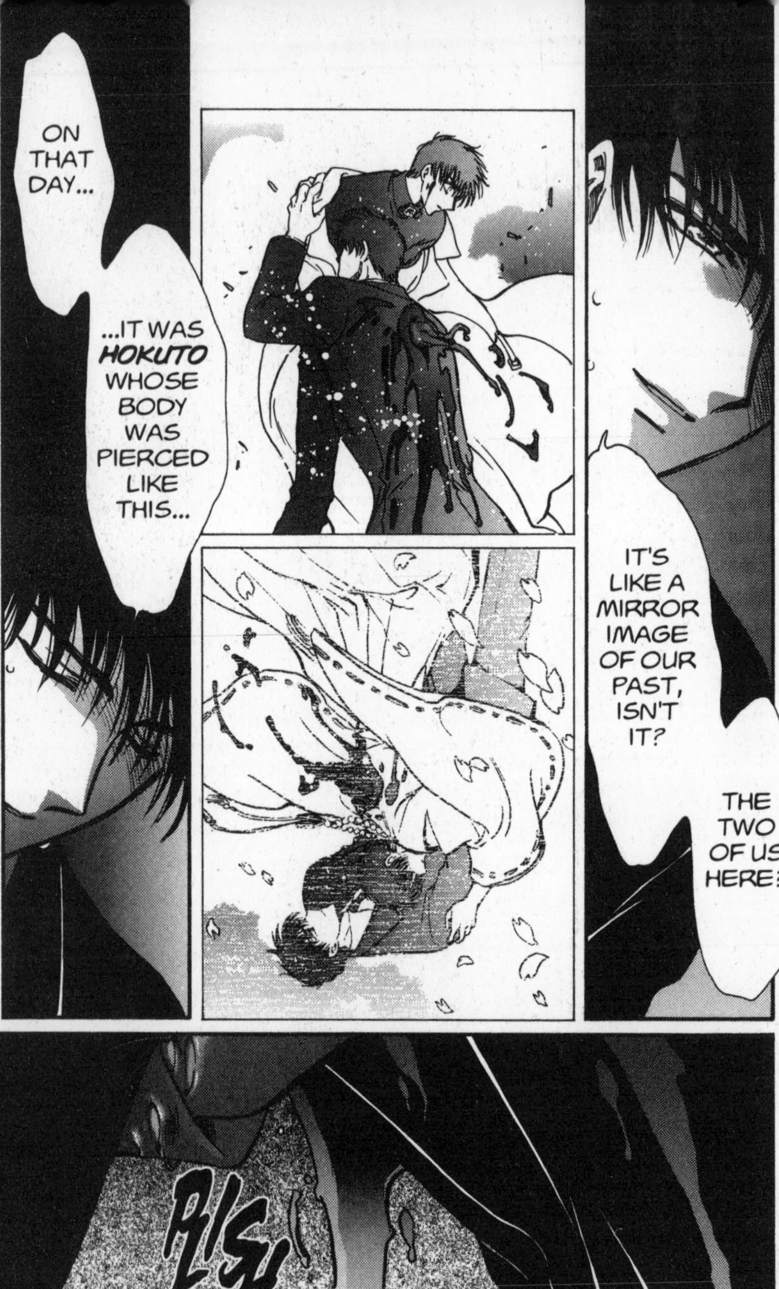
IT'S LIKE A MIRROR IMAGE OF OUR PAST, ISN'T IT?
THE TWO OF US HERE?
ON THAT DAY...
...IT WAS **HOKUTO** WHOSE BODY WAS PIERCED LIKE THIS...
PLISH

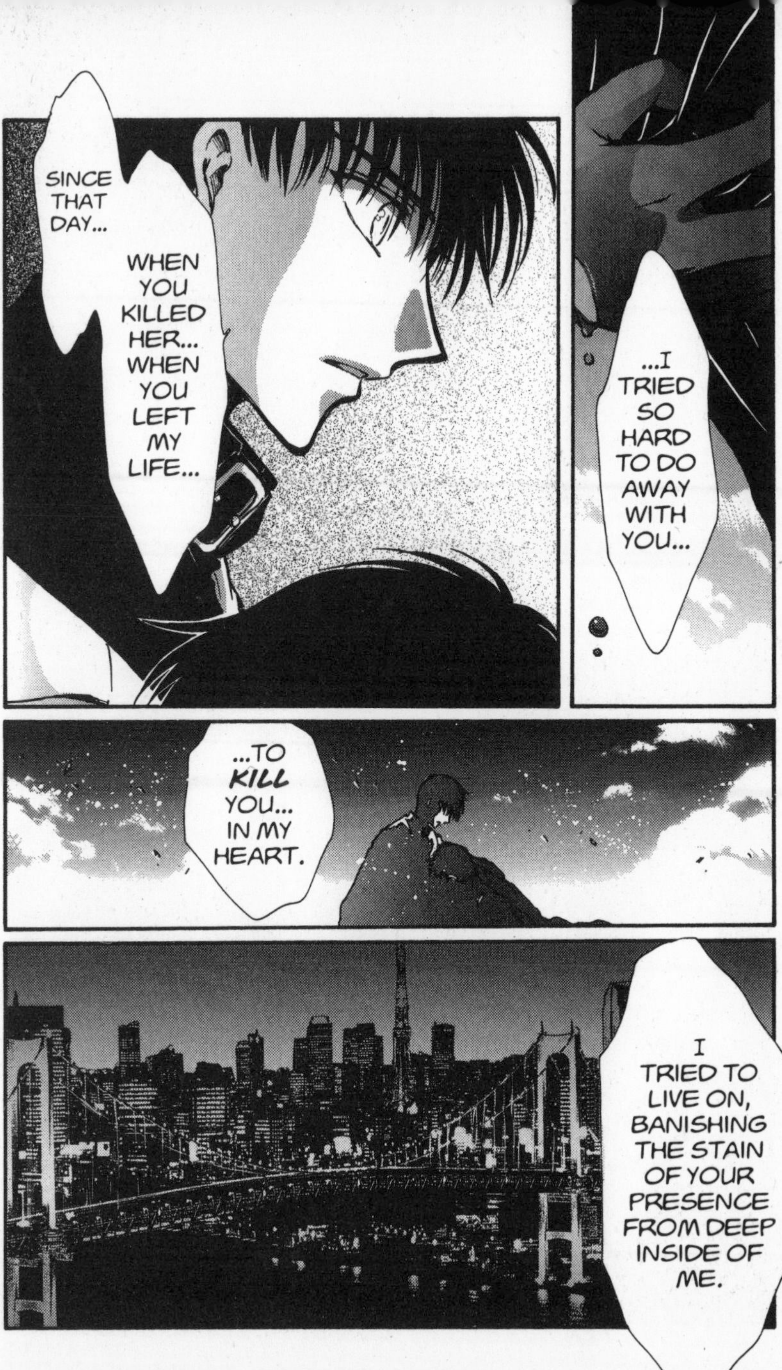
...I TRIED SO HARD TO DO AWAY WITH YOU...
SINCE THAT DAY...
WHEN YOU KILLED HER... WHEN YOU LEFT MY LIFE...
...TO KILL YOU... IN MY HEART.
I TRIED TO LIVE ON, BANISHING THE STAIN OF YOUR PRESENCE FROM DEEP INSIDE OF ME.

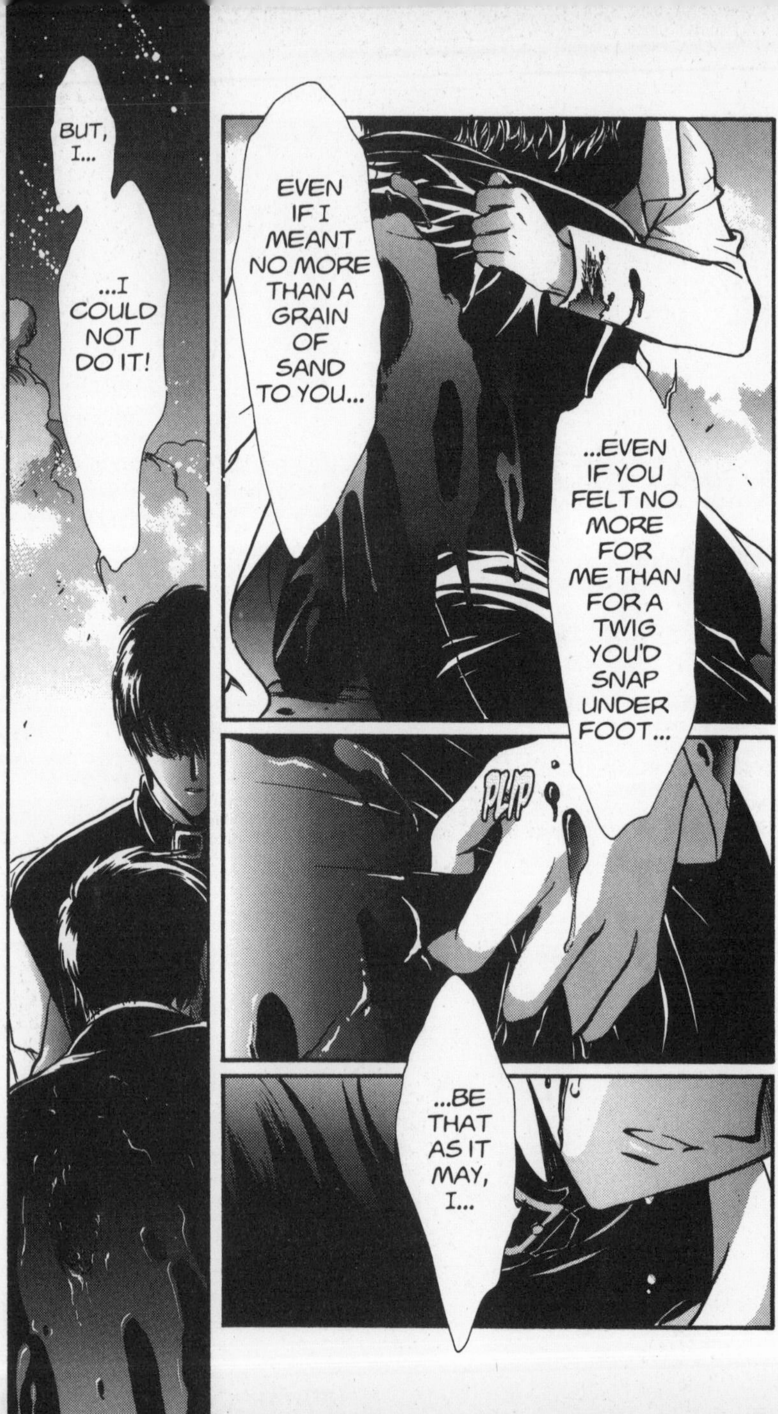
EVEN IF I MEANT NO MORE THAN A GRAIN OF SAND TO YOU...
...EVEN IF YOU FELT NO MORE FOR ME THAN FOR A TWIG YOU'D SNAP UNDER FOOT...
PLIP
...BE THAT AS IT MAY, I...
BUT, I...
...I COULD NOT DO IT!

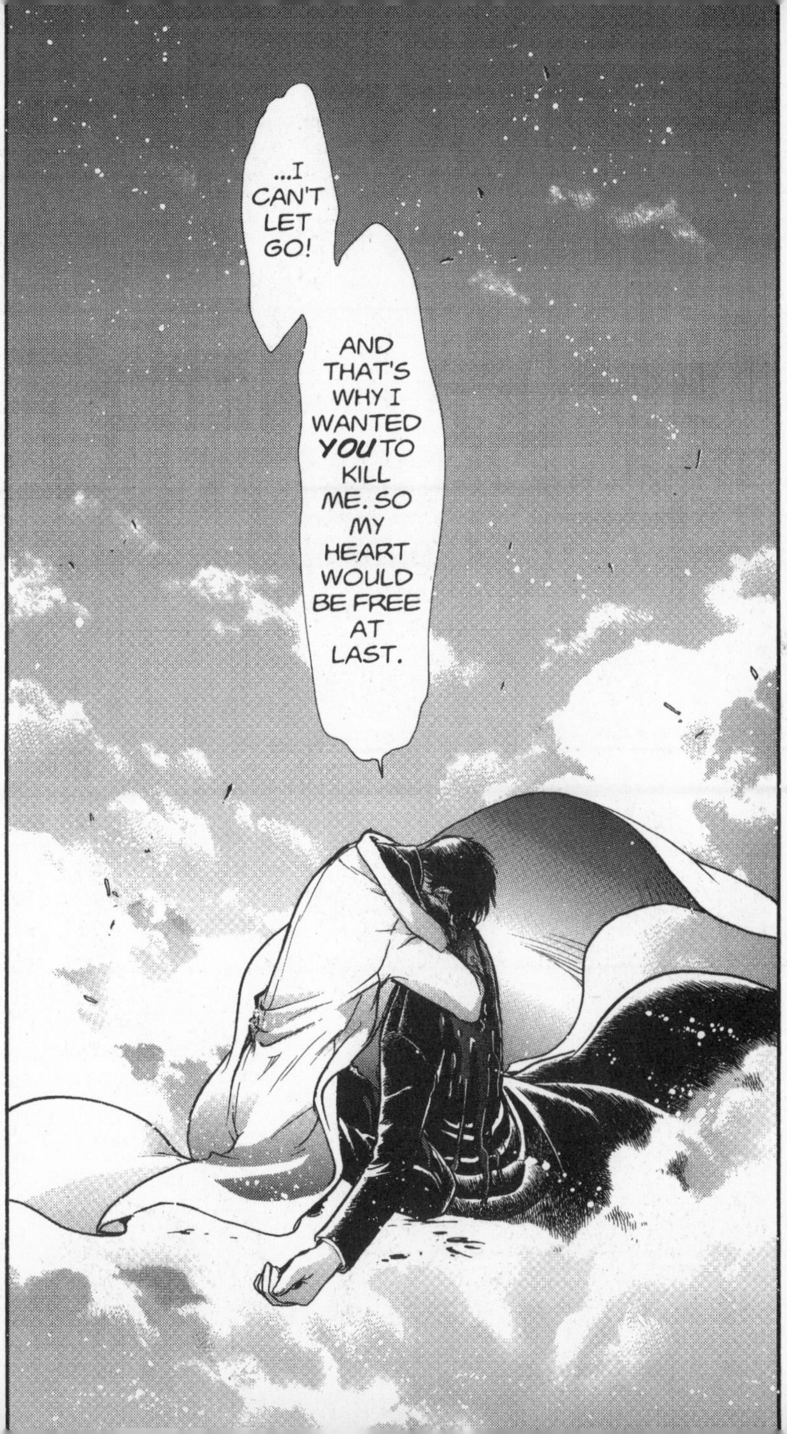
...I CAN'T LET GO!
AND THAT'S WHY I WANTED YOU TO KILL ME. SO MY HEART WOULD BE FREE AT LAST.

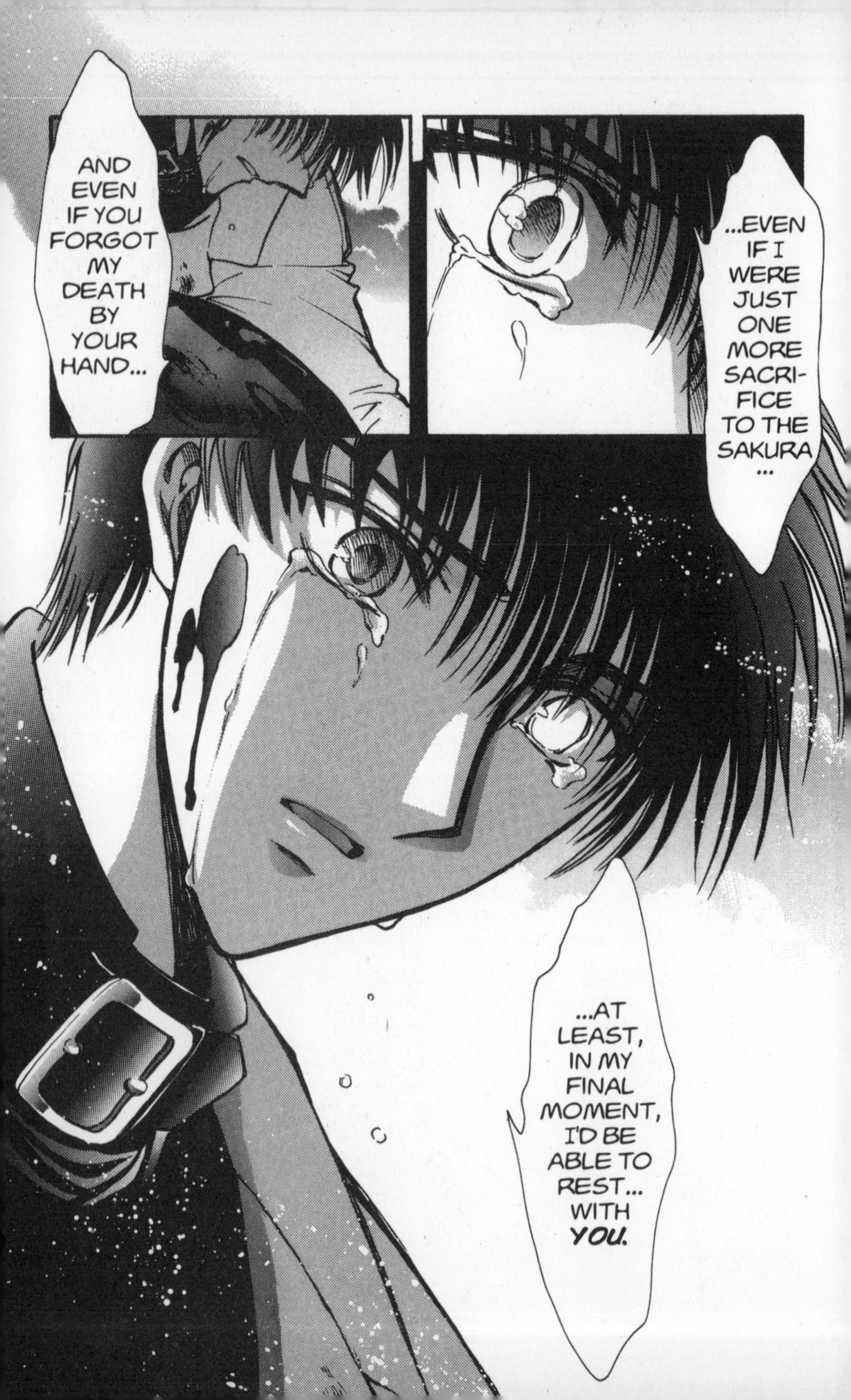
AND EVEN IF YOU FORGOT MY DEATH BY YOUR HAND...
...EVEN IF I WERE JUST ONE MORE SACRI-FICE TO THE SAKURA ...
...AT LEAST, IN MY FINAL MOMENT, I'D BE ABLE TO REST... WITH **YOU.**

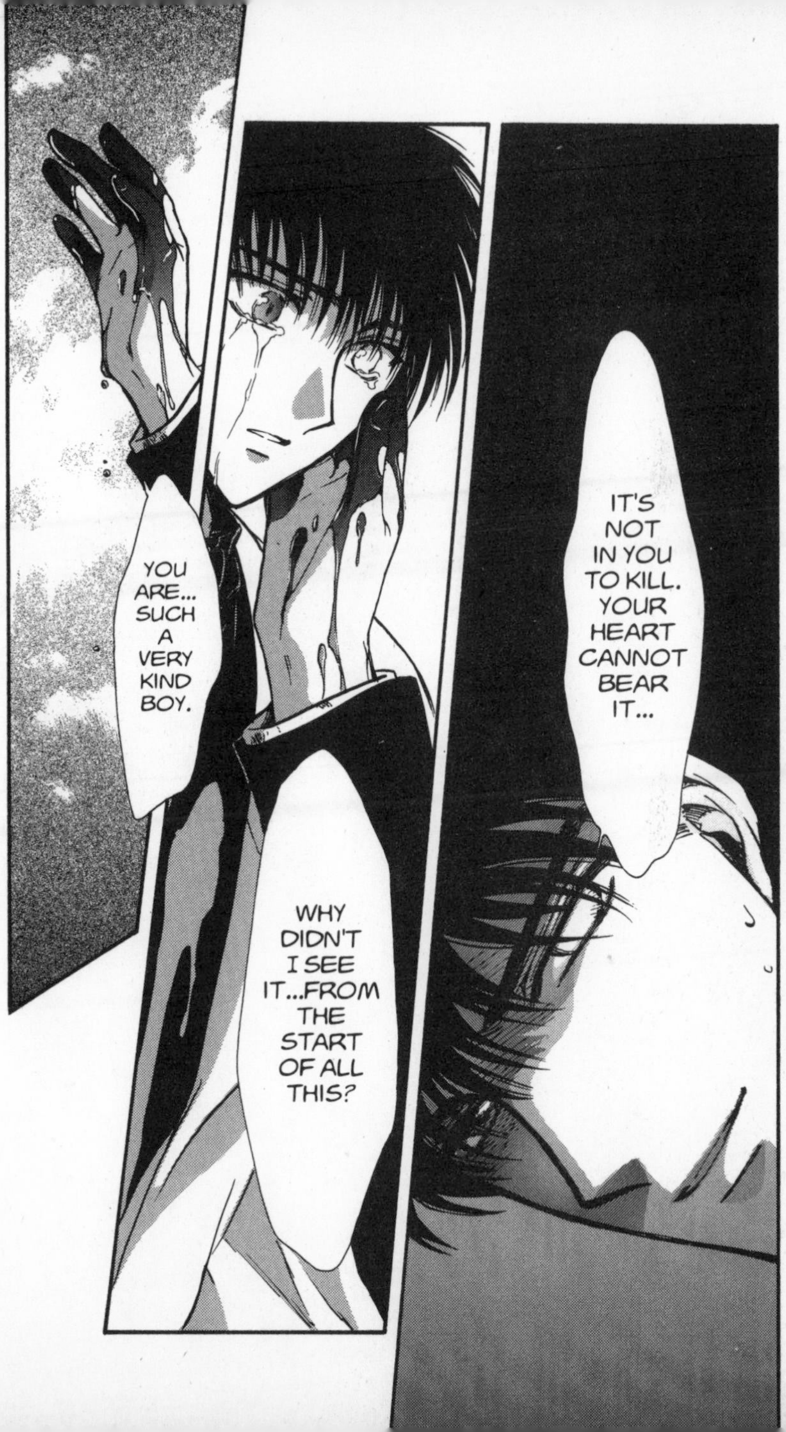
IT'S NOT IN YOU TO KILL. YOUR HEART CANNOT BEAR IT...
YOU ARE... SUCH A VERY KIND BOY.
WHY DIDN'T I SEE IT...FROM THE START OF ALL THIS?

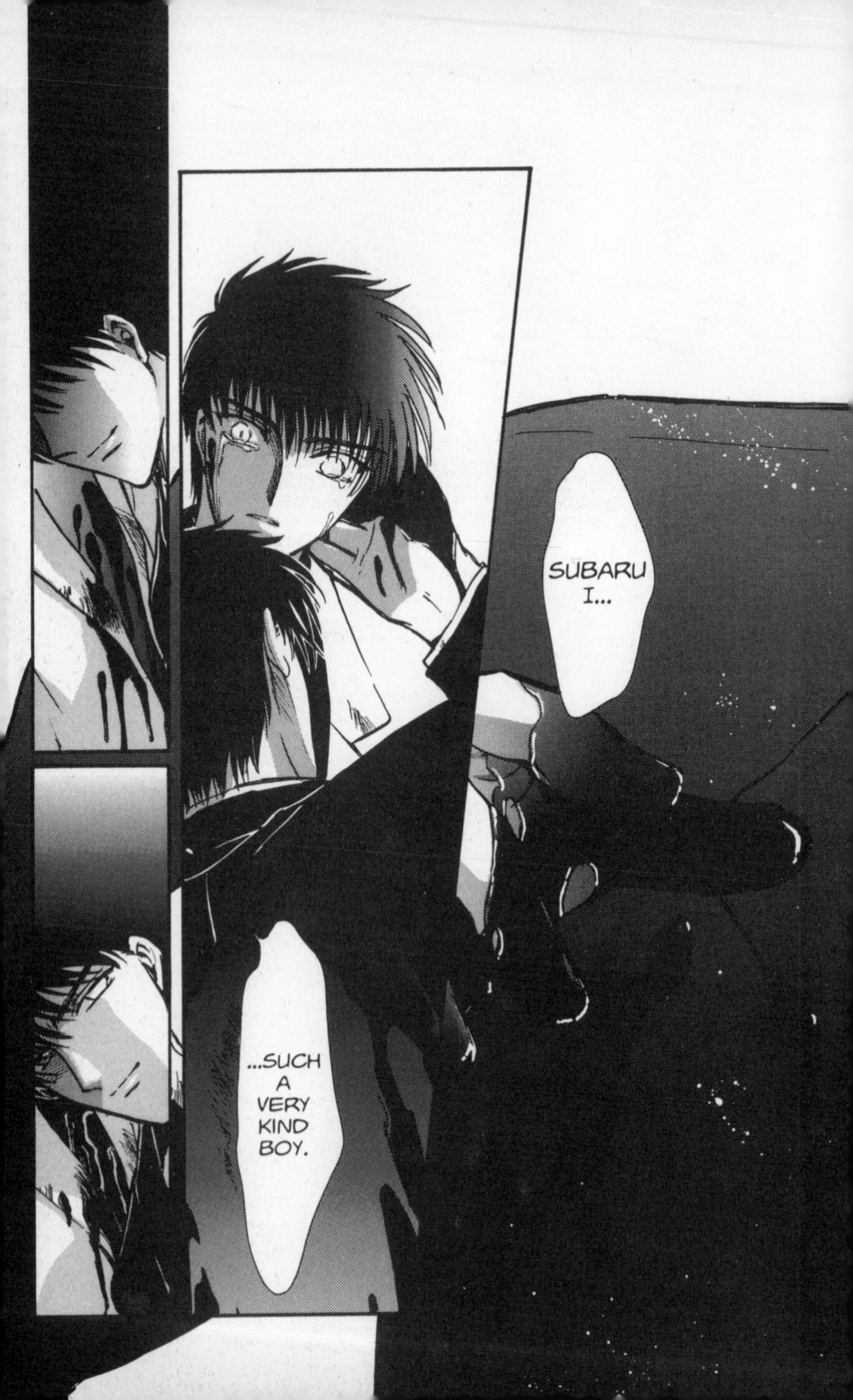
SUBARU I...
...SUCH A VERY KIND BOY.

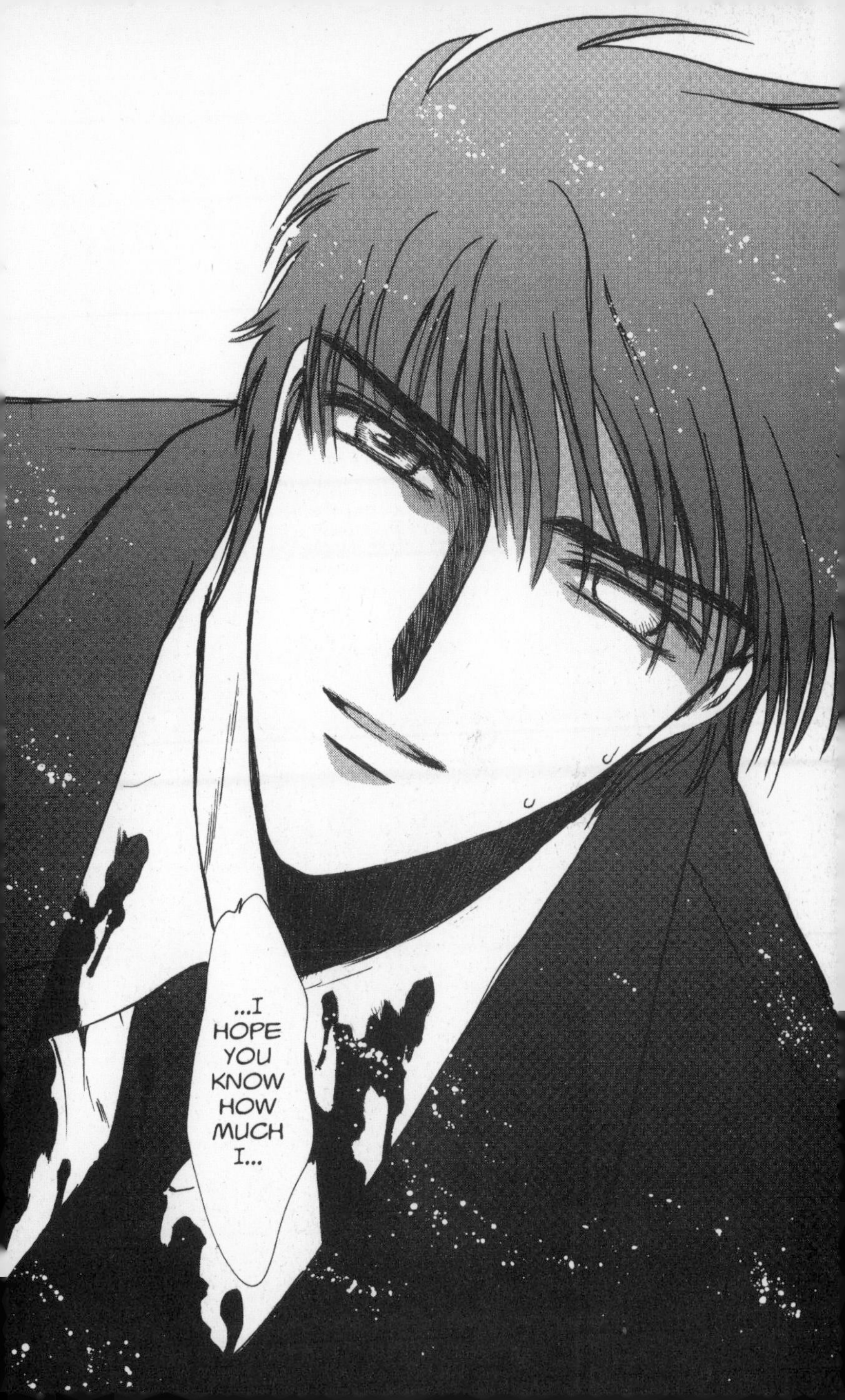
...I HOPE YOU KNOW HOW MUCH I...

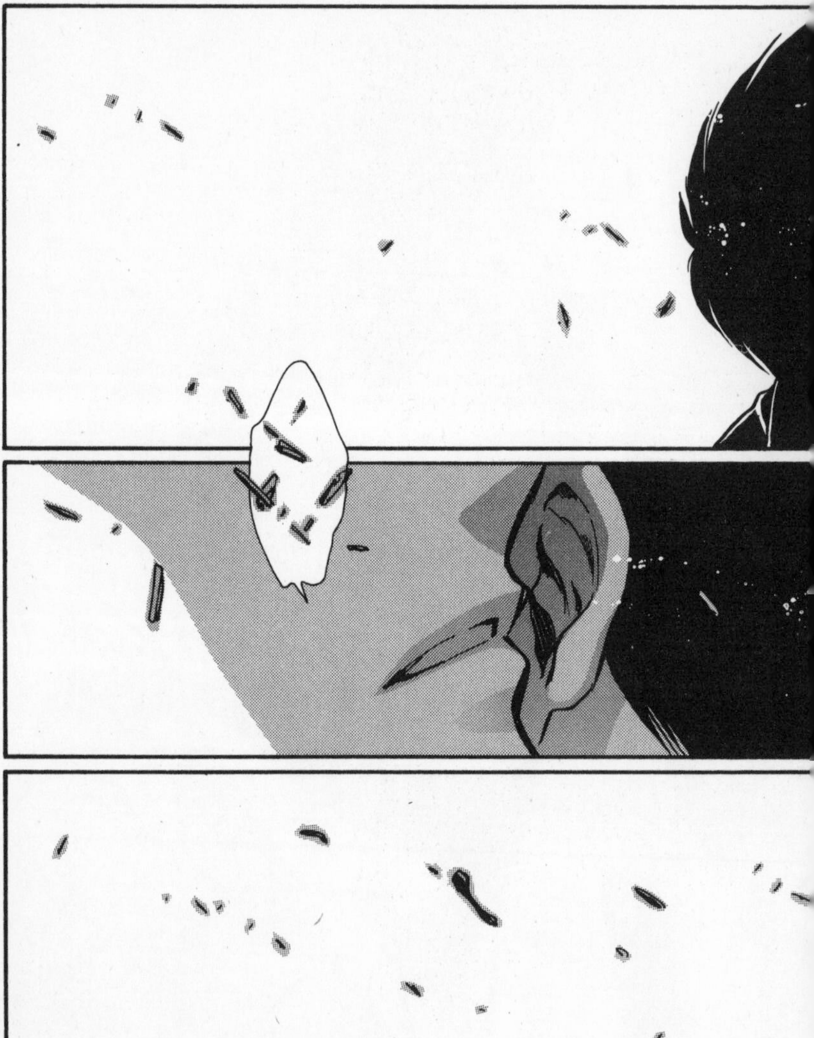

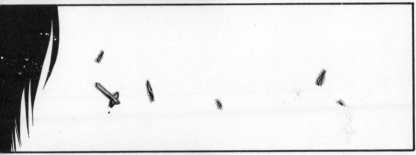

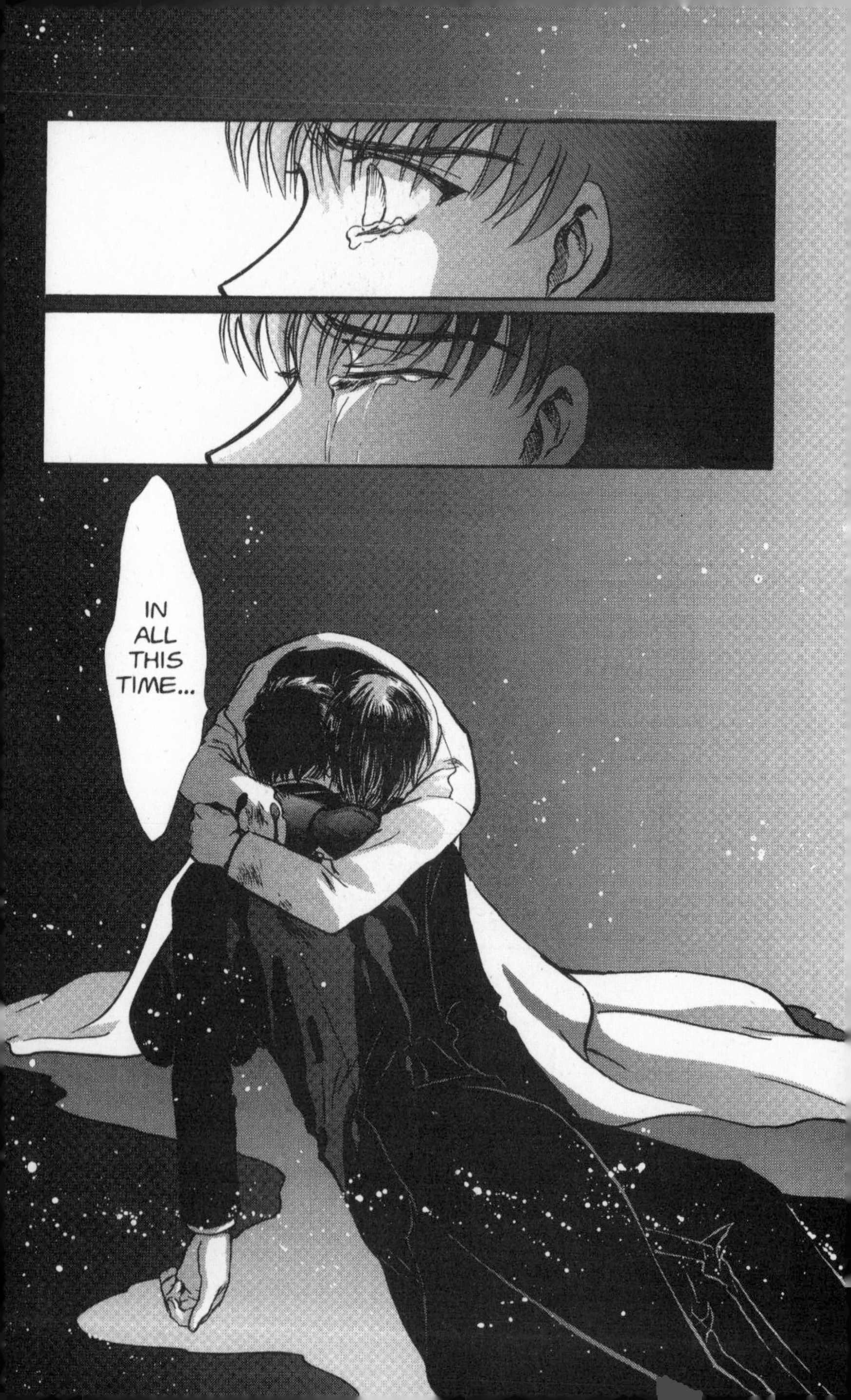
IN ALL THIS TIME...

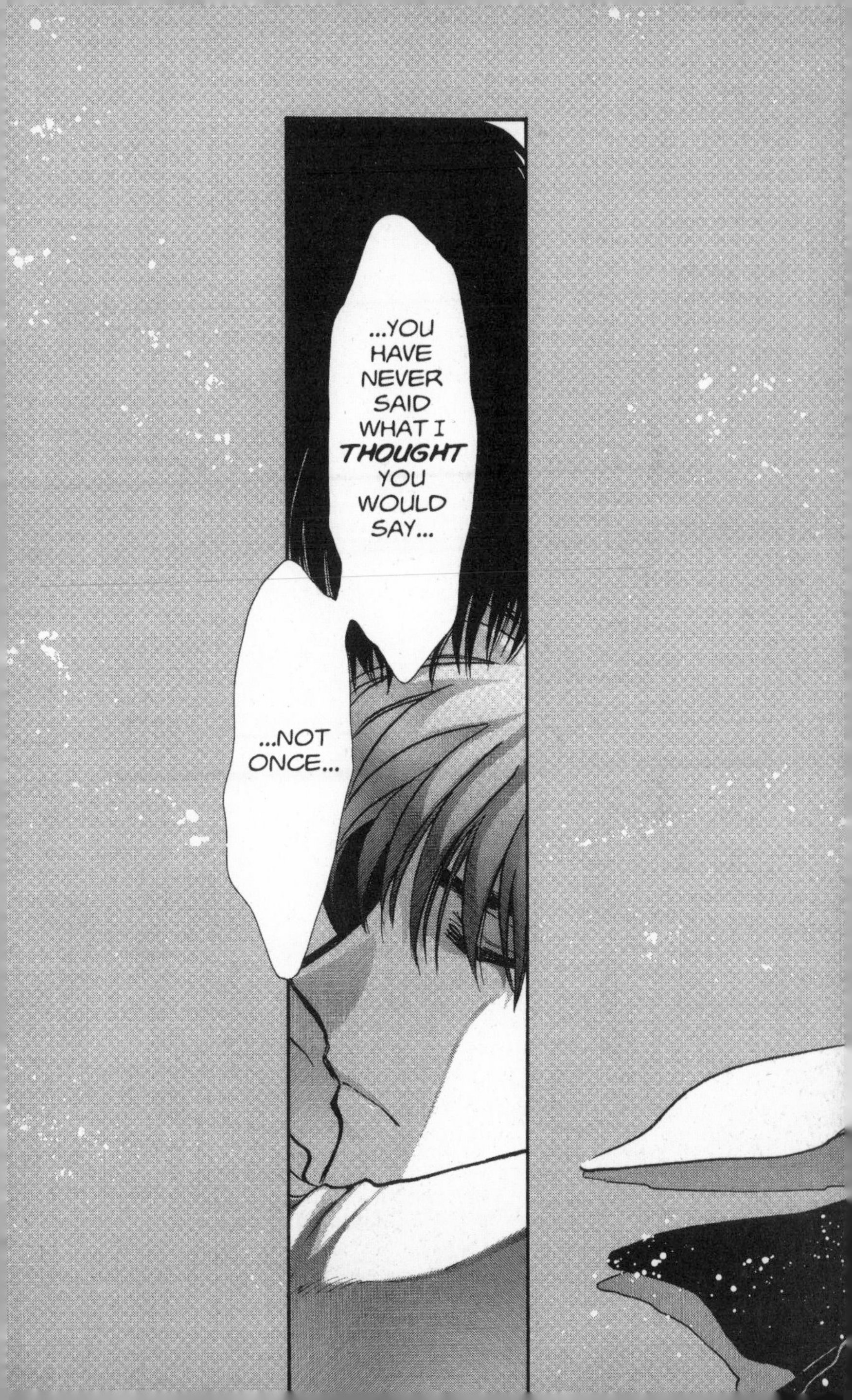
...YOU HAVE NEVER SAID WHAT I **THOUGHT** YOU WOULD SAY...
...NOT ONCE...

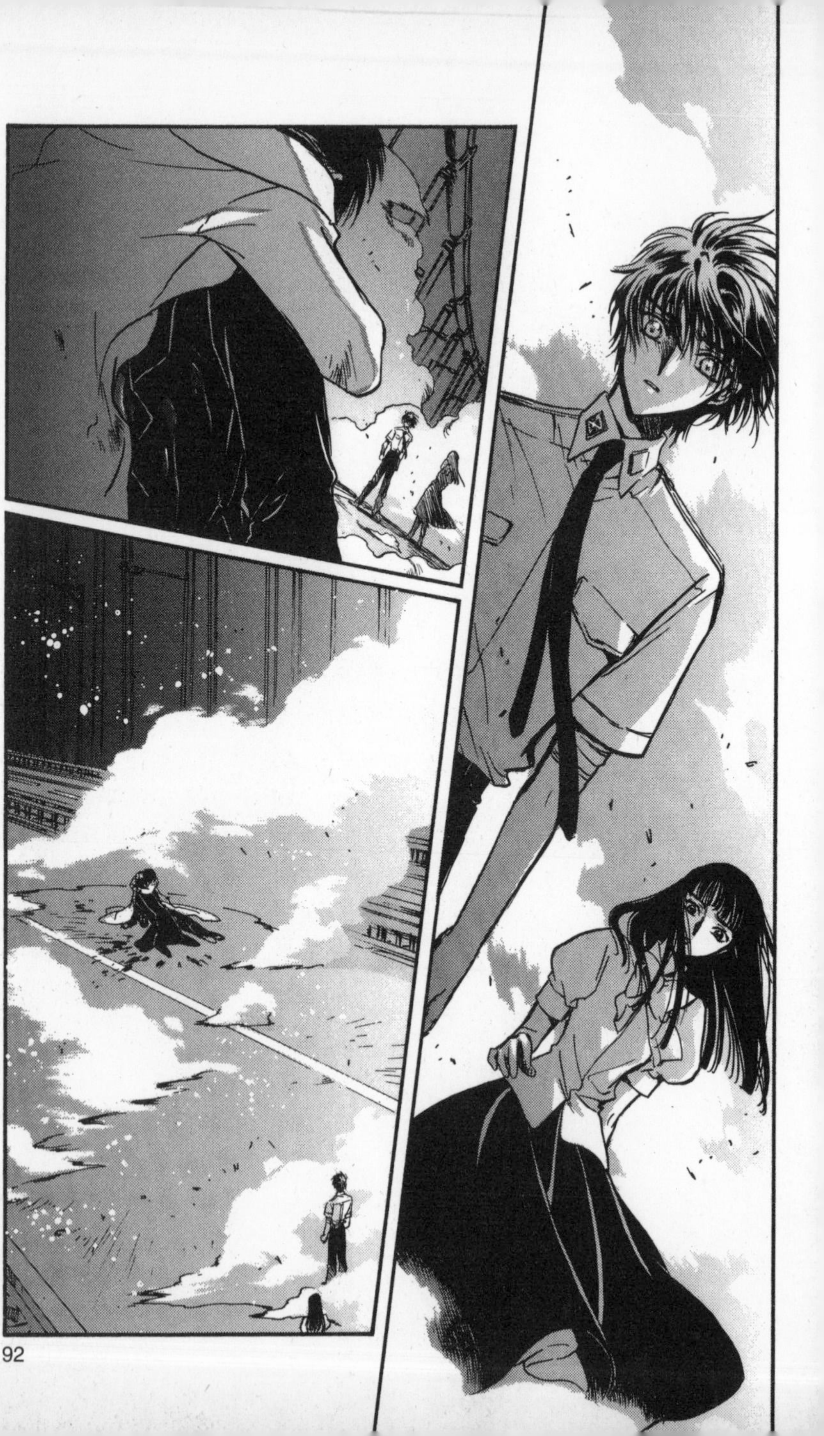

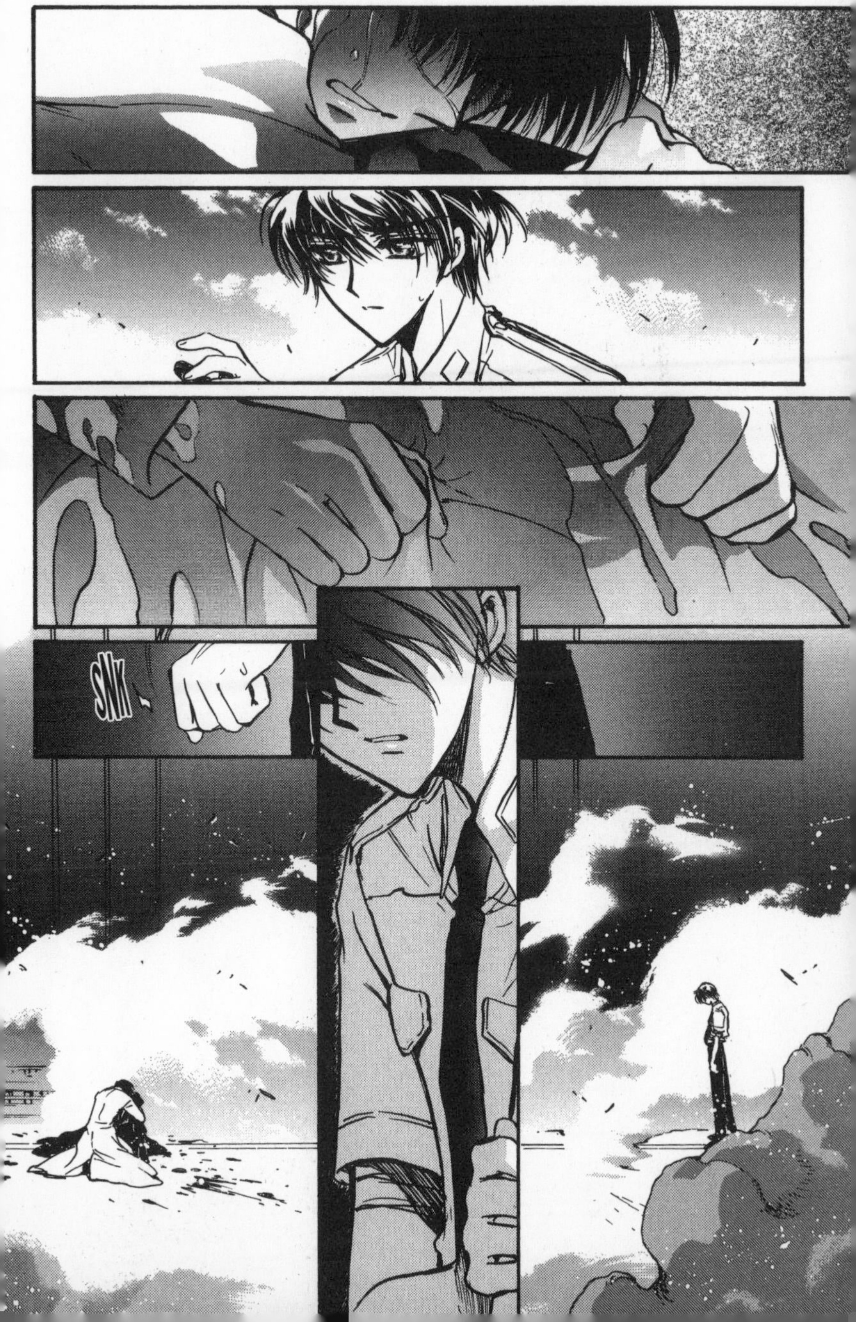
SNK

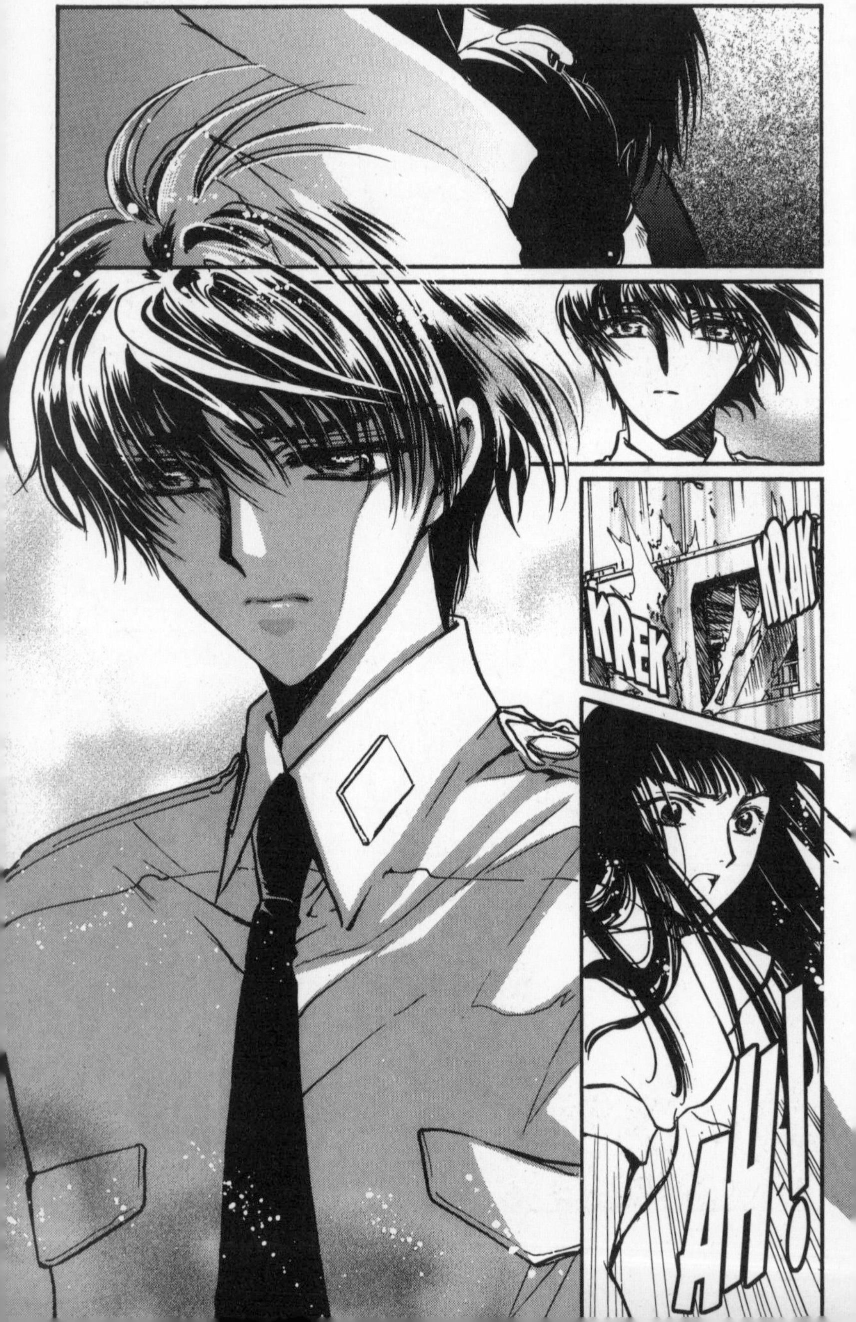
KRAK
KREK
AH!

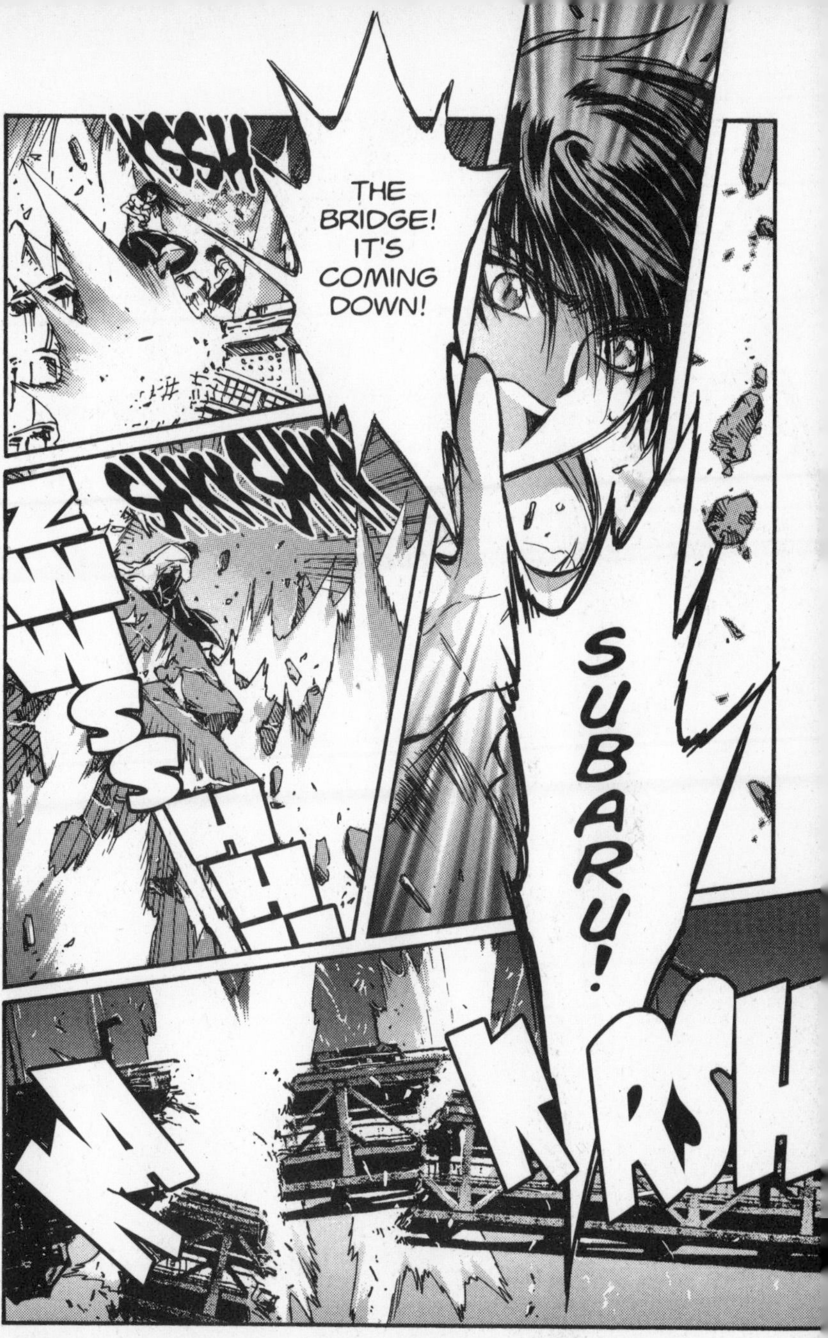
THE BRIDGE! IT'S COMING DOWN!
KSSH
SUBARU!
CHK CHK
ZWSSHH
KRSH

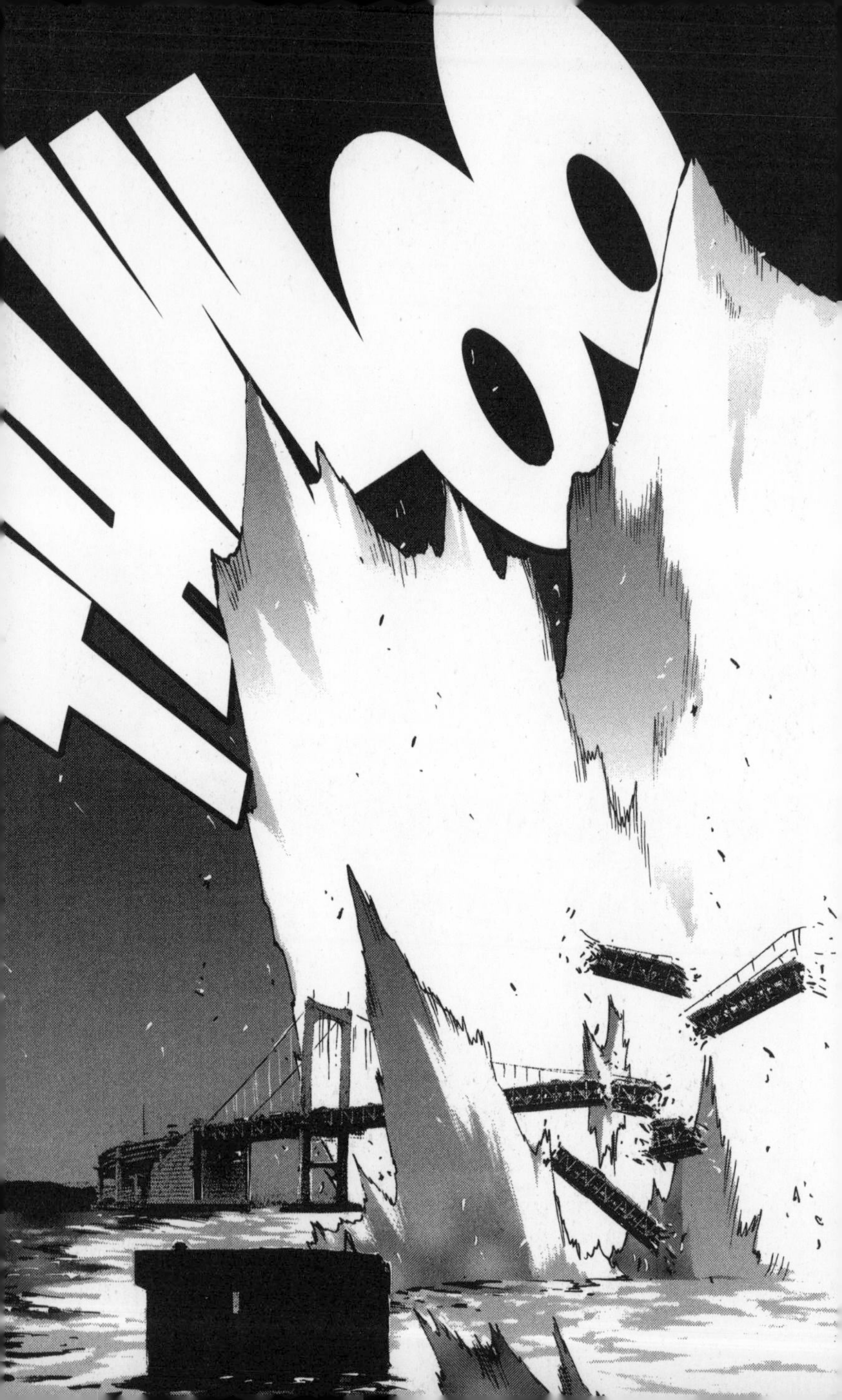

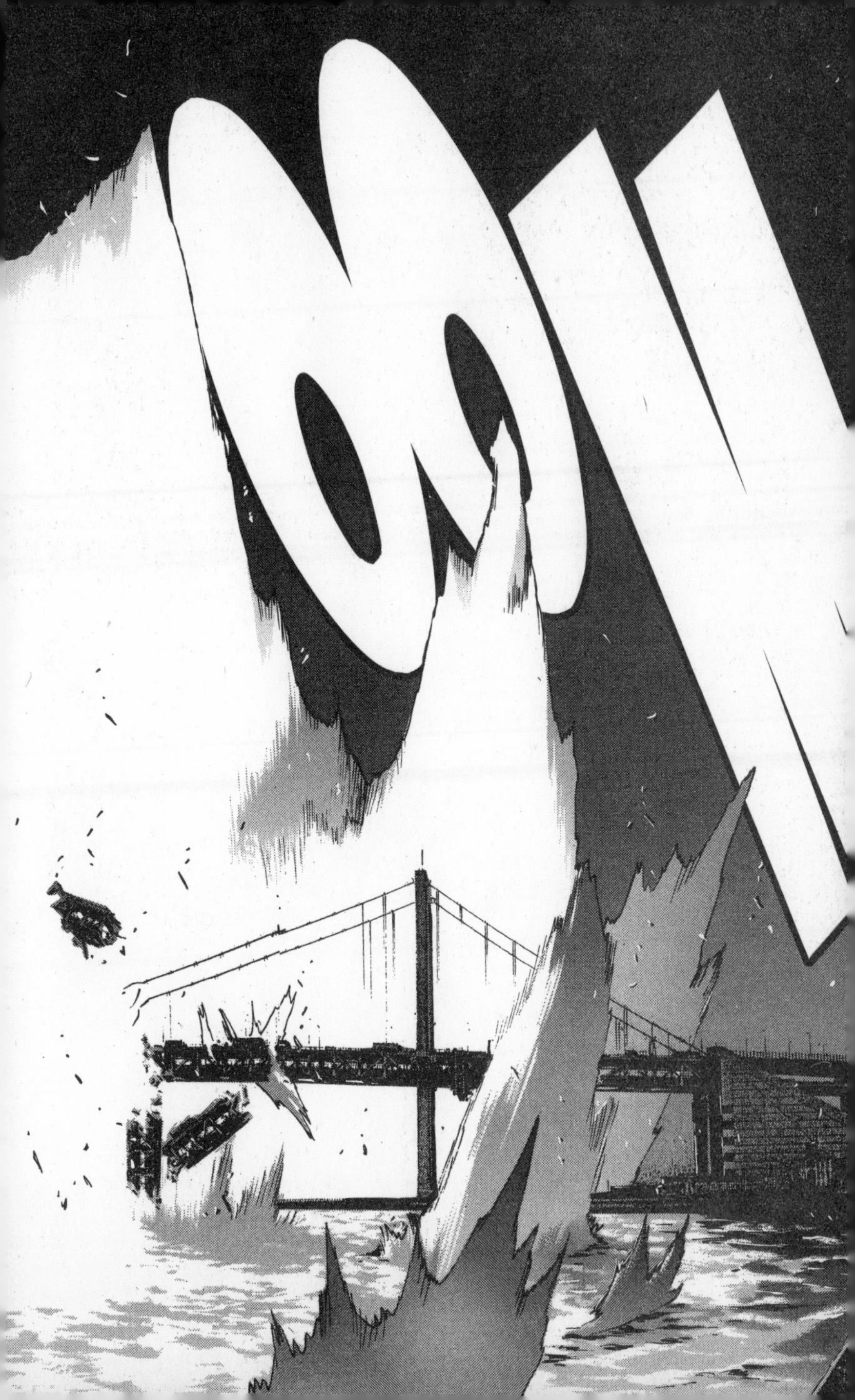

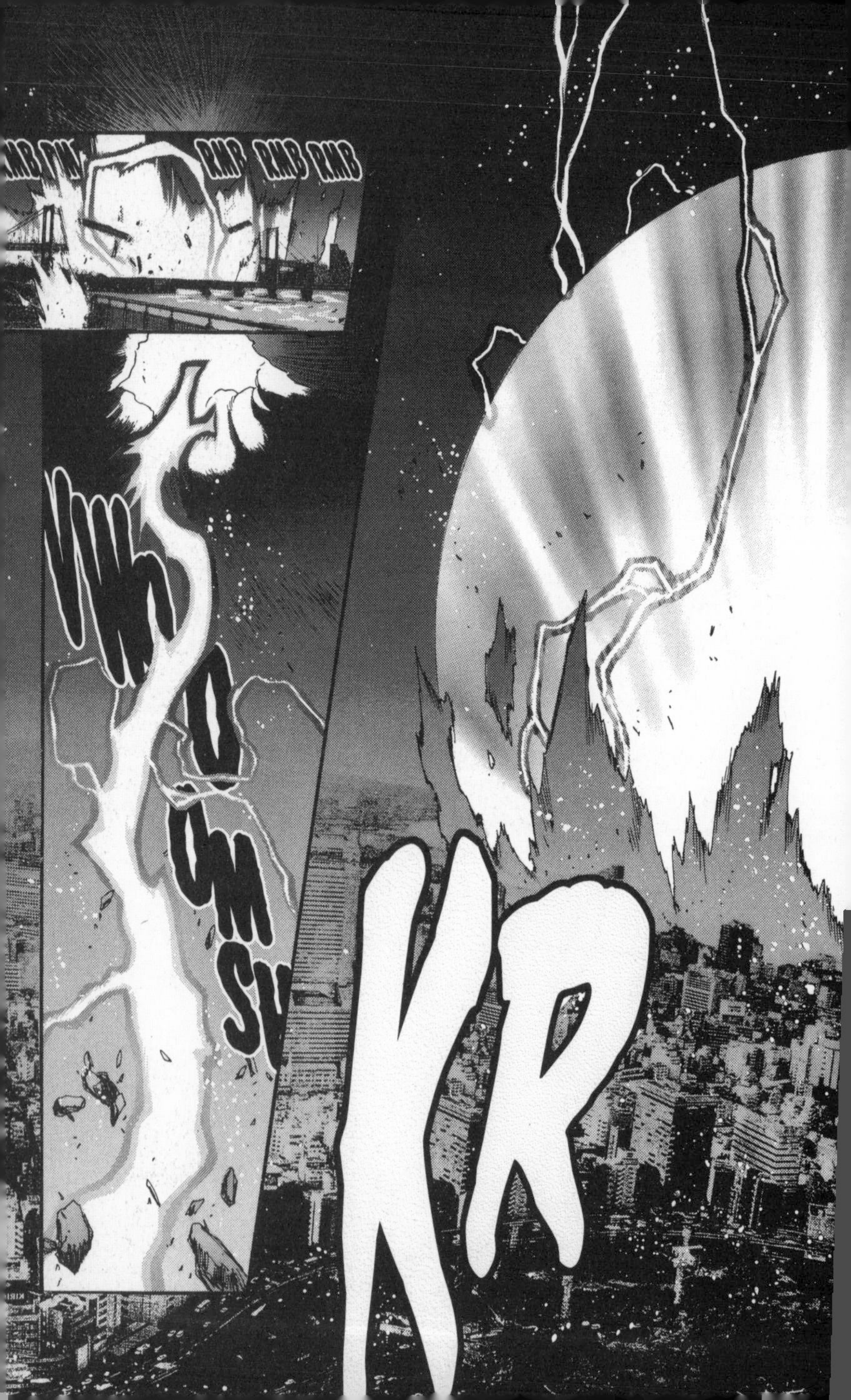
RMB RMB RMB
RMB RM
VWOOOM
SV
KR

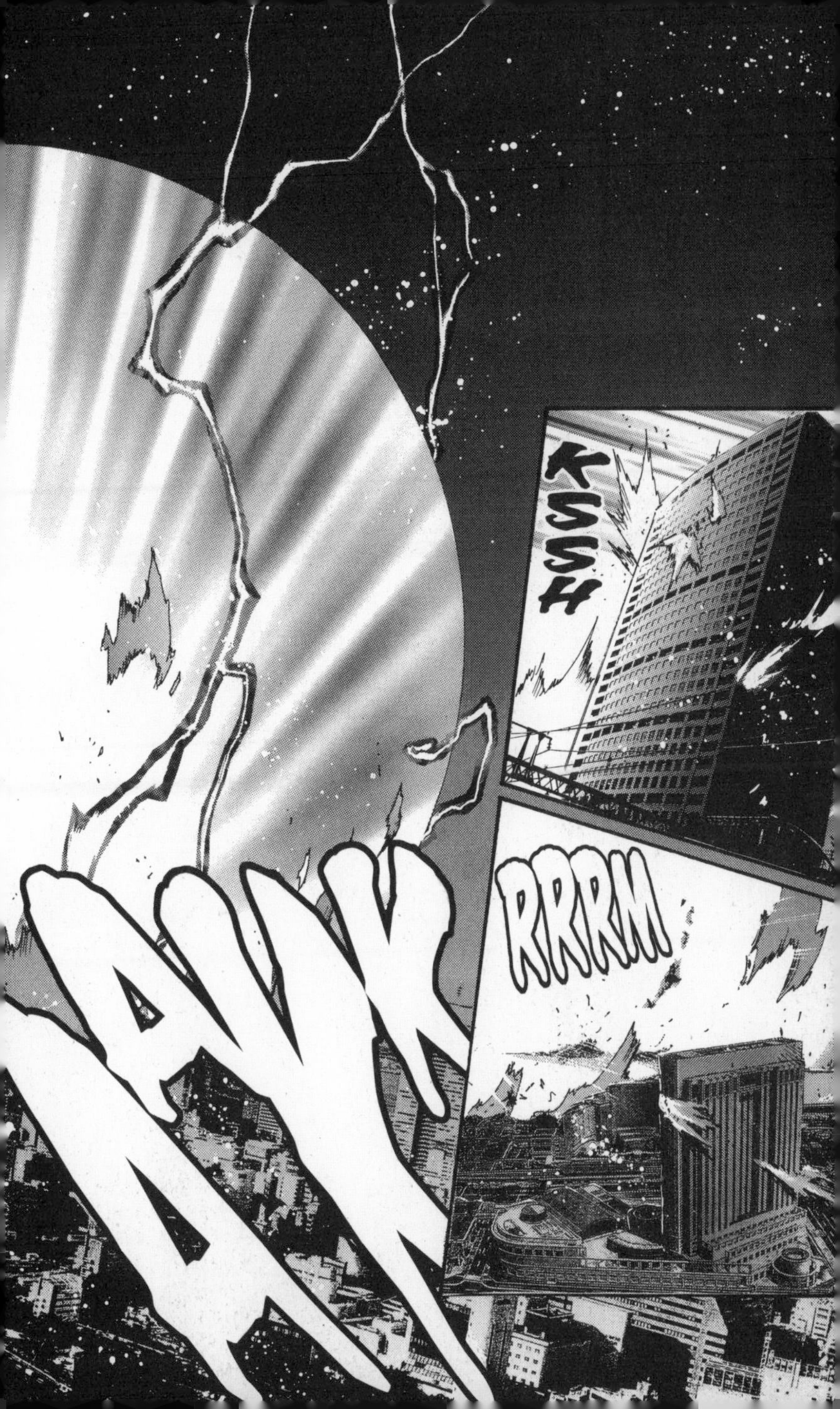
KSSH
RRRM

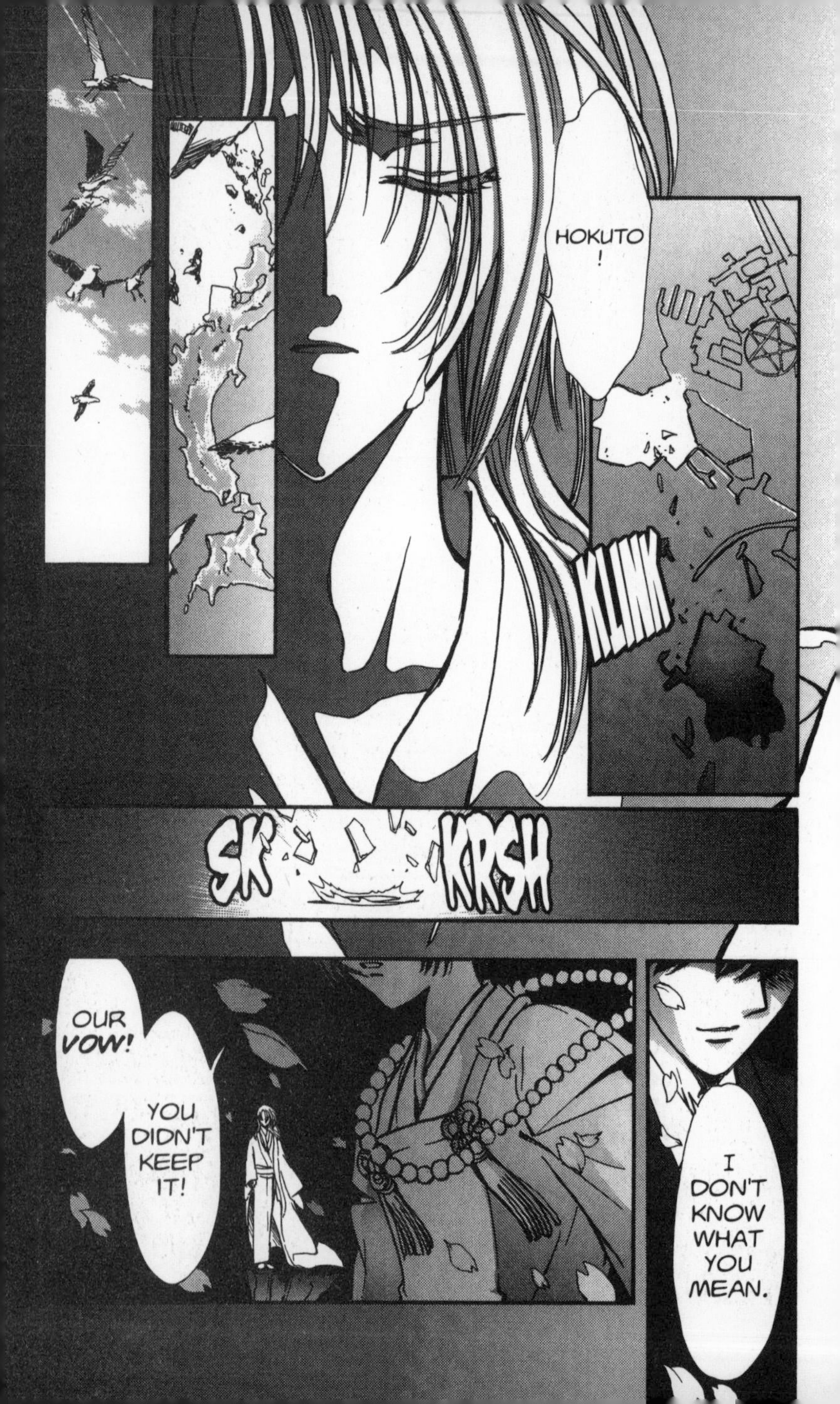
HOKUTO!
KLINK
SK KRSH
I DON'T KNOW WHAT YOU MEAN.
OUR VOW!
YOU DIDN'T KEEP IT!

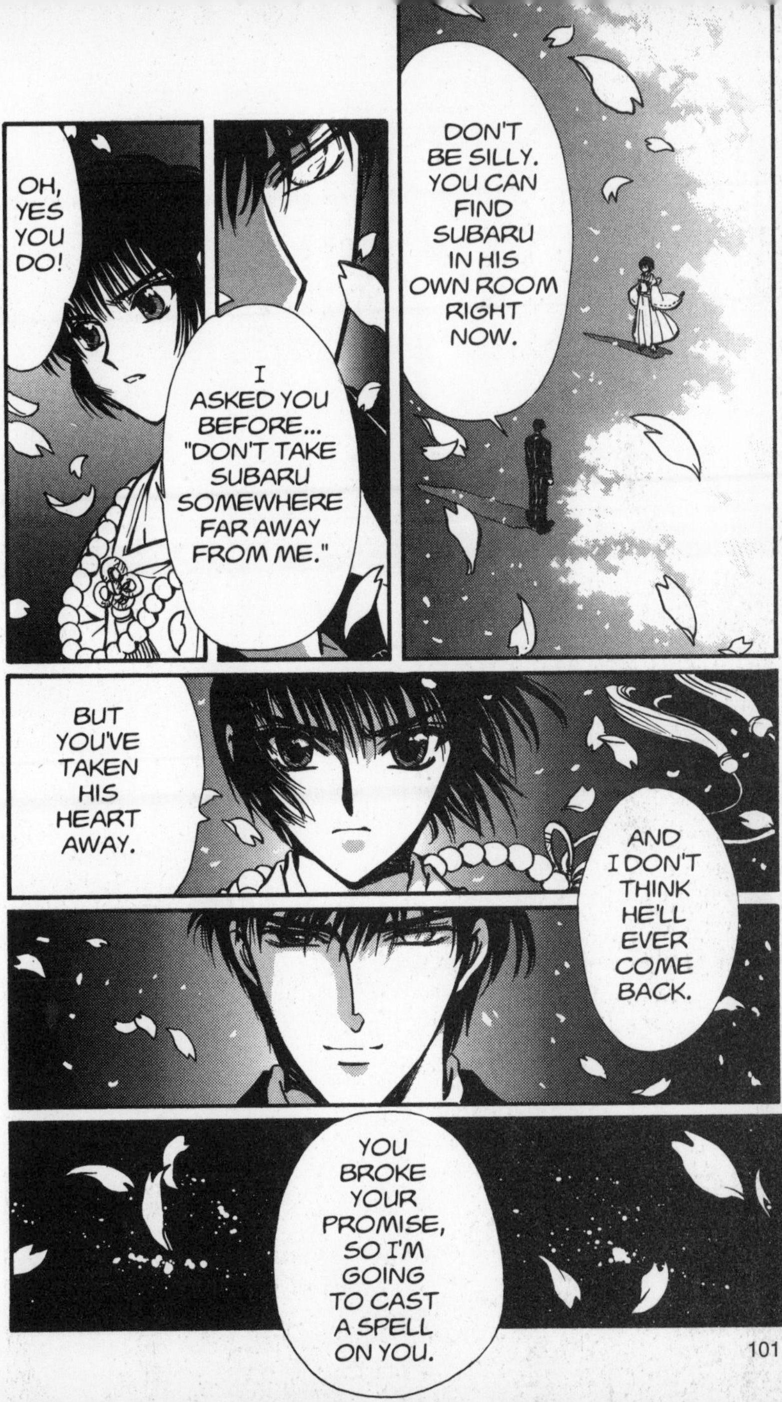
DON'T BE SILLY. YOU CAN FIND SUBARU IN HIS OWN ROOM RIGHT NOW.
I ASKED YOU BEFORE... "DON'T TAKE SUBARU SOMEWHERE FAR AWAY FROM ME."
OH, YES YOU DO!
BUT YOU'VE TAKEN HIS HEART AWAY.
AND I DON'T THINK HE'LL EVER COME BACK.
YOU BROKE YOUR PROMISE, SO I'M GOING TO CAST A SPELL ON YOU.

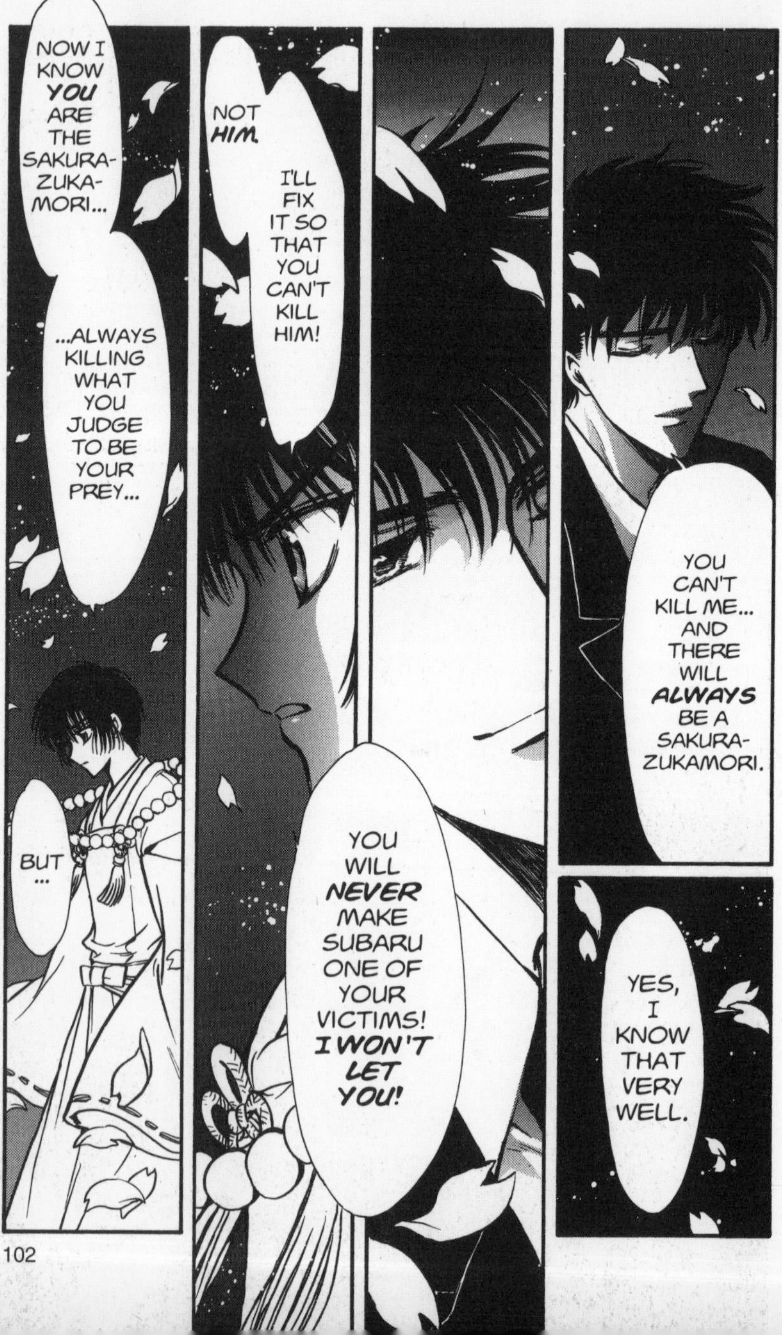
NOW I KNOW **YOU** ARE THE SAKURA-ZUKA-MORI...
...ALWAYS KILLING WHAT YOU JUDGE TO BE YOUR PREY...
BUT ...
NOT **HIM**.
I'LL FIX IT SO THAT YOU CAN'T KILL HIM!
YOU WILL **NEVER** MAKE SUBARU ONE OF YOUR VICTIMS! **I WON'T LET YOU!**
YOU CAN'T KILL ME... AND THERE WILL **ALWAYS** BE A SAKURA-ZUKAMORI.
YES, I KNOW THAT VERY WELL.

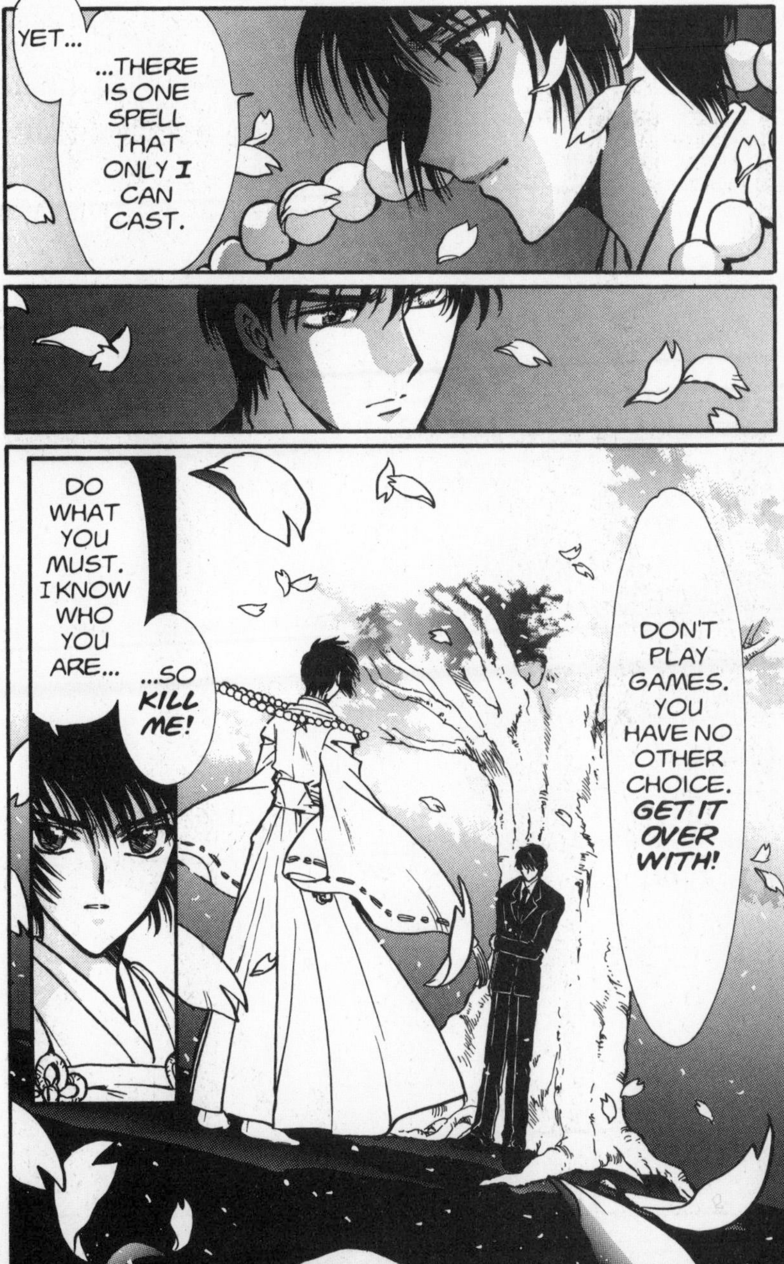
YET...
...THERE IS ONE SPELL THAT ONLY **I** CAN CAST.
DON'T PLAY GAMES. YOU HAVE NO OTHER CHOICE. ***GET IT OVER WITH!***
DO WHAT YOU MUST. I KNOW WHO YOU ARE...
...SO ***KILL ME!***

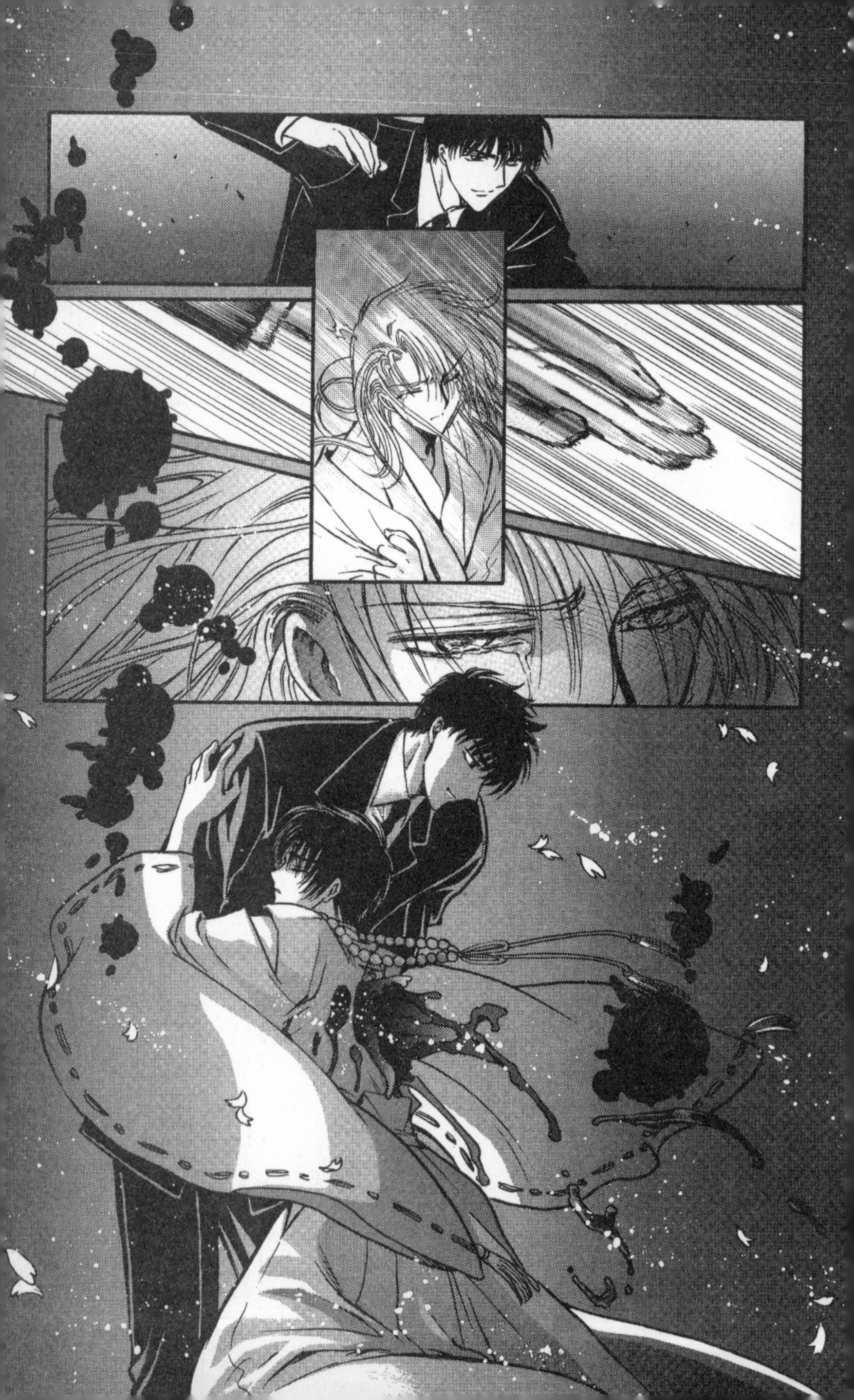

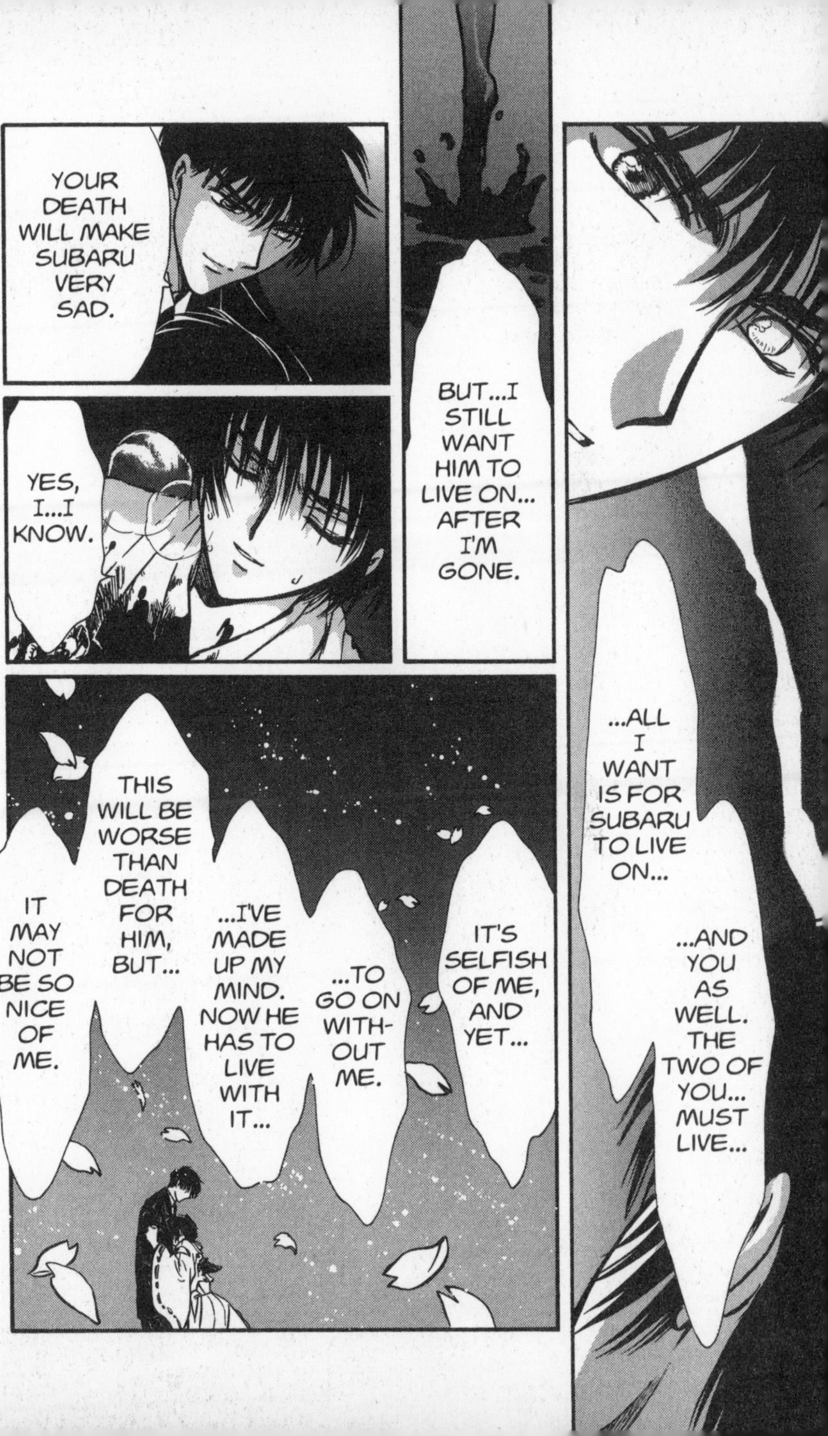
YOUR DEATH WILL MAKE SUBARU VERY SAD.
YES, I...I KNOW.
BUT...I STILL WANT HIM TO LIVE ON... AFTER I'M GONE.
IT'S SELFISH OF ME, AND YET...
...TO GO ON WITH-OUT ME.
...I'VE MADE UP MY MIND. NOW HE HAS TO LIVE WITH IT...
THIS WILL BE WORSE THAN DEATH FOR HIM, BUT...
IT MAY NOT BE SO NICE OF ME.
...ALL I WANT IS FOR SUBARU TO LIVE ON...
...AND YOU AS WELL. THE TWO OF YOU... MUST LIVE...

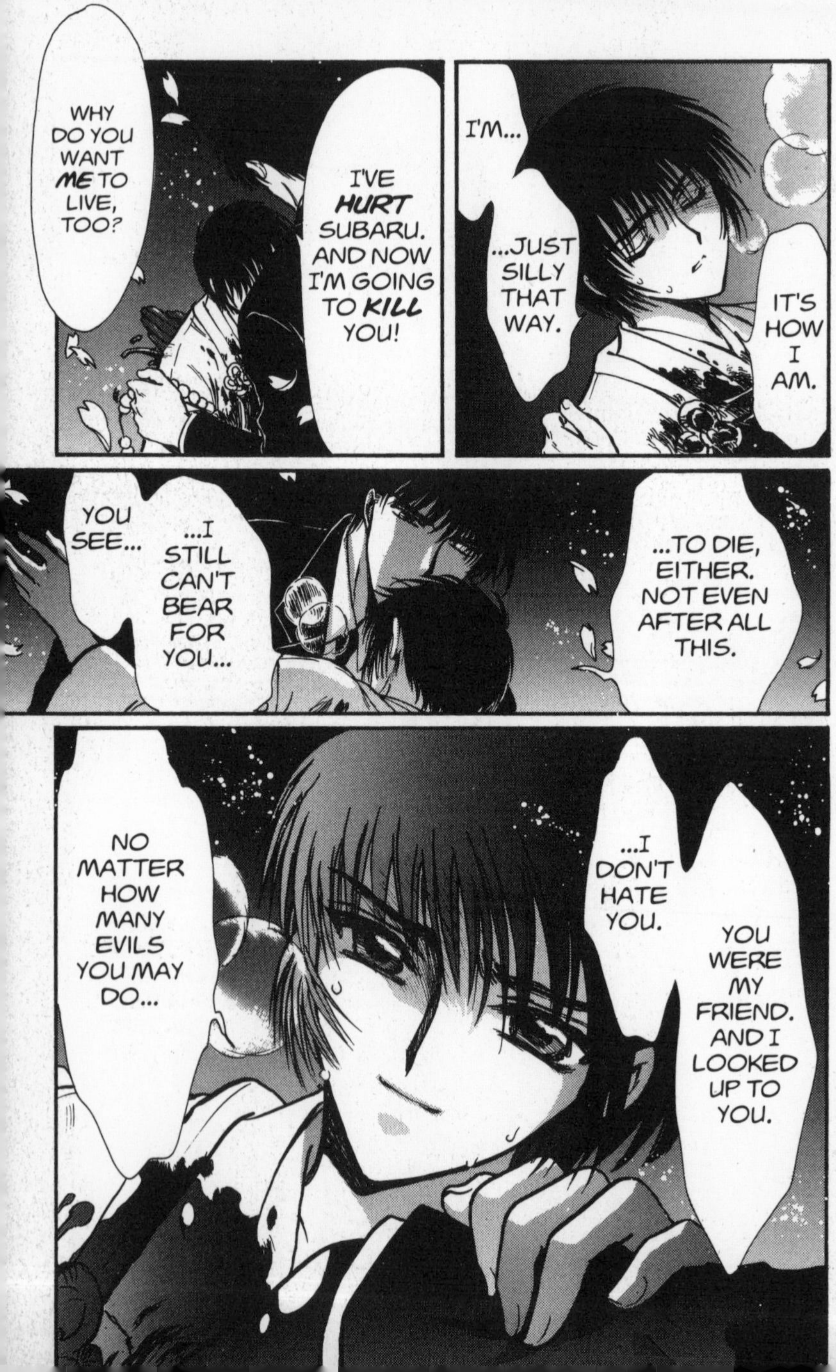
I'M...
...JUST SILLY THAT WAY.
IT'S HOW I AM.
I'VE HURT SUBARU. AND NOW I'M GOING TO KILL YOU!
WHY DO YOU WANT ME TO LIVE, TOO?
YOU SEE...
...I STILL CAN'T BEAR FOR YOU...
...TO DIE, EITHER. NOT EVEN AFTER ALL THIS.
...I DON'T HATE YOU.
YOU WERE MY FRIEND. AND I LOOKED UP TO YOU.
NO MATTER HOW MANY EVILS YOU MAY DO...

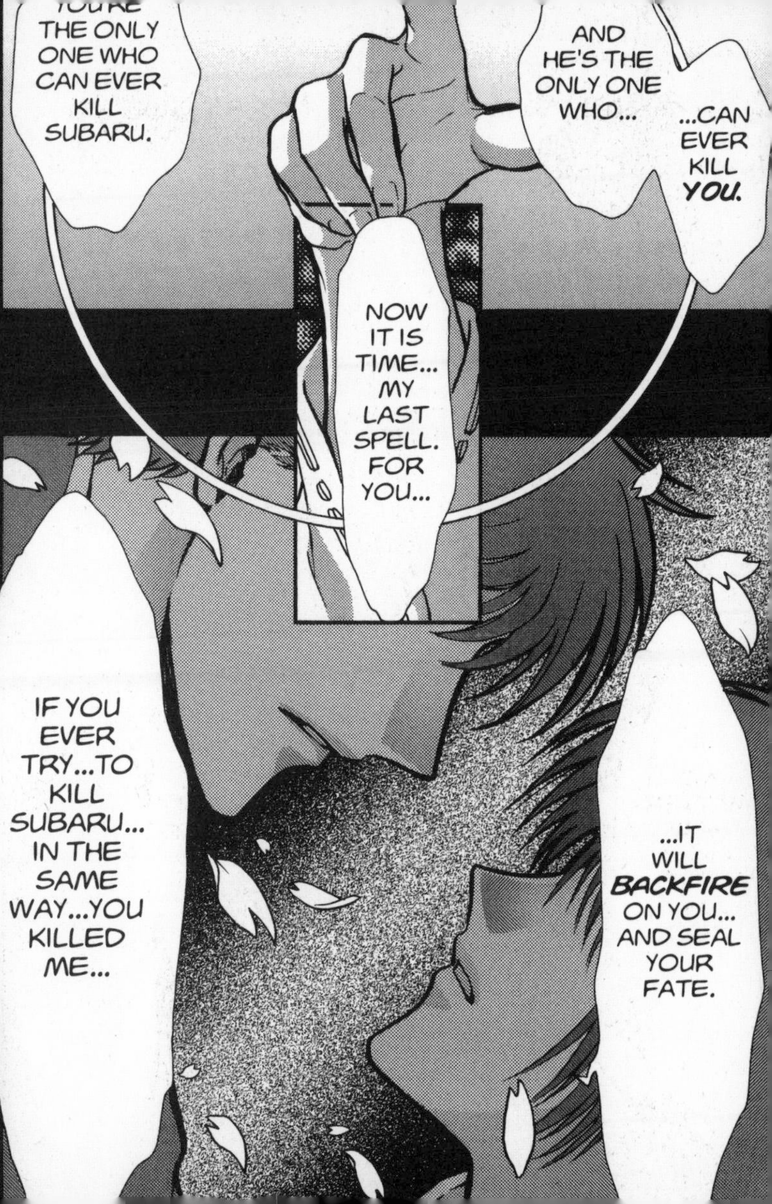
THE ONLY ONE WHO CAN EVER KILL SUBARU.
AND HE'S THE ONLY ONE WHO...
...CAN EVER KILL *YOU.*
NOW IT IS TIME... MY LAST SPELL. FOR YOU...
IF YOU EVER TRY...TO KILL SUBARU... IN THE SAME WAY...YOU KILLED ME...
...IT WILL **BACKFIRE** ON YOU... AND SEAL YOUR FATE.

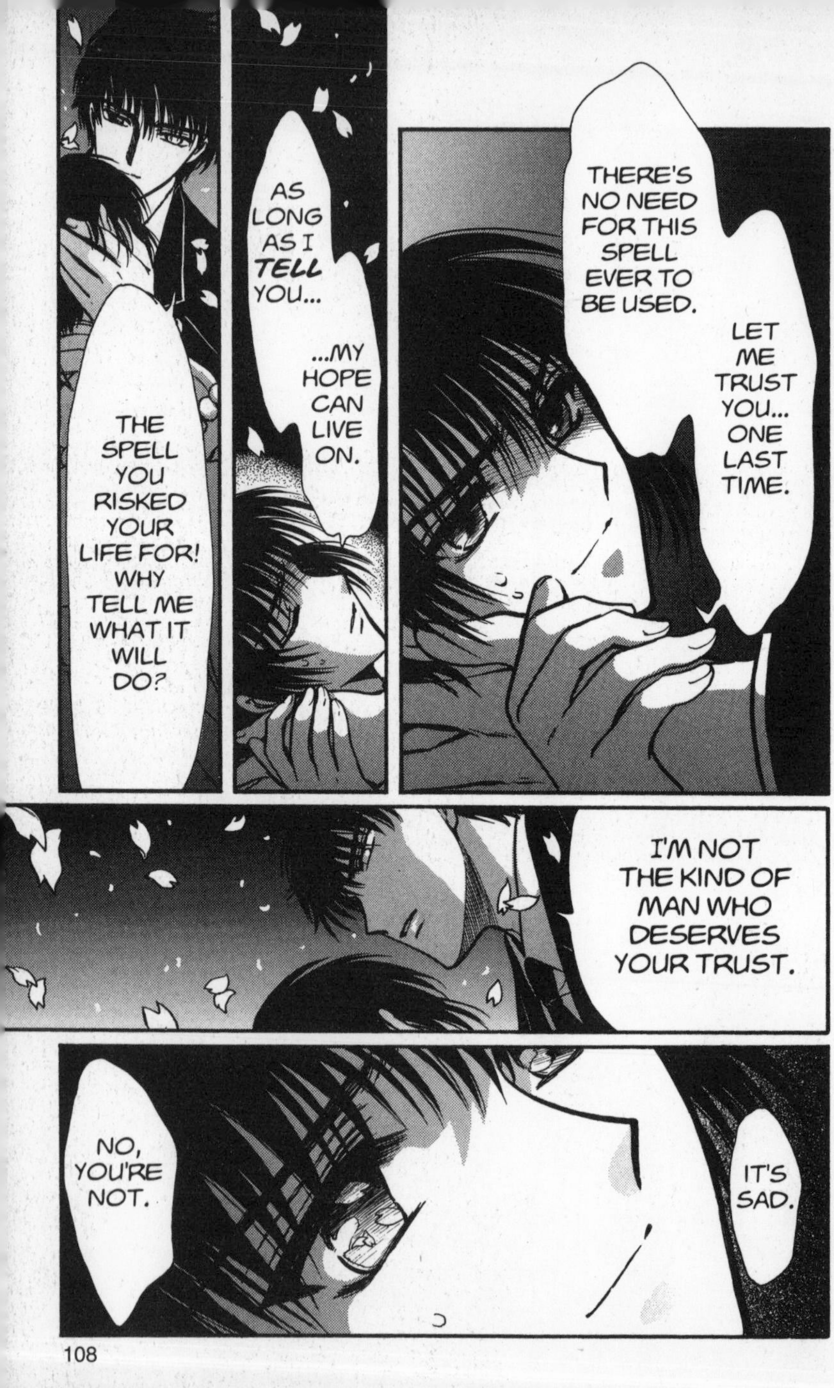
THE SPELL YOU RISKED YOUR LIFE FOR! WHY TELL ME WHAT IT WILL DO?
AS LONG AS I **TELL** YOU...
...MY HOPE CAN LIVE ON.
THERE'S NO NEED FOR THIS SPELL EVER TO BE USED.
LET ME TRUST YOU... ONE LAST TIME.
I'M NOT THE KIND OF MAN WHO DESERVES YOUR TRUST.
NO, YOU'RE NOT.
IT'S SAD.

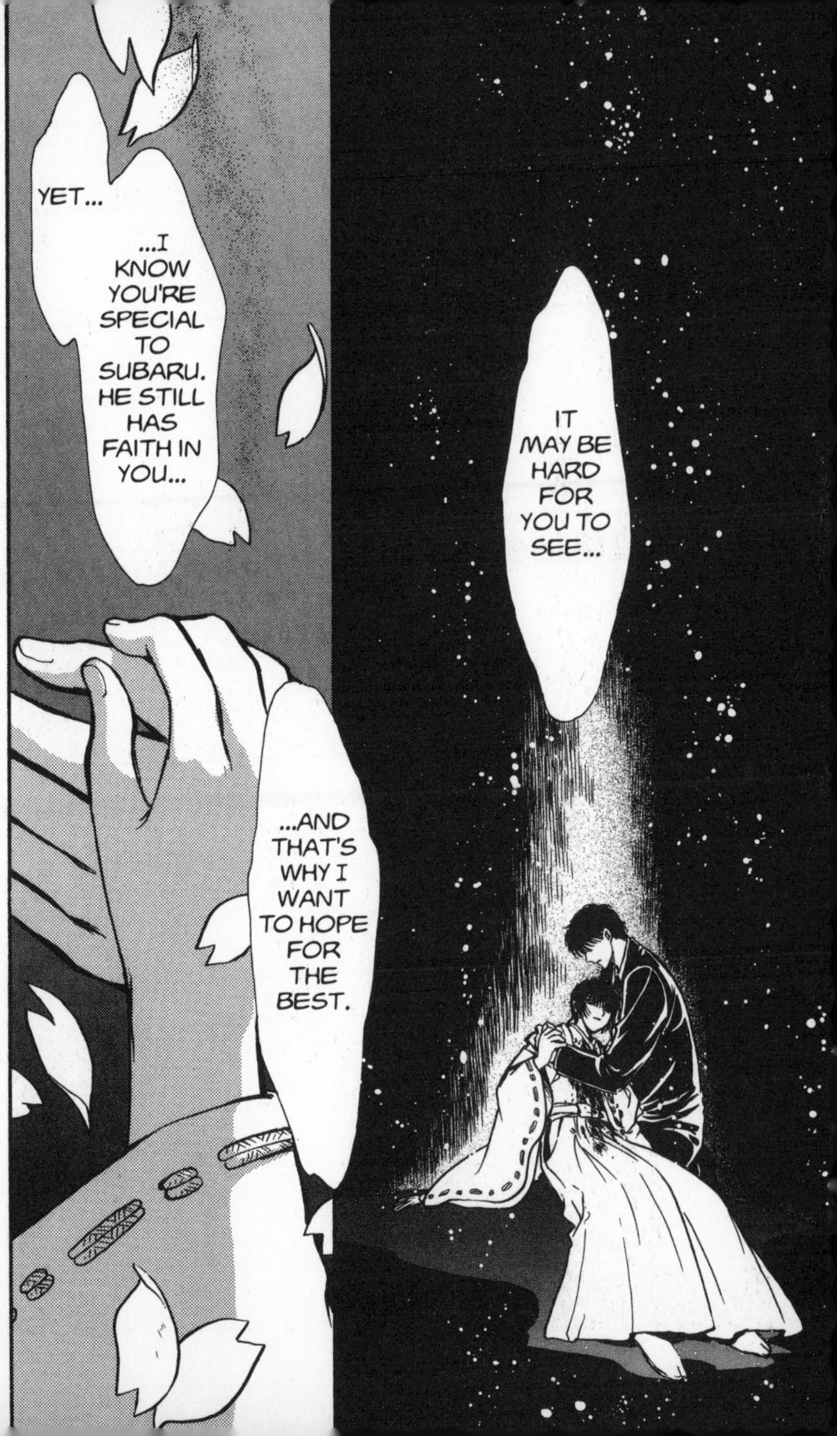
IT MAY BE HARD FOR YOU TO SEE...
YET...
...I KNOW YOU'RE SPECIAL TO SUBARU. HE STILL HAS FAITH IN YOU...
...AND THAT'S WHY I WANT TO HOPE FOR THE BEST.

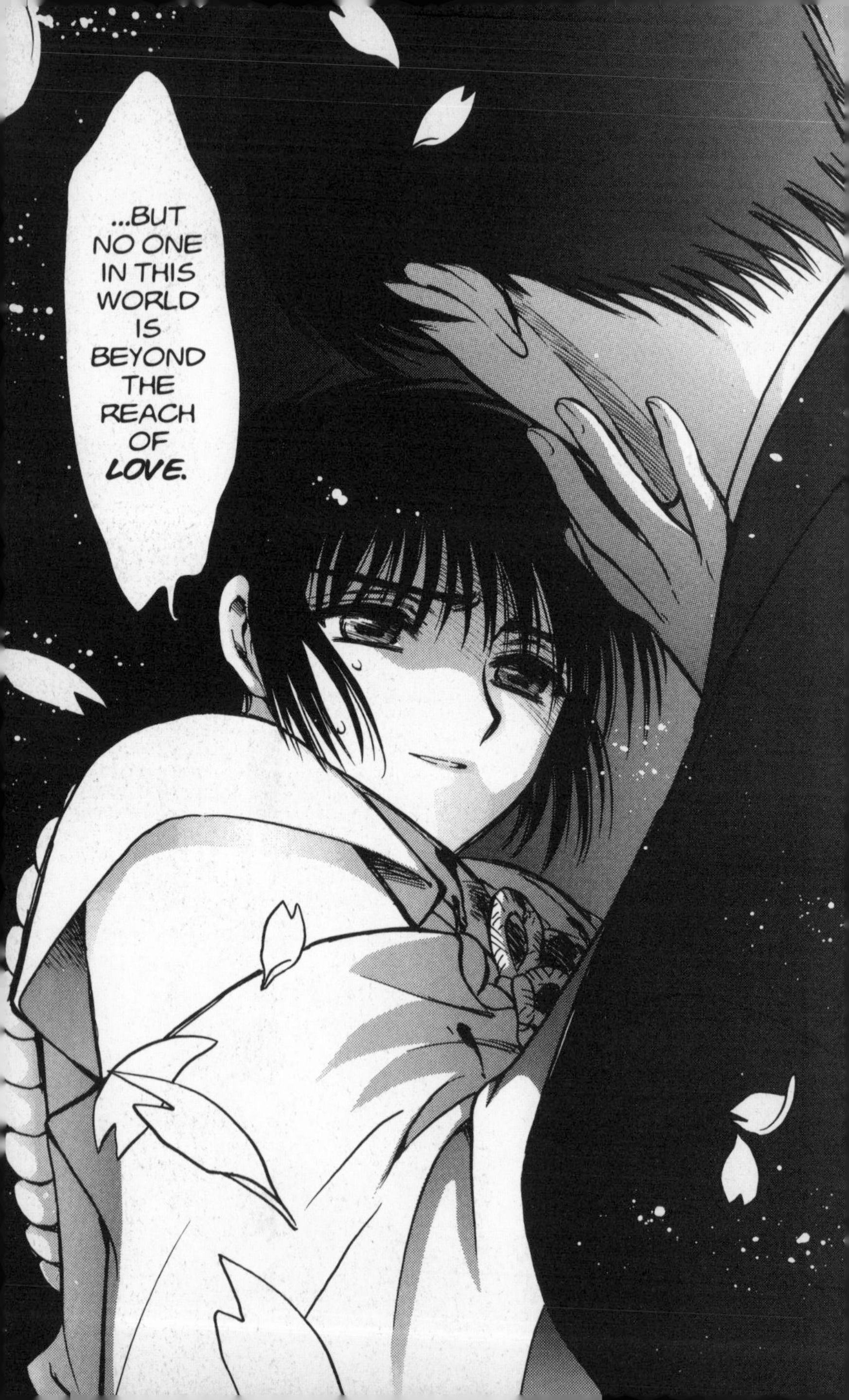
...BUT NO ONE IN THIS WORLD IS BEYOND THE REACH OF LOVE.

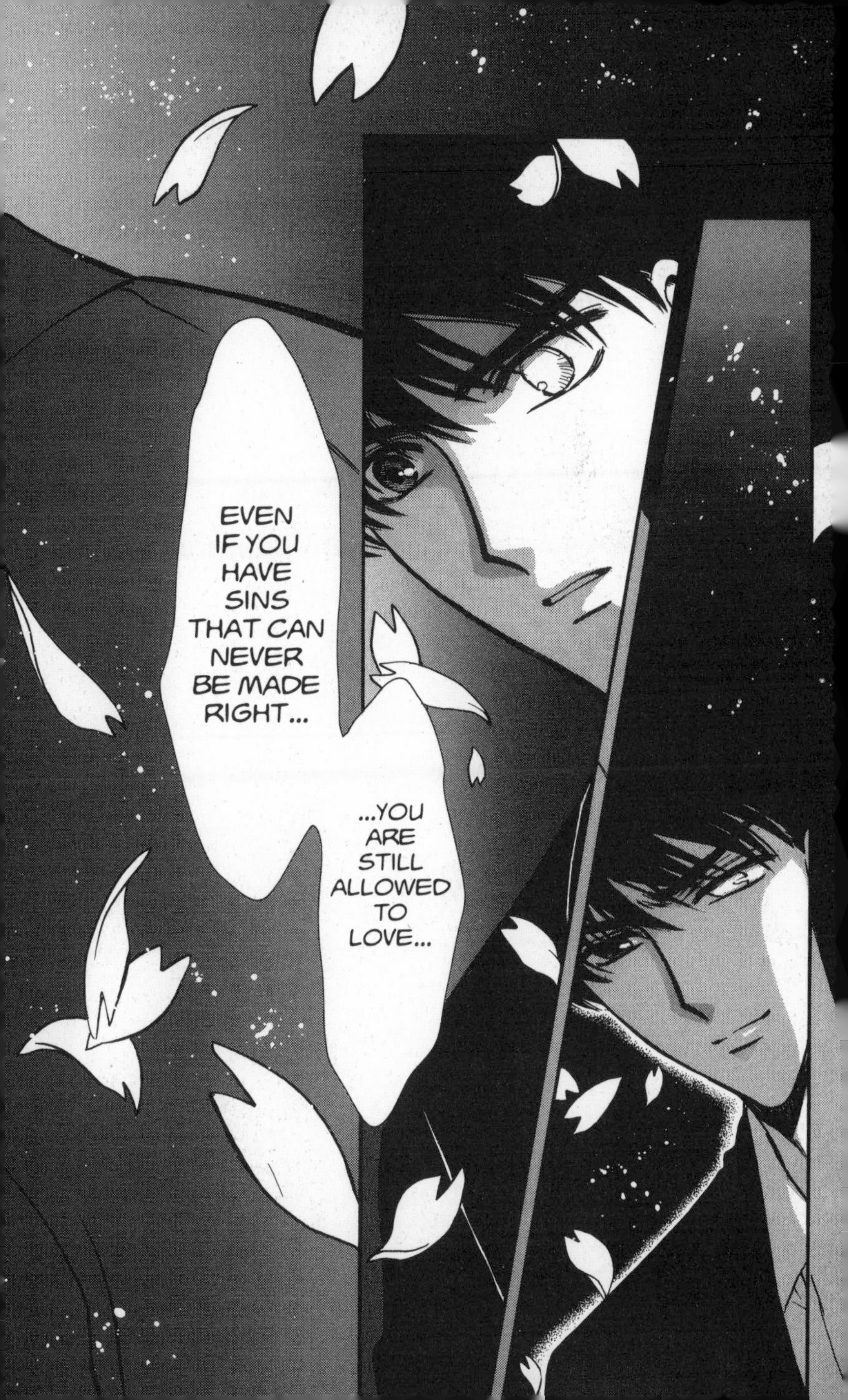
EVEN IF YOU HAVE SINS THAT CAN NEVER BE MADE RIGHT...
...YOU ARE STILL ALLOWED TO LOVE...

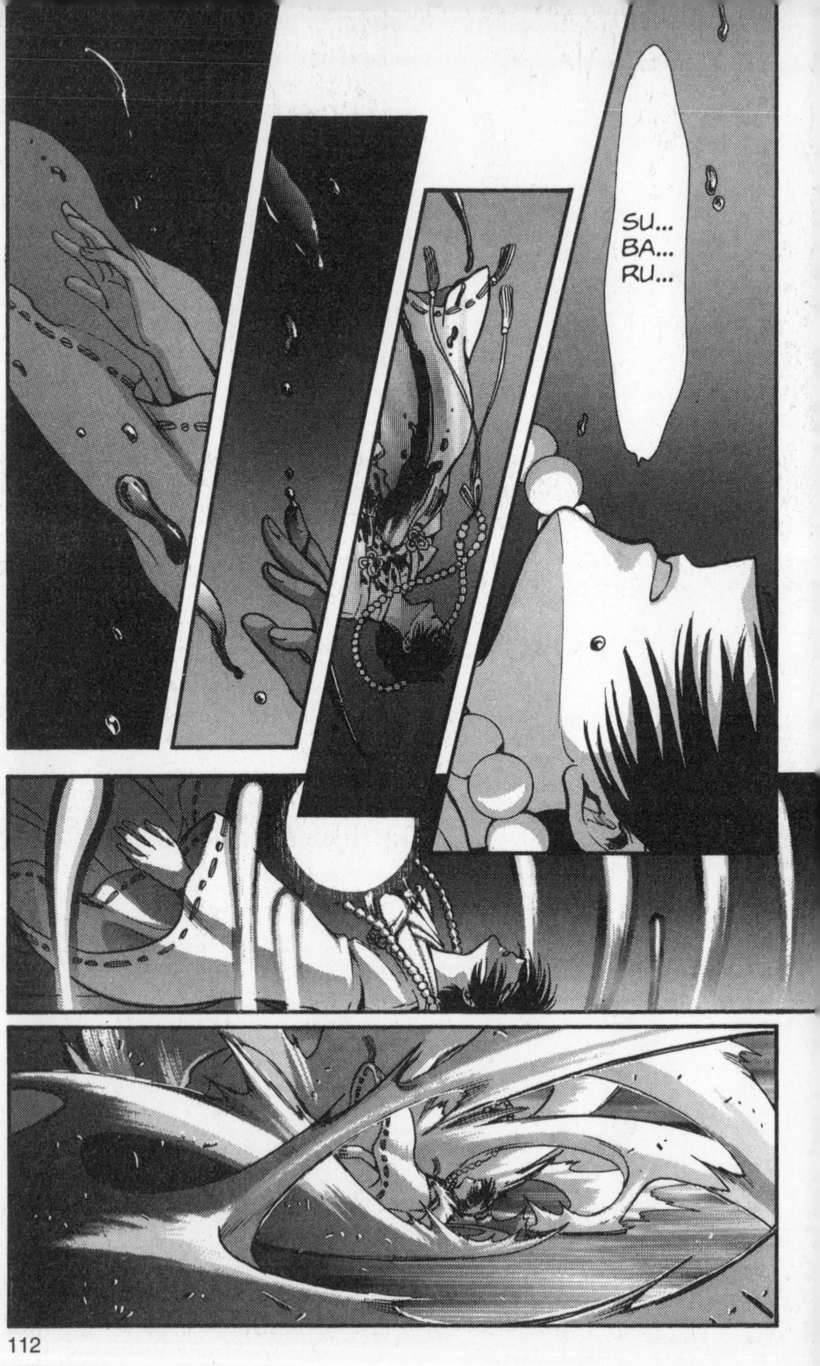
SU...
BA...
RU...

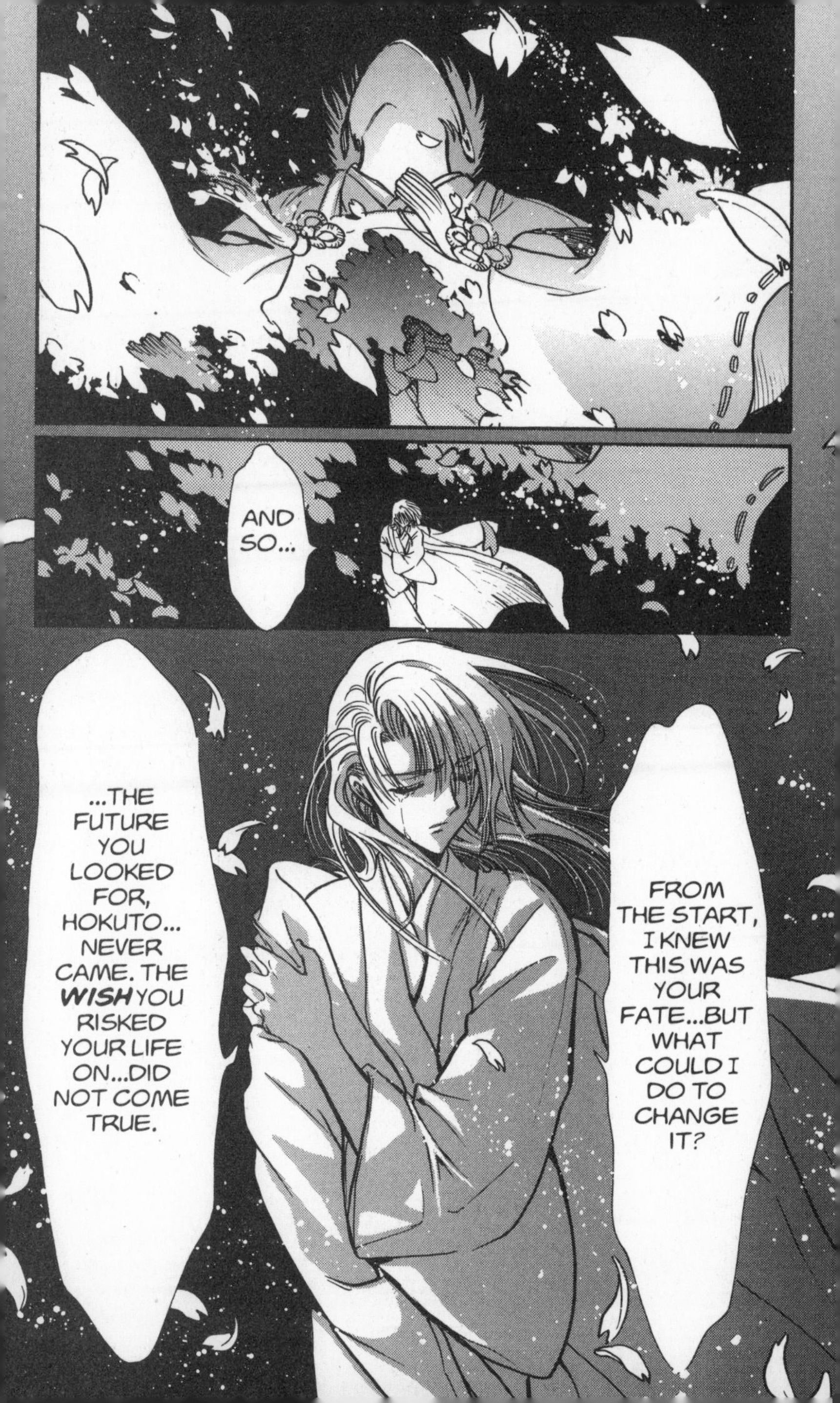
AND SO...
FROM THE START, I KNEW THIS WAS YOUR FATE...BUT WHAT COULD I DO TO CHANGE IT?
...THE FUTURE YOU LOOKED FOR, HOKUTO... NEVER CAME. THE WISH YOU RISKED YOUR LIFE ON...DID NOT COME TRUE.

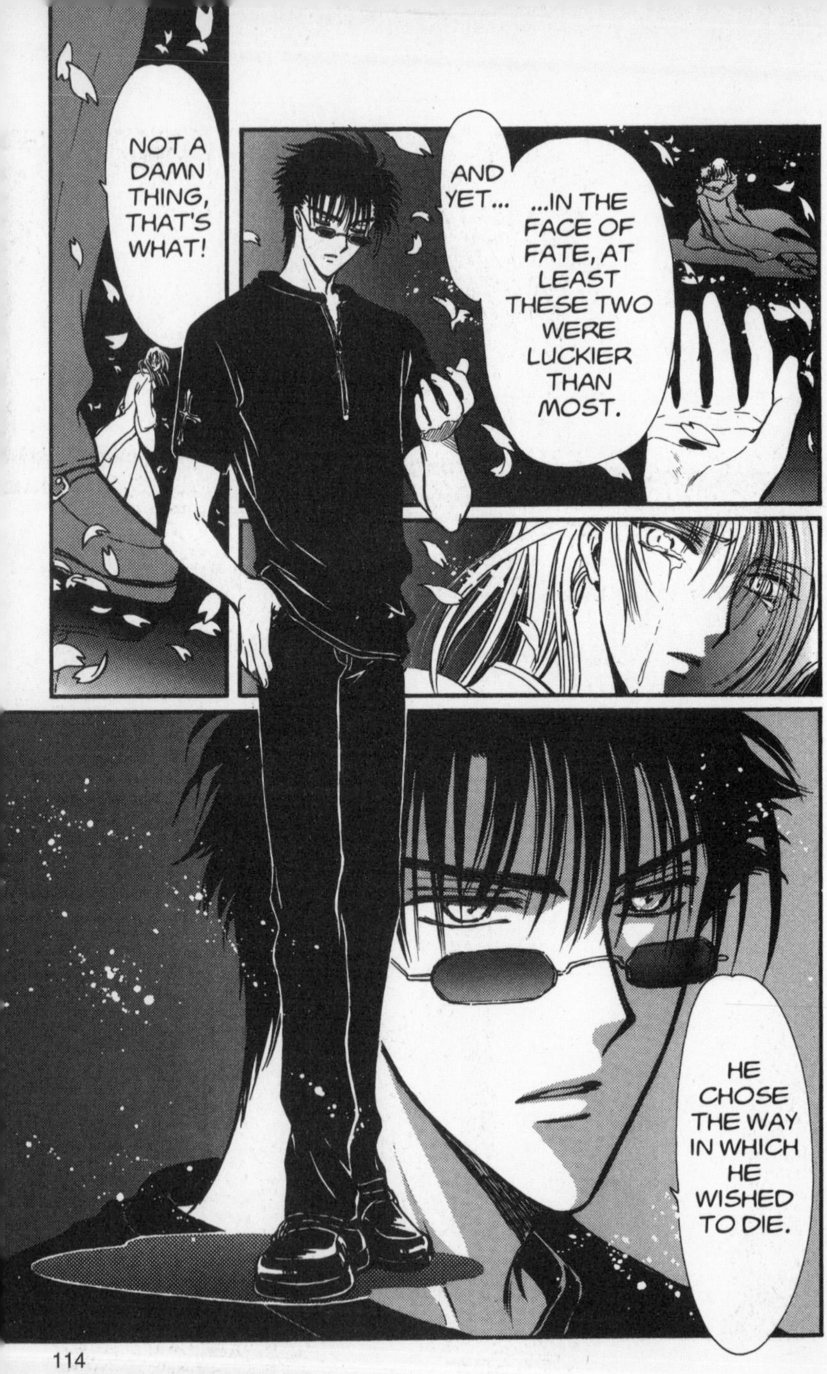
NOT A DAMN THING, THAT'S WHAT!
AND YET...
...IN THE FACE OF FATE, AT LEAST THESE TWO WERE LUCKIER THAN MOST.
HE CHOSE THE WAY IN WHICH HE WISHED TO DIE.

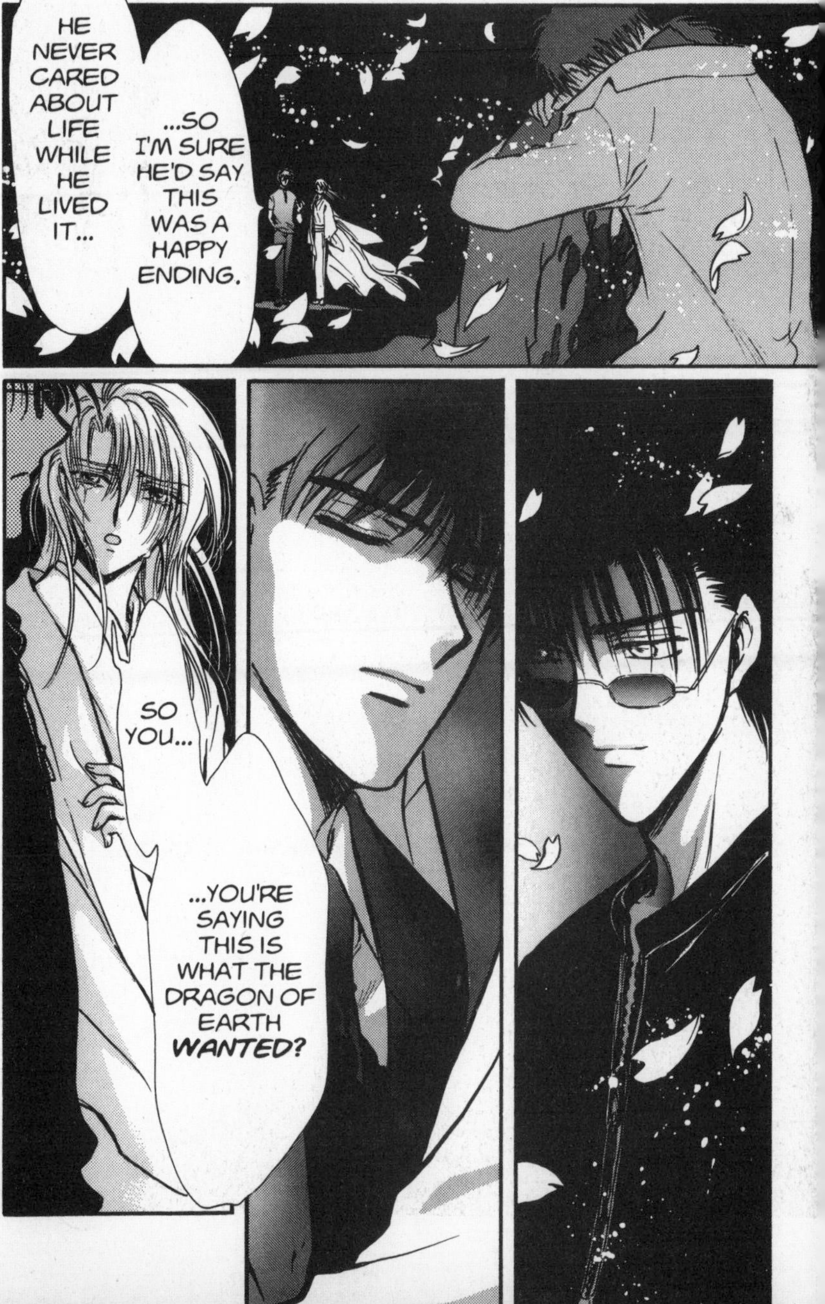
HE NEVER CARED ABOUT LIFE WHILE HE LIVED IT...
...SO I'M SURE HE'D SAY THIS WAS A HAPPY ENDING.
SO YOU...
...YOU'RE SAYING THIS IS WHAT THE DRAGON OF EARTH *WANTED?*

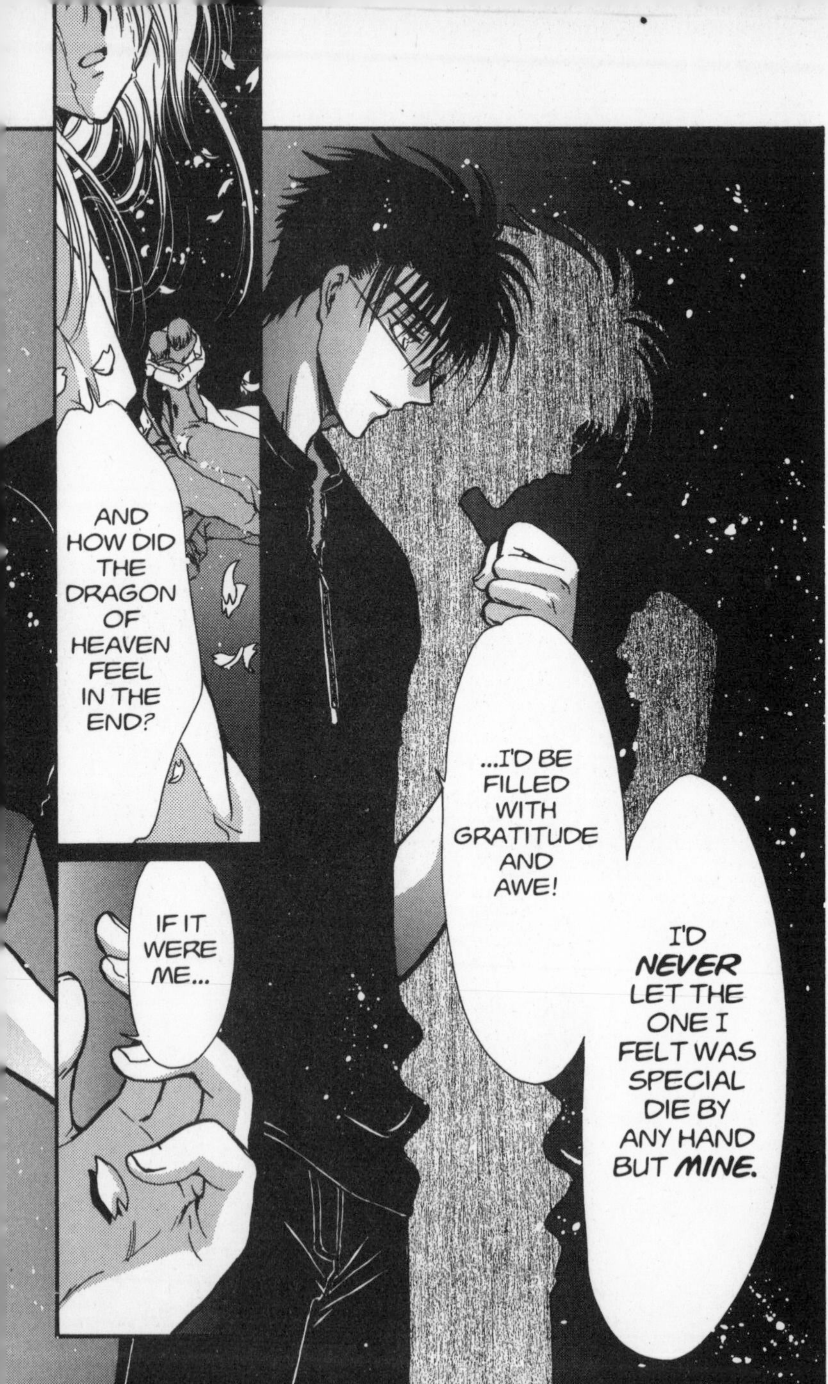
AND HOW DID THE DRAGON OF HEAVEN FEEL IN THE END?
IF IT WERE ME...
...I'D BE FILLED WITH GRATITUDE AND AWE!
I'D ***NEVER*** LET THE ONE I FELT WAS SPECIAL DIE BY ANY HAND BUT ***MINE.***

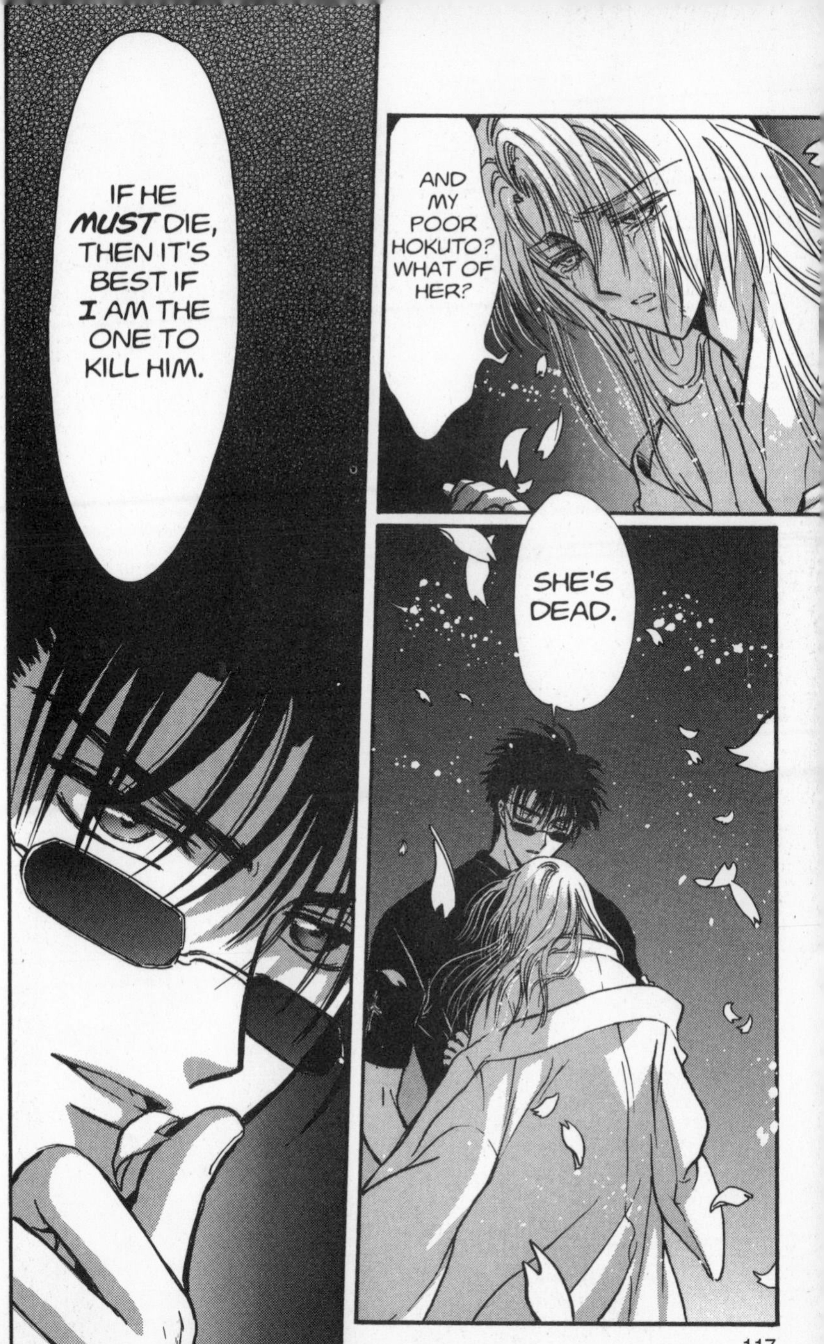
AND MY POOR HOKUTO? WHAT OF HER?
SHE'S DEAD.
IF HE MUST DIE, THEN IT'S BEST IF I AM THE ONE TO KILL HIM.

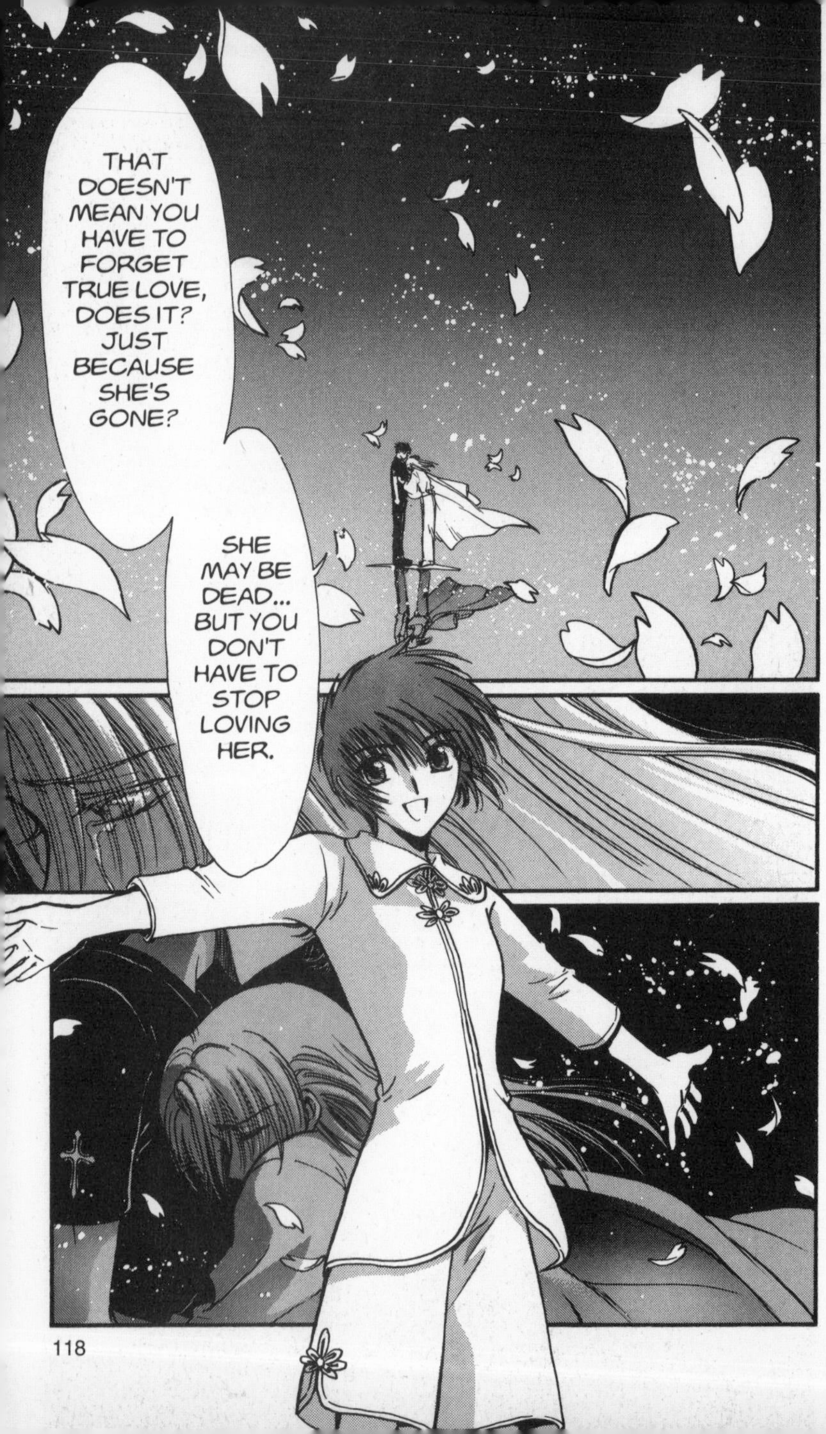
THAT DOESN'T MEAN YOU HAVE TO FORGET TRUE LOVE, DOES IT? JUST BECAUSE SHE'S GONE?
SHE MAY BE DEAD... BUT YOU DON'T HAVE TO STOP LOVING HER.

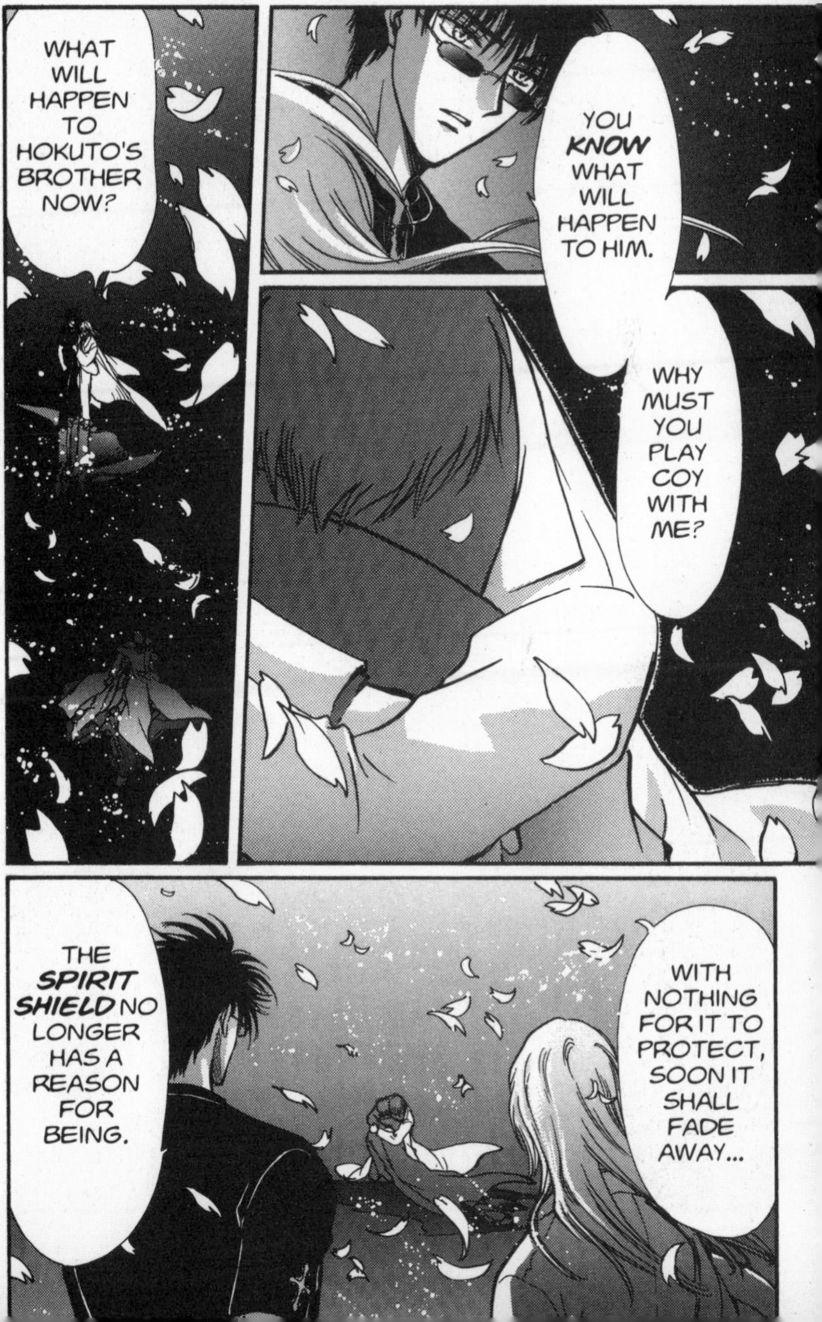
WHAT WILL HAPPEN TO HOKUTO'S BROTHER NOW?
YOU KNOW WHAT WILL HAPPEN TO HIM.
WHY MUST YOU PLAY COY WITH ME?
THE SPIRIT SHIELD NO LONGER HAS A REASON FOR BEING.
WITH NOTHING FOR IT TO PROTECT, SOON IT SHALL FADE AWAY...

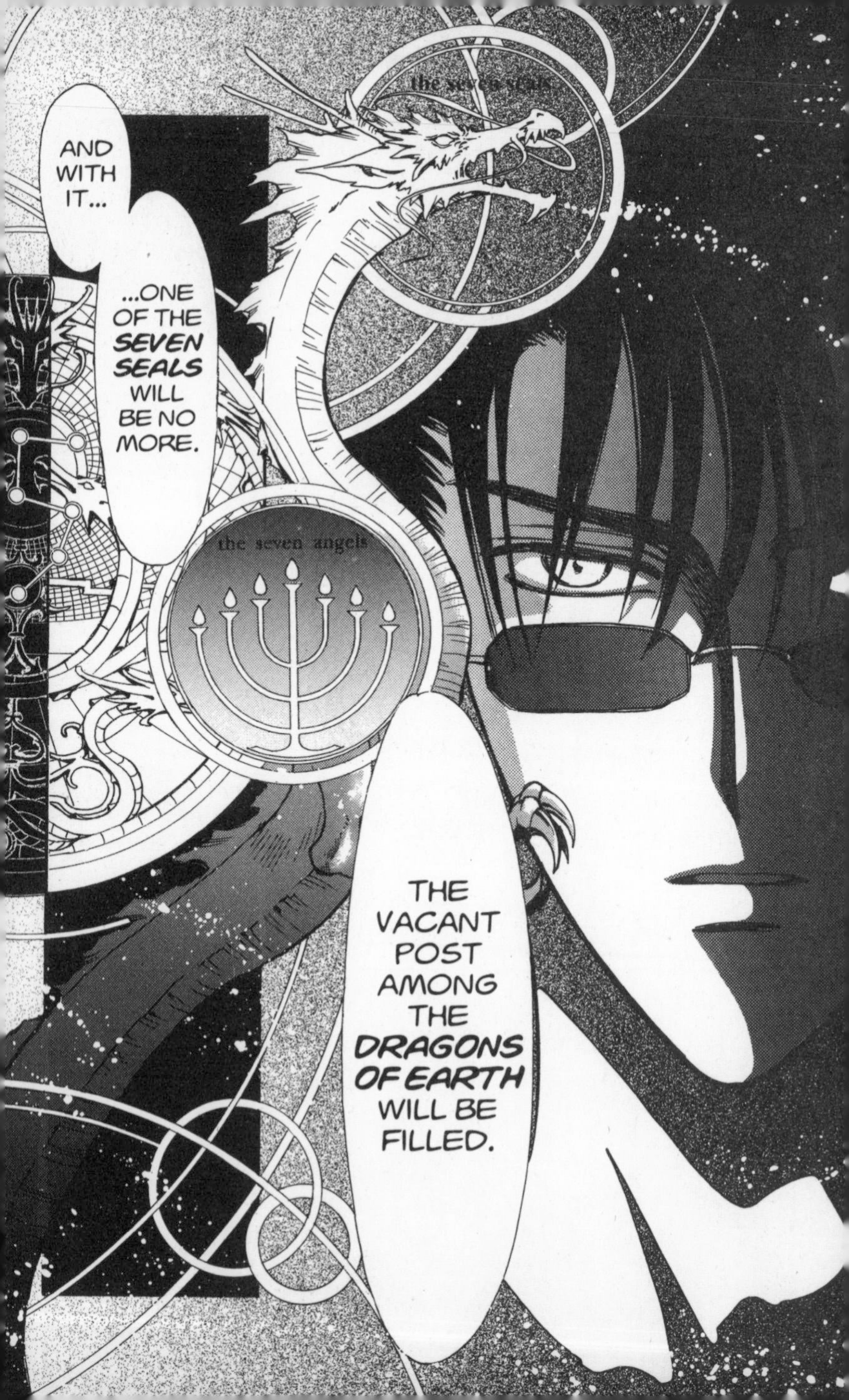
the seven seals
the seven angels
AND WITH IT...
...ONE OF THE SEVEN SEALS WILL BE NO MORE.
THE VACANT POST AMONG THE DRAGONS OF EARTH WILL BE FILLED.

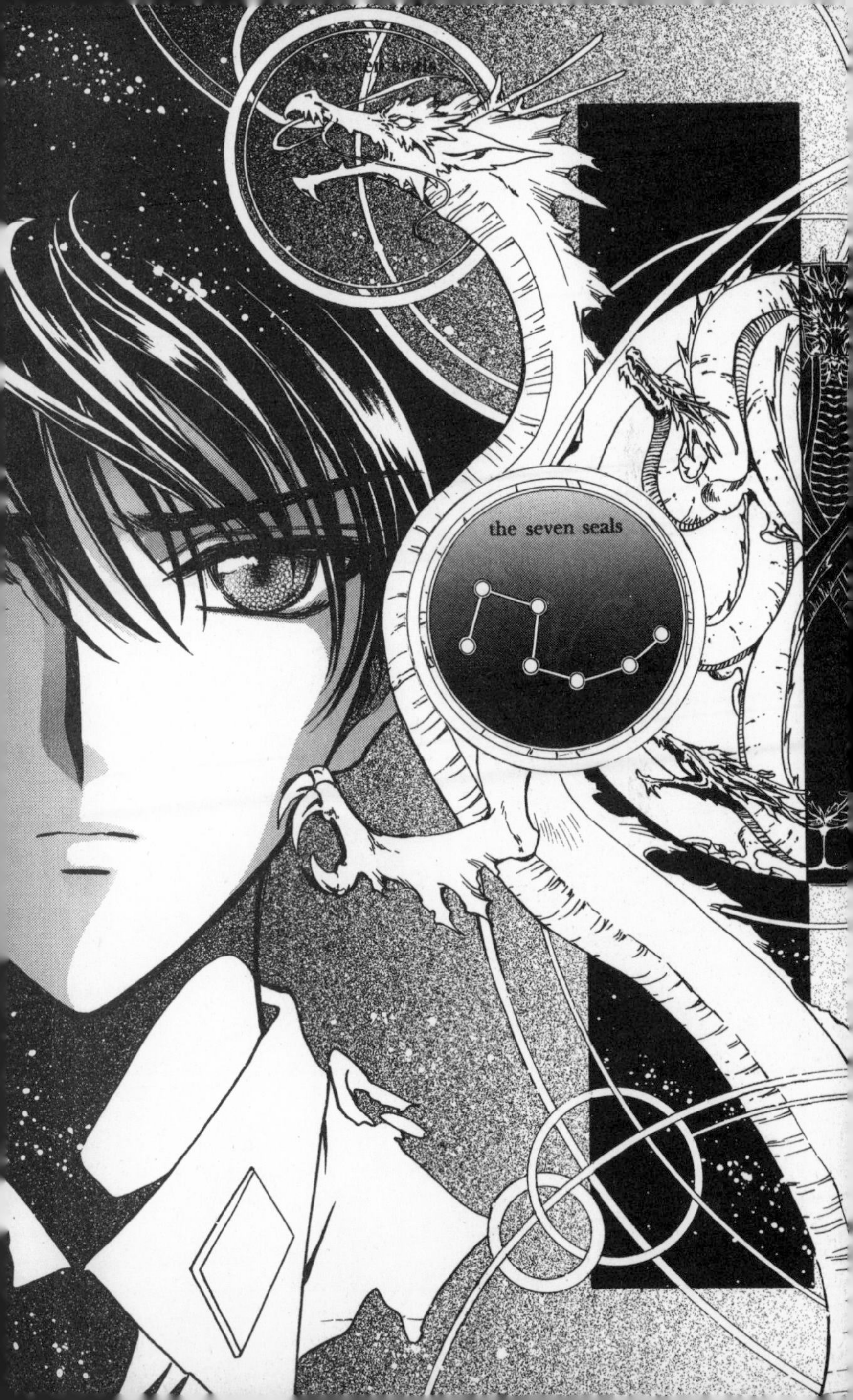
the seven seals

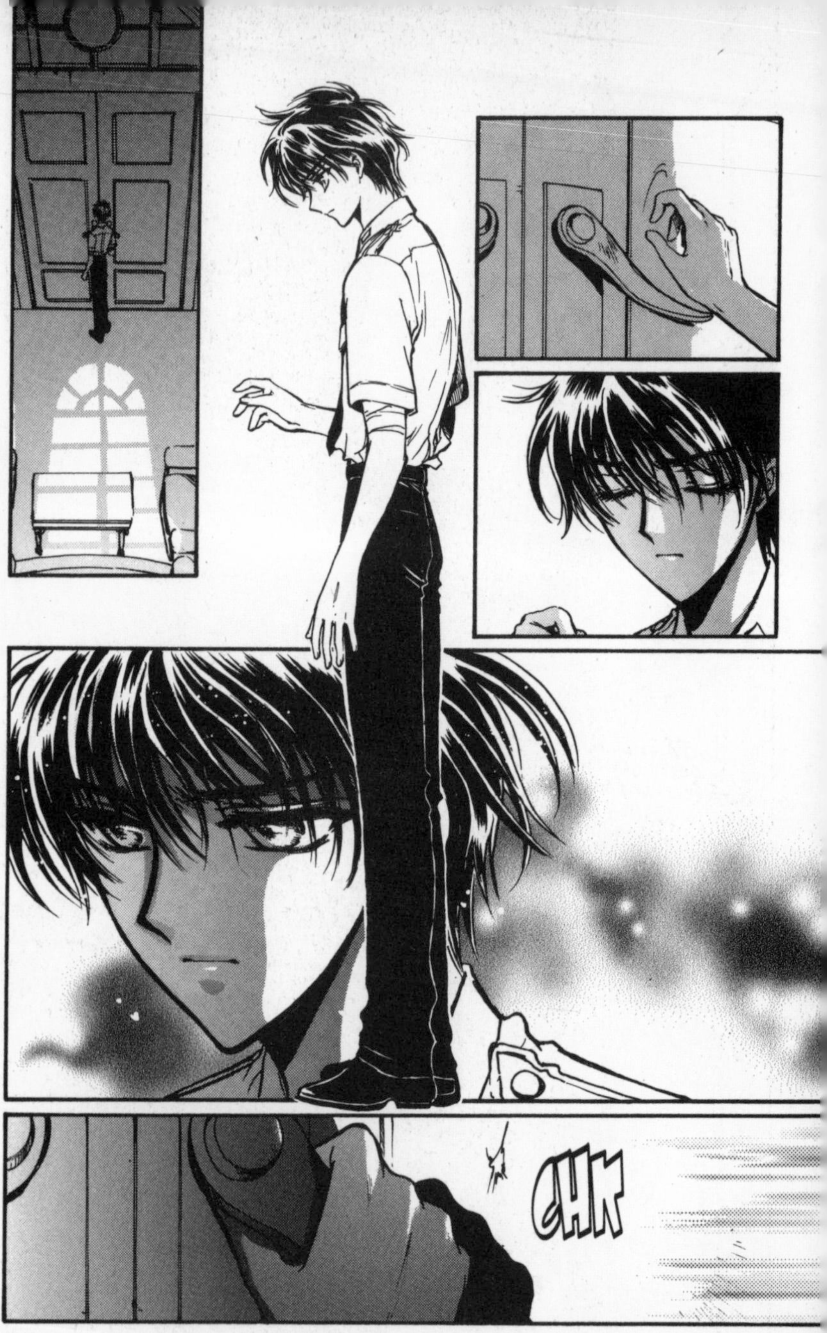
CHK

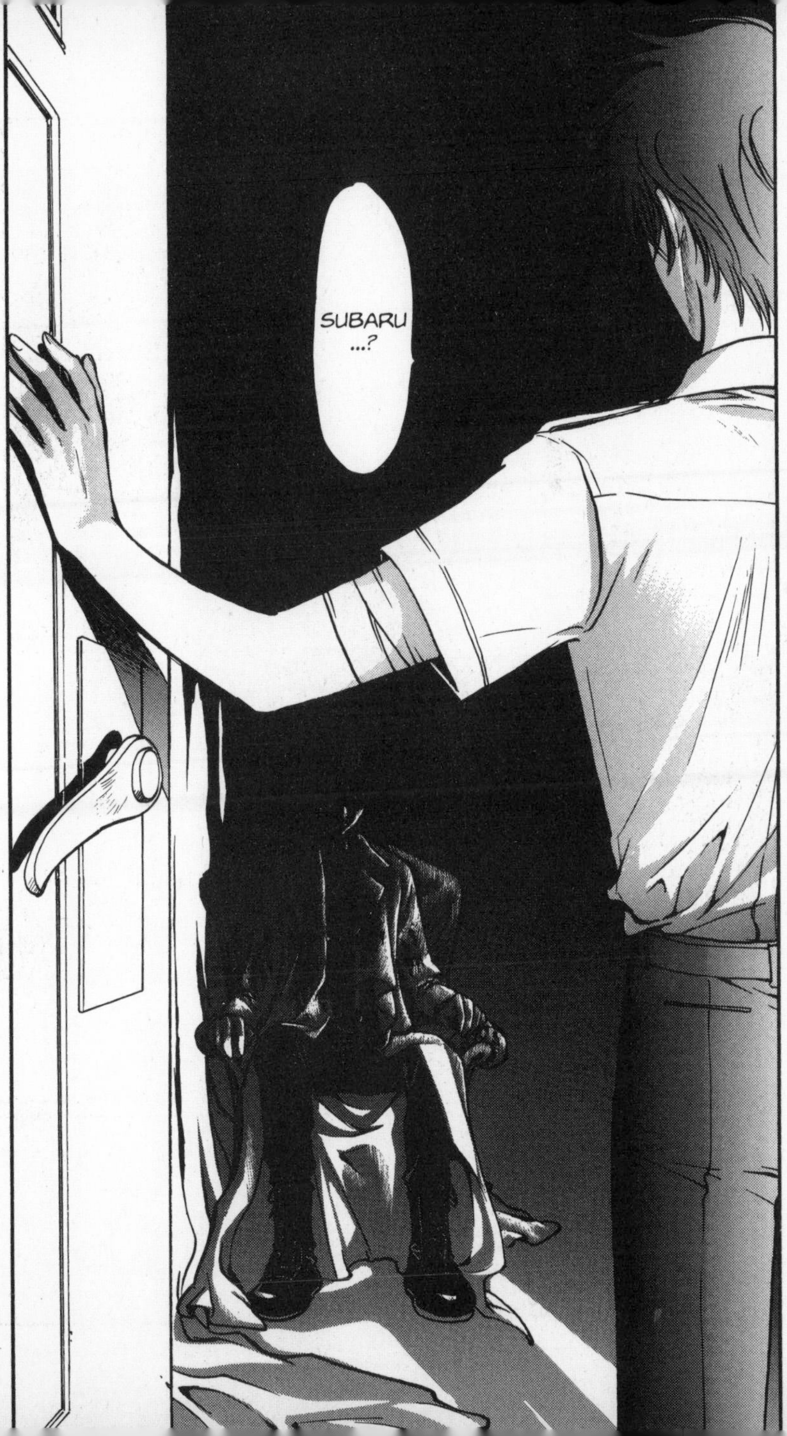
SUBARU ...?

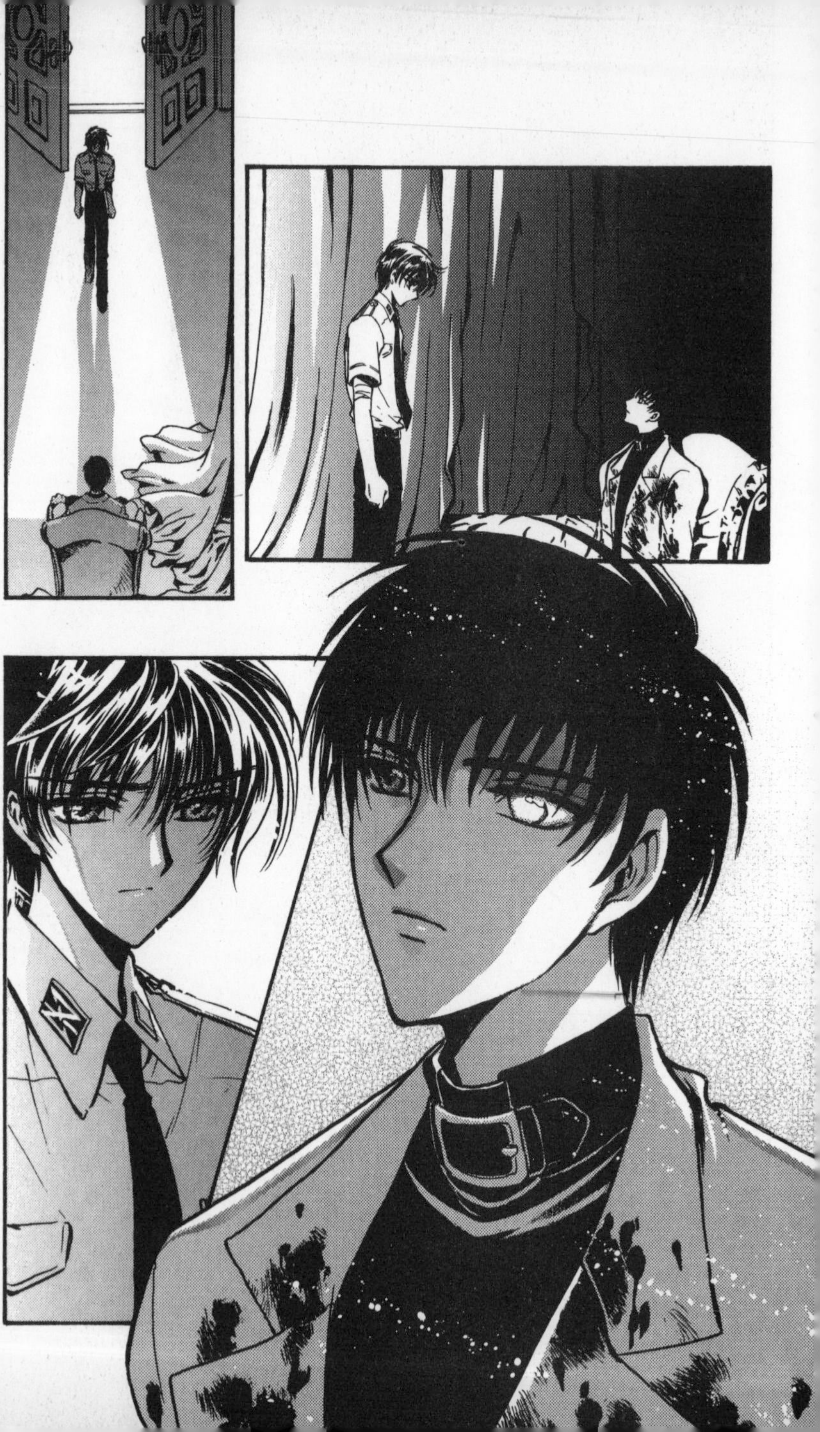

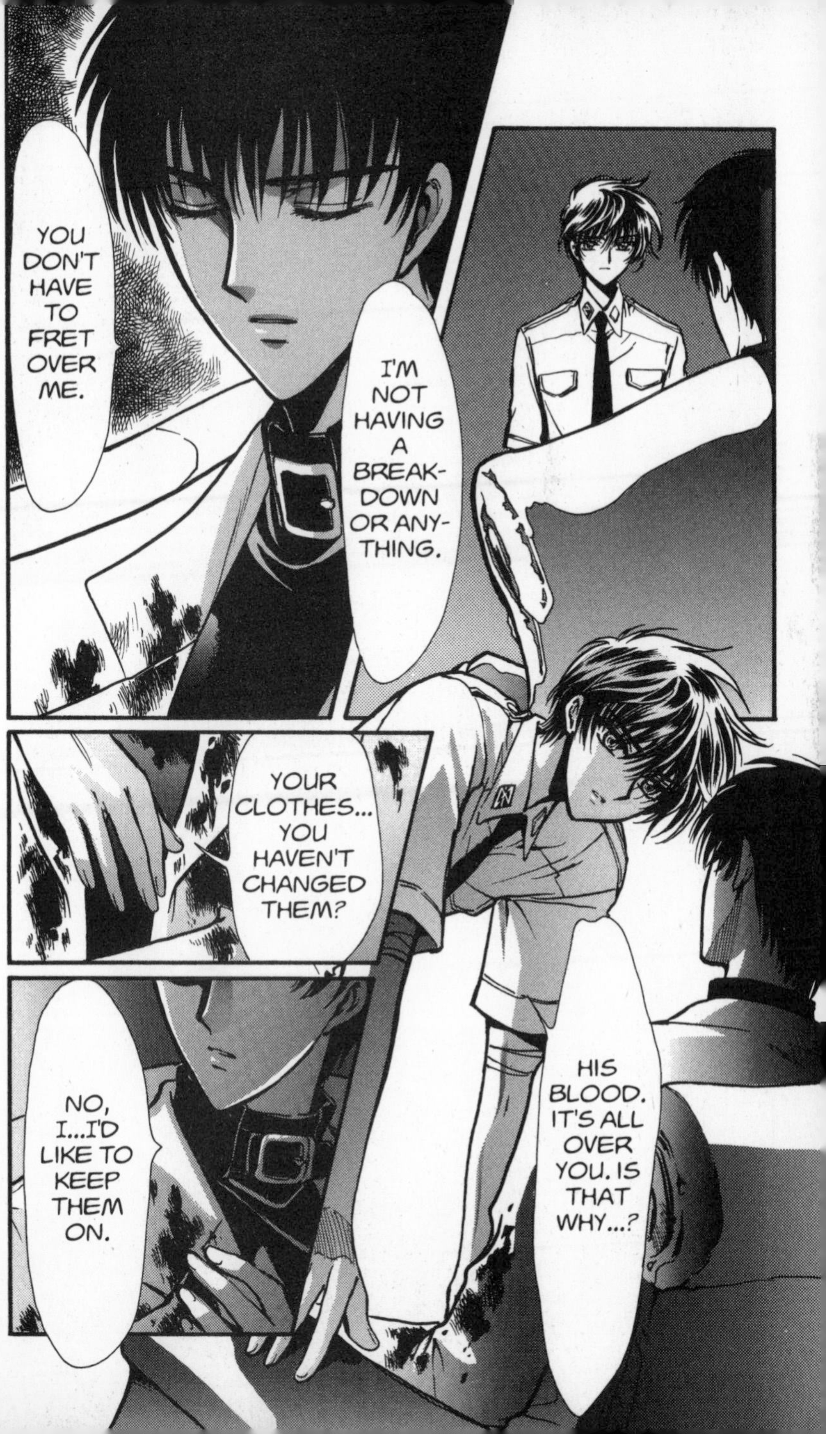
I'M NOT HAVING A BREAK-DOWN OR ANY-THING.
YOU DON'T HAVE TO FRET OVER ME.
YOUR CLOTHES... YOU HAVEN'T CHANGED THEM?
HIS BLOOD. IT'S ALL OVER YOU. IS THAT WHY...?
NO, I...I'D LIKE TO KEEP THEM ON.

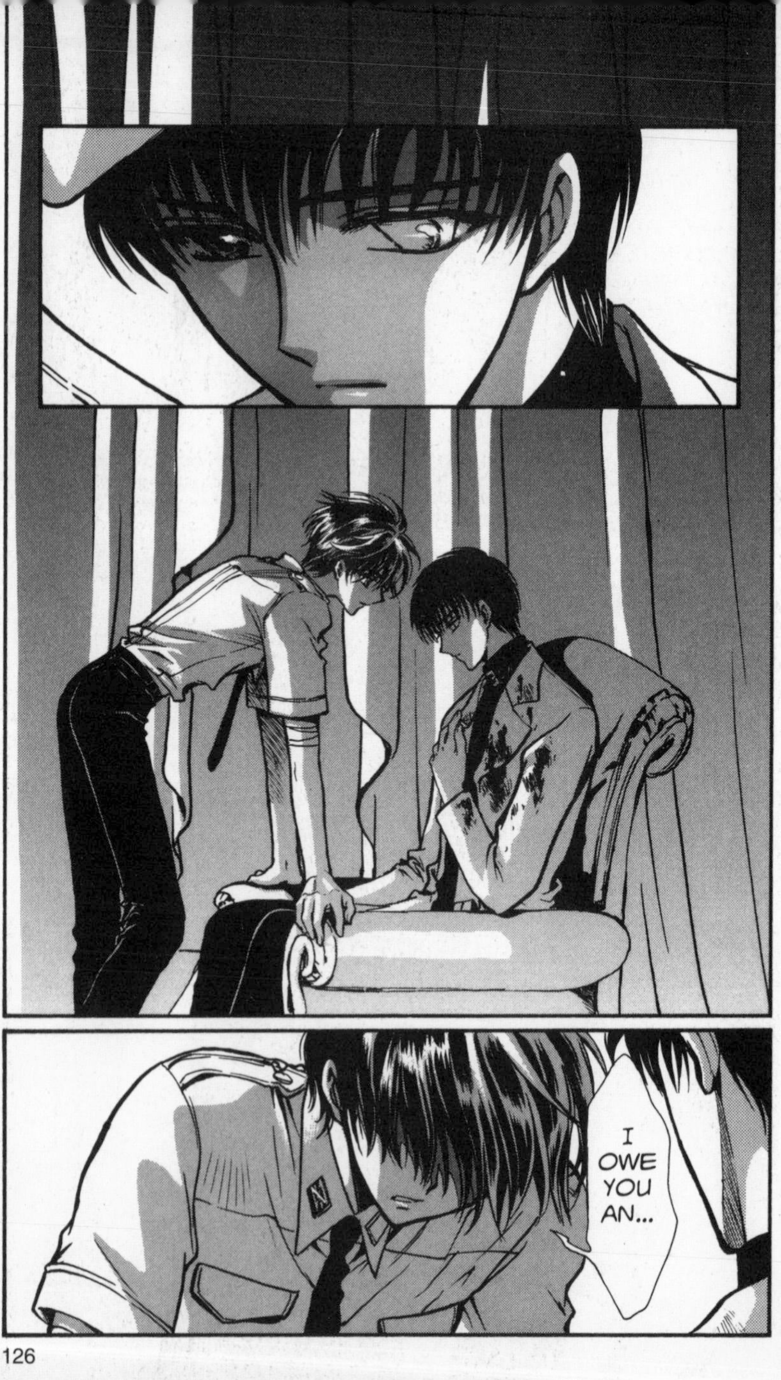
I OWE YOU AN...

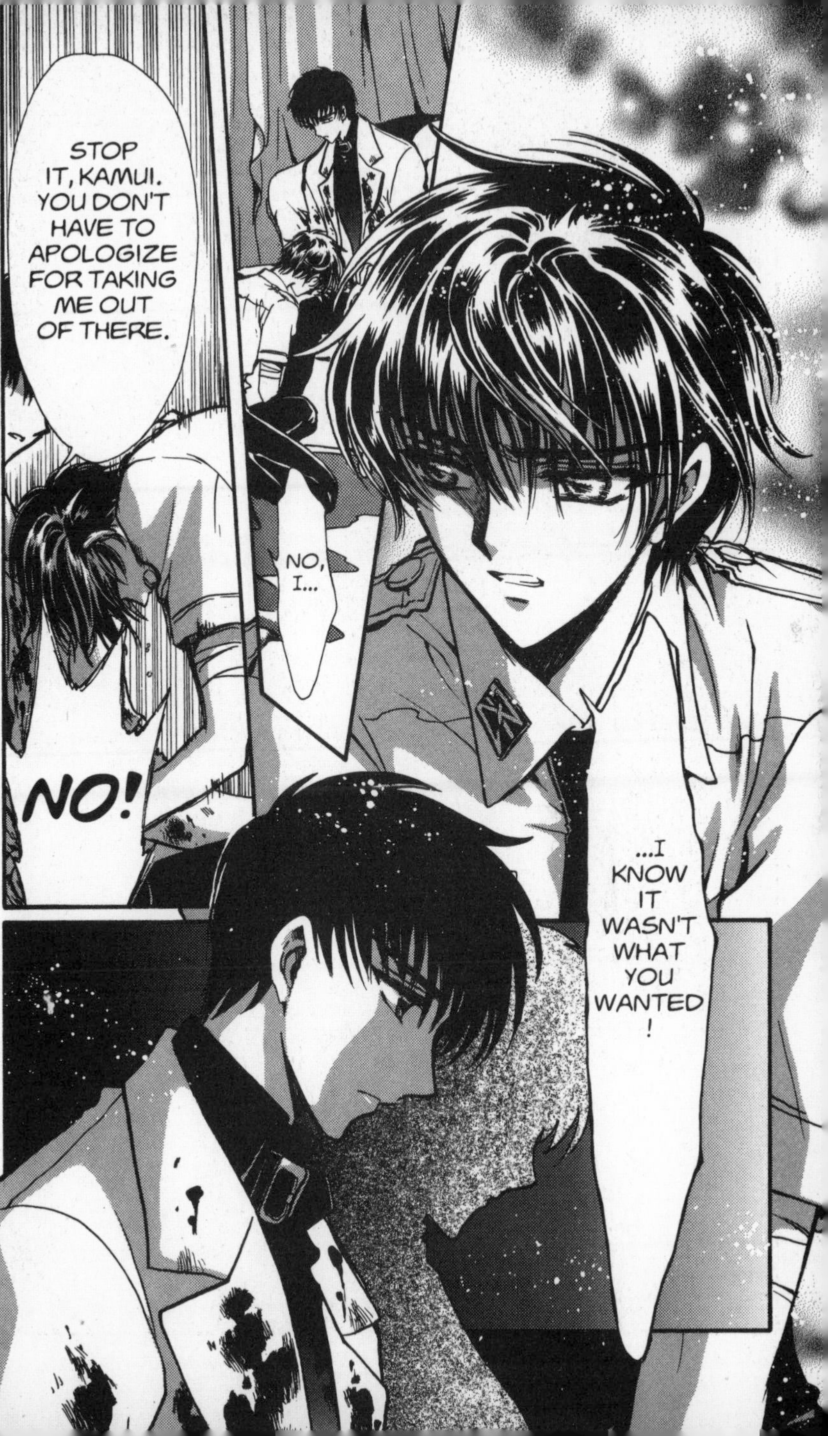
STOP IT, KAMUI. YOU DON'T HAVE TO APOLOGIZE FOR TAKING ME OUT OF THERE.
NO, I...
NO!
...I KNOW IT WASN'T WHAT YOU WANTED!

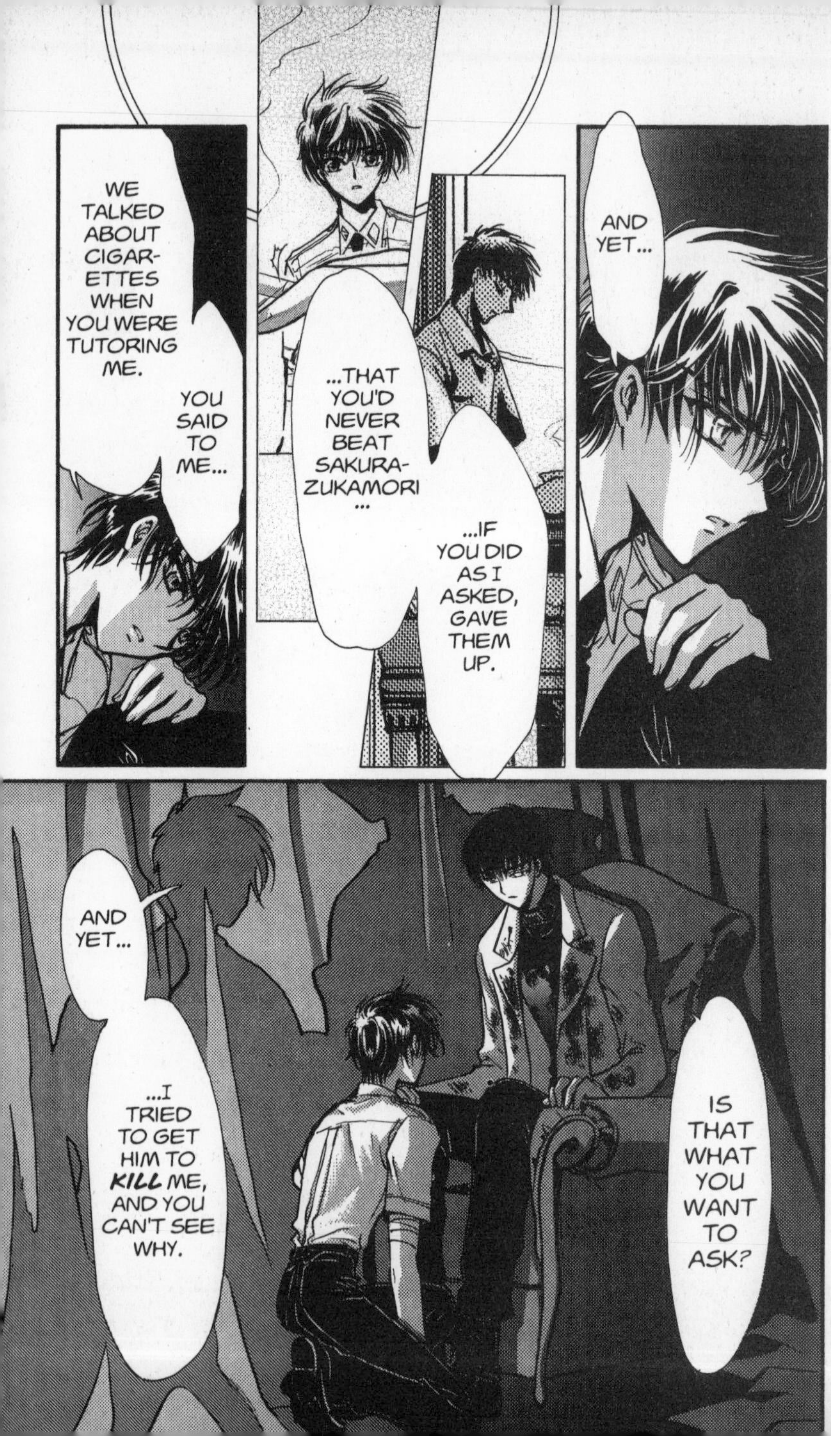
WE TALKED ABOUT CIGAR-ETTES WHEN YOU WERE TUTORING ME.
YOU SAID TO ME...
...THAT YOU'D NEVER BEAT SAKURA-ZUKAMORI ...
...IF YOU DID AS I ASKED, GAVE THEM UP.
AND YET...
AND YET...
...I TRIED TO GET HIM TO KILL ME, AND YOU CAN'T SEE WHY.
IS THAT WHAT YOU WANT TO ASK?

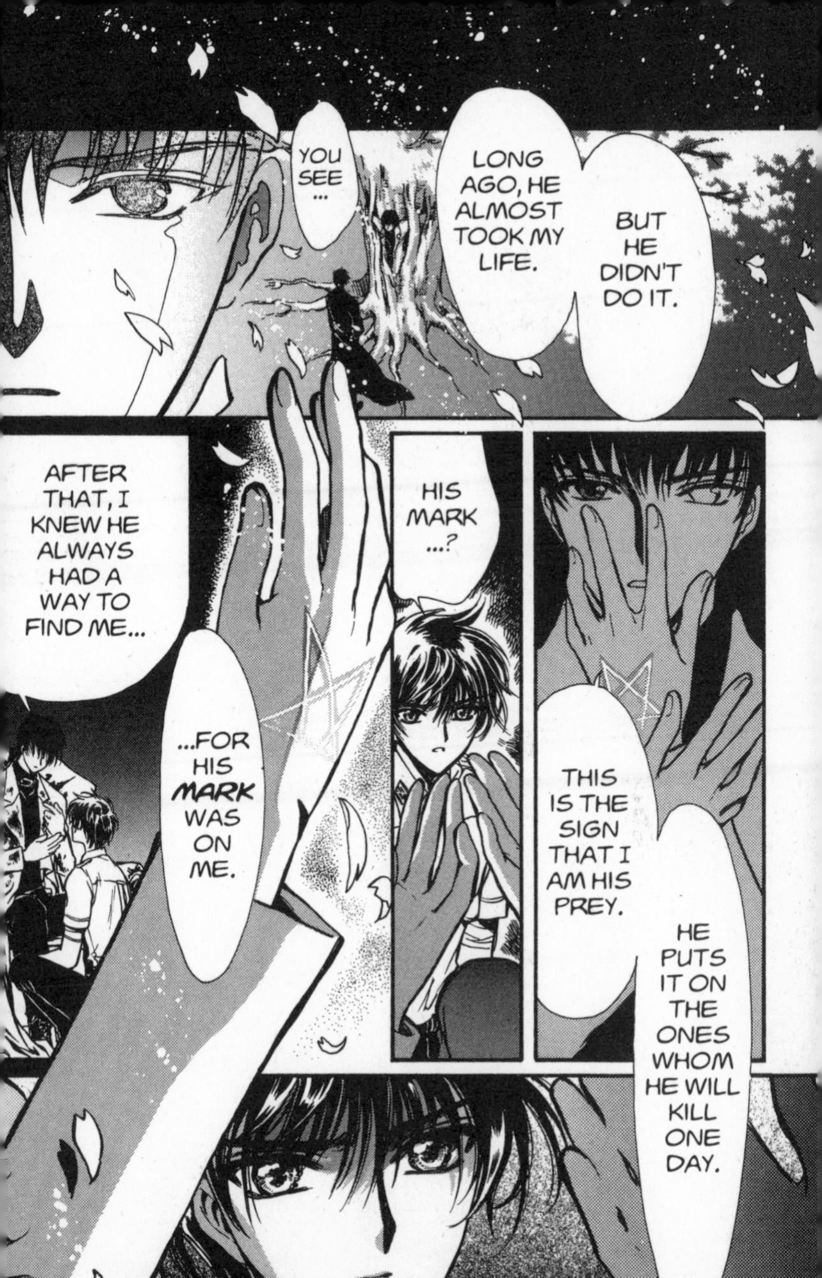
YOU SEE ...
LONG AGO, HE ALMOST TOOK MY LIFE.
BUT HE DIDN'T DO IT.
AFTER THAT, I KNEW HE ALWAYS HAD A WAY TO FIND ME...
...FOR HIS MARK WAS ON ME.
HIS MARK ...?
THIS IS THE SIGN THAT I AM HIS PREY.
HE PUTS IT ON THE ONES WHOM HE WILL KILL ONE DAY.

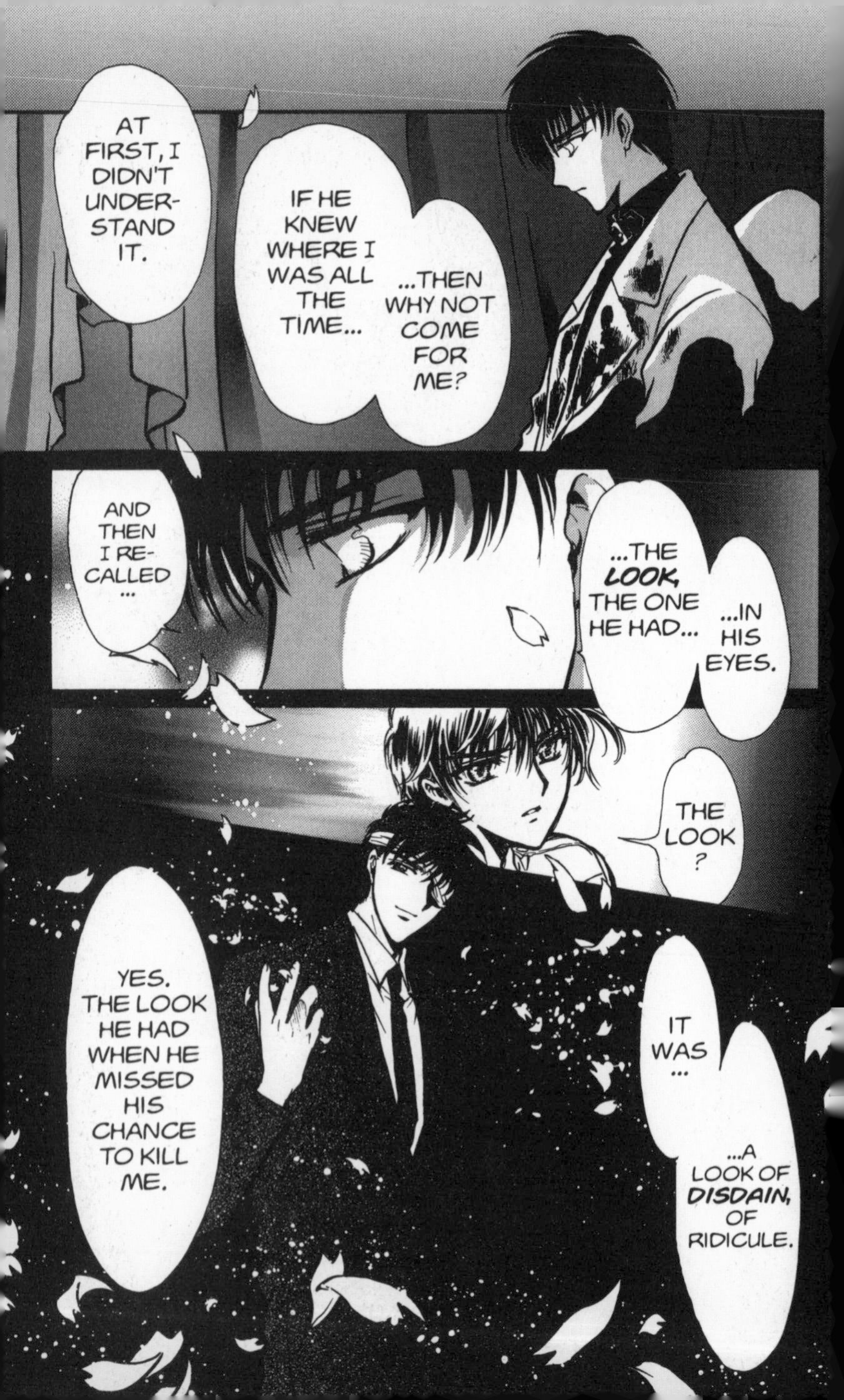
AT FIRST, I DIDN'T UNDER-STAND IT.
IF HE KNEW WHERE I WAS ALL THE TIME...
...THEN WHY NOT COME FOR ME?
AND THEN I RE-CALLED ...
...THE *LOOK*, THE ONE HE HAD...
...IN HIS EYES.
THE LOOK ?
YES. THE LOOK HE HAD WHEN HE MISSED HIS CHANCE TO KILL ME.
IT WAS ...
...A LOOK OF *DISDAIN*, OF RIDICULE.

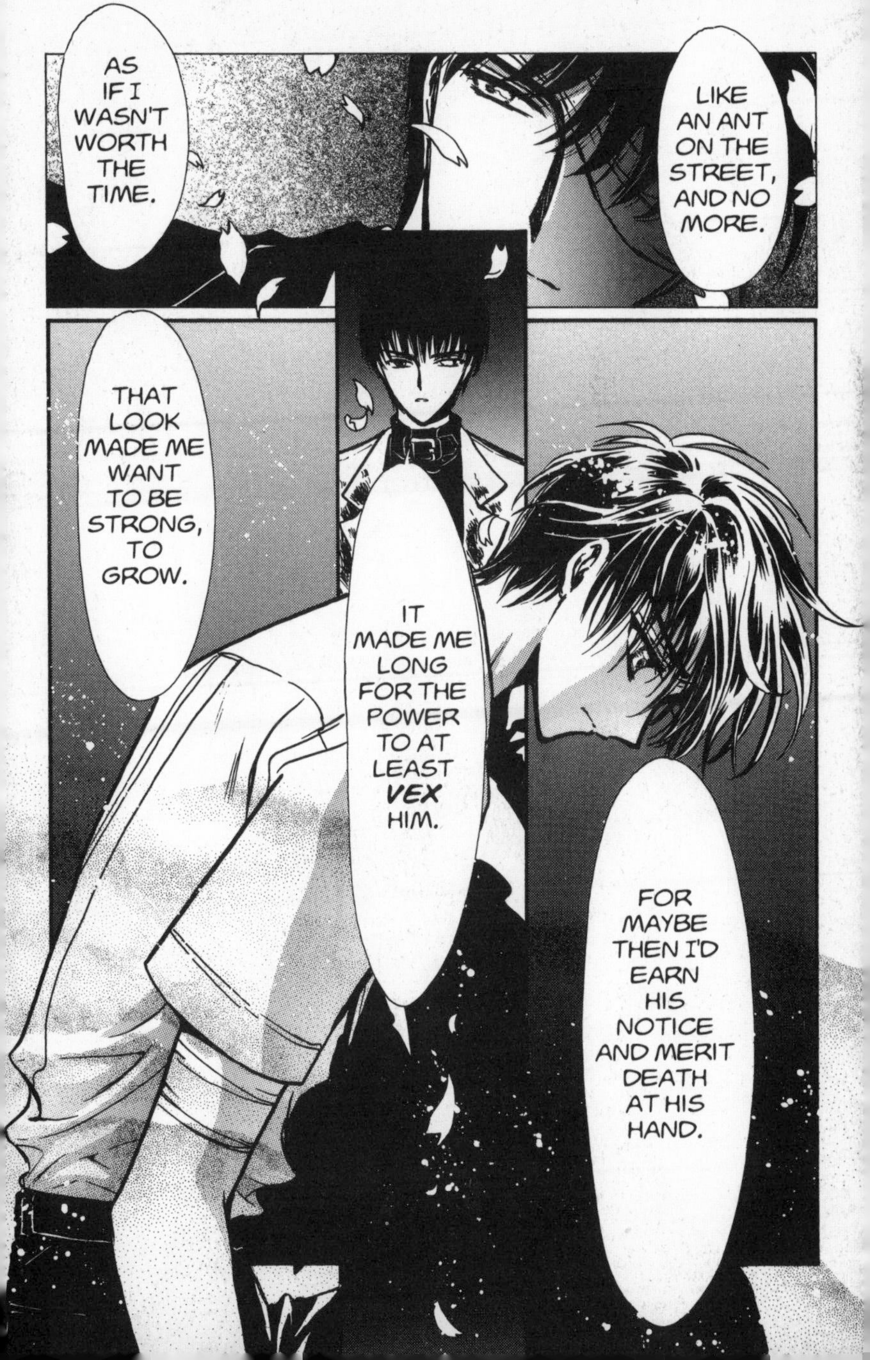
LIKE AN ANT ON THE STREET, AND NO MORE.
AS IF I WASN'T WORTH THE TIME.
THAT LOOK MADE ME WANT TO BE STRONG, TO GROW.
IT MADE ME LONG FOR THE POWER TO AT LEAST ***VEX*** HIM.
FOR MAYBE THEN I'D EARN HIS NOTICE AND MERIT DEATH AT HIS HAND.

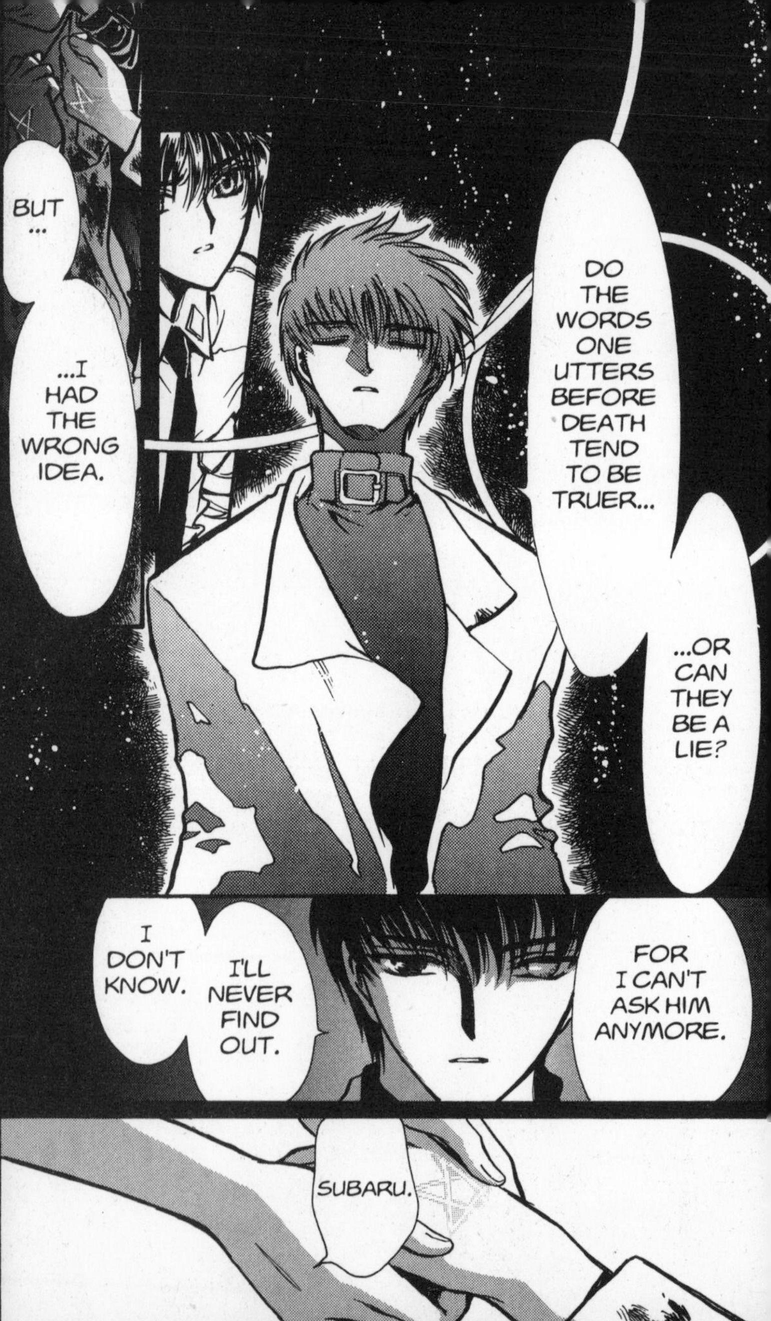
DO THE WORDS ONE UTTERS BEFORE DEATH TEND TO BE TRUER...
...OR CAN THEY BE A LIE?
BUT ...
...I HAD THE WRONG IDEA.
FOR I CAN'T ASK HIM ANYMORE.
I'LL NEVER FIND OUT.
I DON'T KNOW.
SUBARU.

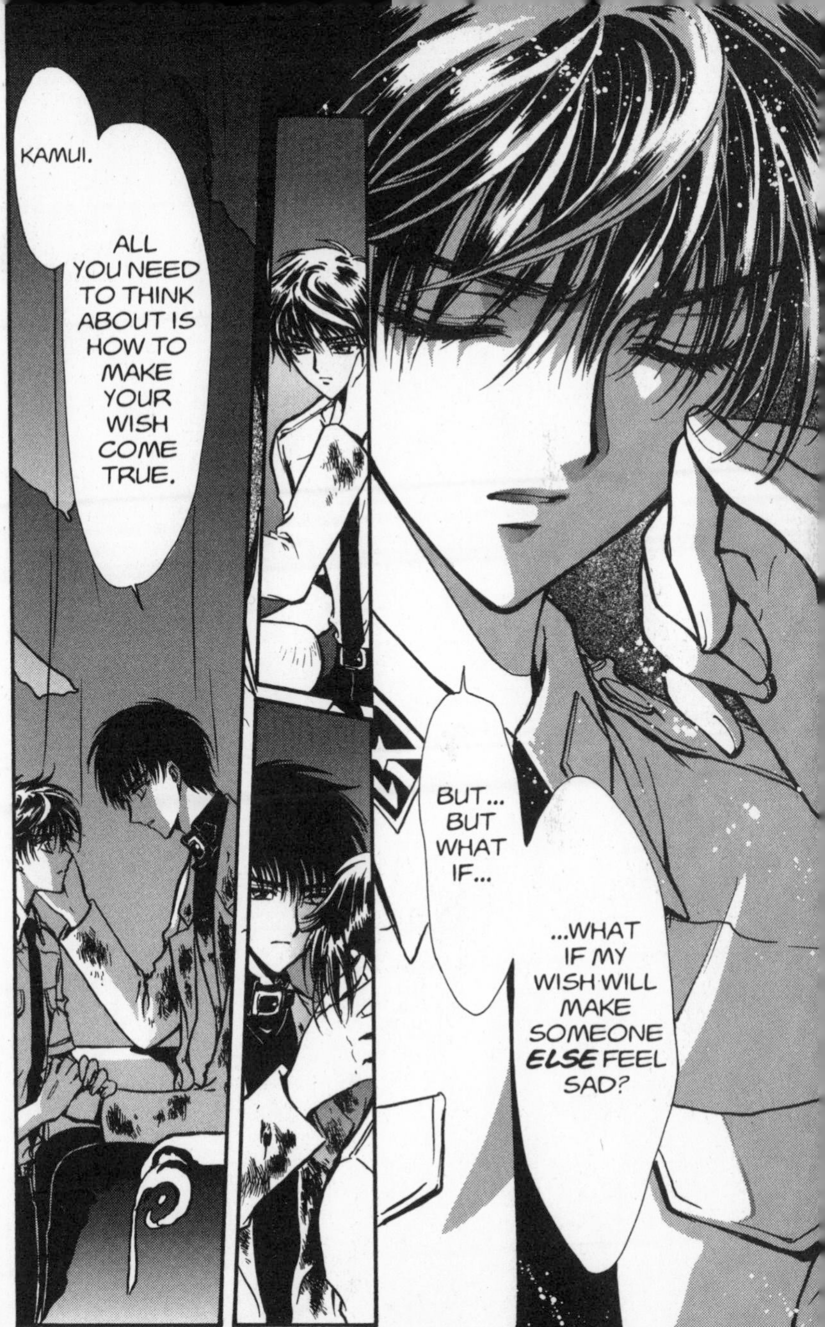
KAMUI.
ALL YOU NEED TO THINK ABOUT IS HOW TO MAKE YOUR WISH COME TRUE.
BUT... BUT WHAT IF...
...WHAT IF MY WISH WILL MAKE SOMEONE *ELSE* FEEL SAD?

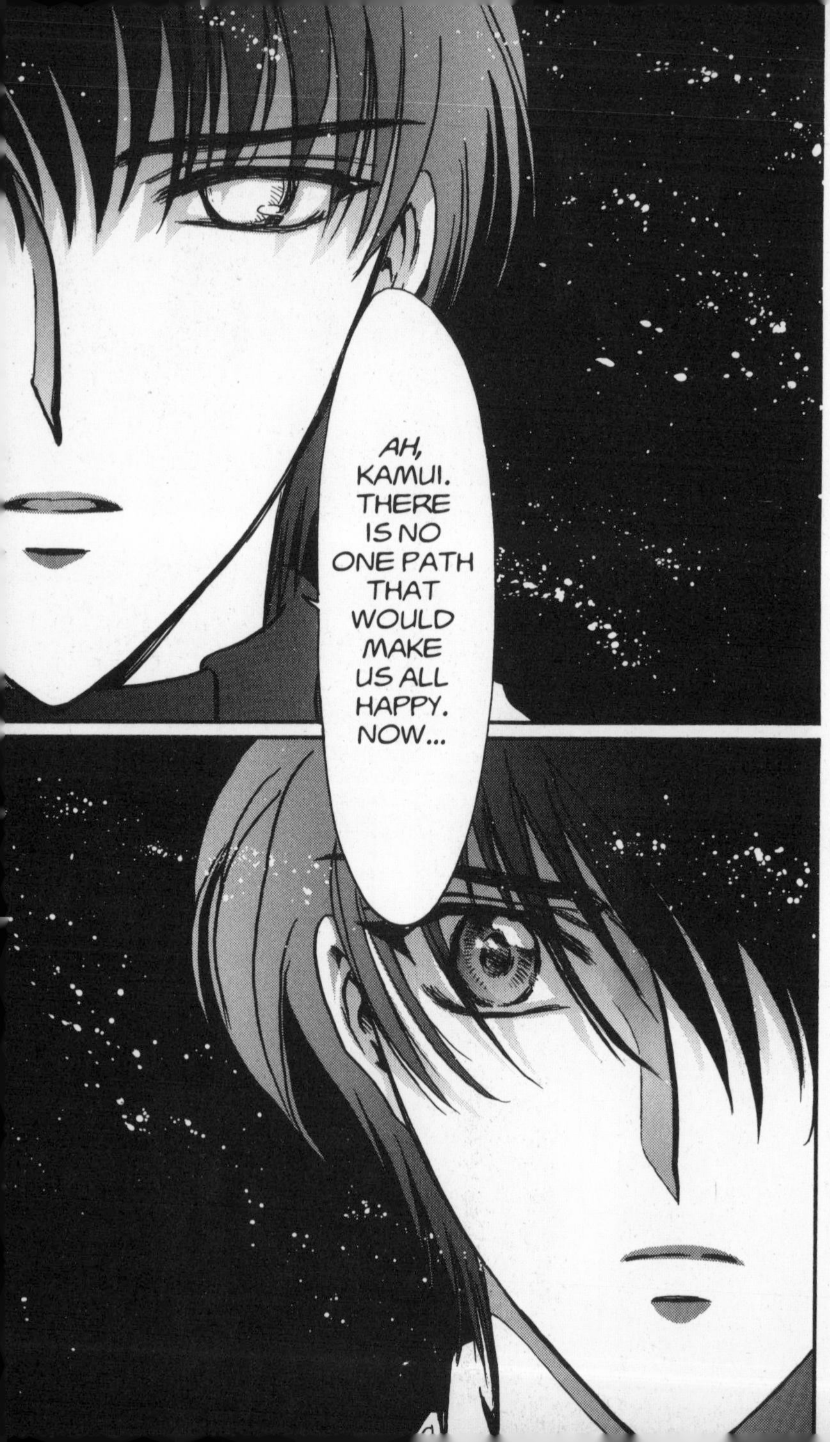
AH, KAMUI. THERE IS NO ONE PATH THAT WOULD MAKE US ALL HAPPY. NOW...

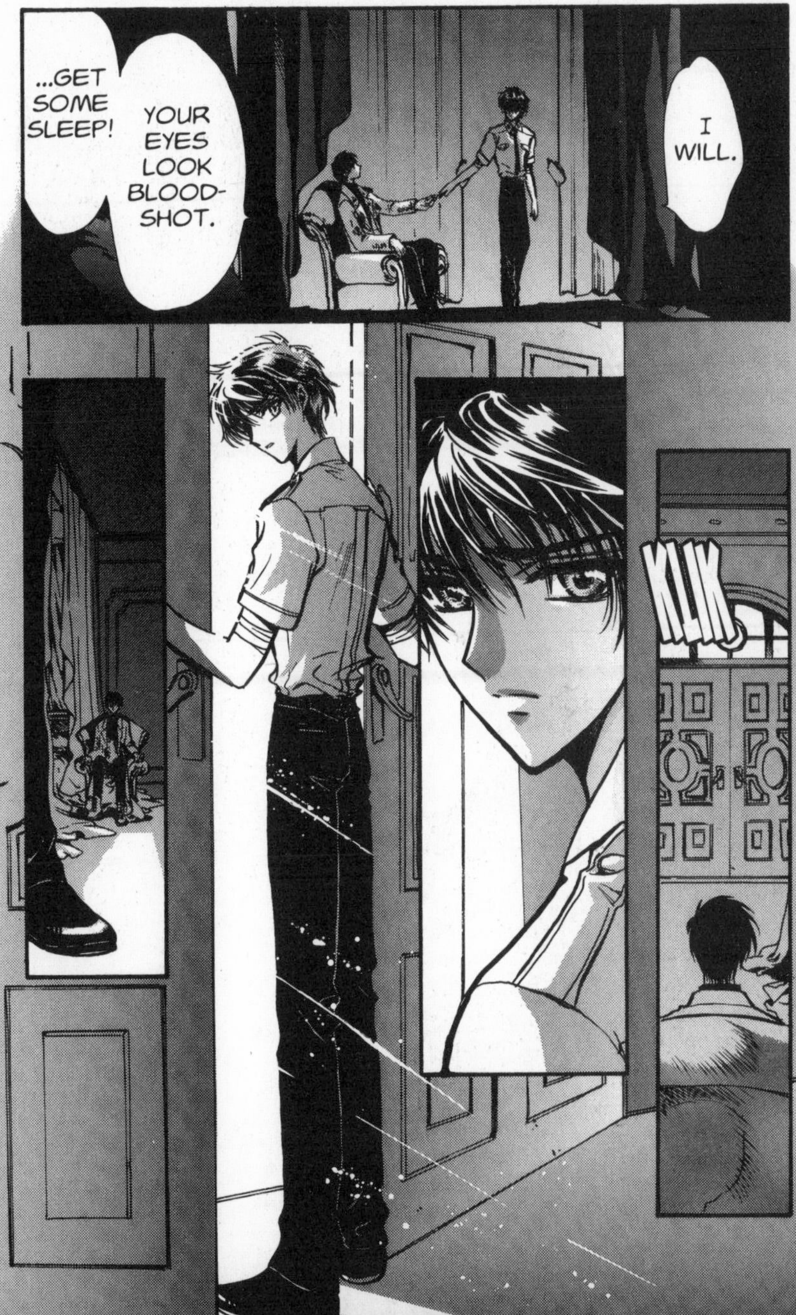
...GET SOME SLEEP!
YOUR EYES LOOK BLOOD-SHOT.
I WILL.
KLIK

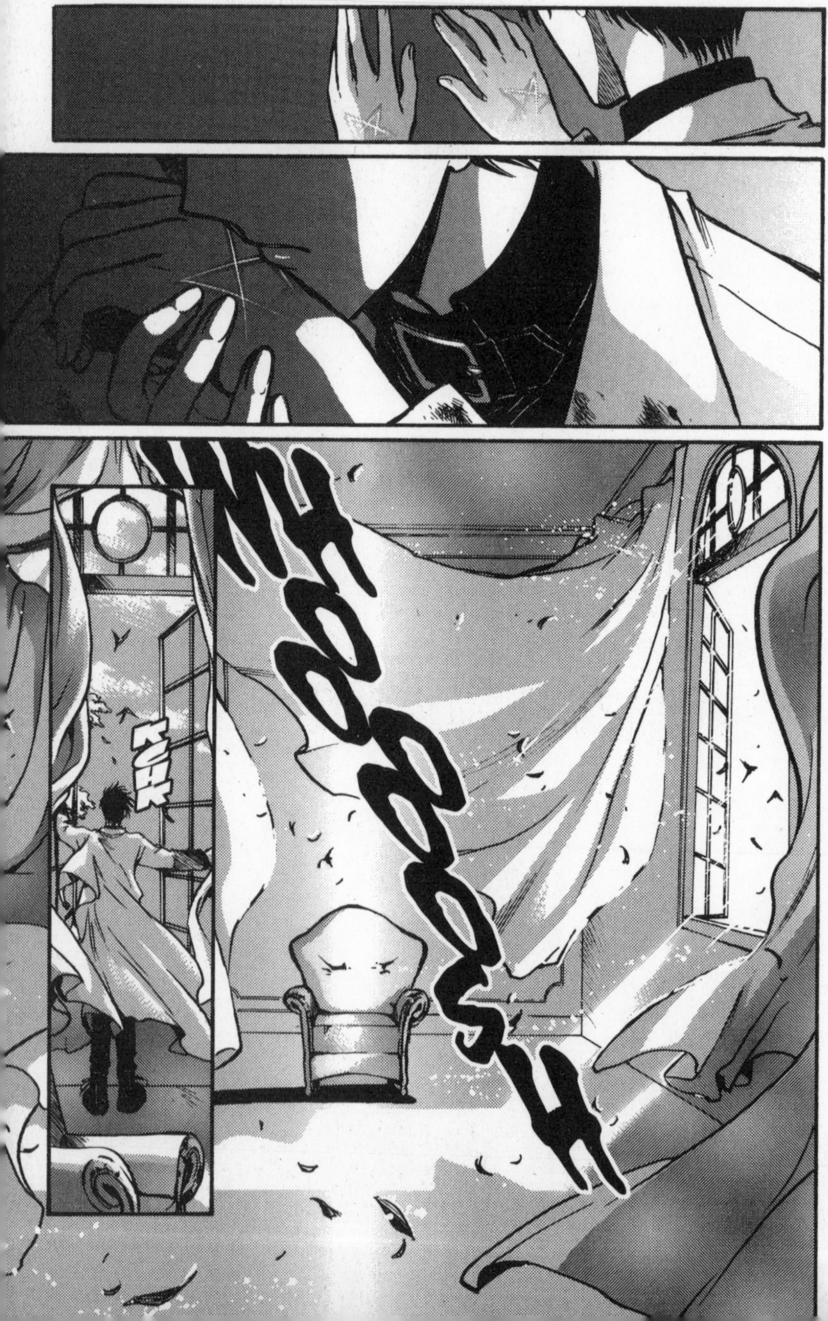
WHOOOOSH
KUHK

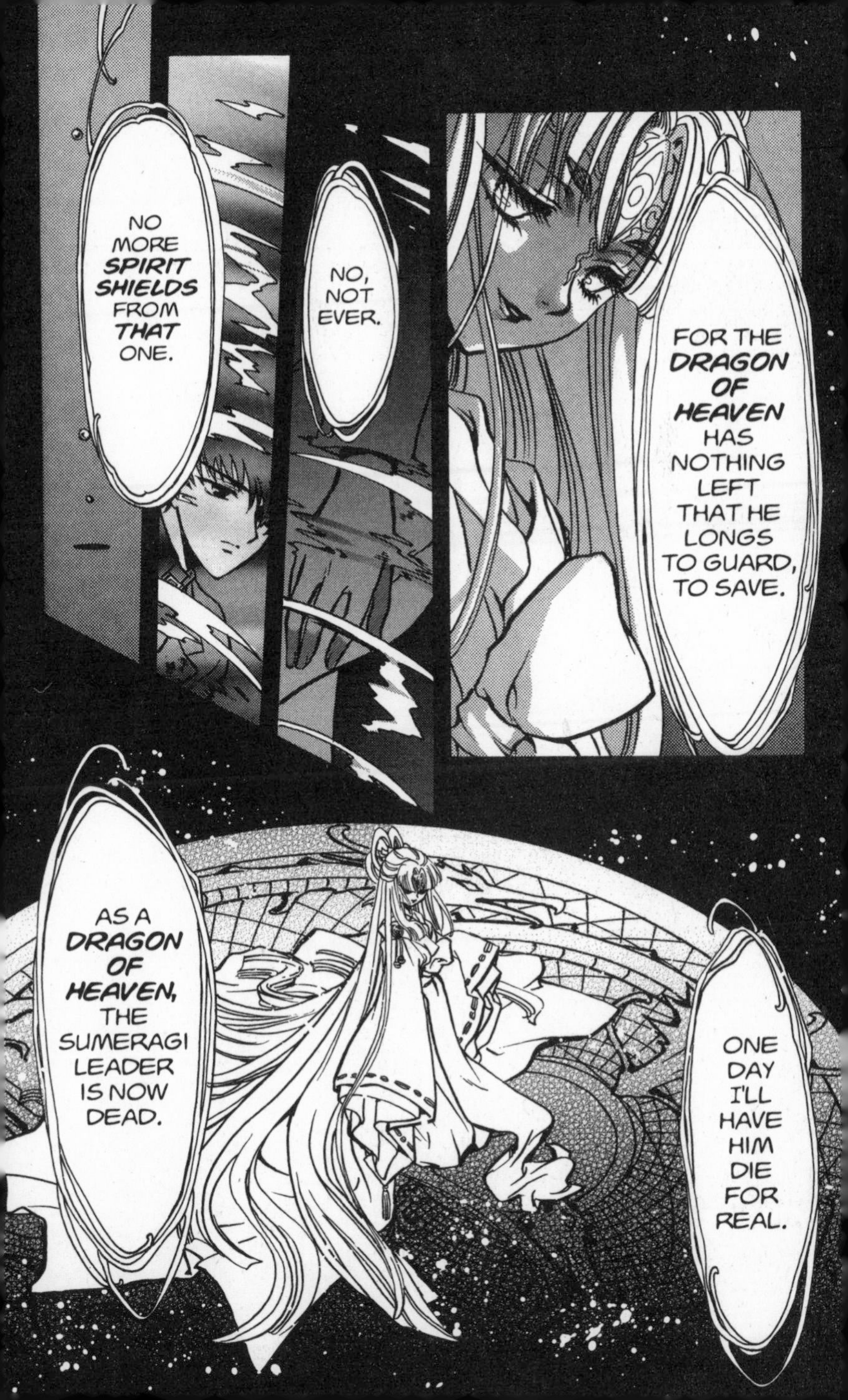
NO MORE SPIRIT SHIELDS FROM THAT ONE.
NO, NOT EVER.
FOR THE DRAGON OF HEAVEN HAS NOTHING LEFT THAT HE LONGS TO GUARD, TO SAVE.
AS A DRAGON OF HEAVEN, THE SUMERAGI LEADER IS NOW DEAD.
ONE DAY I'LL HAVE HIM DIE FOR REAL.

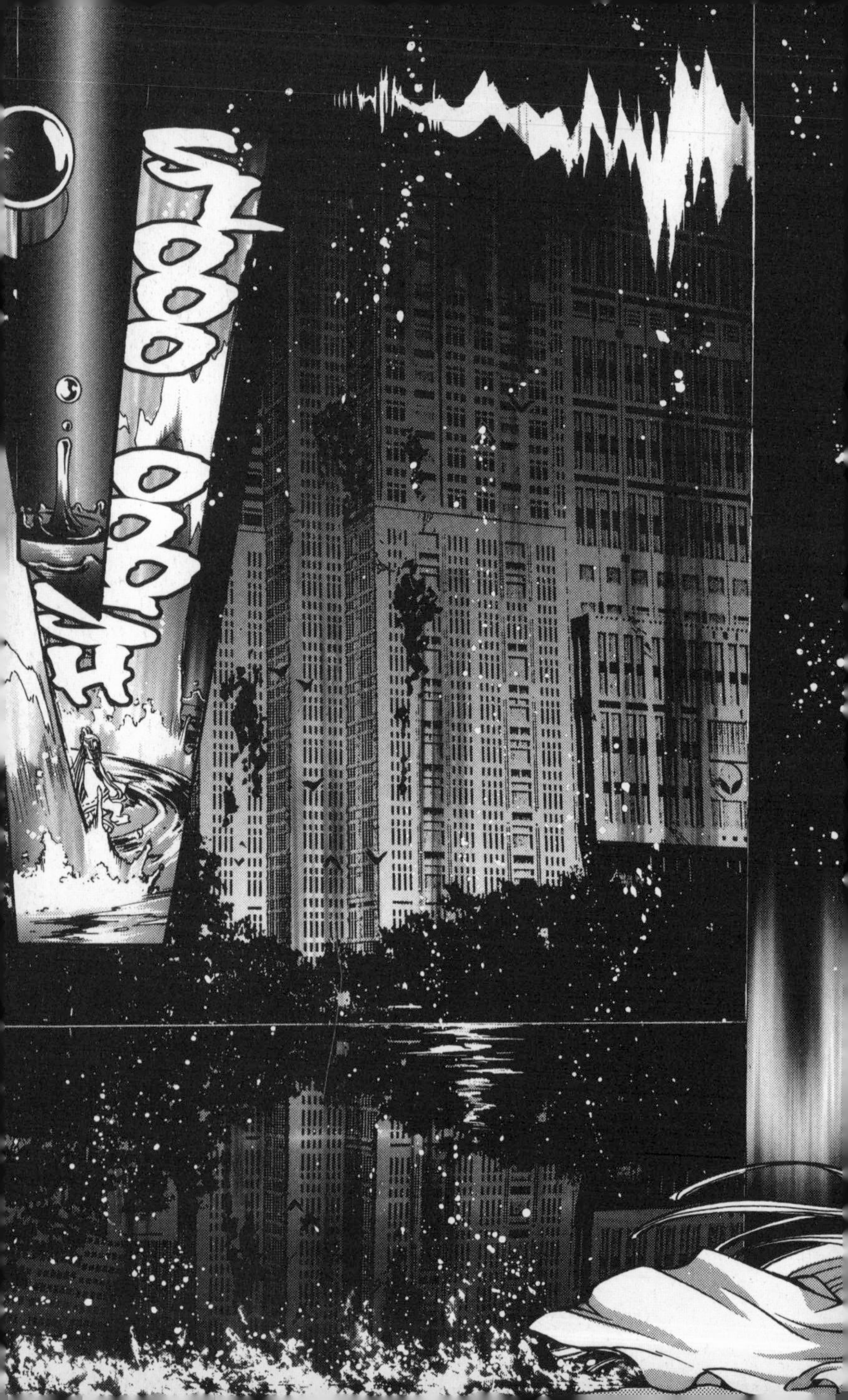
SHOOOOOOSH

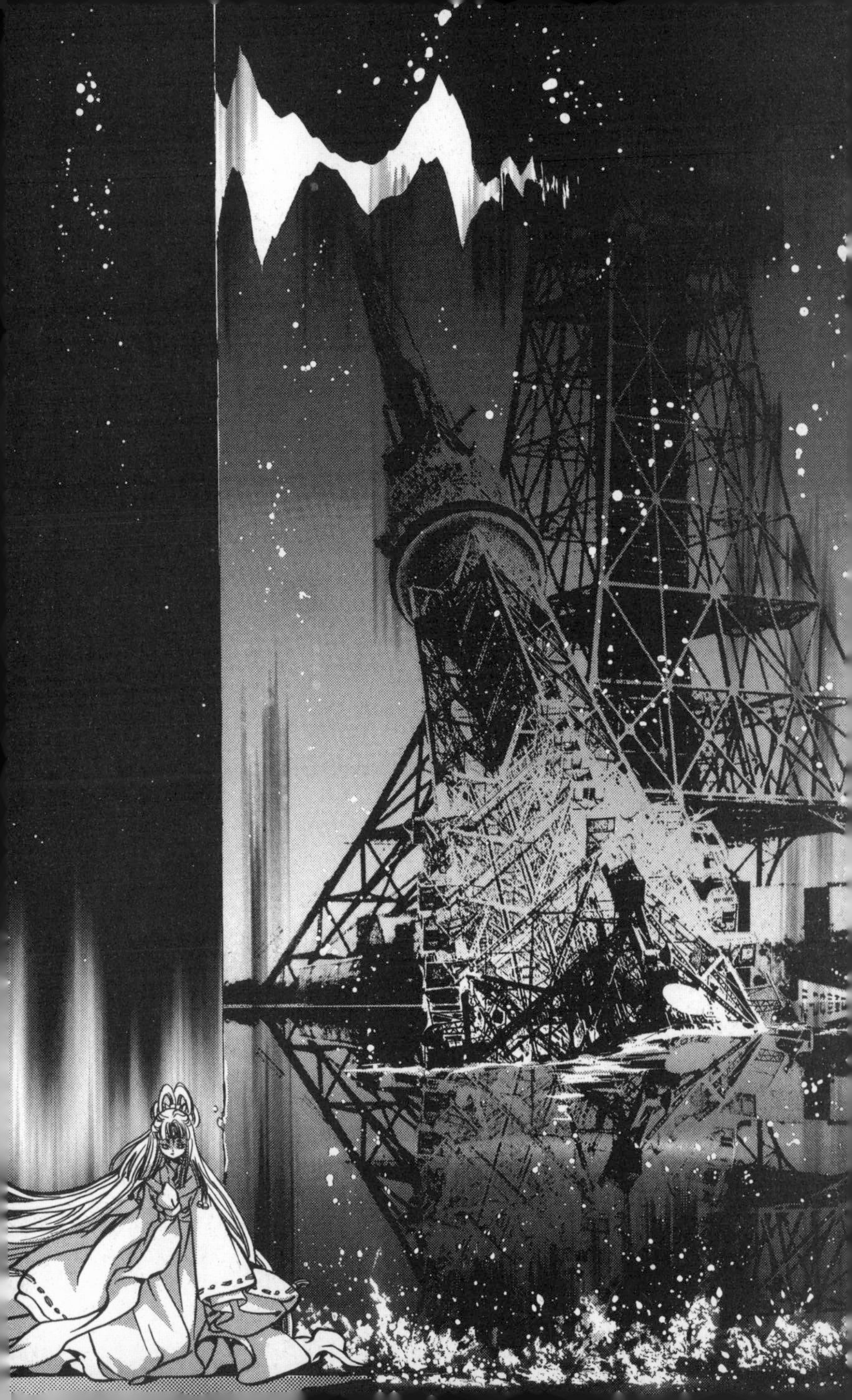

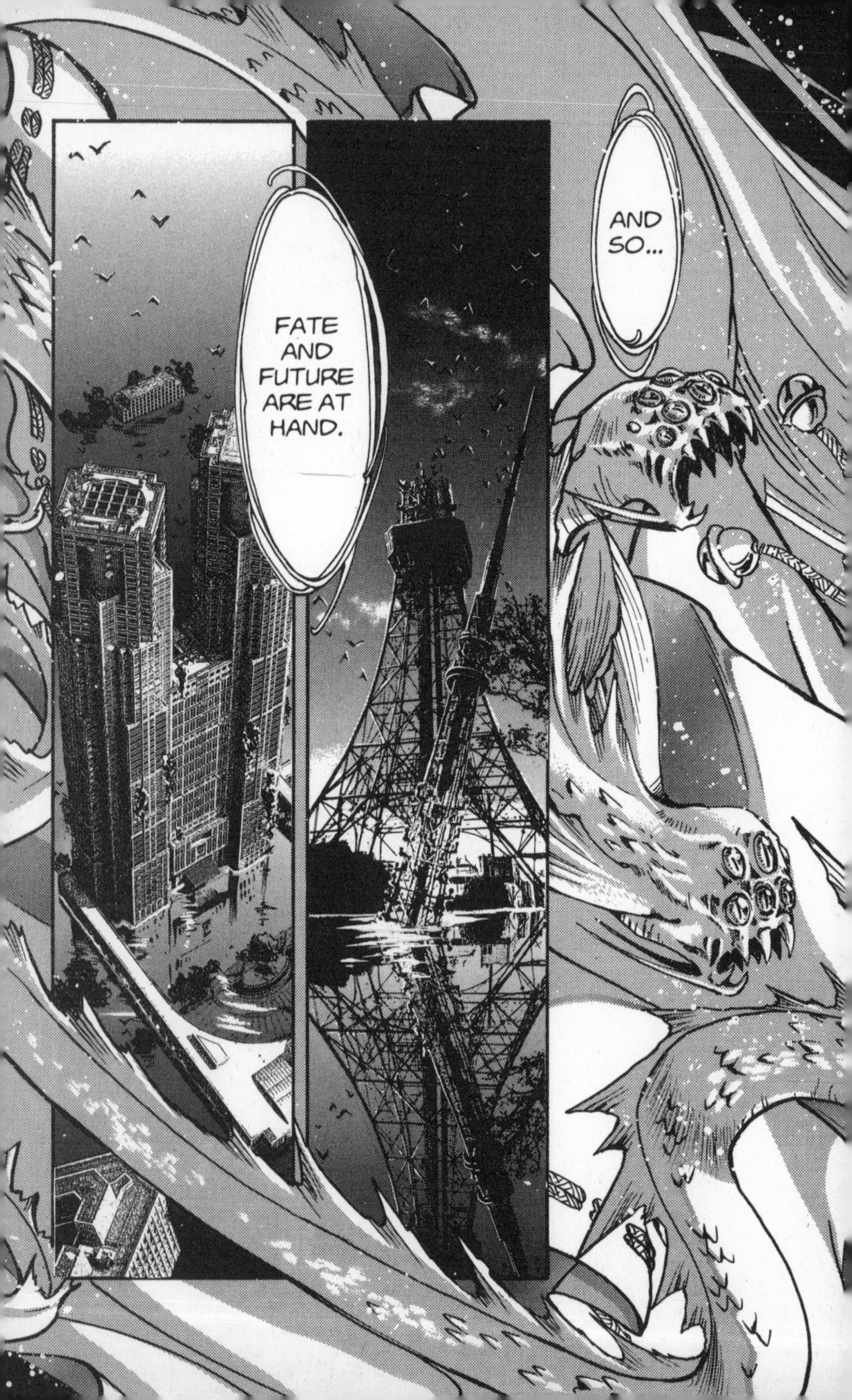
AND SO...
FATE AND FUTURE ARE AT HAND.

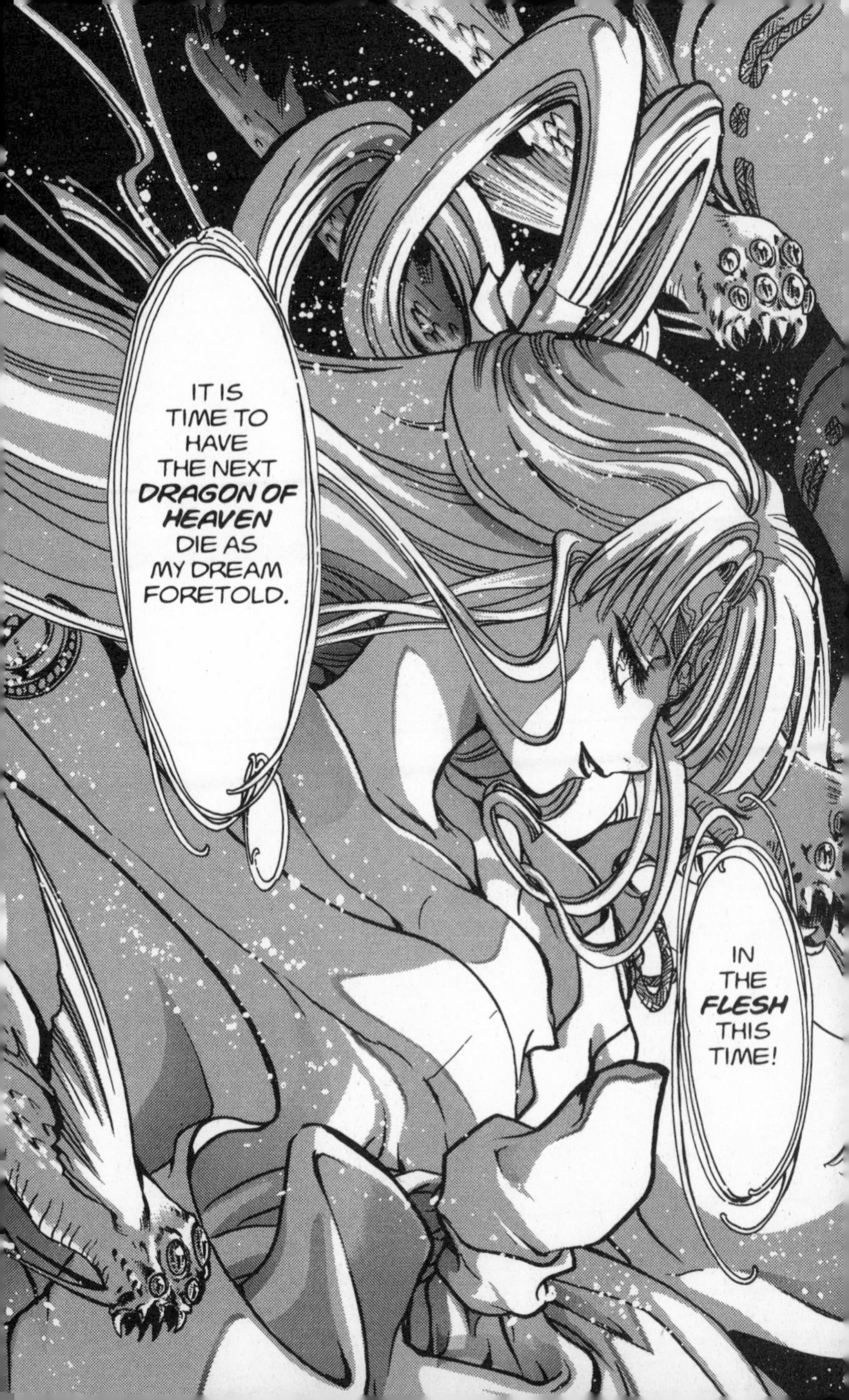
IT IS TIME TO HAVE THE NEXT ***DRAGON OF HEAVEN*** DIE AS MY DREAM FORETOLD.
IN THE ***FLESH*** THIS TIME!

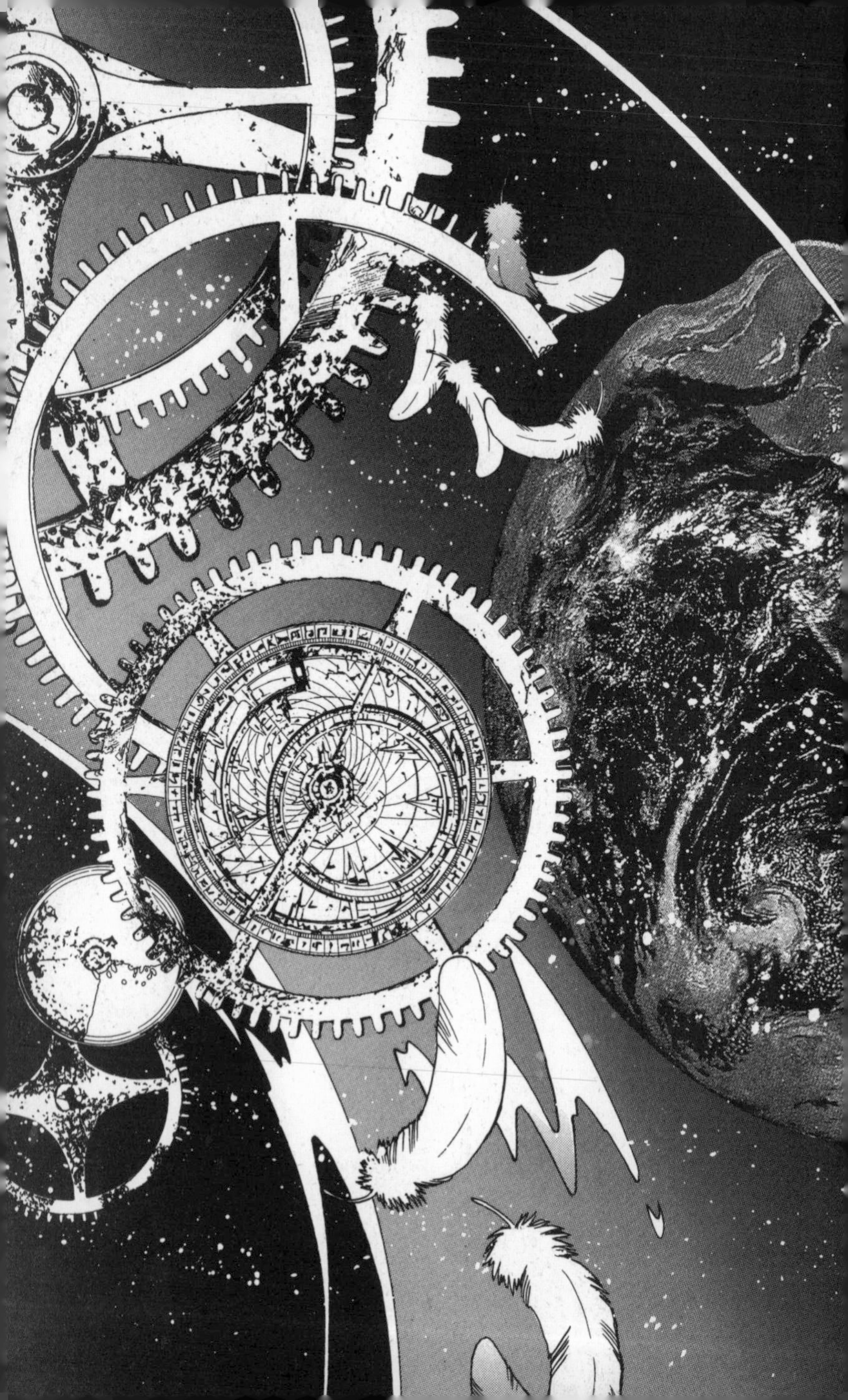

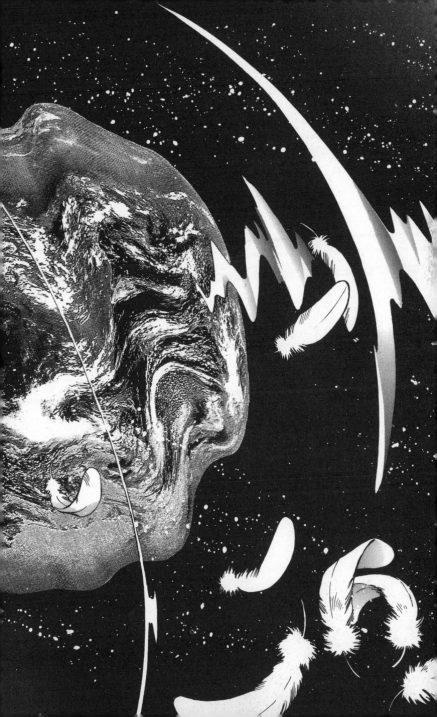

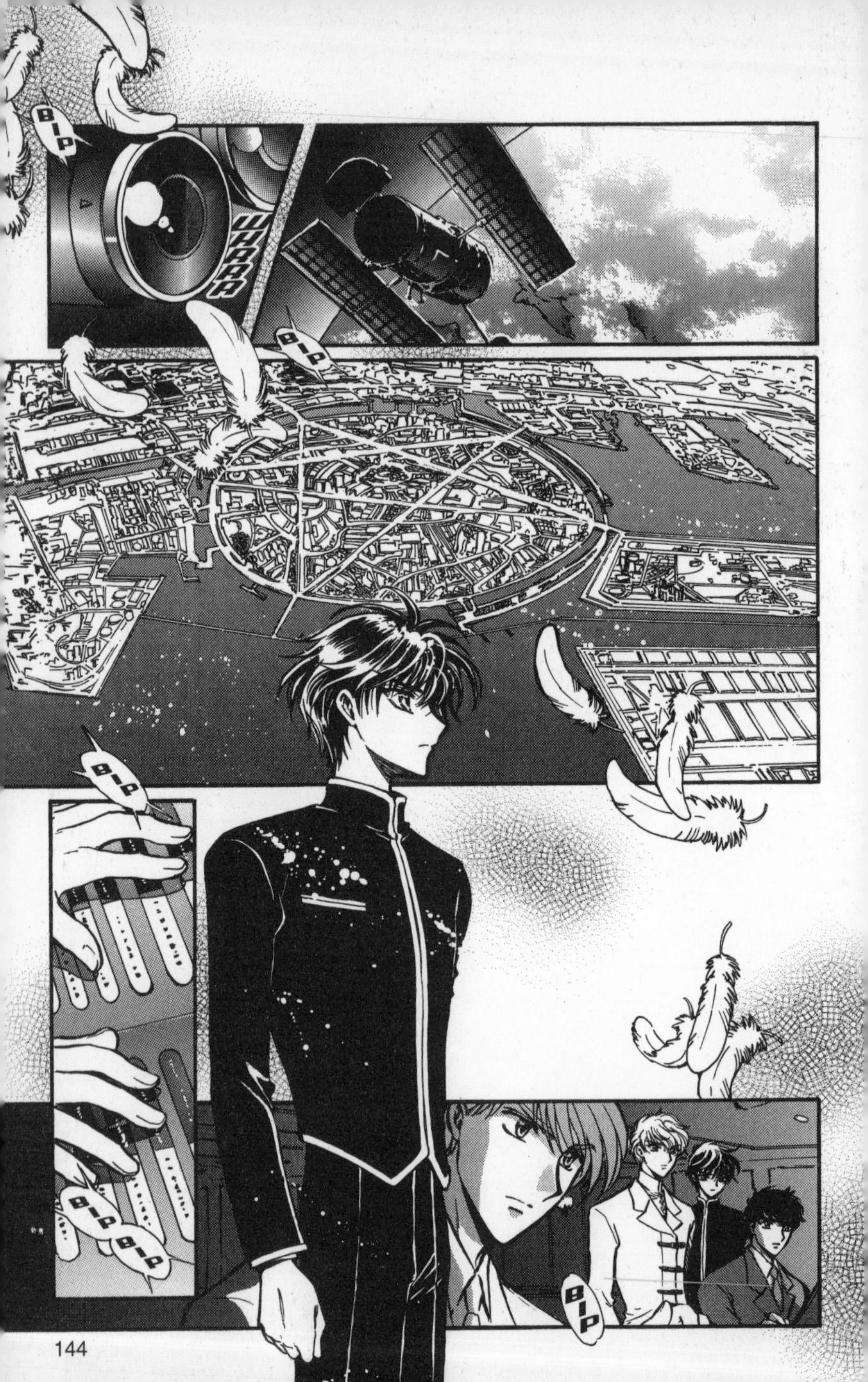
BIP
WHRRR
BIP
BIP
BIP
BIP
BIP

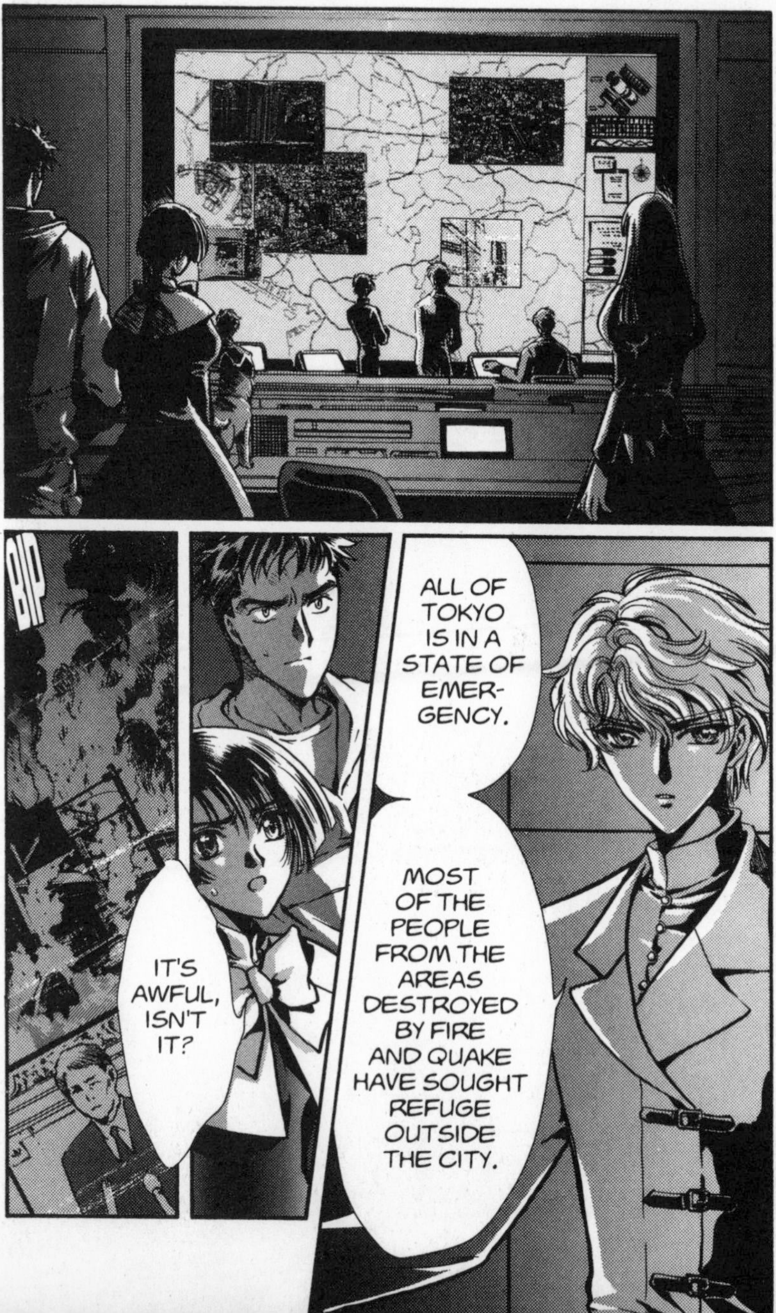
ALL OF TOKYO IS IN A STATE OF EMER-GENCY.
MOST OF THE PEOPLE FROM THE AREAS DESTROYED BY FIRE AND QUAKE HAVE SOUGHT REFUGE OUTSIDE THE CITY.
IT'S AWFUL, ISN'T IT?
BIP

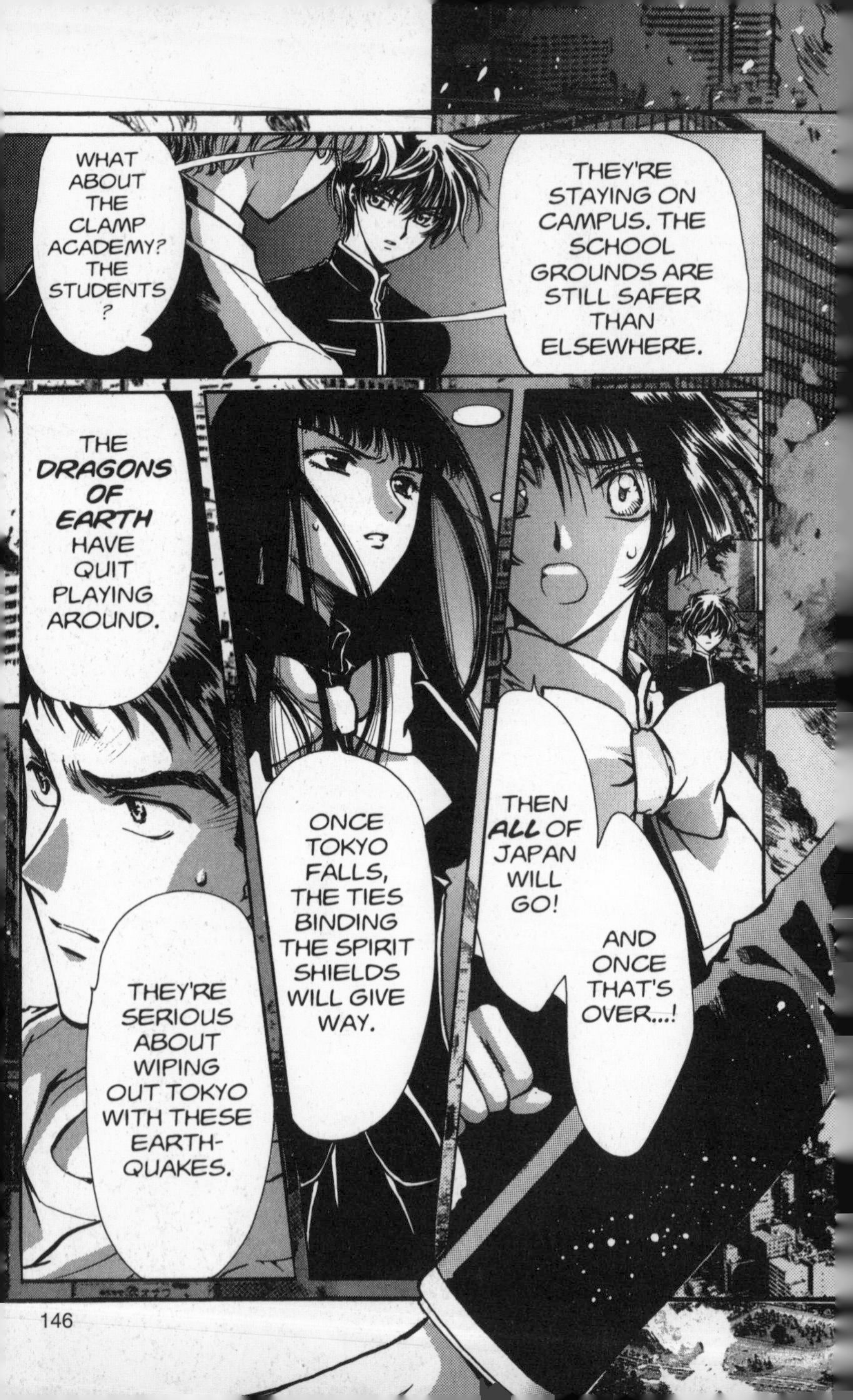
WHAT ABOUT THE CLAMP ACADEMY? THE STUDENTS?
THEY'RE STAYING ON CAMPUS. THE SCHOOL GROUNDS ARE STILL SAFER THAN ELSEWHERE.
THE DRAGONS OF EARTH HAVE QUIT PLAYING AROUND.
THEY'RE SERIOUS ABOUT WIPING OUT TOKYO WITH THESE EARTH-QUAKES.
ONCE TOKYO FALLS, THE TIES BINDING THE SPIRIT SHIELDS WILL GIVE WAY.
THEN ALL OF JAPAN WILL GO!
AND ONCE THAT'S OVER...!

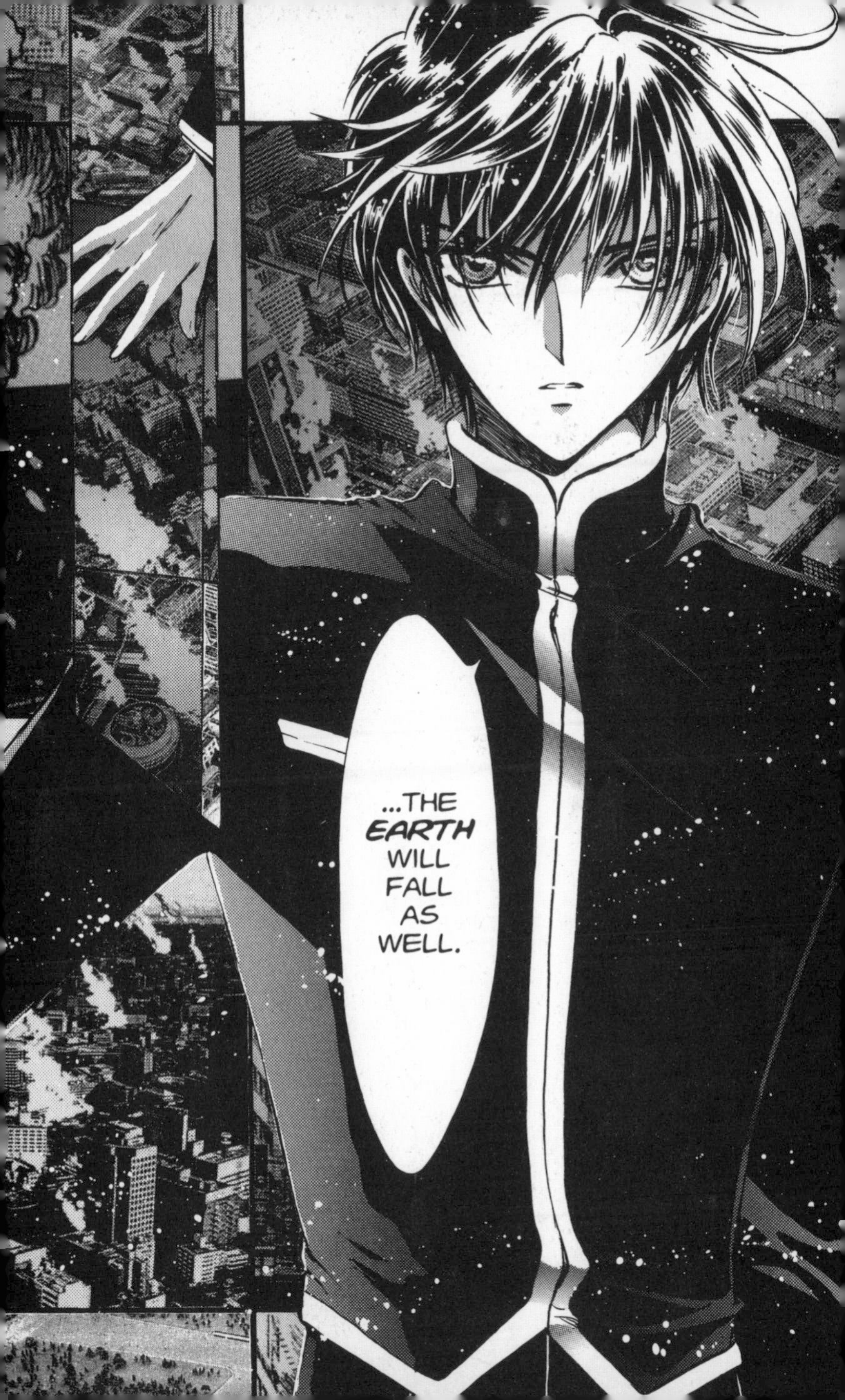
...THE EARTH WILL FALL AS WELL.

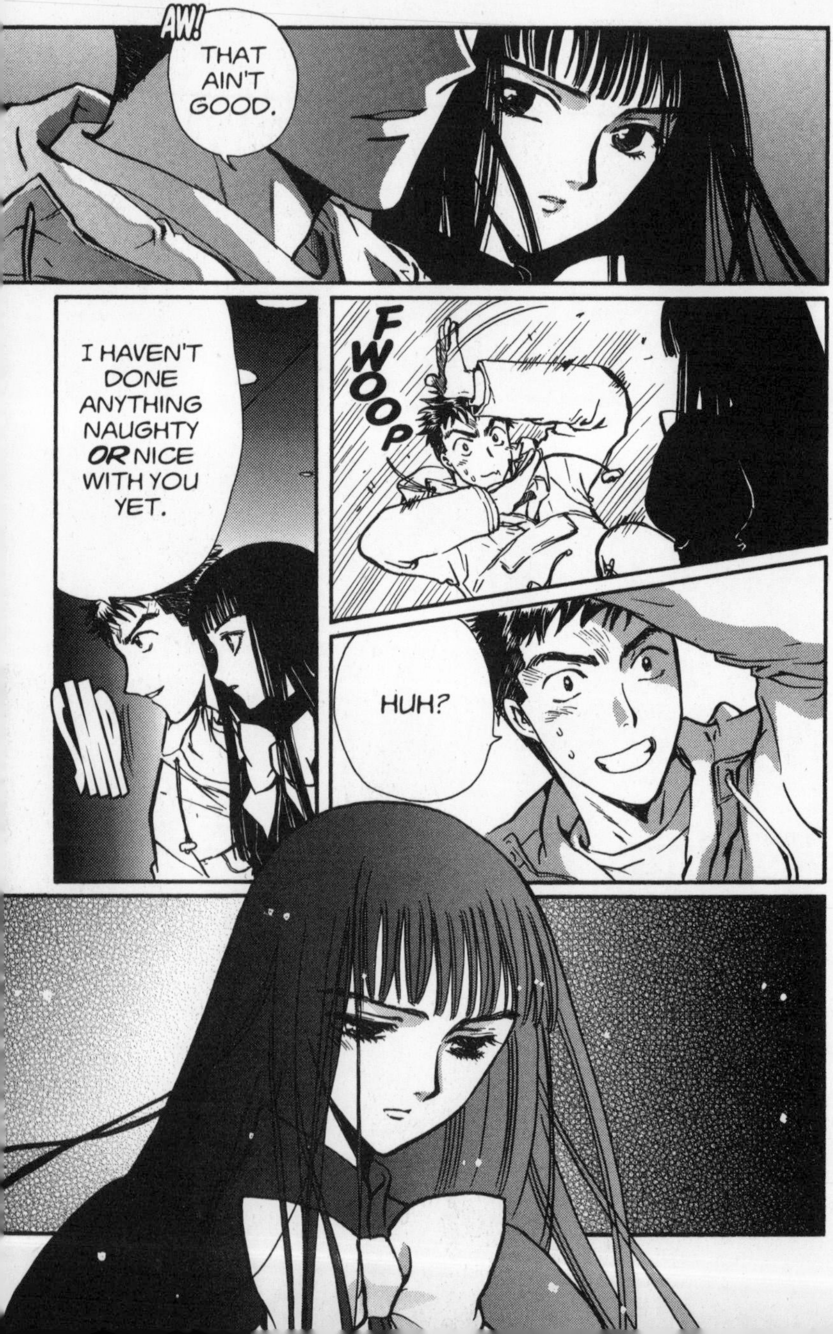
AW!
THAT AIN'T GOOD.
FWOOOP
HUH?
I HAVEN'T DONE ANYTHING NAUGHTY OR NICE WITH YOU YET.
SMP

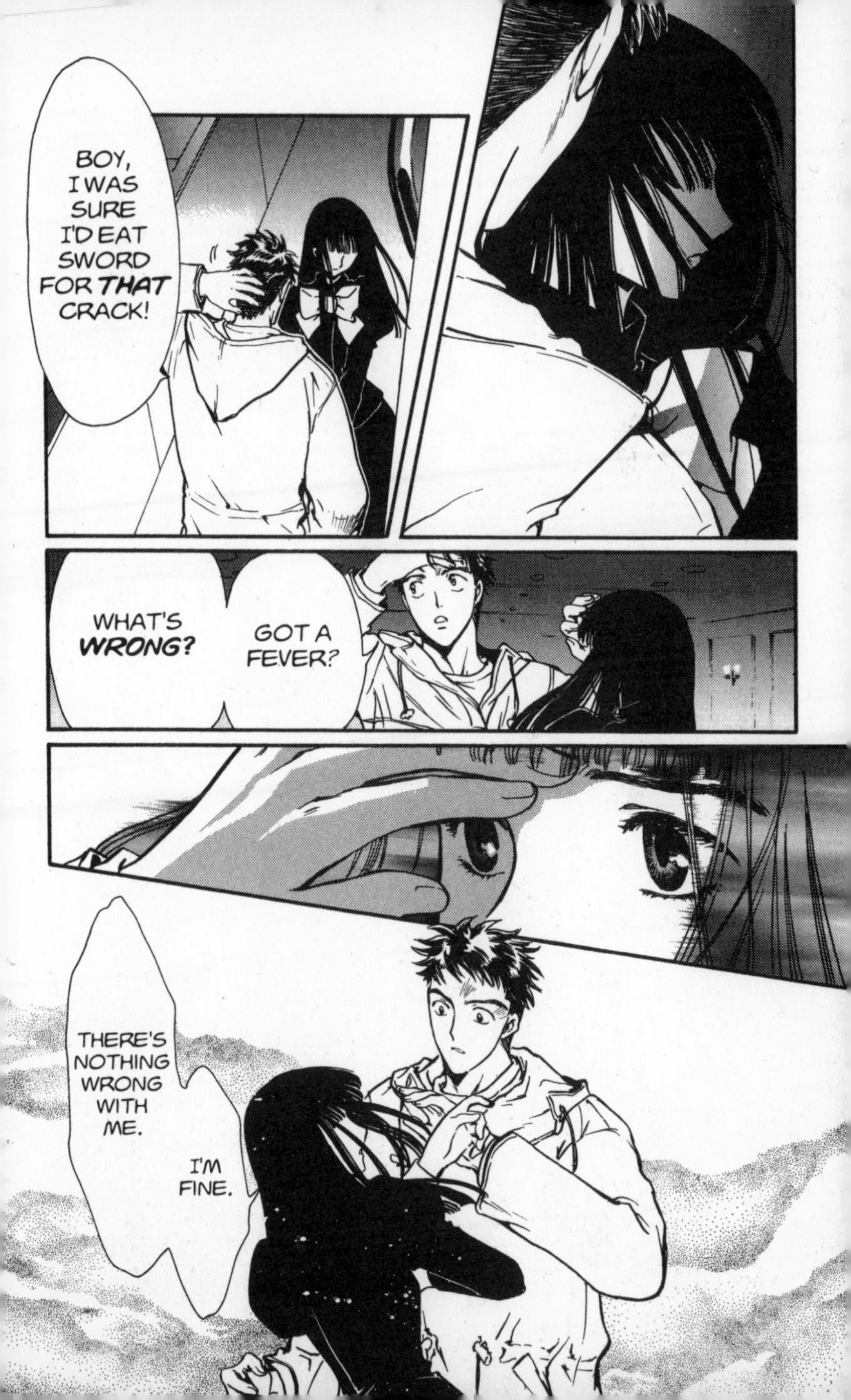
BOY, I WAS SURE I'D EAT SWORD FOR **THAT** CRACK!
GOT A FEVER?
WHAT'S **WRONG?**
THERE'S NOTHING WRONG WITH ME.
I'M FINE.

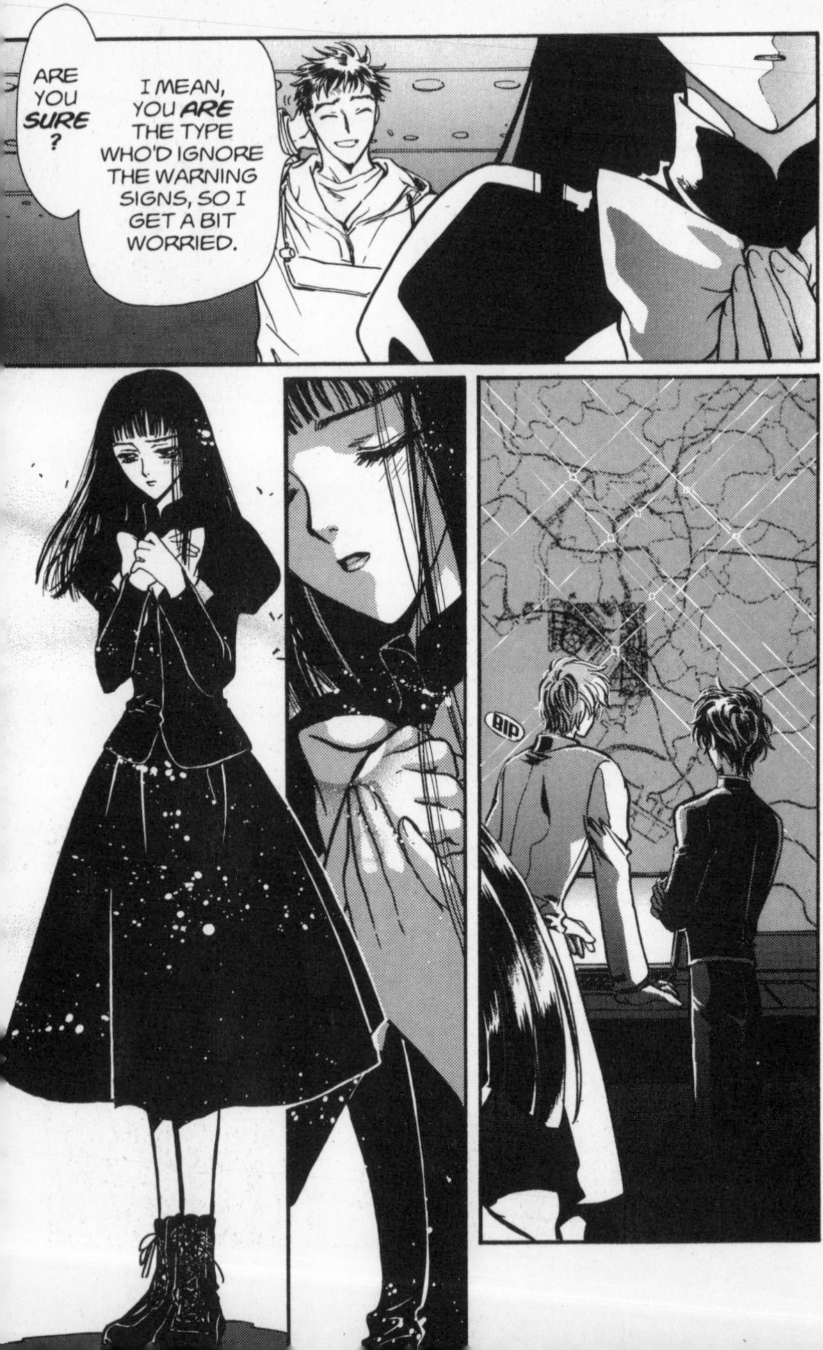
ARE YOU SURE ?
I MEAN, YOU ARE THE TYPE WHO'D IGNORE THE WARNING SIGNS, SO I GET A BIT WORRIED.
BIP

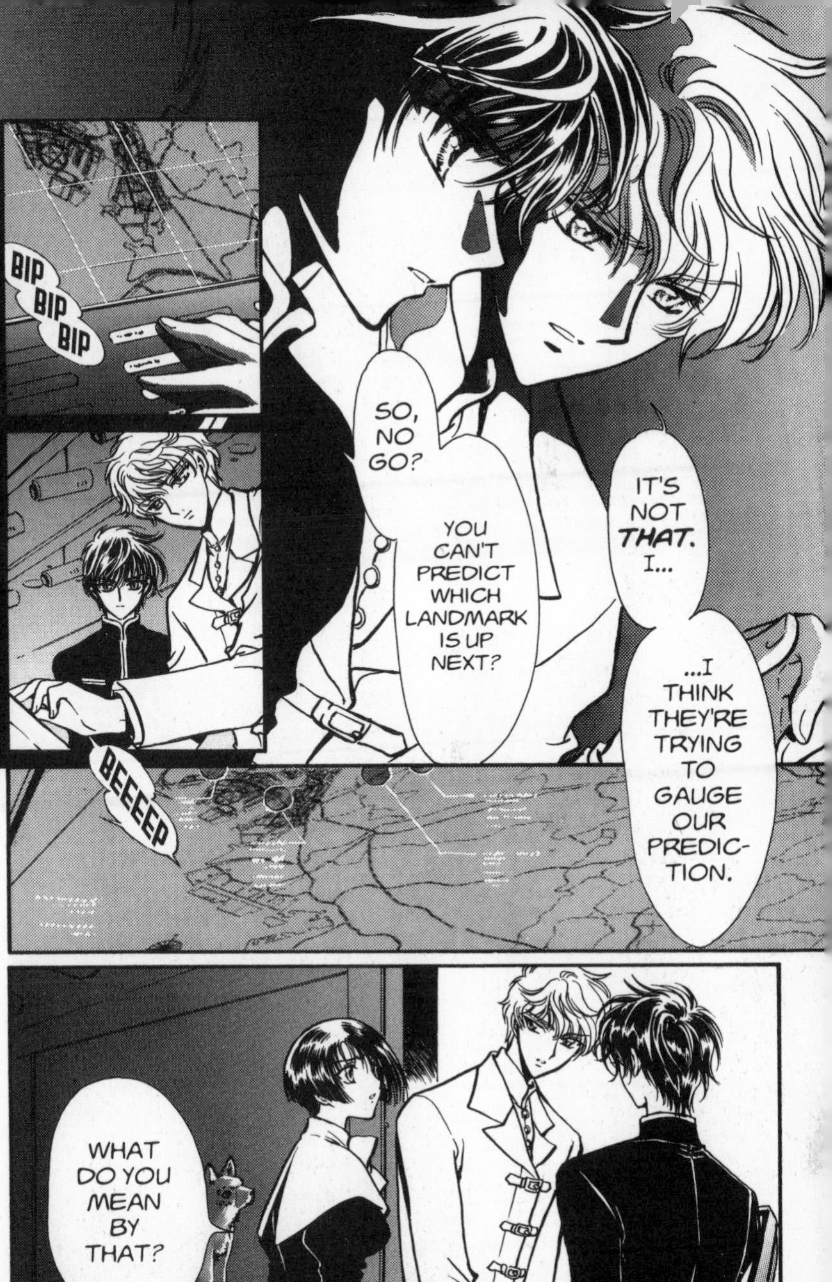
SO, NO GO?
YOU CAN'T PREDICT WHICH LANDMARK IS UP NEXT?
IT'S NOT *THAT*. I...
...I THINK THEY'RE TRYING TO GAUGE OUR PREDIC-TION.
BIP BIP BIP
BEEEEP
WHAT DO YOU MEAN BY THAT?

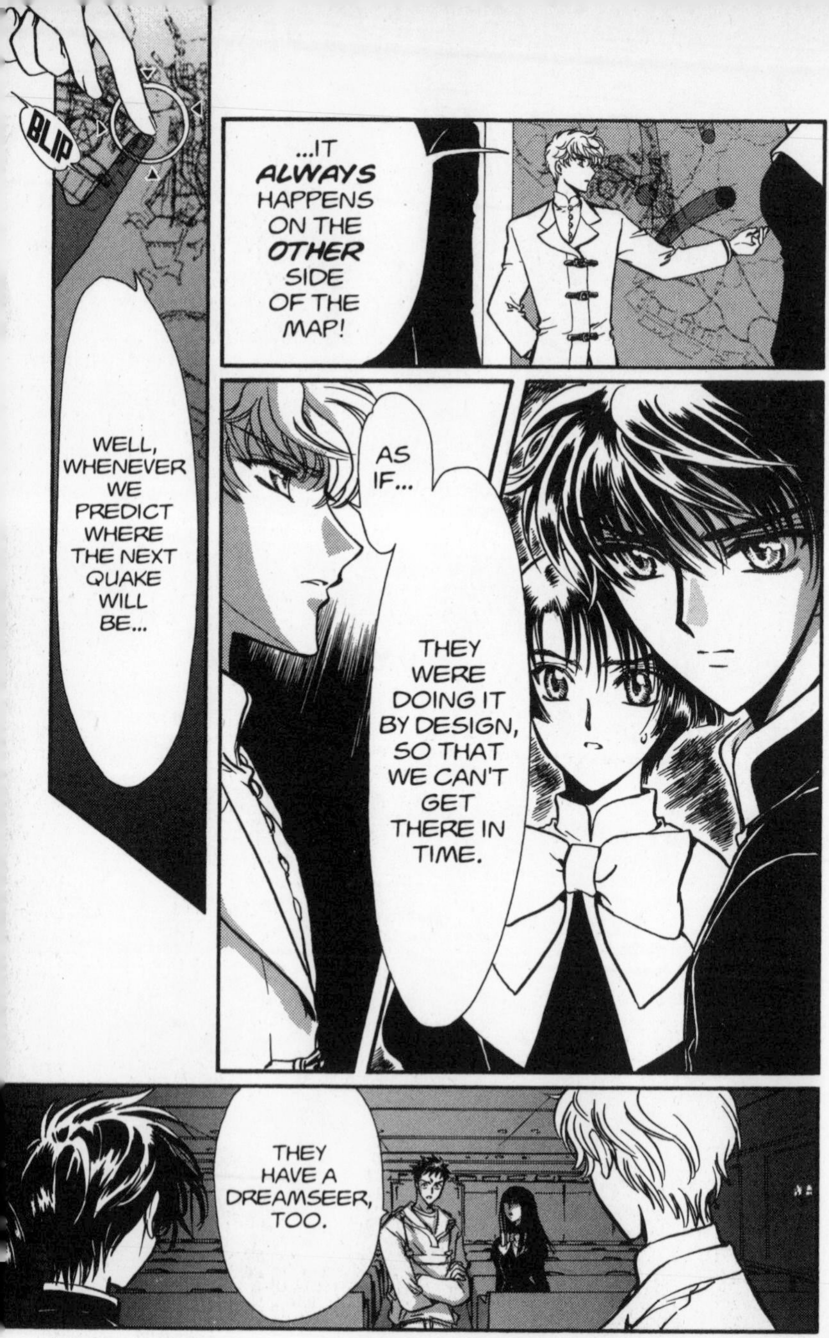
BLIP
WELL, WHENEVER WE PREDICT WHERE THE NEXT QUAKE WILL BE...
...IT ALWAYS HAPPENS ON THE OTHER SIDE OF THE MAP!
AS IF...
THEY WERE DOING IT BY DESIGN, SO THAT WE CAN'T GET THERE IN TIME.
THEY HAVE A DREAMSEER, TOO.

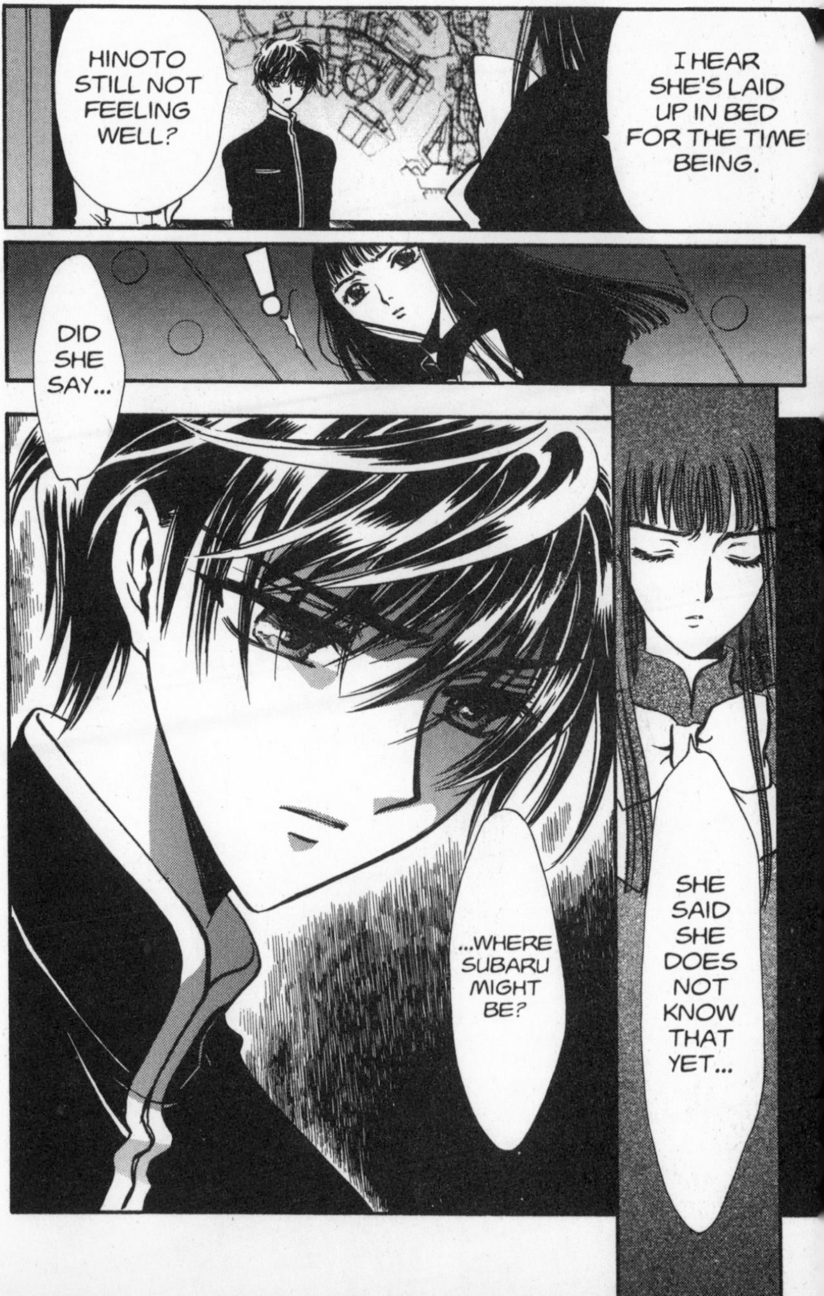
HINOTO STILL NOT FEELING WELL?
I HEAR SHE'S LAID UP IN BED FOR THE TIME BEING.
!
DID SHE SAY...
...WHERE SUBARU MIGHT BE?
SHE SAID SHE DOES NOT KNOW THAT YET...

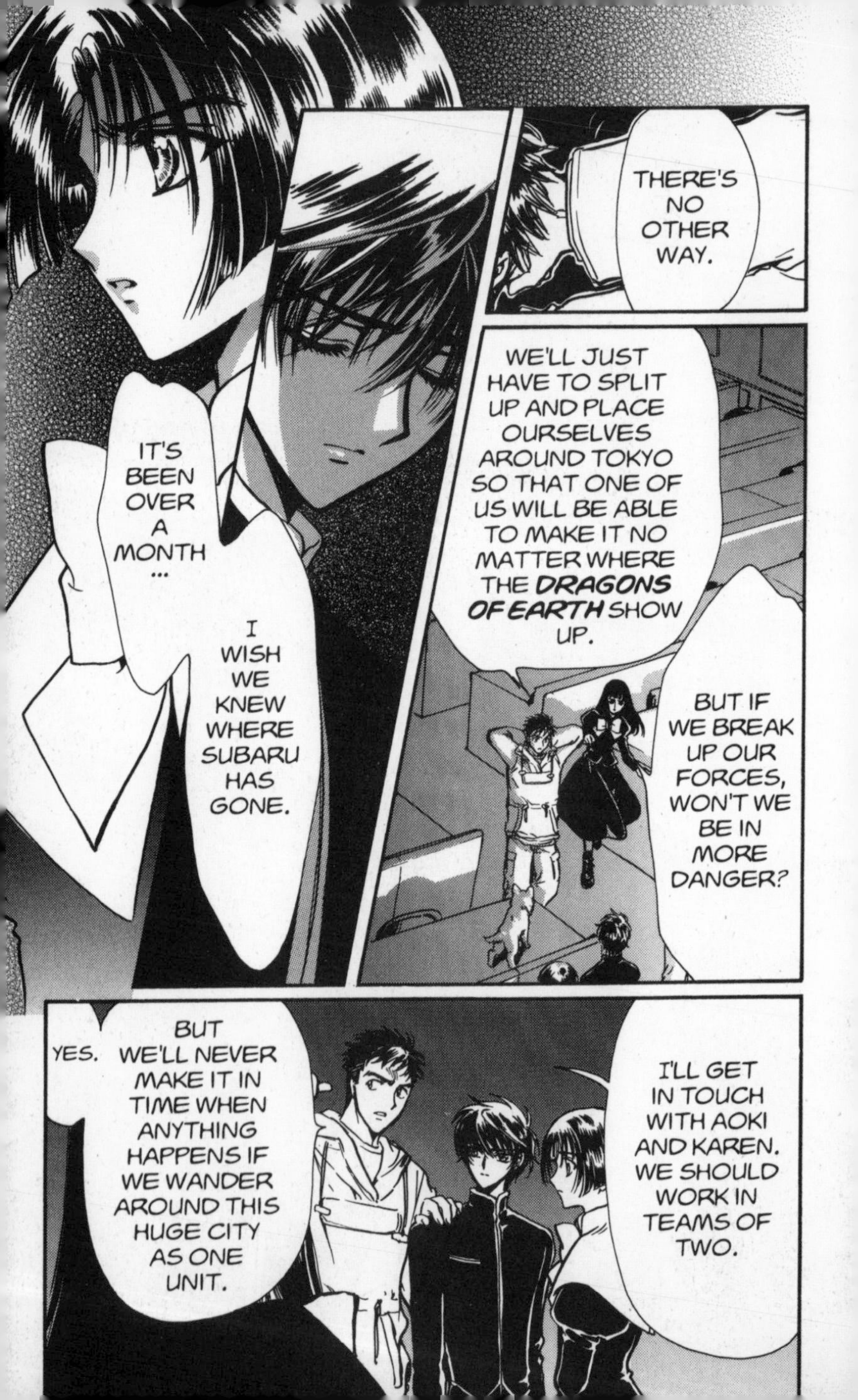
THERE'S NO OTHER WAY.
WE'LL JUST HAVE TO SPLIT UP AND PLACE OURSELVES AROUND TOKYO SO THAT ONE OF US WILL BE ABLE TO MAKE IT NO MATTER WHERE THE ***DRAGONS OF EARTH*** SHOW UP.
BUT IF WE BREAK UP OUR FORCES, WON'T WE BE IN MORE DANGER?
IT'S BEEN OVER A MONTH ...
I WISH WE KNEW WHERE SUBARU HAS GONE.
I'LL GET IN TOUCH WITH AOKI AND KAREN. WE SHOULD WORK IN TEAMS OF TWO.
BUT WE'LL NEVER MAKE IT IN TIME WHEN ANYTHING HAPPENS IF WE WANDER AROUND THIS HUGE CITY AS ONE UNIT.
YES.

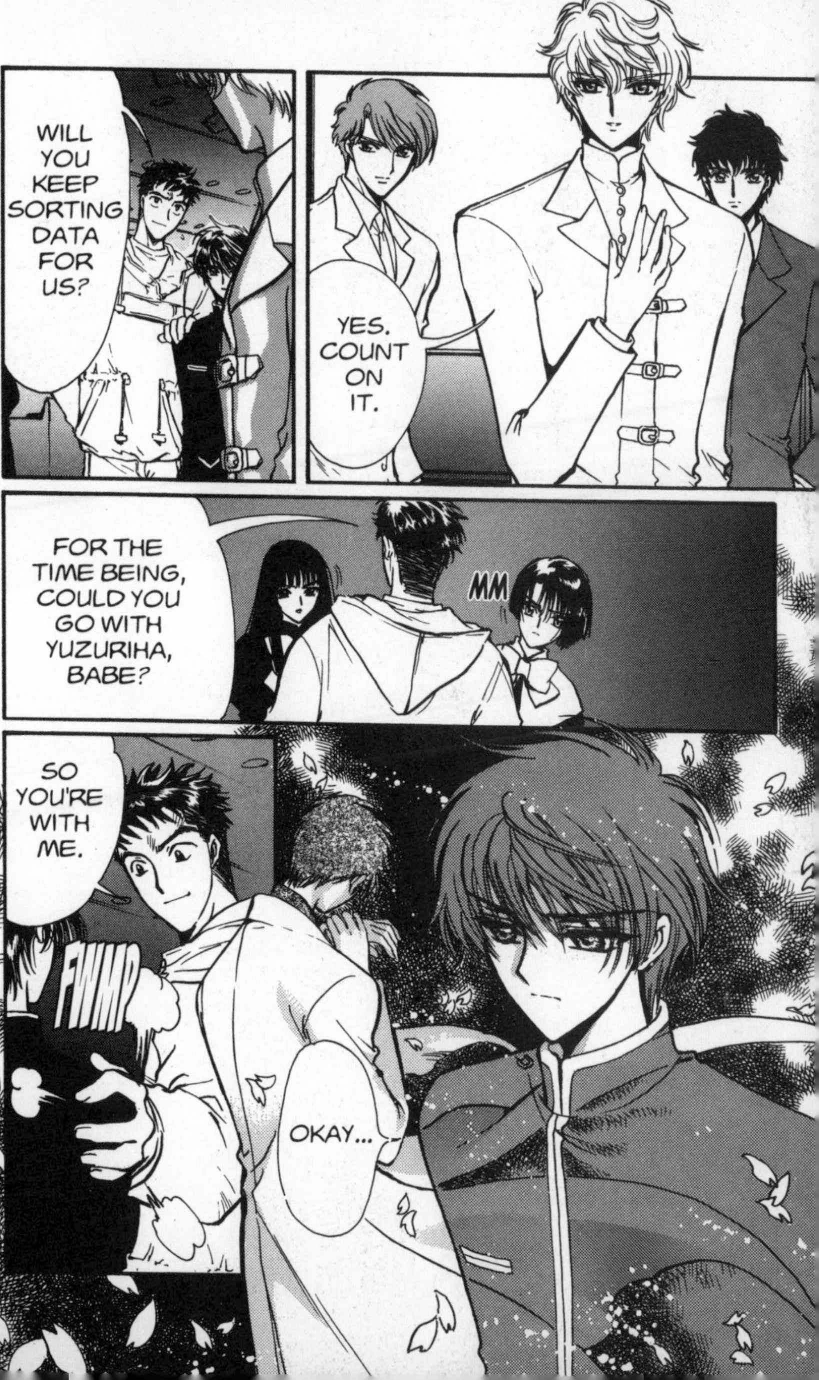
WILL YOU KEEP SORTING DATA FOR US?
YES. COUNT ON IT.
FOR THE TIME BEING, COULD YOU GO WITH YUZURIHA, BABE?
MM
SO YOU'RE WITH ME.
FWMP
OKAY...

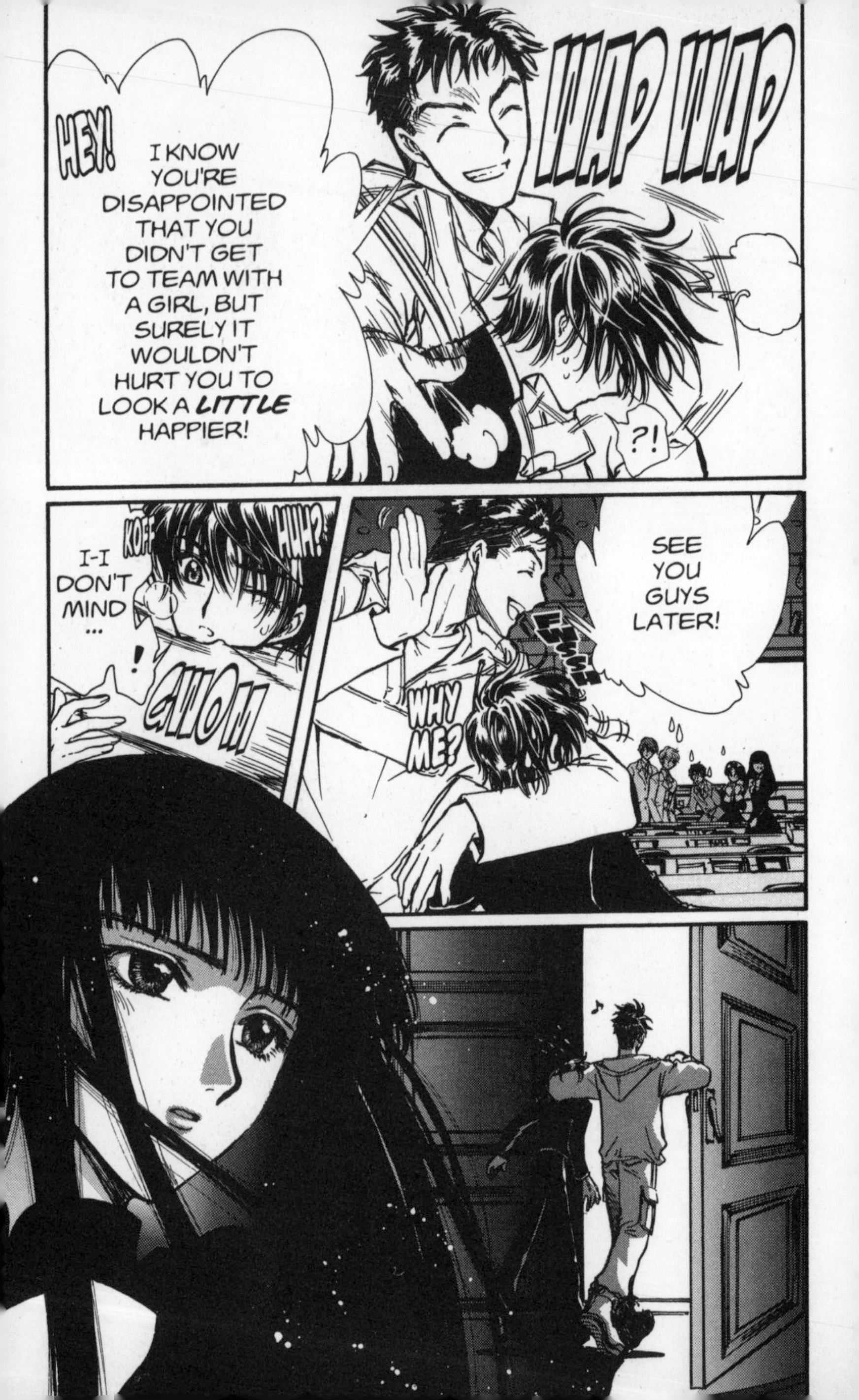
WAP WAP
HEY!
I KNOW YOU'RE DISAPPOINTED THAT YOU DIDN'T GET TO TEAM WITH A GIRL, BUT SURELY IT WOULDN'T HURT YOU TO LOOK A ***LITTLE*** HAPPIER!
?!
SEE YOU GUYS LATER!
FWSSH
WHY ME?
HUH?
KOFF
I-I DON'T MIND ...
!

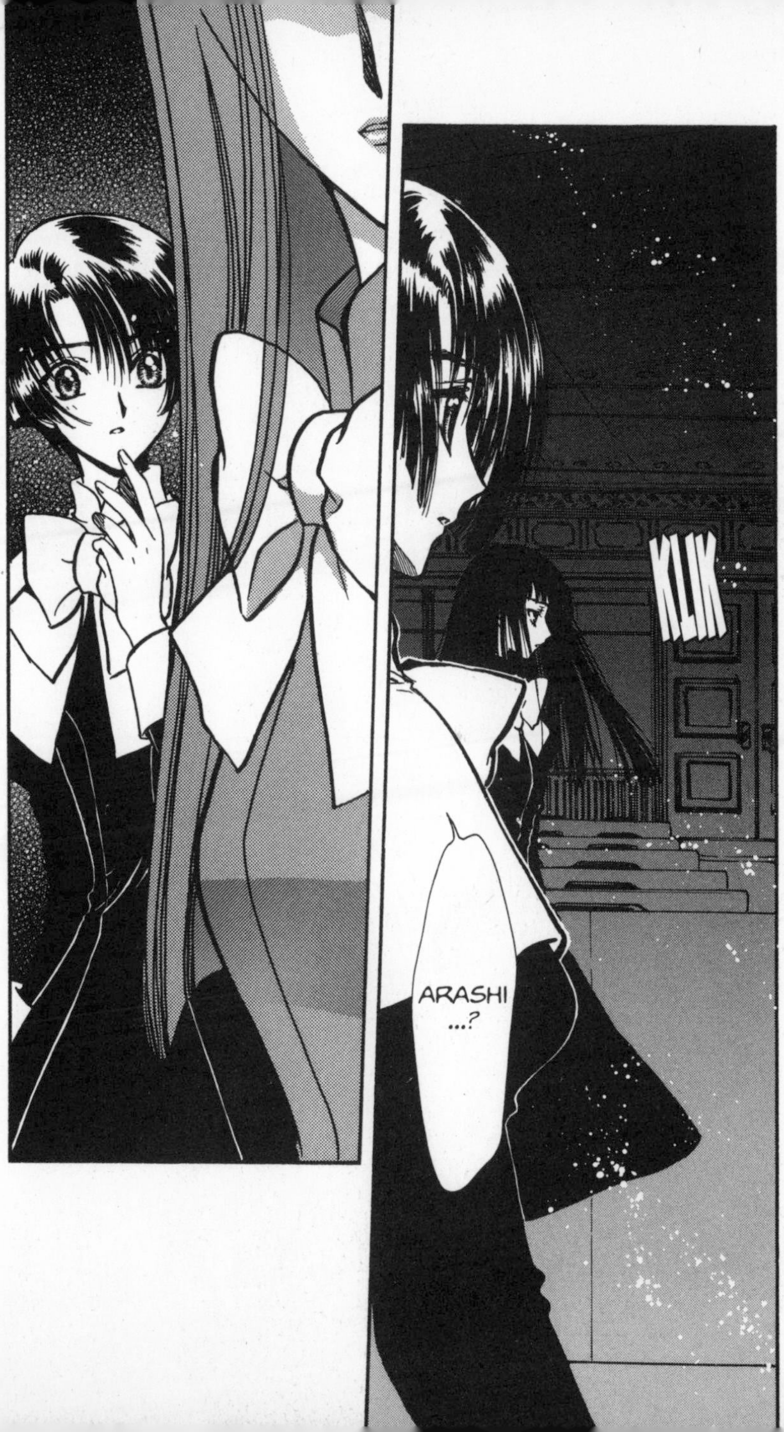
KLIK
ARASHI
...?

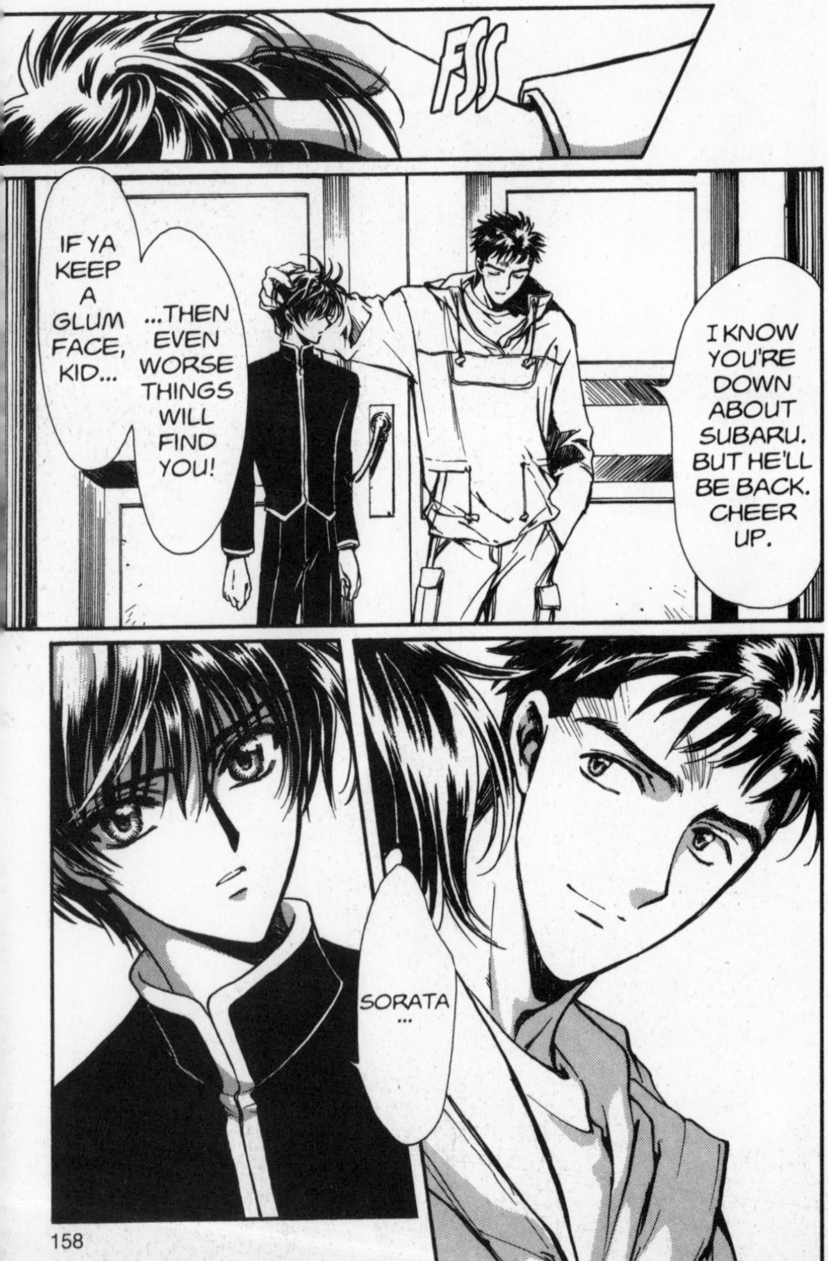
FSS
I KNOW YOU'RE DOWN ABOUT SUBARU. BUT HE'LL BE BACK. CHEER UP.
IF YA KEEP A GLUM FACE, KID...
...THEN EVEN WORSE THINGS WILL FIND YOU!
SORATA ...

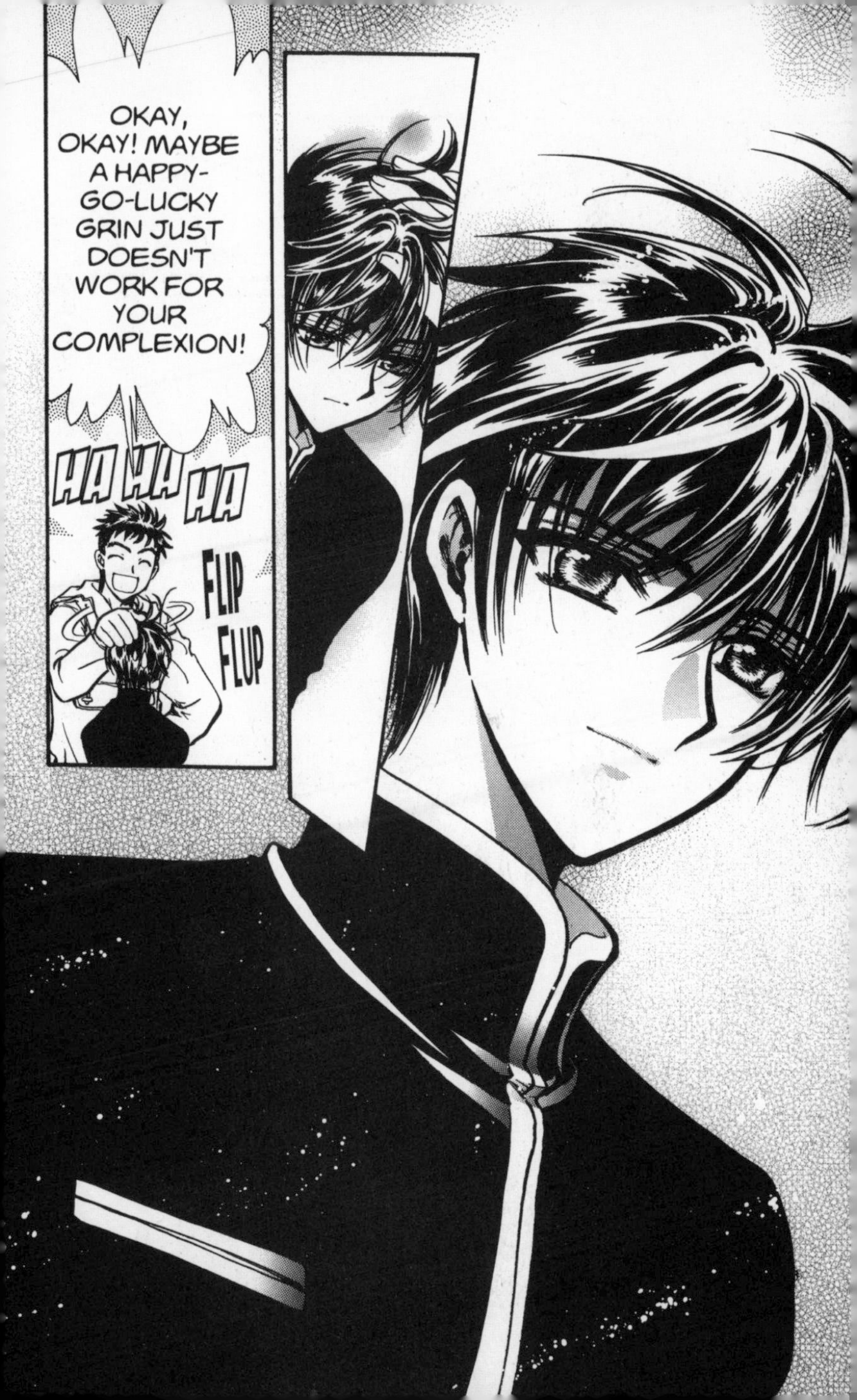
OKAY, OKAY! MAYBE A HAPPY-GO-LUCKY GRIN JUST DOESN'T WORK FOR YOUR COMPLEXION!
HA HA HA
FLIP FLUP

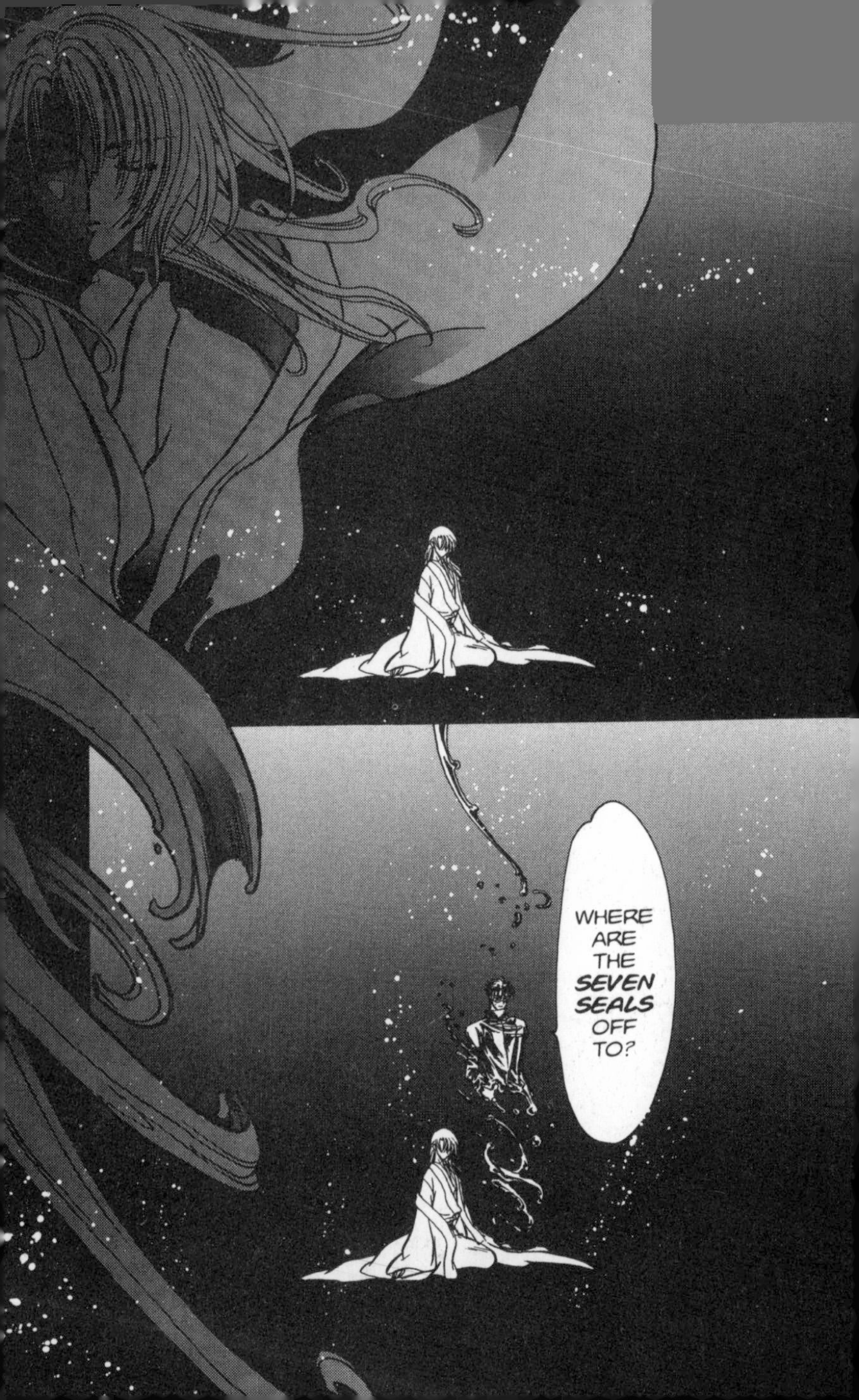
WHERE ARE THE SEVEN SEALS OFF TO?

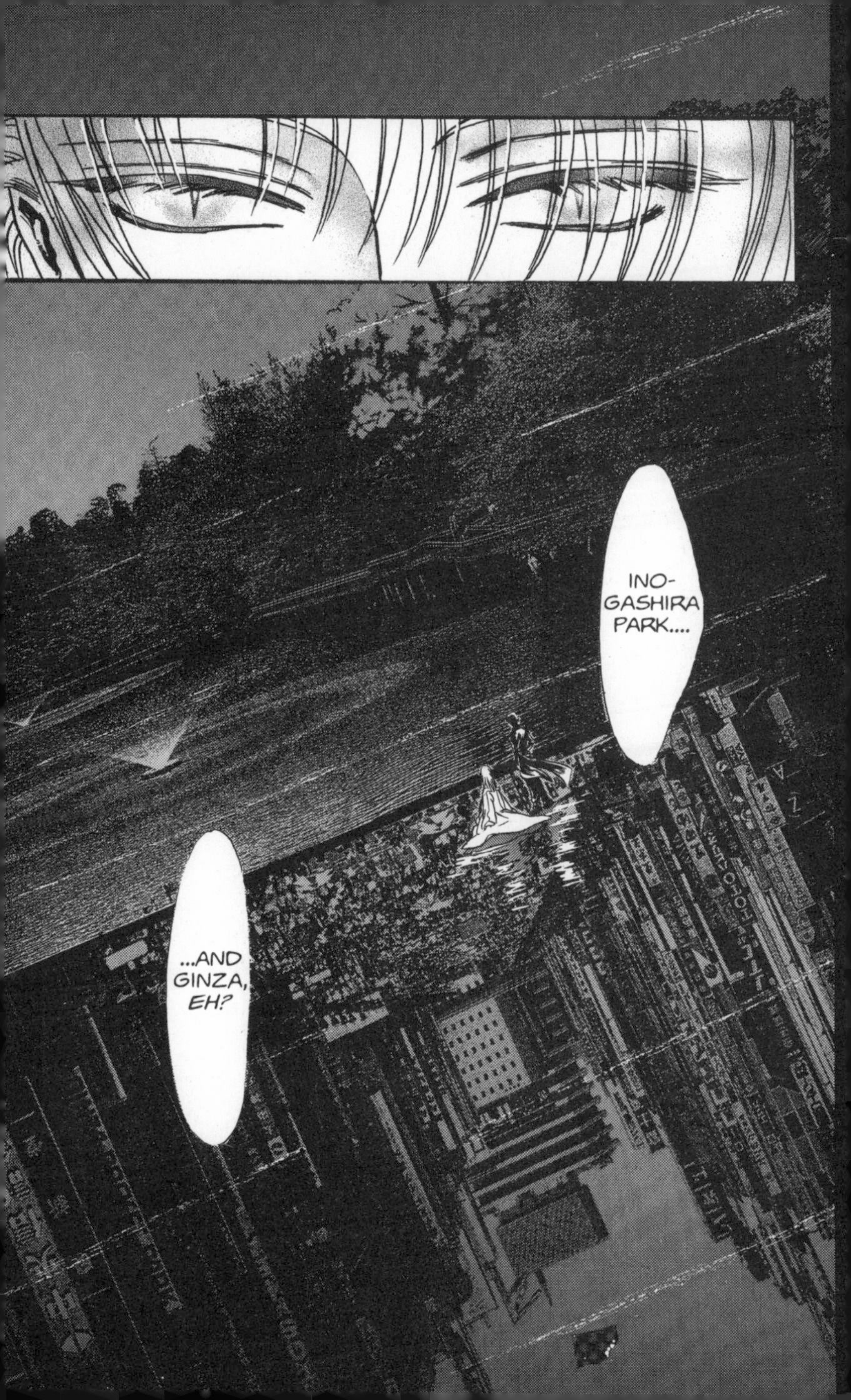
INO-GASHIRA PARK....
...AND GINZA, EH?

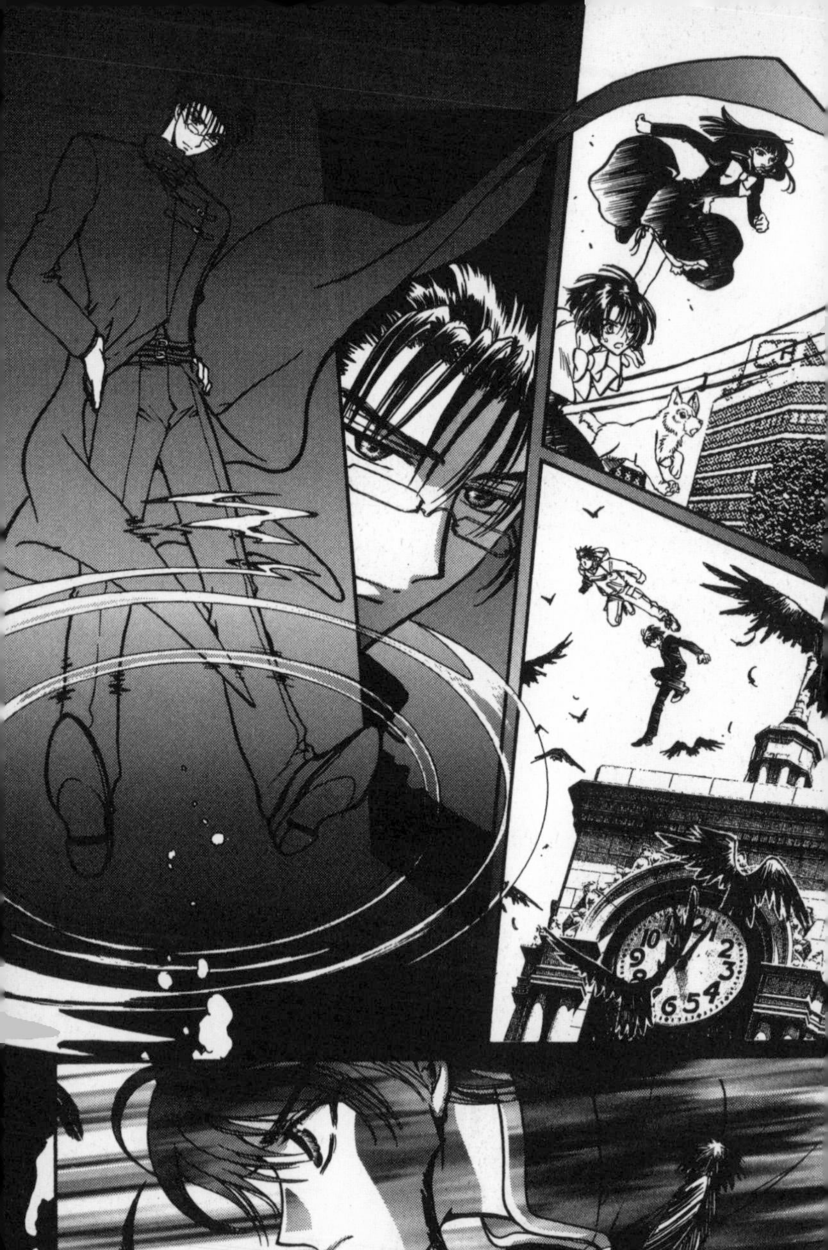

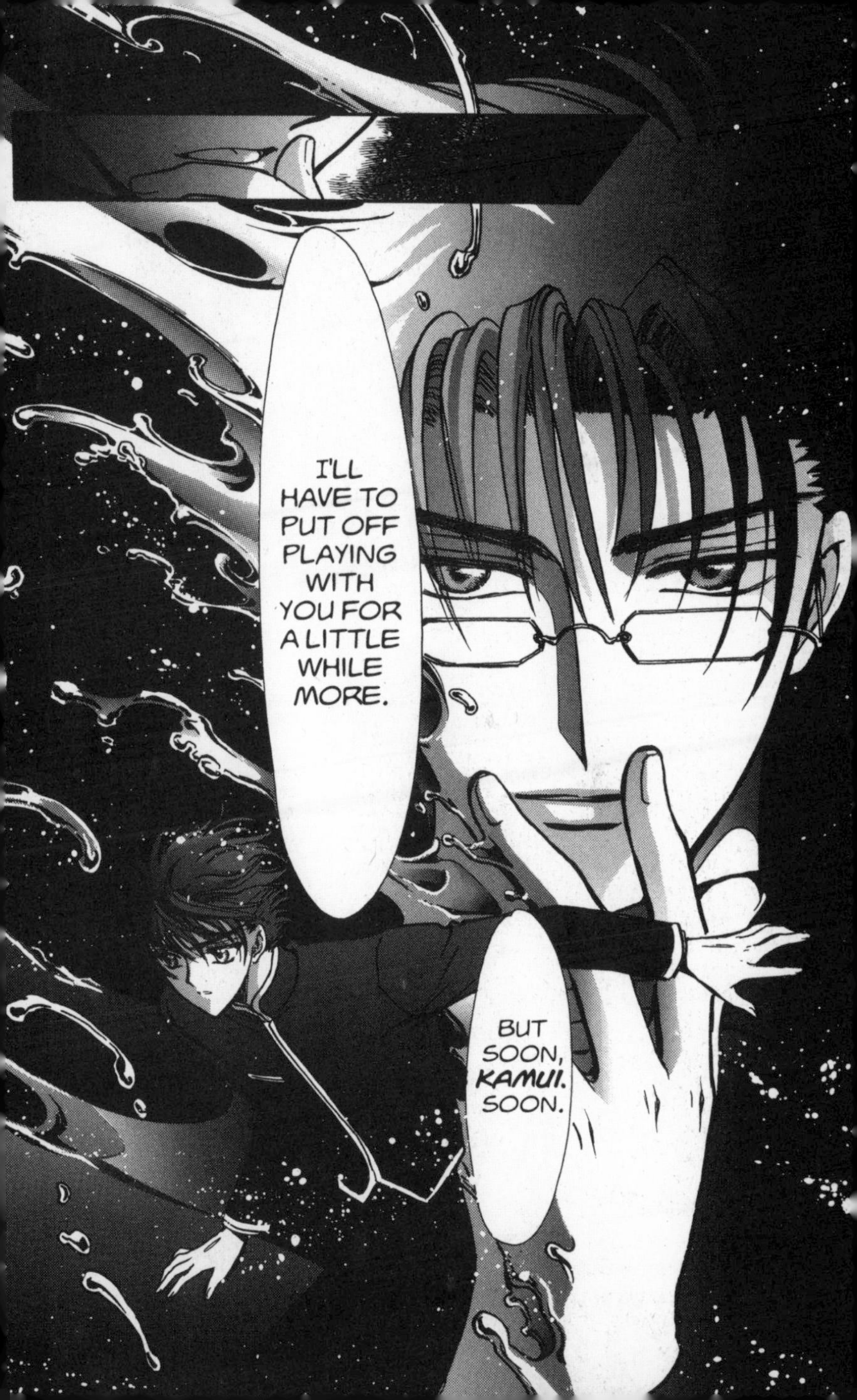
I'LL HAVE TO PUT OFF PLAYING WITH YOU FOR A LITTLE WHILE MORE.
BUT SOON, *KAMUI*. SOON.

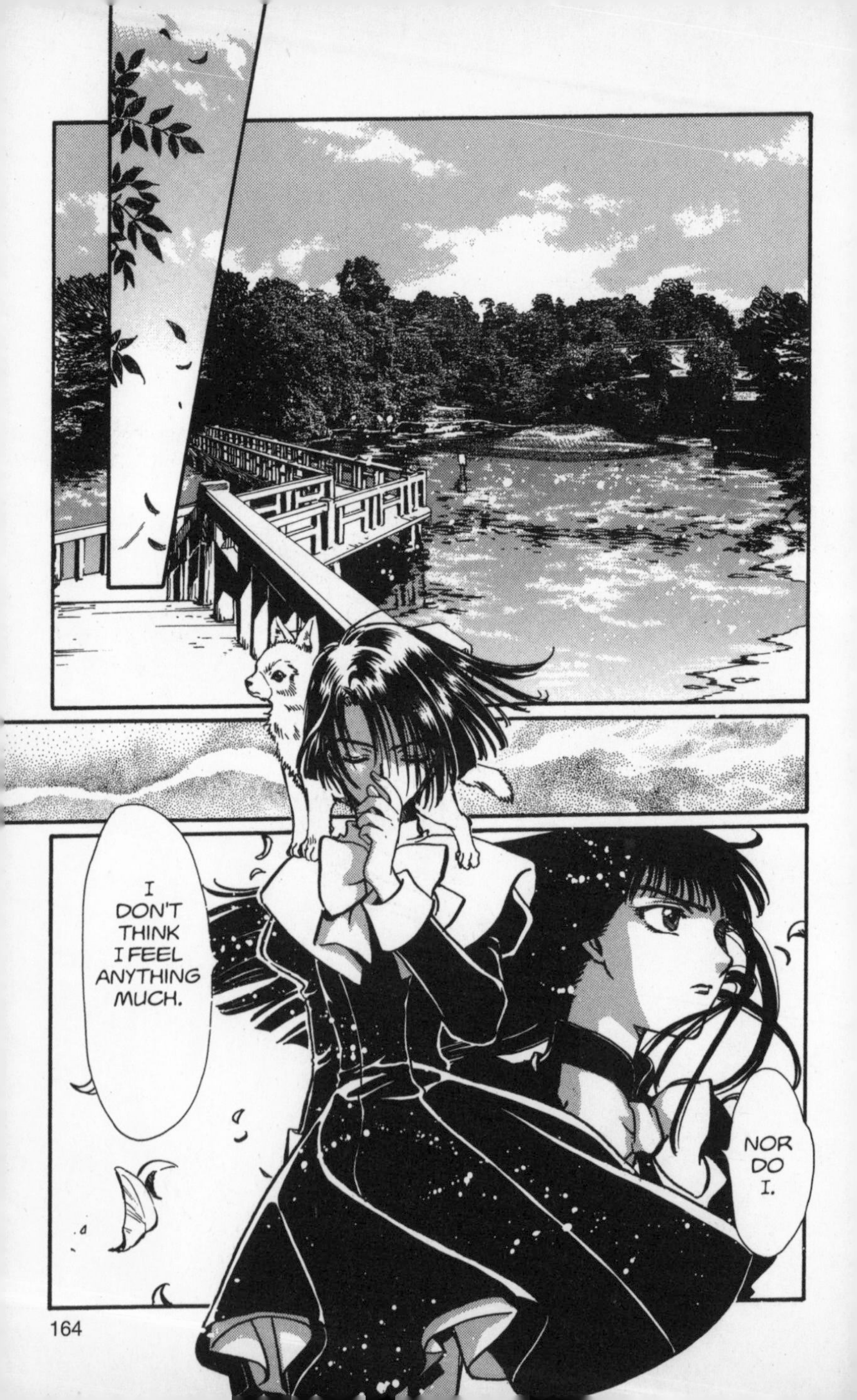
NOR DO I.
I DON'T THINK I FEEL ANYTHING MUCH.

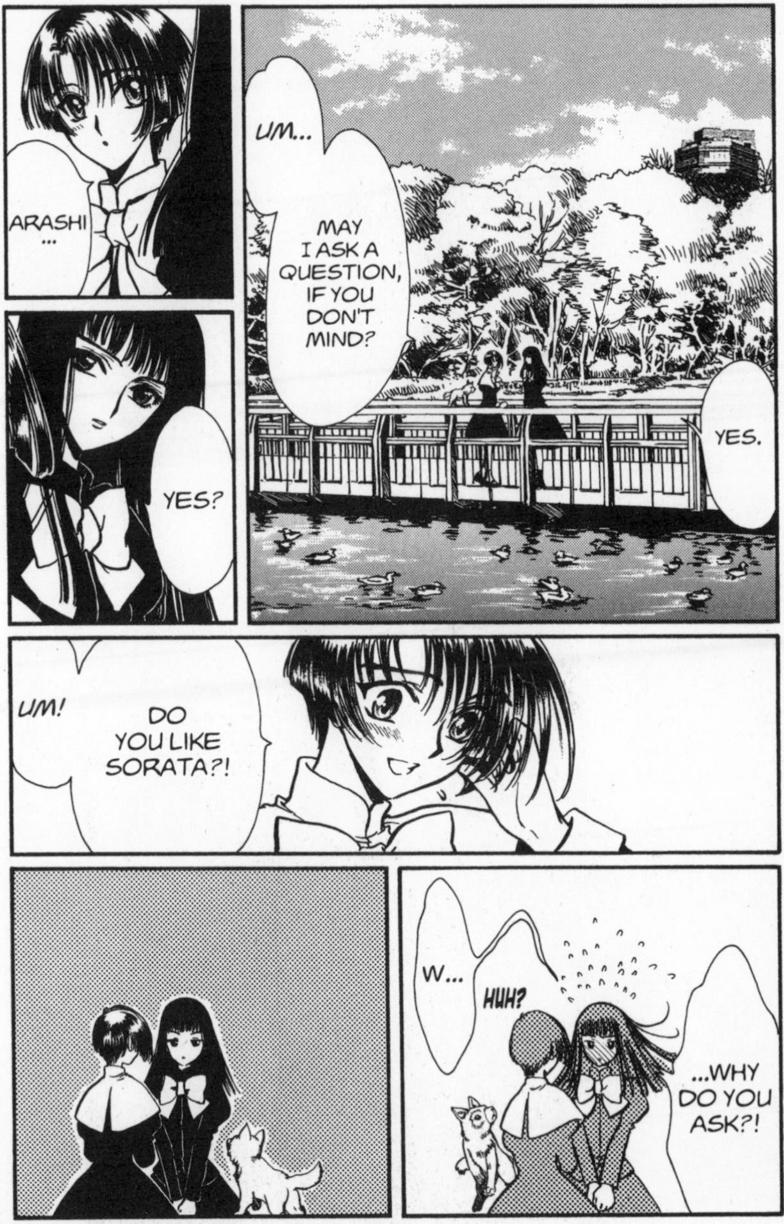
ARASHI ...
YES?
UM...
MAY I ASK A QUESTION, IF YOU DON'T MIND?
YES.
UM!
DO YOU LIKE SORATA?!
W...
HUH?
...WHY DO YOU ASK?!

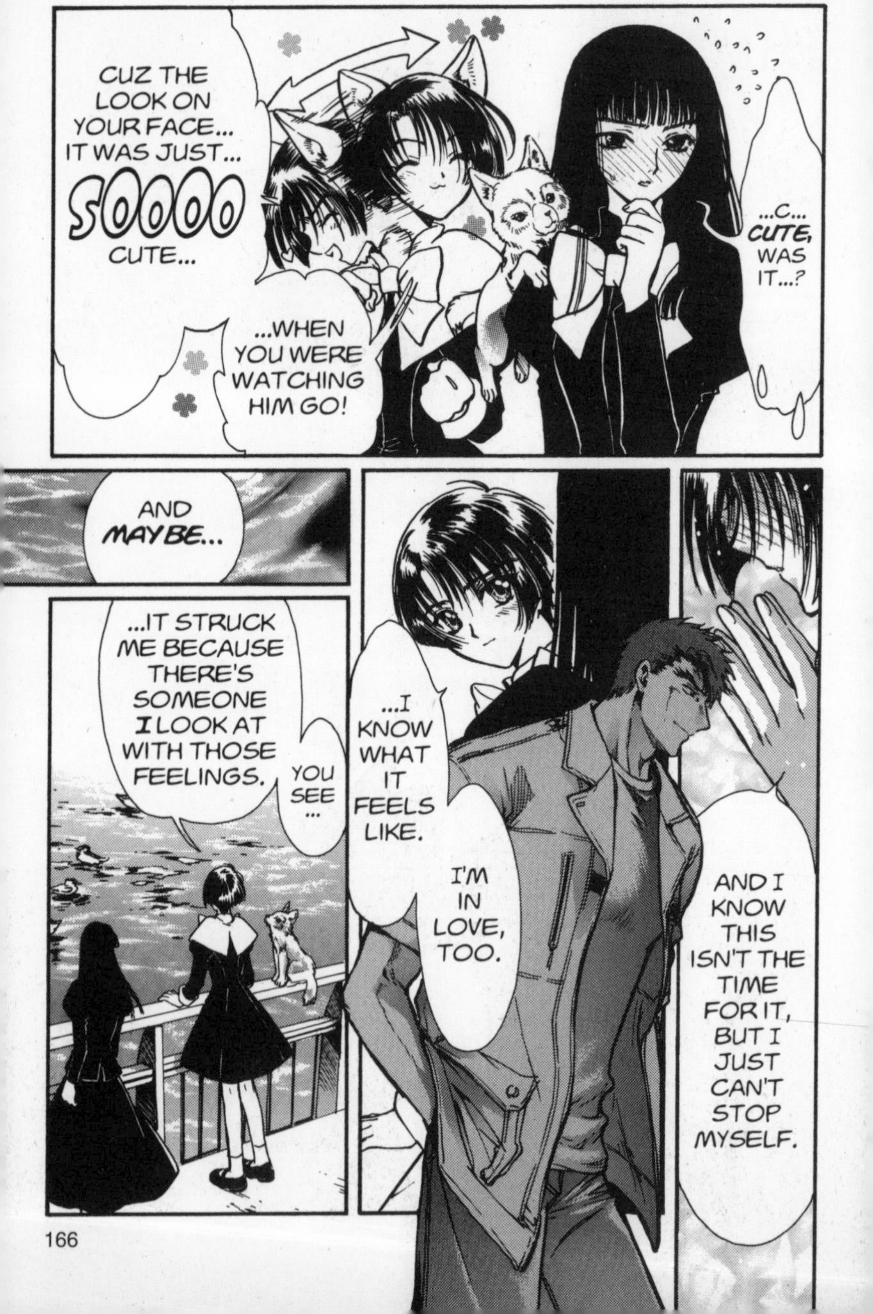
CUZ THE LOOK ON YOUR FACE... IT WAS JUST... SOOOO CUTE...
...WHEN YOU WERE WATCHING HIM GO!
...C... CUTE, WAS IT...?
AND MAYBE...
...IT STRUCK ME BECAUSE THERE'S SOMEONE I LOOK AT WITH THOSE FEELINGS.
YOU SEE ...
...I KNOW WHAT IT FEELS LIKE.
I'M IN LOVE, TOO.
AND I KNOW THIS ISN'T THE TIME FOR IT, BUT I JUST CAN'T STOP MYSELF.

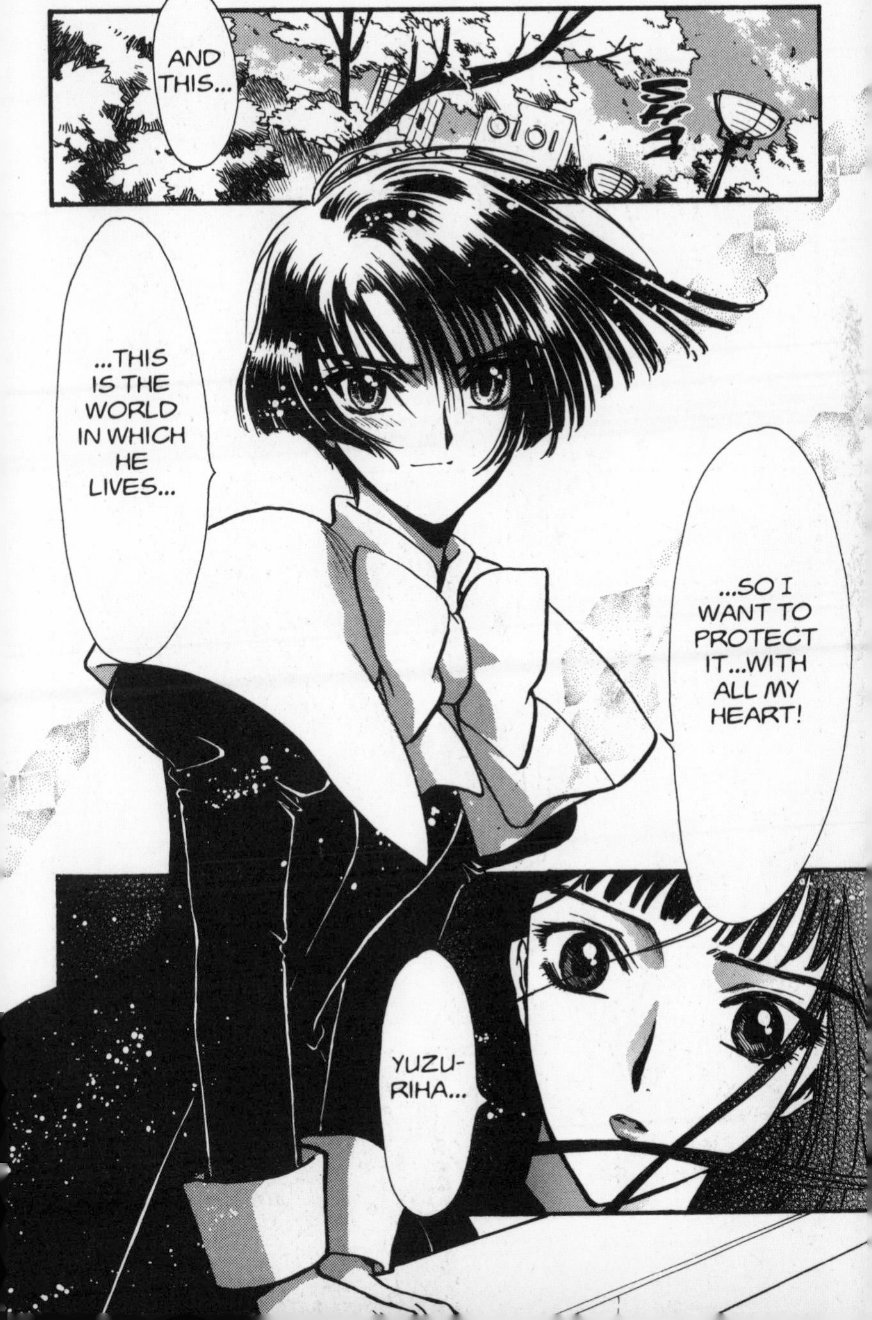
SHA
AND THIS...
...THIS IS THE WORLD IN WHICH HE LIVES...
...SO I WANT TO PROTECT IT...WITH ALL MY HEART!
YUZU-RIHA...

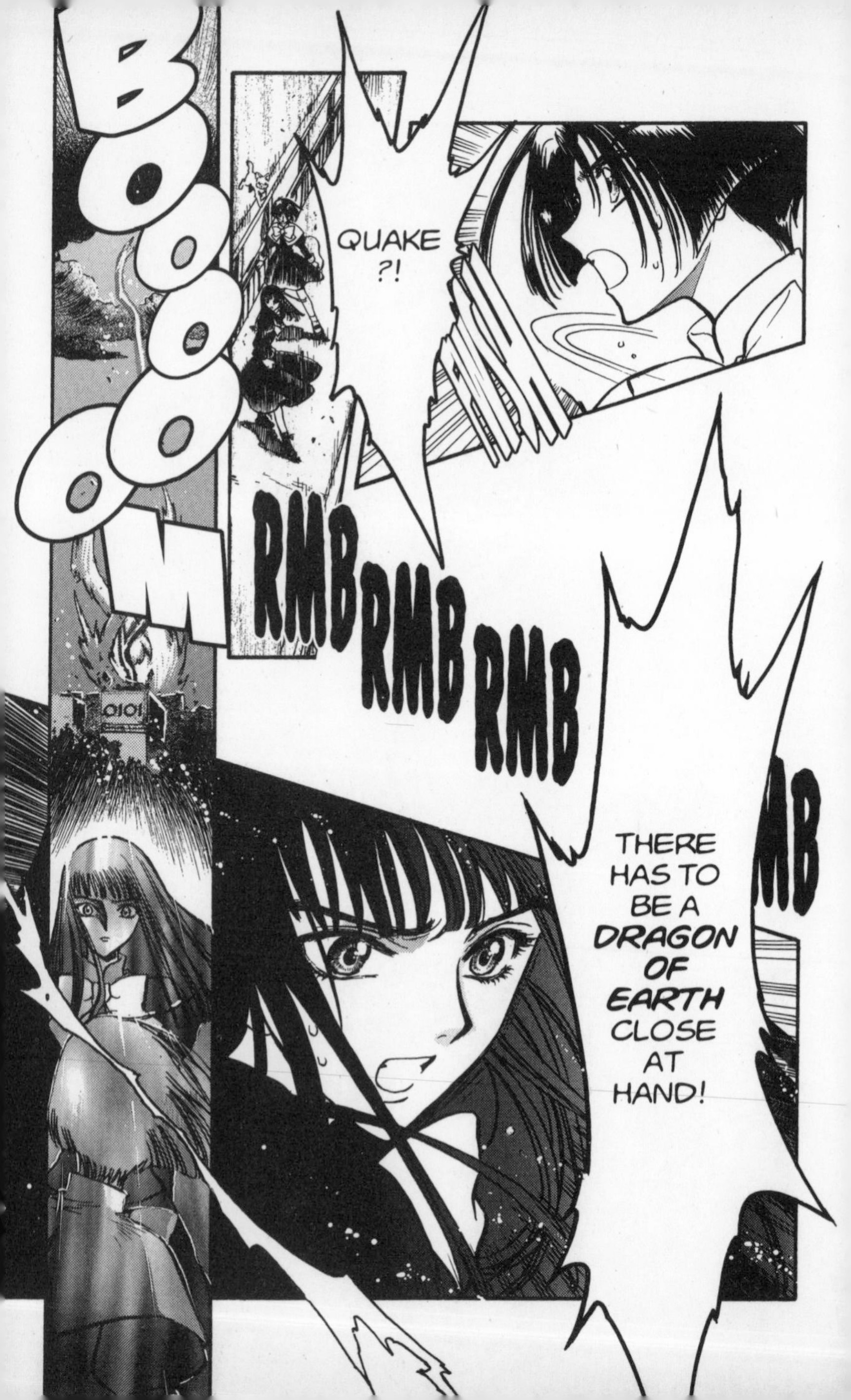
QUAKE ?!
BOOOOOOM
RMB RMB RMB RMB
THERE HAS TO BE A DRAGON OF EARTH CLOSE AT HAND!

$$X \boxed{16} \textbf{END}$$

X

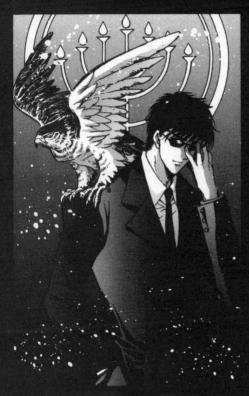

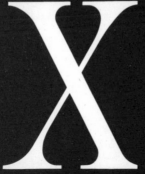

SEISHIRO SAKURAZUKA

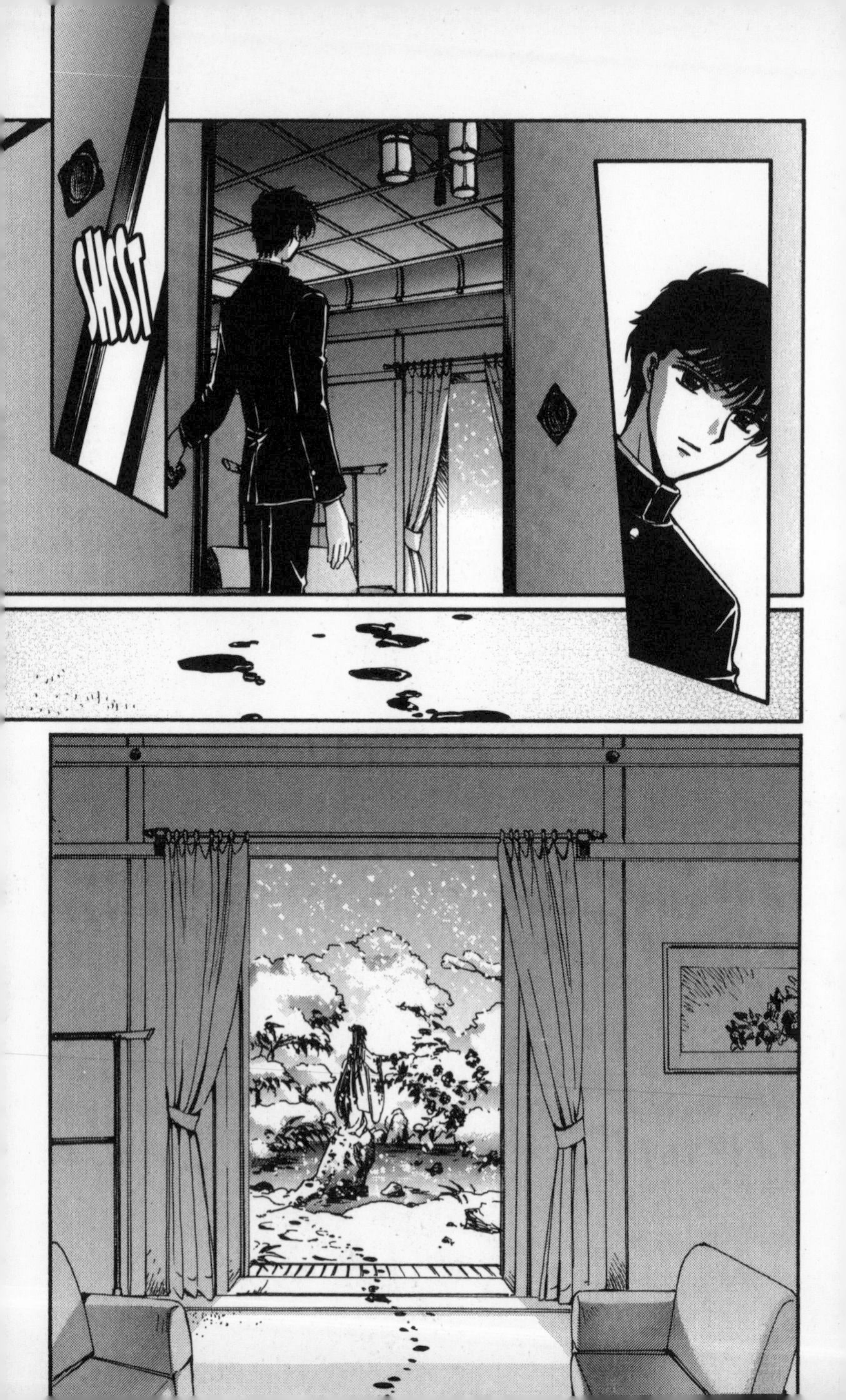
SHSST

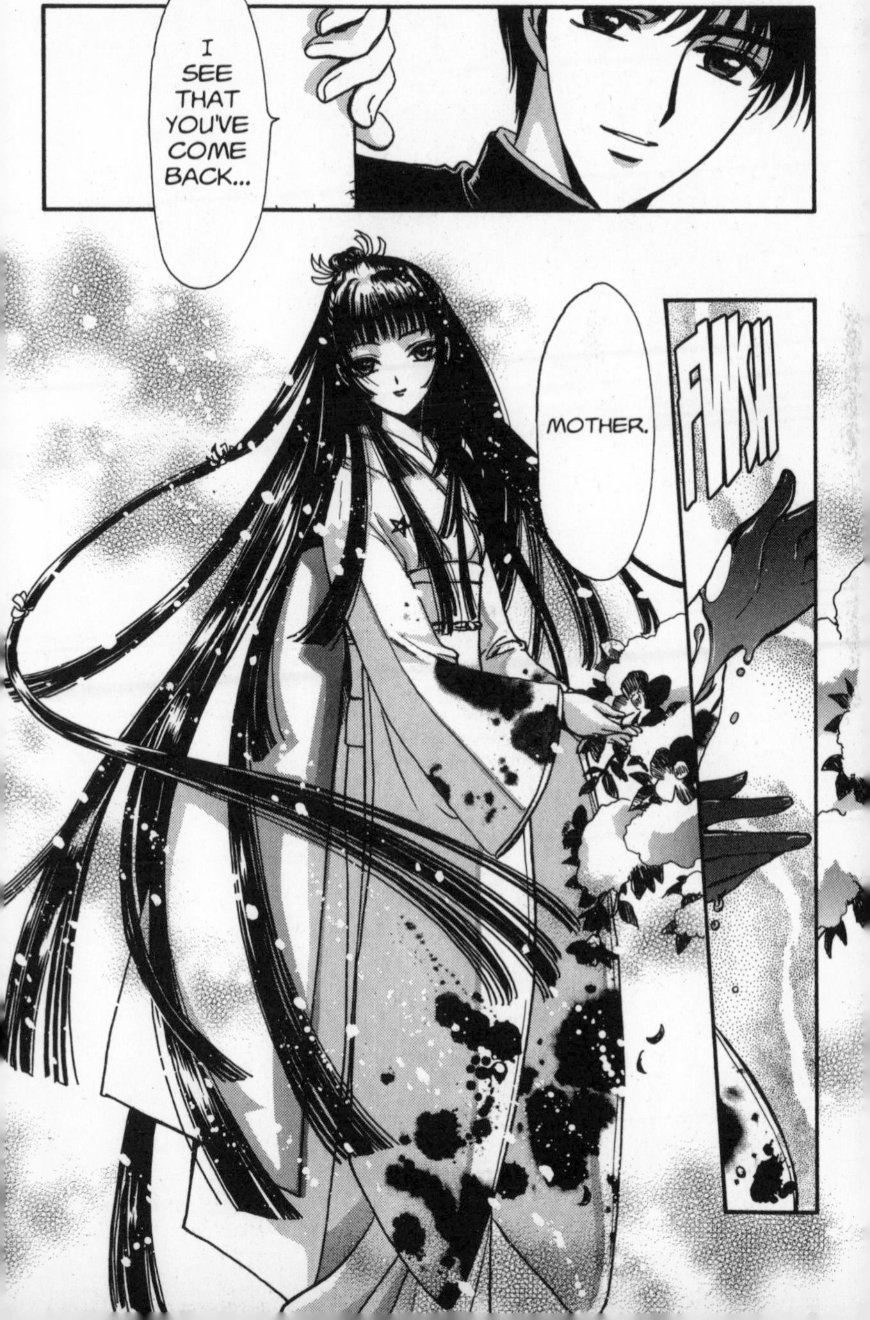
I SEE THAT YOU'VE COME BACK...
MOTHER.
FWISH

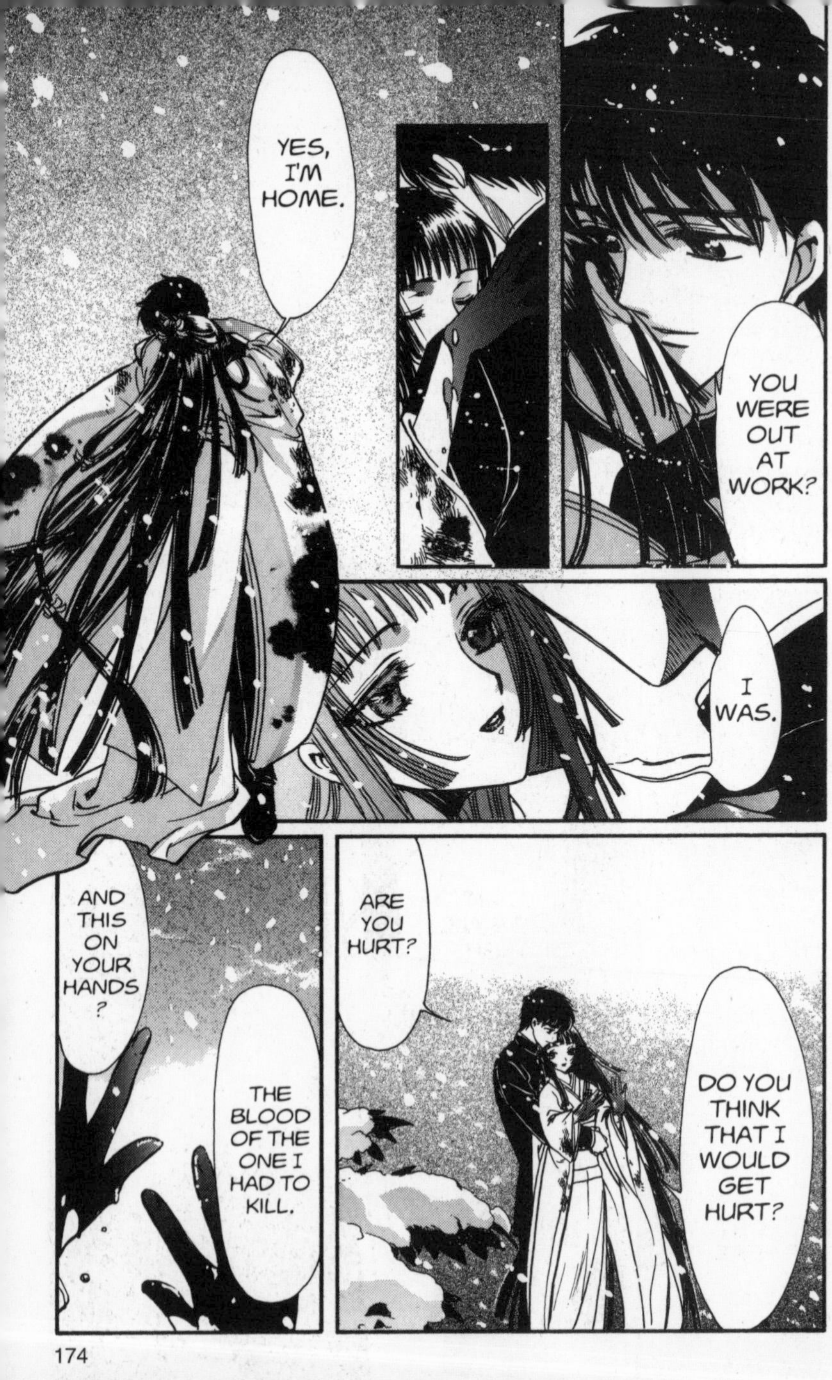
YES, I'M HOME.
YOU WERE OUT AT WORK?
I WAS.
ARE YOU HURT?
DO YOU THINK THAT I WOULD GET HURT?
AND THIS ON YOUR HANDS?
THE BLOOD OF THE ONE I HAD TO KILL.

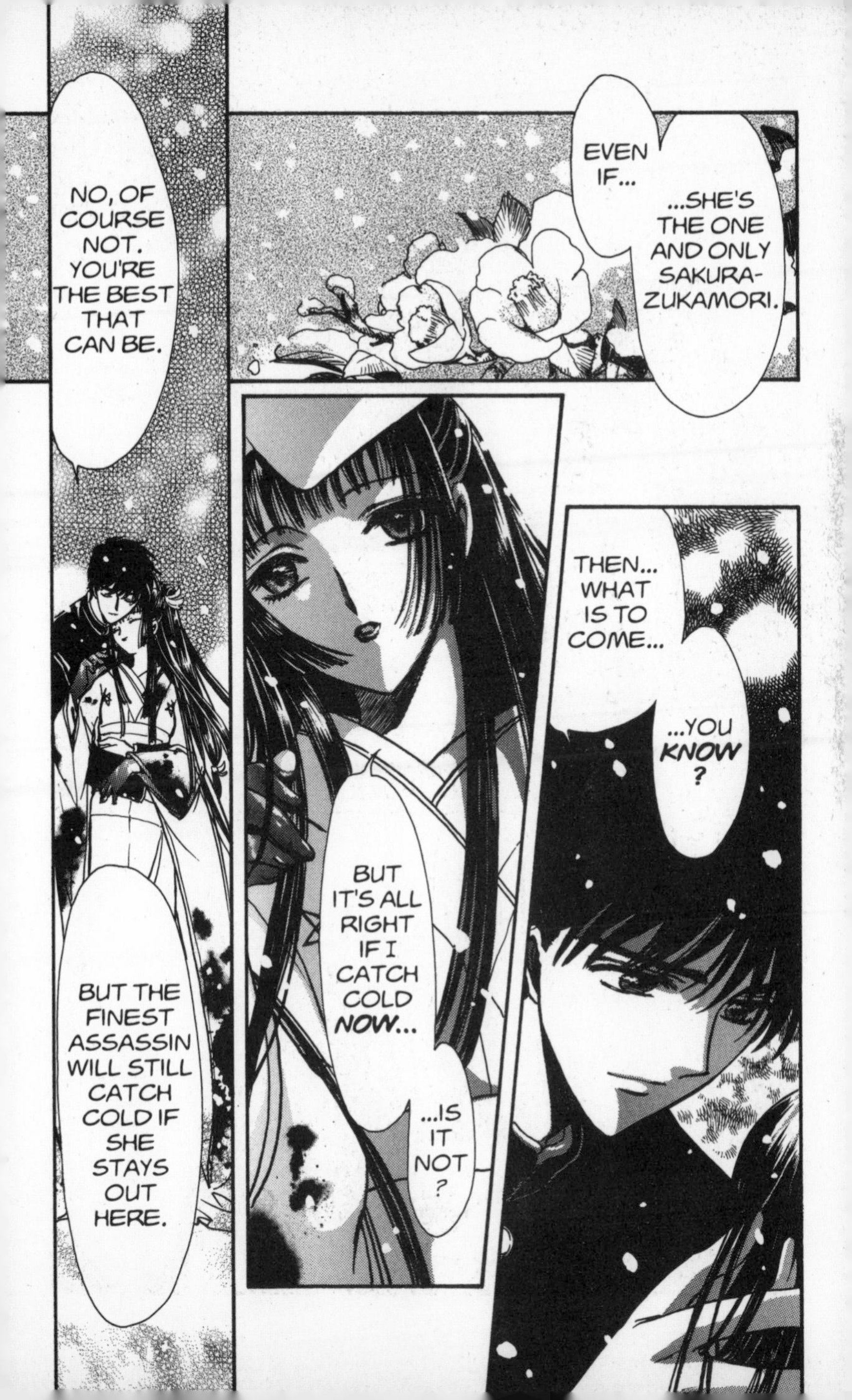
EVEN IF...
...SHE'S THE ONE AND ONLY SAKURA-ZUKAMORI.
THEN... WHAT IS TO COME...
...YOU *KNOW* ?
BUT IT'S ALL RIGHT IF I CATCH COLD *NOW*...
...IS IT NOT ?
NO, OF COURSE NOT. YOU'RE THE BEST THAT CAN BE.
BUT THE FINEST ASSASSIN WILL STILL CATCH COLD IF SHE STAYS OUT HERE.

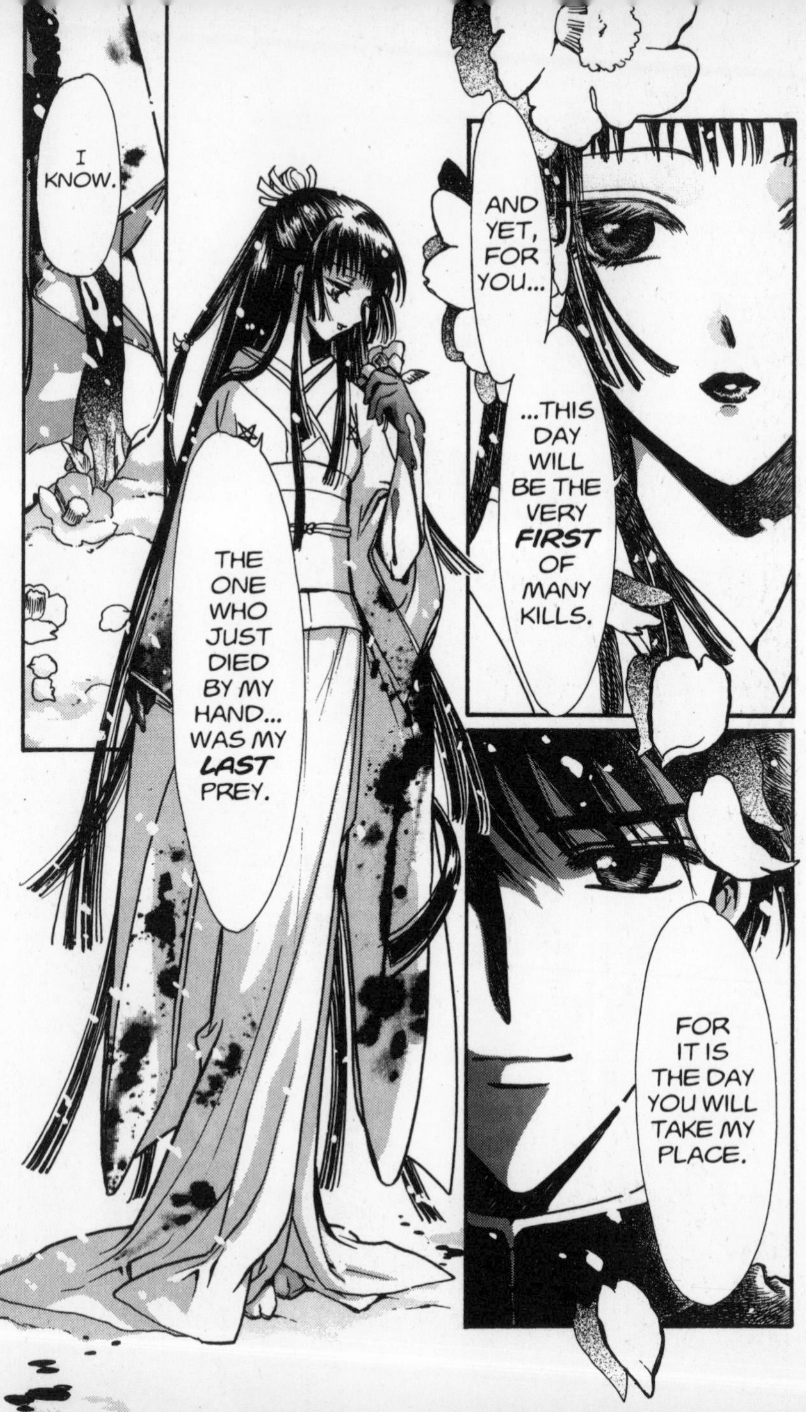
THE ONE WHO JUST DIED BY MY HAND... WAS MY *LAST* PREY.
I KNOW.
AND YET, FOR YOU...
...THIS DAY WILL BE THE VERY *FIRST* OF MANY KILLS.
FOR IT IS THE DAY YOU WILL TAKE MY PLACE.

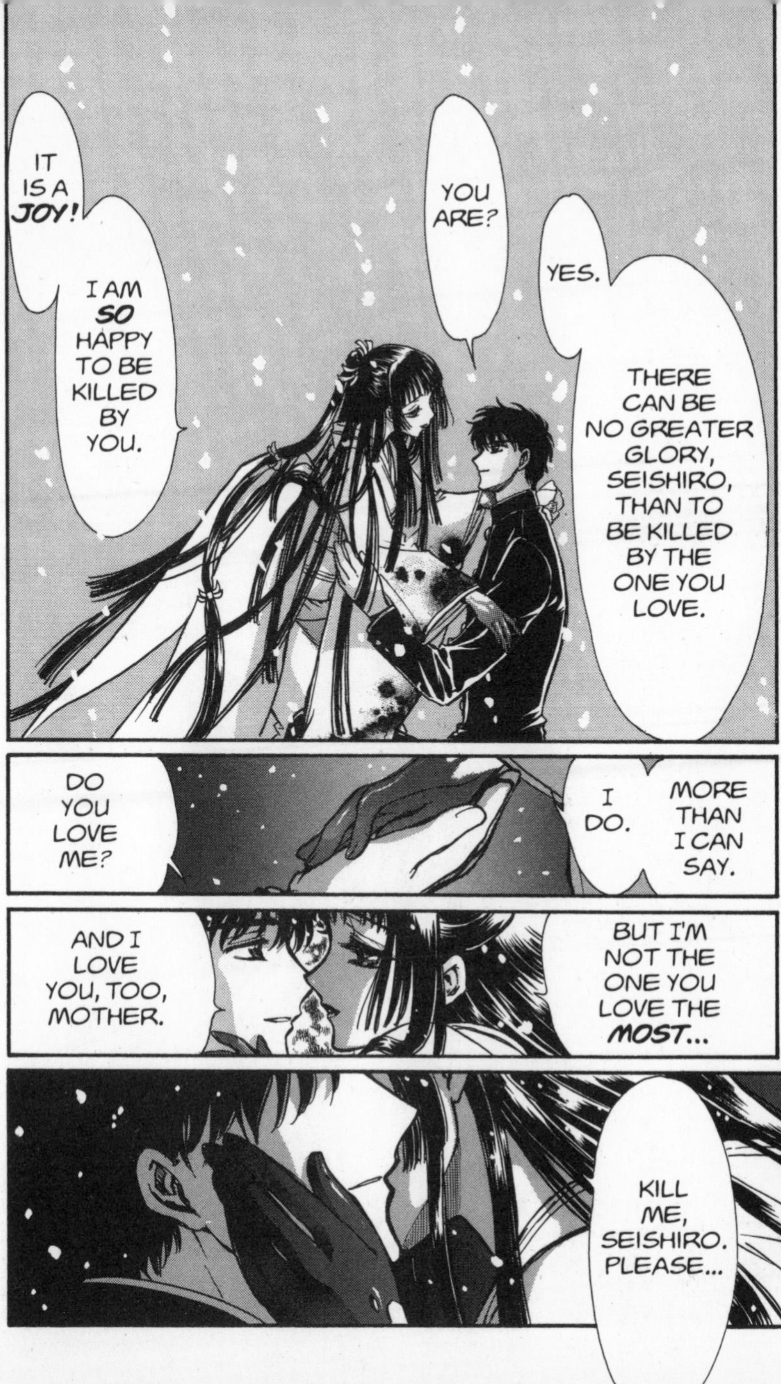

IT IS A ***JOY!***
I AM ***SO*** HAPPY TO BE KILLED BY YOU.
YOU ARE?
YES.
THERE CAN BE NO GREATER GLORY, SEISHIRO, THAN TO BE KILLED BY THE ONE YOU LOVE.
DO YOU LOVE ME?
I DO.
MORE THAN I CAN SAY.
AND I LOVE YOU, TOO, MOTHER.
BUT I'M NOT THE ONE YOU LOVE THE ***MOST...***
KILL ME, SEISHIRO. PLEASE...

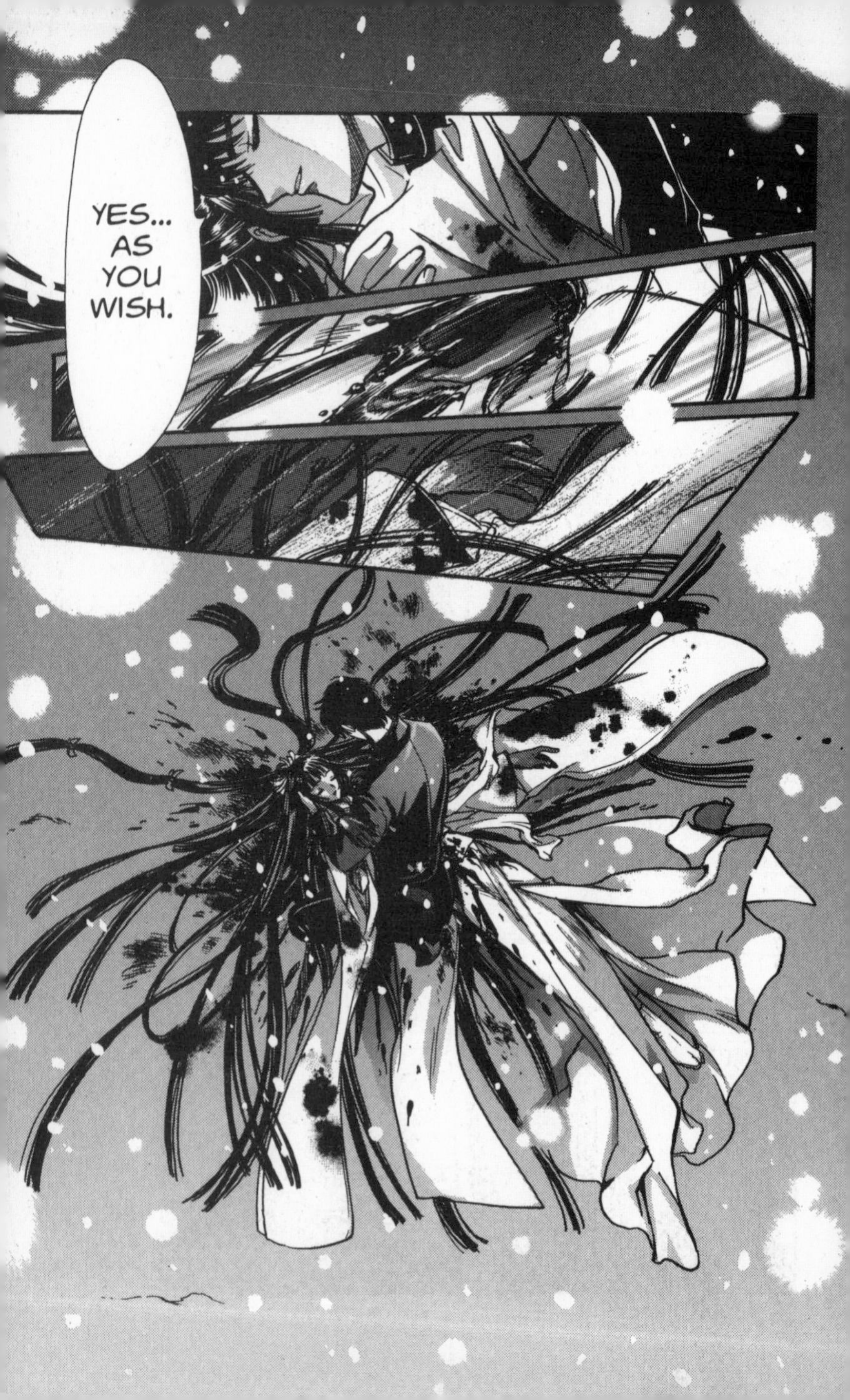
YES... AS YOU WISH.

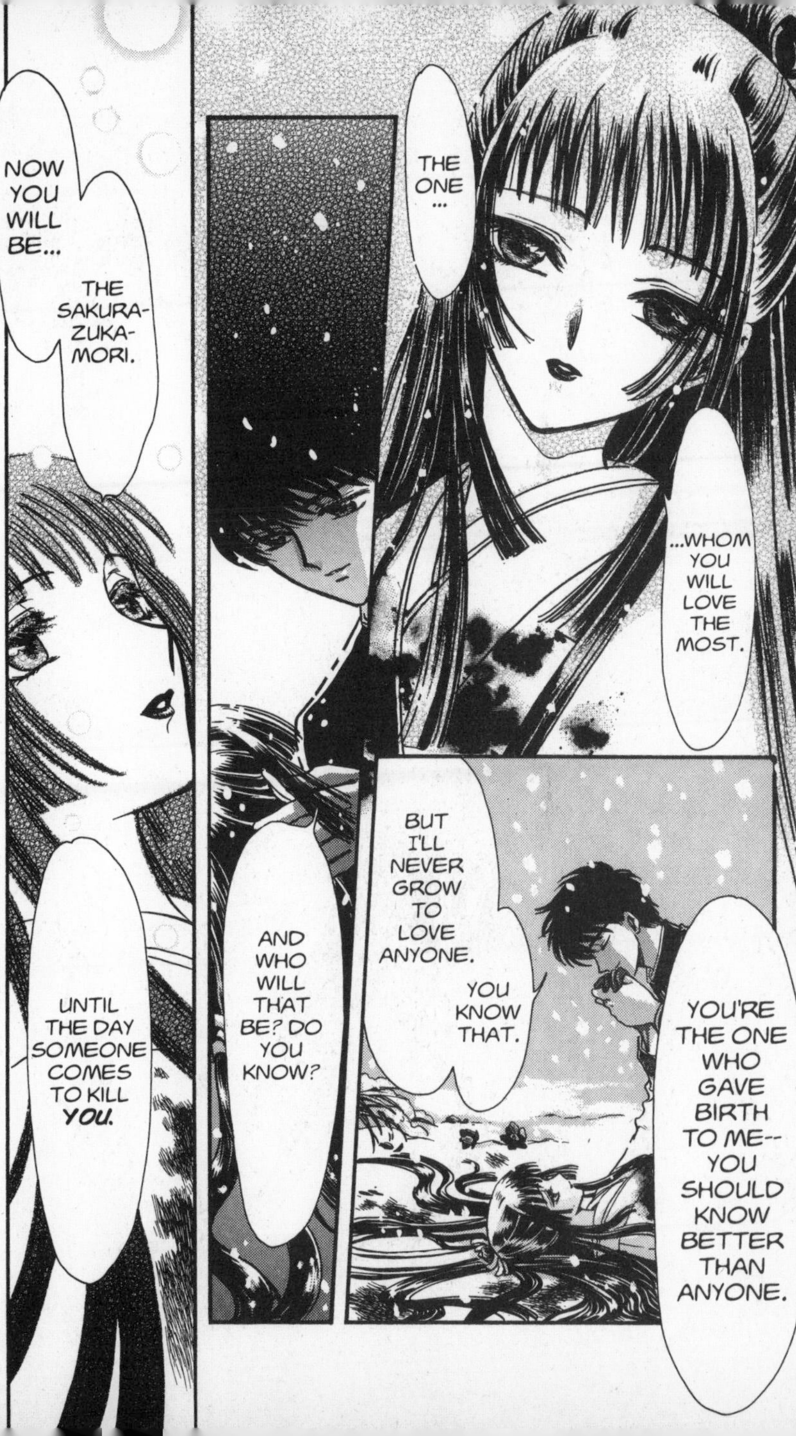
THE ONE...
...WHOM YOU WILL LOVE THE MOST.
AND WHO WILL THAT BE? DO YOU KNOW?
YOU'RE THE ONE WHO GAVE BIRTH TO ME--YOU SHOULD KNOW BETTER THAN ANYONE.
BUT I'LL NEVER GROW TO LOVE ANYONE.
YOU KNOW THAT.
NOW YOU WILL BE...
THE SAKURA-ZUKA-MORI.
UNTIL THE DAY SOMEONE COMES TO KILL ***YOU***.

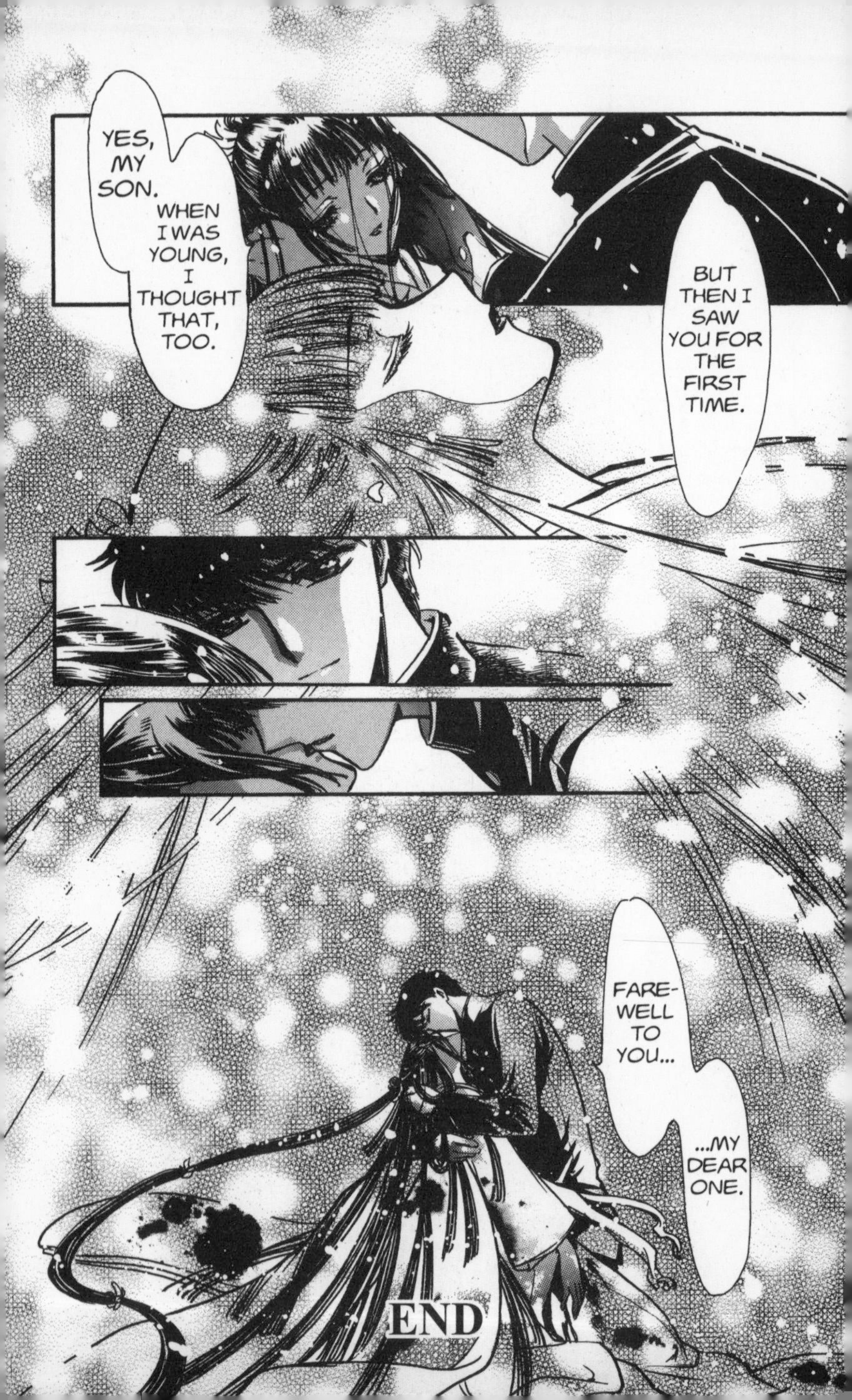
BUT THEN I SAW YOU FOR THE FIRST TIME.
YES, MY SON. WHEN I WAS YOUNG, I THOUGHT THAT, TOO.
FARE-WELL TO YOU...
...MY DEAR ONE.
END

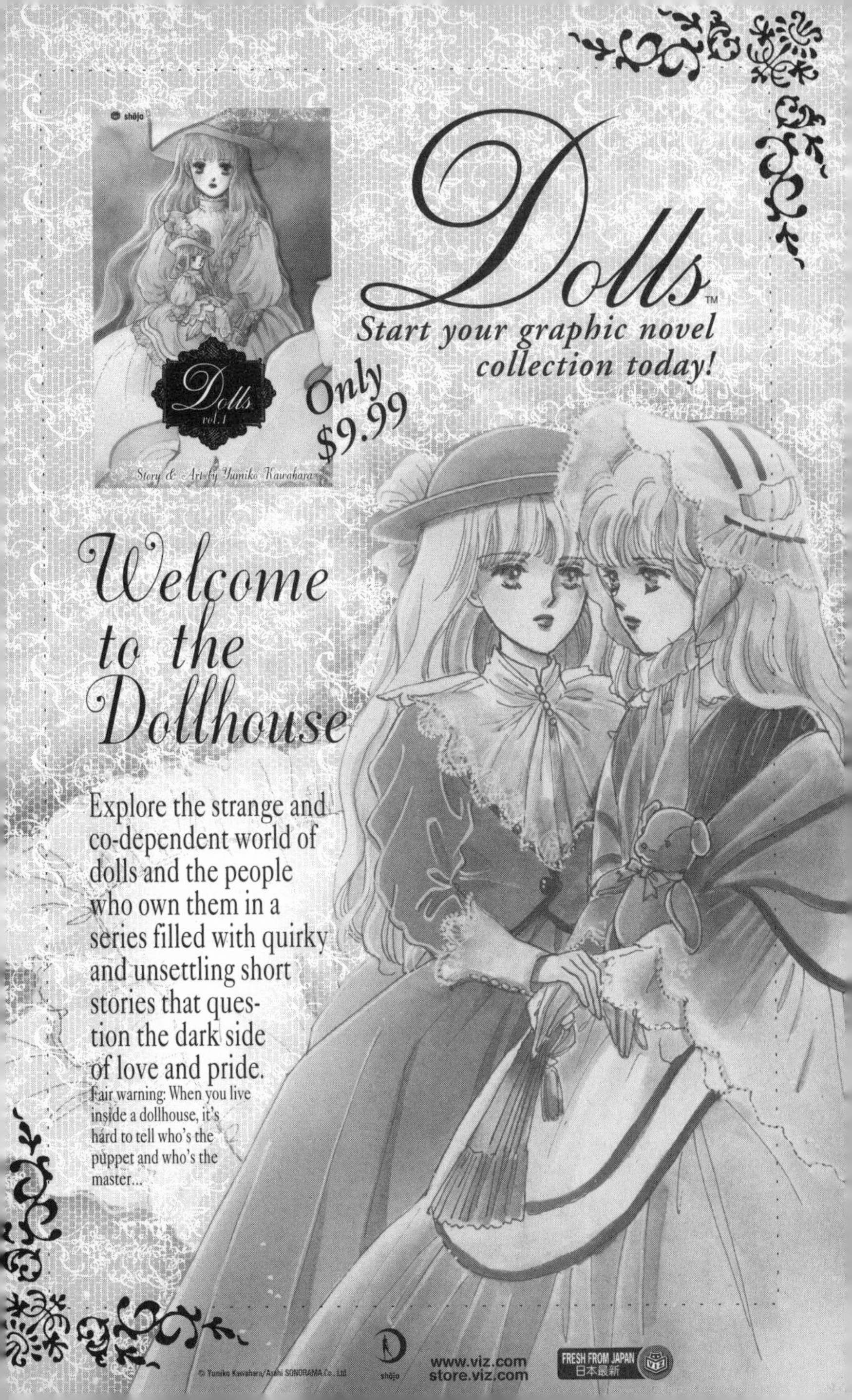
shōjo
Dolls
vol.1
Story & Art by Yumiko Kawahara
Only $9.99
Dolls™
Start your graphic novel collection today!
Welcome to the Dollhouse
Explore the strange and co-dependent world of dolls and the people who own them in a series filled with quirky and unsettling short stories that question the dark side of love and pride.
Fair warning: When you live inside a dollhouse, it's hard to tell who's the puppet and who's the master...
© Yumiko Kawahara/Asahi SONORAMA Co., Ltd.
shōjo
www.viz.com
store.viz.com
FRESH FROM JAPAN
日本最新
VIZ

shôjo

AT THE HEART OF THE MATTER

- Alice 19th
- Angel Sanctuary
- Banana Fish
- Basara
- B.B. Explosion
- Boys Over Flowers *
- Ceres, Celestial Legend *
- Descendants of Darkness
- Dolls
- From Far Away
- Fushigi Yûgi
- Hana-Kimi
- Here Is Greenwood
- Hot Gimmick
- Imadoki
- Kare First Love
- Please Save My Earth *
- Red River
- Revolutionary Girl Utena
- Sensual Phrase
- W Juliet
- Wedding Peach
- Wild Com.
- X/1999

Start Your Shôjo Graphic Novel Collection Today!

COMPLETE OUR SURVEY AND LET
US KNOW WHAT YOU THINK!

☐ Please do NOT send me information about VIZ products, news and events, special offers, or other information.

☐ Please do NOT send me information from VIZ's trusted business partners.

Name: _____

Address: _____

City: _____ **State:** _____ **Zip:** _____

E-mail: _____

☐ Male ☐ Female **Date of Birth** (mm/dd/yyyy): ___/___/_____ (Under 13? Parental consent required)

What race/ethnicity do you consider yourself? (please check one)

☐ Asian/Pacific Islander ☐ Black/African American ☐ Hispanic/Latino

☐ Native American/Alaskan Native ☐ White/Caucasian ☐ Other: _____

What VIZ product did you purchase? (check all that apply and indicate title purchased)

☐ DVD/VHS _____

☐ Graphic Novel _____

☐ Magazines _____

☐ Merchandise _____

Reason for purchase: (check all that apply)

☐ Special offer ☐ Favorite title ☐ Gift

☐ Recommendation ☐ Other _____

Where did you make your purchase? (please check one)

☐ Comic store ☐ Bookstore ☐ Mass/Grocery Store

☐ Newsstand ☐ Video/Video Game Store ☐ Other: _____

☐ Online (site: _____)

What other VIZ properties have you purchased/own? _____

_____

How many anime and/or manga titles have you purchased in the last year? How many were VIZ titles? (please check one from each column)

ANIME

☐ None
☐ 1-4
☐ 5-10
☐ 11+

MANGA

☐ None
☐ 1-4
☐ 5-10
☐ 11+

VIZ

☐ None
☐ 1-4
☐ 5-10
☐ 11+

I find the pricing of VIZ products to be: (please check one)

☐ Cheap   ☐ Reasonable   ☐ Expensive

What genre of manga and anime would you like to see from VIZ? (please check two)

☐ Adventure   ☐ Comic Strip   ☐ Science Fiction   ☐ Fighting
☐ Horror   ☐ Romance   ☐ Fantasy   ☐ Sports

What do you think of VIZ's new look?

☐ Love It   ☐ It's OK   ☐ Hate It   ☐ Didn't Notice   ☐ No Opinion

Which do you prefer? (please check one)

☐ Reading right-to-left
☐ Reading left-to-right

Which do you prefer? (please check one)

☐ Sound effects in English
☐ Sound effects in Japanese with English captions
☐ Sound effects in Japanese only with a glossary at the back

THANK YOU! Please send the completed form to:

NJW Research
42 Catharine St.
Poughkeepsie, NY 12601

All information provided will be used for internal purposes only. We promise not to sell or otherwise divulge your information.